Urban Education 1

The City Experience

Edited by

John Raynor and Elizabeth Harris

Ward Lock Educational
in association with
The Open University Press

ISBN 0 7062 3635 1 paperback
    0 7062 3636 x hardback

First published 1977

W 17631(1) £3.80. 10.81

Set in 11 on 12 point Plantin by
Computacomp (UK) Limited, Fort William
and printed by Robert MacLehose and Company Limited, Glasgow
for Ward Lock Educational
116 Baker Street, London W1M 2BB
A member of the Pentos Group
Made in Great Britain

Contents

Acknowledgments

The Open University and publishers would like to thank the following for permission to reproduce copyright material. All possible care has been taken to trace ownership of the selections included and to make full acknowledgment for their use.

George Allen & Unwin Ltd for 'The origins: urban growth in England 1801–1939' by Peter Hall from *The Containment of Urban England* Vol. 1, by Peter Hall *et al* 1973; and for 'The diploma disease – England' from *The Diploma Disease* by Robert Dore 1976; Cambridge University Press for 'Poverty and the urban system' by R. E. Pahl, M.A., Ph.D., Professor of Sociology, from *Spatial Policy Problems of the British Economy* by Michael Chisholm and Gerald Manners (eds) 1971; Jonathan Cape Ltd for 'The uses of city neighbourhoods' from *The Death and Life of Great American Cities* by Jane Jacobs 1962 © 1961 by Jane Jacobs. Originally published in America by Random House Inc; Dr James Coleman and The Johns Hopkins University for 'How do the young become adults?', Report No. 130, May 1972, of the Center for Social Organization of Schools, The Johns Hopkins University, Baltimore, Maryland; David & Charles for 'Delinquency on the move' from *A View from the Boys* by Howard J. Parker 1974; Professor John Kenneth Galbraith for 'The Metropolis' from *The Listener* 24 March 1977; Heinemann Educational Books Ltd for 'Beyond the ghetto: the illusion of choice' by Nicholas Deakin and Clare Ungerson from *London: Urban Patterns, Problems and Policies* by David Donnison and David Eversley (eds) 1973; Little, Brown & Company for 'The imperatives of class' from *The Unheavenly City Revisited* by Edward C. Banfield 1973; Liverpool University Press for 'Community' by A. Buttimer from *Town Planning Review* Vol. 42, No. 2, 1971; The Literary Executors of the Colin MacInnes Estate for 'Portrait of working-class culture' by Colin

MacInnes from *The Times Educational Supplement* 5 October 1973; *New Left Review* for 'Factory time' by Dennis Johnson, from *New Left Review* 1965; New Science Publications for 'Population and community in London' by Peter Willmott from *New Society* 24 October 1974. This article first appeared in *New Society London* the weekly review of the Social Sciences; Richard Peet, General Editor of *Antipode Monographs in Social Geography* and David Harvey for 'Social justice and spatial systems' by David Harvey from *Antipode Monographs in Social Geography* No. 1, 1972, reprinted in *Social Justice and the City* by David Harvey 1973, published by Edward Arnold; 'The good uses of the city' from *The Uses of Disorder* (1971) pp.113–38 © Richard Sennett 1970, reprinted by permission of Penguin Books Ltd; Routledge & Kegan Paul Ltd for 'Urbanism and suburbanism as ways of life' by H. J. Gans from *Human Behaviour and Social Processes* by Arnold M. Rose (ed) 1962; and for 'The flaw in the pluralist heaven' by John Benington from *Action Research in Community Development* by Ray Lees and George Smith (eds) 1975; and for 'The long shadow of work' from *Schooling in Capitalist America* by Samuel Bowles and Herbert Gintis 1976, originally published by Basic Books Inc; The Royal Town Planning Institute for 'Physical planning and social policy' by J. M. Simmie from *Journal of the Royal Town Planning Institute* 57 (10) 1971; Wendy Sarkissian, *Urban Studies* and Longman Group Ltd for 'The idea of social mix in town planning: an historical review' by Wendy Sarkissian from *Urban Studies* Vol. 13, No. 3, October 1976; Thames and Hudson Ltd for 'Status of the worker' from *The Rise of the Meritocracy* by Michael Young 1958; *Three Banks Review* for 'Ideas for town planners' by David Donnison from *Three Banks Review* No. 96, December 1972, published by the National and Commercial Banking Group Ltd; University of Birmingham Centre for Contemporary Cultural Studies and Phil Cohen for 'Subcultural conflict and the working-class community' by Phil Cohen from *Working Papers in Cultural Studies* No. 2, 1972; University of Chicago Press for 'The growth of the city' by E. W. Burgess from *The City* by R.E. Park *et al* 1925; Raymond Williams and Chatto & Windus Ltd for 'Cities and countries' from *The Country and the City* by Raymond Williams 1973.

General introduction

Three companion volumes of readings: *The City Experience*, *Schooling in the City* and *The Political Context*, have been prepared for the third-level course *Education and the Urban Environment* offered by the Faculty of Educational Studies at the Open University. As many people will now know the readers form only one component of Open University courses which also include correspondence texts, BBC radio and television programmes, personal tuition and summer schools. In the preparation of these readers we have deliberately excluded material which will appear in other components of the course. This accounts for the non-appearance of names and materials which might otherwise be expected.

Taken together the three Readers are designed to provide students with:

1 a sample of perspectives on the city and of the social processes at work within urban settings
2 a survey of some of the principal debates encountered in urban schooling
3 an introduction to a variety of political and economic issues in urban education.

It is only four years since the previous course, E351 *Urban Education*, was prepared with its two readers: *Cities, Communities and the Young* and *Equality and City Schools* (published by Routledge and Kegan Paul, 1973) and in that short space of time it is interesting to note the differences in emphasis in the two courses. In the earlier course one of our central concerns was the problem of urban poverty and the disadvantaged learners in our city schools, and the course preparation period coincided with the Educational Priority Area and the Community Development Programmes. Again, we were writing against a background of high truancy rates, high teacher turnover and the reported crises taking place within many of our large secondary schools. Not surprisingly therefore, our attention came to be focused on the process of institution-building within schools, on community relations and on alternative strategies for education. Today's educational picture has changed, and the new course reflects that change. As might be expected at a time of cut-backs and economic stringency, considerable time is given to examining resource implications for urban schooling. Again, though the earlier course gave some attention to an understanding of urban processes, the new course contains even more material reflecting our greater awareness of the way in which the city serves as a distributive agency; of the plight of the 'inner city' areas, of cultural dislocation within different groups and the implications all of these have for urban schooling. Further, we are, today, much more conscious of the difficulties of searching for a multicultural education in a period of economic recession and unemployment, when the racism which lies so close to the surface manifests itself in hostility towards minorities.

This is not to suggest that *Urban Education* is nothing more than a loose collective title for a number of disparate topics conveniently gathered under one heading susceptible to whim, current concern or the crisis of the moment. In any course on urban education one would now expect to find students examining some, if not all, of the following issues:

1   *the urban setting* covering the main urban processes, not only in terms of location and structure but also in terms of interests, community and culture
2   *urban politics* introducing students to the questions raised by the priorities, activities and judgments of urban decision-makers in terms of physical planning, city governance and educational policies.

From these two basic considerations a whole number of issues branch out. Among these can be identified:

(a)   *issues of equity* – the debates, the research and the programmes for equal educational opportunity; compensatory programmes; multicultural education; bilingual education and affirmative action
(b)   *management, finance and government* – the structure, plans, methods and budgetary considerations of urban education
(c)   *institutional issues* – the most appropriate kinds of provision for education for different groups at different ages in different parts of the city. Here, too, is that debate on the nature of the curricular objectives that are being pursued in urban schools and the way they relate to parents and to community.

The three readers in this series reflect the issues outlined above. They have been compiled to enrich the course which starts from a study of the urban experience, examines various political and economic questions and concludes by looking at a number of issues in urban schooling. However, each volume can be read separately from the course and give the reader a useful introduction to the field of study.

Reader 1 focuses on the first part of the course with a range of papers under the broad title of *The City Experience*. We have brought together, in section 1, a sample of perspectives ranging from the writings of economists and of urban geographers to essays in the area of cultural analysis. Clearly we have had to be very selective for in this area the literature is extremely rich. The second section, entitled 'Urban processes' concentrates on two broad themes. The first is that of social justice in the city (with a key paper by David Harvey) and, attendant on it, the relationship between poverty and the urban system. The second of these themes is that of the assumptions and claims of the physical planners and their relationship to social policy generally. The third section looks briefly at the area of 'Community and neighbourhood' and includes a paper by John Benington which casts a critical look at community development programmes in cities. Finally, in section 4, we have gathered together an eclectic range of papers under the general heading of 'Living and working in the city'. We have concentrated on working-class experience though inevitably these are more descriptions about a way of life, rather than experiences revealed from within.

1   Urban perspectives

Introduction

How can we come to grips with the entity called the city? If the last thing a fish is aware of is the sea, similarly (because we are all urban dwellers to some degree or other) reflecting on urban experience is not something most of us do. Rather the city and the experiences we have from living within it are part of our taken-for-granted world. Perhaps the city is too big and complex to understand as a whole and, moreover, it is always on the move – always changing from being one thing to becoming something else. We do not lack books on 'cities' these days but could anyone do for late twentieth-century Manchester what Engels did for it in the nineteenth century? 'Reading' the city is now an almost impossible task because the original structure, plan and groundwork have been destroyed under constant redevelopment. Of course, insights into the city are not denied us whether we approach it, say, from the literature of urban sociology or from film or fiction. Few would deny the contribution to our developing sensibility made by Jane Jacobs in 'The death and life of American cities', but what complementary insights are provided by, for example, Martin Scorscese's film *Mean Streets*? Do we learn more about Chicago from Burgess and Park or from novels such as James T. Farrell's *Studs Lonigan* or, more contemporaneously, Saul Bellow or Studs Terkel?

The perspectives chosen here are very varied, ranging from Galbraith's ironic detatchment (1.1), looking at the relationship of the modern metropolis with the industrial economy, to Raymond Williams' (1.2) cultural analysis of the relationship between city and country and the connection with contemporary capitalism. Burgess' classic essay (1.3) on urban structural analysis is included. Hall (1.6) examines the concept of urbanism and the growth of British cities up to the Second World War. Donnison's essay (1.4) looks at the interlocking nature of the urban system and the constraints on planning. The by now almost classic essay by Gans

(1.5) gives an analysis of different ways of life within city and suburb, and finally, we conclude with a paper by Sennett (1.7), who sees the bureaucratic organization of cities as cramping the development of human beings, reducing community and restricting conviviality, but also advances his own diagnosis of the relationship between personal identity and city life.

1.1 The metropolis

John Kenneth Galbraith

What is the physical face of modern industrial society? The question arose in ghoulish fashion, in World War Two: what should Allied bombers destroy? An historic dispute developed. The American desk-warriors held that the vital things were factories, refineries, railroad yards. The British planners argued for the city; this was the industrial society. Destroy the city and you destroyed all.

The difference was not based on compassion, or on deep philosophical insight. Proceeding at night, the RAF bombers could find only cities; going by day, the US air force could see, although they could not reliably hit, factories, so military convenience was, as often, the parent of thought. But there is much to be said for the British view. The factory is only one part of the physical paraphernalia of the industrial civilization; and the city is nearly all. It is the mirror of social achievement; and of misfortune, too.

Poverty is a case in point. Poverty, in by far its most common form, as we now know, is a problem of land and people, and for such poverty, the city is the escape-hatch. So it has been for centuries. People are forced off the land by deprivation, and they are drawn to the cities by the chances of wages or, if not wages, then better social services, more compassionate standards of welfare. It is not that the city is good, but that the alternatives are always worse. There were other reasons, of course: some of us were refugees from that hard work on a farm.

The city, then, is the focus of the problems of the modern society. Its uncertainty, its crises, hope, despair – all are there. To understand the modern city is to understand the social ills that most oppress us. Understanding begins with the realization that there is not one kind of city, but several. The modern metropolis is a combination of all the different

Source: *The Listener* 24 March 1977, pp. 359–64. (The eleventh programme in the series *The Age of Uncertainty*, shown on BBC2.)

kinds of cities that have gone before. Classification is the first step in science, but it seems to me that it has lagged where the urban culture is concerned.

There are five distinct types of cities. Some had their greatest glory in the past, but all of them have a modern counterpart. Names are necessary: of cities, there are the Royal Household – or, possibly, we might call it the Political Household; the Merchant City; the Industrial City; the Great Camp – sometimes called the Suburb; and now the Polyglot Metropolis. To understand the modern metropolis, we must see the cities that went before.

The most potent, still, of the ancestral images is the city of the princes. As an expression of one man's taste and personality, as a manifestation of the grandeur of his realm, this is without equal.

Fatehpur Sikri, in India, has been called 'the world's most perfectly preserved ghost town'. It was built by Akbar the Great, on a low, rocky ridge twenty-four miles from Agra. The site was chosen, it is said, because there, in the village of Sikri, lived a holy man whom Akbar had visited when he was in despair over the prospect for a son and heir. As a result of the visit, a son, Jahangir, was forthcoming. In gratitude, around 1571, Akbar quarried the beautiful, salmon-red stone of the ridge, made a lake some twenty miles around, and built a new capital. It was larger than London, and its public buildings, by a wide margin, more elegant. It is still there. That this city was the extension of one personality is not in doubt. At Fatehpur Sikri we see in the clearest possible form the city that I have called the 'royal' or 'political household'. Over the centuries, nothing has been so used to enhance royal personality, armed slaughter apart, as the architectural embellishment of the seat of government. Fatehpur Sikri is our purest case.

The royal household is mostly of the past, but it remains powerfully in our mind as the basic image of what a city should be like, and it has also a modern prototype. The idea lends itself well to modern political rhetoric. The greatness of the capital measures the greatness of the state. President Kubitschek of Brazil said:

> From this central plateau, from which will emanate decisions of vital national importance, I look, once more, to the future of my country, and foresee this dawn with unshakeable belief in the greatness of our destiny.

From the royal household came the notion that government has a special claim to architectural magnificence and civic grandeur, as with Brasilia.

Industrialists are expected to work, though not to live, in cities of considerable squalor. Their office buildings may be tall, but they must be functional. Politicians, even bureaucrats, should have more refined surroundings: their cities should be planned; their buildings embellished, however crudely, as was the royal household. What rejoices the eye must be nicely balanced with what might distress the taxpayer. From this calculation have come the modern capitals – Washington, New Delhi, Canberra, Islamabad, Brasilia – cities that, like Fatehpur Sikri, have been built in accordance with a ruling conception and design. Their order and symmetry have a strong claim on the eye. It is worth a thought that these are almost the only modern cities that the modern tourist ever wants to visit.

The merchant city, the second of our five cities, also had a strong unity of design. This was less the result of central authority than of a unity of taste: merchants must be sensitive to fashion and, at any time, in architecture as in dress, there is a ruling style. Bruges, in Belgium, was a member of the Hanseatic League, and once it was the northern counterpart of Venice itself – the Venice of the North. It was saved from the modern world when its access to the sea silted up, in the fifteenth century, and when fate put it a mere twenty miles behind the guns in World War One.

The strong sense of collective interest of the merchants was manifested in both the design of the houses and the plan of the town. Within this larger framework, there was, then, a rewarding competition. The quality and style of the house advertised the quality and style of the merchandise available therefrom. So Bruges, like the other merchant cities – Venice, Florence, Genoa, Bremen, Lubeck – such of them as survived the wars, had much of the order and elegance of the royal household. In 1438, a visiting merchant gave his impression of Bruges. Note well the admiring tone:

The products of the whole world are brought here, so that they have everything in abundance, in exchange for the work of their hands. The people of this part of the country are exceedingly cleanly in their apparel, but very extravagant. Without doubt, the great goddess of luxury has great power here – but it is not a place for poor men, who would be badly received. But anyone who has money and wishes to spend it will find, in this town alone, everything which the whole world produces. I saw there oranges and lemons from Castille, fruits and wines from Greece, confections and spices from Alexandria, furs from the Black Sea ...

The guildhall, town hall and cathedral each had a function in the merchant city. They proclaimed, regulated and sanctified the gains from trade. The houses and palaces of the merchants were places of business, places of residence, and a sure source of community esteem. So they were the subject of much thought: in the merchant city, men were valued less for what they were than for where they lived − a nice, straightforward, objective test of merit for which many must still yearn.

With the Industrial Revolution, civic pride withered, the very connotation of the word 'city' changed. Before 1776, it had an overtone of grandeur: the phrase 'heavenly city' seemed not to be a contradiction in terms. Had the Bible been written after the Industrial Revolution, paradise would not have been a city − whatever the paving of the streets. Slowly but certainly, a reference to a city became a reference to something not grand, but sordid.

There was much about the industrial city, to which we now come, which assured this reputation. The people of its factories were a utility − a servo-mechanism. They were important only for their effort, and this was not diminished by their being shabby, unwashed, rough of manner and ripe of smell. These attributes minimized personal expenditure − living costs − and, in the industrial city, men sought not elegance but low cost. Nor was this entirely to be deplored; the industrial city, unlike its predecessors, produced goods in quantity for those who were also poor.

The people of the industrial city were not very beautiful, nor was their housing. Nor − a commonplace point − were the processes by which goods were made. On the contrary, these almost invariably involved smoke and grime, for coal had to be dug and washed, ore had to be fired, steam-engines had to be fuelled; and all of these operations spread filth. In considering the effect of economic growth on our surroundings, on the environment, we might remember that industrial progress has been a remarkably steady march from foul processes to clean − from dirty coal to clean gas, from dirty foundries to clean control-rooms, from the belching steam-engine to the wholly antiseptic electric motor. We now have pollution, not because industrial processes are dirtier, but because we produce and consume so much more. But early industrial processes *were* dirty, and the industrial city was rightly thought squalid.

Finally, among the things affecting the character of the industrial city, were the industrialists. The merchant had to be, like his customers, a man of some style and taste; users of coal and steel and chemicals and machinery were not concerned with style, only with cost and performance. And the early consumer products of the industrial city − cloth and more cloth and cheap tin trays − were not stylish either. So the early manufacturer was, like his products, solid, efficient, without grace. He built his house above the mills, and it, too, was solid and often ugly. But beauty is in the eye of the beholder. Here is the view of Dr Andrew Ure, a chemist and scientific writer of the last century and, as would now be said, an articulate defender of 'the system':

> Factories are magnificent edifices, surpassing far in number, value, usefulness and ingenuity of construction the boasted monuments of Asiatic, Egyptian and Roman despotism. In these spacious halls, the benignant power of steam summons around him his myriads of willing menials. Yet, even at the present day, when the system is perfectly organized and its labours lightened to the utmost, it is found nearly impossible to convert persons past the age of puberty into useful factory hands. After struggling for a while to conquer their listless or restive habits, they either renounce the employment spontaneously or are dismissed by the overlookers on account of inattention. They are readily moved to outrage by crafty demagogues and are apt to regard their best benefactor, the enterprising and frugal capitalist who employs them, with a jealous eye.

One who would qualify for Ure's denunciation was Friedrich Engels, Karl Marx's great collaborator. In 1844, he described Manchester:

> And as for the dirt! Everywhere one sees heaps of garbage, refuse and filth. There are stagnant pools instead of gutters, and the stench alone is so overpowering that no person, even partially civilized, would think it bearable to live in such a district. There is to be found under the railway bridge a court which is even filthier and more revolting than the others. In a hole barely six feet long and five feet wide, I saw two beds (and what beds and what bedding!) which filled the room.
>
> When all comes to all, what really matters to the Englishman is his own interest and, above all, his desire to make money. One day I walked with one of these middle-class gentlemen into Manchester. I spoke to him about the disgraceful, unhealthy slums and drew his attention to the disgusting condition in which the factory workers lived. I declared I had never seen so badly built a town in my life. He listened patiently and, at the corner of the street at which we parted company, he remarked: 'And yet a great deal of money is made here. Good morning, sir.'

In the industrial city, the industrialist was free from restraint. He could do as he needed with air, steam, landscape – and he did. It was a place to shelter the work stock at the lowest possible cost. Given that the purpose of the city was to produce goods cheaply, not much more was to be asked.

In one variant of the industrial city, the industrialist did take responsibility for inception, design and administration. He laid out streets, built and owned the houses, built and operated the company store, and he laid on water supply and sewage, if any. This, like the cities of the princes, was an imposed order – an industrial household. Its purpose, however, was to keep down costs and ensure that the inmates, if sullen, would not be mutinous. I am speaking here of the company town. Few creations of man have been so reviled, hated. It is a warning against order without consent.

There were exceptions: in the 1840s, Brunel's Great Western Railway built a housing estate for the workers at its new locomotive works, at Swindon. The company believed that everything possible should be done to ensure a happy, healthy, intelligent – and non-mutinous – workforce. It was a housing estate where people lived in comparative comfort, with a decent amount of space. There *was* consent. The houses were small, but each had a garden, two bedrooms and a toilet. (The average for the period was one lavatory for every four houses.) There was a mechanics institute for education, and a Wesleyan chapel for spiritual development.

The cost of Swindon was not very high, but it was only possible for a sizeable enterprise, like a railway – and a very enlightened one. For both of these reasons, Swindon was the exception, and it had to be. The ruling doctrine of the age was *laissez-faire*, free enterprise, and this the industrial city was bound to reflect. One could not expect the city to be an island of order in an unplanned world. Sheffield, Rochdale, Essen, Pittsburgh, Gary are the industrial city in its purest form. But the image is now blurred. Time, change and economics have melded the industrial city into the final form – the great, modern metropolis.

New York is the ultimate city – the polyglot metropolis. There is a political household here, the United Nations; also a merchant city; also industry. Around it is our fourth city, the camp. From the earliest days of the industrial city, those who could afford it sought to escape its smoke and its grime and, even more, its unlovely landscape. But the suburban camp owes much to developments since – to the appearance in the economy of a new, well-paid managerial and professional élite. In the camp, the rich and the merely affluent live in comparatively clear air with their private trees and grass. And they have schools, churches, recreation, all of superior quality, the quality insured and the cost kept down by their not having to be shared with the poor.

Unlike the other cities, the camp has no political or economic function – it does not rule, sell or make. It is a place where people find space; and thus its name. A housewife of Montclair, New Jersey:

I think one can achieve a certain state of serenity here; it is very nice to be able to come away from the city, come away from the dirty air, the crowds of people, the noise, and to come into the cleaner air, the quieter environment, the lovely, lovely, lush trees and a place where our children can grow up. I find, however, for me, the hardest part is the lack of mental work, of mental stimulation. I need something for my head. For instance, the winters can be very lonely here. You can feel very isolated unless you are involved in a lot of things that take you outside. You can feel very, very secluded in your house. I think women are very, very private, and we are all stuck away from each other in our houses. At times, I think this is no place for me to be; but then I think, that is the ambivalence of life. One minute, 'Oh, this is just terrific!' – the next minute, you want to be back where you were. You want to be back in the city.

Well, when I lived in the city, there was a lot of violence in the area. When I began to walk around with the baby in a stroller or in a carriage, I quickly began to feel uncomfortable carrying a purse or a handbag. I felt I would be better off not having it – just put my money in my pocket. I carried as little cash as I possibly could: this was a necessary way of life. I don't think like that out here. For me, right now, this happens to be the place I'm at – and I am trying to make the best of it. It is lovely to be able to plunge in my own swimming-pool, or to have twenty people on a weekend. And I am trying to be happy here, just as one tries everywhere.

'Sir,' Dr Johnson said, 'when a man is tired of London, he is tired of life.' I have always felt exactly that way about New York; in fact, I used to feel that a week when I did not go there was a week wasted. In the great polyglot metropolis, all of the earlier cities come together. What is it that most distinguishes this metropolis from the industrial city? I should say it was money. Money – rising real income – is a far greater force for change than we commonly imagine. The industrial city had two classes: capitalist and proletariat. In the modern metropolis, there is a vast, new, merchant, professional, technical, governmental and artistic community, all of which is called into being by the increase in income. This has altered the face of the city, for its needs must be met. And it also introduces new tensions – tensions that are different from those of the industrial city, but not in any way less real.

These we now see and, as always, we see them most vividly in New York, where life is always a trifle larger than life itself. As the affluent move to the camps, the poor take their place and the very poor then replace the merely poor. All see the well-to-do go; not so many notice that it is a prime function of the modern metropolis to rescue the truly deprived from the world around. In New York, the menial jobs are done by the refugees from something worse; and so it is in every world metropolis, only the names – migrant workers, foreign workers, guest workers – are different. Bad as are the New York slums, there can be hope; in the *barrios* of Puerto Rico, not even that. Juan Marquez's letter home tells the difference:

> My beloved mother, hoping for you that when you receive this letter you feel the best of your health. As for me, I'm going to tell you what is happening to me when I get to New York. I have to tell you that I got lost for three days in a subway train, and that somebody helped me to get back to where I was supposed to be.
>
> Well, for the rest I'm all right. I've just found a job and I'm planning to stay working so I can bring my brothers over. You know everybody is saying New York is a big town and there was good jobs and a lot of money here, but in the places I go everybody speaks Spanish, so that makes it difficult for me to learn ...

We saw earlier the oldest remedy for poverty, one of the few within the power of the individual to employ in his own behalf, is to move from the poor country to the rich. It is a hard solution for both. The affluent should not feel, as they sometimes do, that theirs is the only suffering. Juan's letter continues:

> ... Also, I don't like the apartment because there is no landlord, no services, and the ceiling is peeling and the water coming down. Sometimes my old lady, she is very disturbed with her nerves and also the asthma take her real bad, but I don't know if its the condition of the apartment or not. I feel bad because she is sick and I would like to have better things, but there is more opportunity for job here and I wouldn't like to go back the same way I came. But, Ma, I'm going to tell you that over here is real cold – not like home. But I'll get used to it. Regards to my brothers and all the family. Your son, Juan.

In the metropolis, the classic conflict between employer and worker recedes. Instead, there are now two working classes. The old established, relatively well-paid work force feels threatened, both socially and economically, by the new arrivals. They seem a threat to the standards the old work force tried so hard to establish and to raise. This is the new tension. A New York taxi driver:

There are those – black, green, purple, orange or whatever colour – those live pigs that will always remain pigs; and people who want a clean area and clean homes and better schools and better housing for their children and themselves, who keep it clean. But when you get a percentage of people that move into an area, and 80 per cent are pigs, in plain English, let's put it that way, and the rest are decent – it's pretty rough.

In East New York, the particular area where I lived, you had a mother-father type business, garment type, where they manufactured, or they contracted out, women's dresses, skirts, all that, and most of them were Italians in the factories. When they moved out, little by little, the Spanish and the black people came into it and, out of a clear blue sky, it just deteriorated. Now, if you look around, you'll see homes, houses boarded up and they just let it go. Take where I used to live. I cannot believe that, in a span of twenty years, this could ever happen to where I lived. Let's say that I took it personally – as a personal insult. I can't give any other explanation, except that people who live there now just don't care one way or the other what happens. They want to live in filth, slime and garbage ...

The polyglot metropolis, the great metropolis, is the focus of all of the great migrations of our time. This must be kept in perspective. It is something of which we now have a very considerable historical experience. Migrants coming in numbers, whether they have been Irish, Italians or Jews, have always had an unsettling effect on those who were already there: their manners have seemed crude; they were often thought lawless; their personal hygiene seemed questionable; always, it was imagined that the tensions they introduced were permanent. Soon, as in the case of the Irish in Boston, or the Jews and Italians in New York, the manners changed, the tensions eased, and presently the newcomers were the new ruling class.

In recent times, British cities have had their great influx of Indians, Pakistanis and West Indians; Berlin has become one of the largest Turkish cities in the world; Paris is extensively Algerian; and, to the big American cities, have come the blacks and the Puerto Ricans. The old suspicions and the old tensions and the old fears have, everywhere, been recreated; again, it is imagined that they are permanent. There is not the slightest reason to think that the ultimate resolution will be any different, or that it will take any longer than in the case of previous migrations. In looking at the modern polyglot metropolis, it is very important to know what the real problems are. (It is also important to know what the real problems are not.) Meanwhile, of course, the tension: its everyday manifestation is crime –

senseless violence, muggings, vandalism, drugs. The burden falls very heavily on those whom we pay to keep the peace. A police officer in Harlem:

> I'm not afraid too often – though I do get frightened. My major objective, after eight-and-a-half hours here, is to get home. What gets monotonous is driving round at ten miles an hour. It's almost like you're waiting for something to happen. Car stops are where cops get hurt. That's where cops get shot. I have the habit of taking my gun out of the holster and putting it in backwards, because I can get it out faster.

After a night-time walk through Harlem, it is difficult to argue that the modern city is a noticeably safer place than the slums that Engels described more than a century ago: the resemblance is disconcerting:

> It is only when the traveller has visited the slums of this great city that it dawns on him that the inhabitants have had to sacrifice so much that is best in human nature in order to create those wonders of civilization with which their city teems. The more they are packed into a tiny space, the more repulsive and disgraceful becomes the brutal indifference with which they ignore their neighbours and concentrate on their private affairs. Signs of social conflict are to be found everywhere. Everyone turns his house into a fortress to defend himself – under the protection of the law – from the depredations of his neighbours. The observer of such an appalling state of affairs must shudder at the consequences of such feverish activity, and can only marvel that so crazy a social and economic structure should survive at all.

Not all great problems are difficult. Sometimes they are merely made so by people who want to avoid the obvious but very painful solutions. Overwhelmingly, the problem of the polyglot metropolis is money. It takes a truly vast amount of money if people are to live safely and pleasantly in close quarters, and it takes far more money than anyone in the past has realized.

Garbage is the symbol: free enterprise is wonderful at providing what people discard; very poor at picking up the discard. Things work differently for the well-to-do and the poor: the affluent can pay to have garbage picked up, and for security services, and burglar alarms – and, of course, for housing and health care. Nowhere in the world does private enterprise provide good, cheap housing, good health services, good transportation, or police, or schools, or playgrounds. These, the poor and the average citizen need. These, the city – the public – must provide. This may not be the way things should be. It is the way they are.

The modern big city is by nature a social – maybe I should say a socialist – enterprise, and all this is reflected in the cost. In the industrial city, public services required a relatively small deduction from private consumption. The day may come (I think it will come) when, in the great metropolis, public consumption will be greater than private consumption, will cost more. This will not be the result of any ideological preference, it will be a simple matter of necessity.

The singular feature of New York City is its private wealth and its public squalor. The remedy, in principle, is obvious: higher taxes on the affluent, the people who can afford to pay them; more public services for all. The practical solution is more difficult. The affluent can now get much better services for the same or less money, escape the need for having to pay part of the cost for the poor by moving out to the camps. The obvious solution is to tax the whole metropolis. And, sooner or later, it is going to have to be done, because there is not any other way.

The acceptance of the social character of the metropolis involves more than questions of bread, butter, police, taxes. It also involves another dimension – that of art and design. That is a prime lesson of this history. The city was great when these were good. How do we escape from the aesthetic legacy of the Industrial Revolution? How do we recapture the order and the sense of a household of Fatehpur Sikri, the order and elegance of Bruges? There is nothing theoretical or precious about this problem; it is one that the practical administrator must face. A Harlem housing administrator:

> Any job like this requires decisions which are based on expediency rather than principle, and the difficult thing is to know when to put principle aside and do the pragmatic thing. I have more trouble with the politics of land use than I have with the economics of land use. What we have not been able to do is to get political acquiescence in the public use of land, because of the opposition of the local householders or the local residents or the local storekeepers or what-have-you ...

One rule can be laid down as firm: a unified, overall conception for streets, offices, shops, housing, parks, will almost always be better than when there is no governing order at all. There is no place where the substitution of social authority for classical *laissez-faire* is so urgent. To achieve this is a matter of political power and also of trust. We accept the judgment of scientists or physicians on matters of life and death; good design is also important for our lives – we must learn similarly to trust the artist:

> ... The pressure of the multitude gets heavier and heavier. We have had the idea that the multitude, being made up of very different and opposed pressure groups, somehow balances itself out and that the wisest course would emerge. But this does not necessarily happen.
>
> But, of course, one person's principle is another person's obstinacy, so it is very hard to say what is the right thing to do in any circumstances.

But we must also ensure that the design – the imposed order – will be accepted by the community. That means that housing, parks, subway-cars must be a source of pride, not an object for vandalism and graffiti. Citizens must feel the city is theirs. There are, we must believe, forces within the city that can be so used. Every inner city has a network of small villages, small neighbourhoods, small households. Their community – and often their ethnic self-respect – is shown by the care that they take of their streets and their houses: ultimately, it is the people and their identification with where they live who make a city work.

Do we, then, solve all the problems of city life by returning authority to the people? It is a temptingly romantic notion, but I suggest that we respond with some caution. Part of the urban crisis, we have seen, arises from the ability of the affluent to contract out, move to the surrounding camps. This makes the case for larger units, metropolitan or regional governments. Leaving tasks to the people can mean leaving them to the poor of the inner city, who are the least able to pay. Also it was rural poverty that sent people from the rural south, and from Puerto Rico, to New York. People of New York should not be asked to bear the cost of solving the age-old problem of land and people. That is a national responsibility; it is all the more so, for the fiscal systems of most industrial countries – and this includes the United States – give the revenues to national governments, and the costs to the big cities. The money goes one place, and the problems go another.

But for tasks that are within the competence of the local community, there is an equally strong case for local authority and local responsibility. Planning is always an imposed order. It is more likely to be accepted if it reflects local preference, is imposed by people close to home on schools, housing, hospitals, even law enforcement; the citizen needs to have a sense of personal responsibility and participation. And that requires the governing unit to be small. Votes must seem to count, and it is also good that politicians feel the hot breath of their neighbours on their necks. The constitution of the metropolis, in other words, must distinguish between what must be large and what can be small. This is a highly sensitive exercise in democratic design; its test is where we have just been – the modern great metropolis.

1.2   Cities and countries

Raymond Williams

We are touching, and know that we are touching, forms of a general crisis. Looking back, for example, on the English history, and especially on its culmination in imperialism, I can see in the process of the altering relations of country and city the driving force of a mode of production which has indeed transformed the world. I am then very willing to see the city as capitalism, as so many now do, if I can say also that this mode of production began, specifically, in the English rural economy, and produced, there, many of the characteristic effects – increases of production, physical reordering of a totally available world, displacement of customary settlements, a human remnant and force which became a proletariat – which have since been seen, in many extending forms, in cities and colonies and in an international system as a whole. It then does not surprise me that the complaints in Covent Garden echo the complaints of the commoners, since the forces of improvement and development, in those specific forms – an amalgam of financial and political power which is pursuing different ends from those of any local community but which has its own and specific internal rationale – are in a fundamental sense similar, as phases of capitalist enterprise.

What the oil companies do, what the mining companies do, is what landlords did, what plantation owners did and do. And many have gone along with them, seeing the land and its properties as available for profitable exploitation: so clear a profit that the quite different needs of local settlement and community are overridden, often ruthlessly. Difficult and complex as this process is, since the increases in production and the increases in new forms of work and wealth are undoubtedly real, it is usually more necessary to see this kind of contrast – between forms of settlement and forms of exploitation – than to see the more conventional

Source: *The Country and the City* (1973) Chatto and Windus, pp. 292–8.

contrast between agricultural and industrial development: the country as cooperation with nature, the city and industry as overriding and transforming it. There is a visible qualitative difference between the results of farming and the results of mining, but if we see only this contrast we see only some of the results. The effects on human settlements, and on customary or locally self-determined ways of life, are often very similar. The land, for its fertility or for its ore, is in both cases abstractly seen. It is used in an enterprise which overrides, for the time being, all other considerations. Since the dramatic physical transformations of the Industrial Revolution we have found it easy to forget how profoundly and still visibly agriculture altered the land. Some of the earliest and most remarkable environmental effects, negative as well as positive, followed from agricultural practice: making land fertile but also, in places, overgrazing it to a desert; clearing good land but also, in places, with the felling of trees, destroying it or creating erosion. Some of these uses preceded any capitalist order, but the capitalist mode of production is still, in world history, the most effective and powerful agency for all these kinds of physical and social transformation. The city is only one if now conventional way of seeing this kind of change; and the country, as almost all of us now know it, is undoubtedly another. Indeed the change from admiration of cultivated country to the intense attachment to 'unspoiled' places is a precise record of this persistent process and its effects at one of its most active stages.

But we must then also make a distinction between such techniques of production and the *mode* of production which is their particular social form. We call the technical changes improvement and progress, welcome some of their effects and deplore others, and can feel either numbed or divided; a state of mind in which, again and again, the most abstract and illusory ideas of a natural rural way of life tempt or at least charm us. Or we can fall back on saying that this is the human condition: the irresolvable choice between a necessary materialism and a necessary humanity. Often we try to resolve it by dividing work and leisure, or society and the individual, or city and country, not only in our minds but in suburbs and garden cities, town houses and country cottages, the week and the weekend. But we then usually find that the directors of the improvements, the captains of the change, have arrived earlier and settled deeper; have made, in fact, a more successful self-division. The country-house was one of the first forms of this temporary resolution, and in the nineteenth century as many were built by the new lords of capitalist production as survived, improved, from the old lords, sometimes their ancestors, of the agrarian change. It remains remarkable that so much of this settlement has been physically imitated, down to details of semi-detached villas and styles of leisure and weekends. An immensely productive capitalism, in all its stages, has extended both the resources and the modes which, however unevenly, provide and contain forms of response to its effects.

It is then often difficult, past this continuing process which contains the substance of so much of our lives, to recognize, adequately, the specific character of the capitalist mode of production, which is not the use of machines or techniques of improvement, but their minority ownership. Indeed as the persistent concentration of ownership, first of the land, then of all major means of production, was built into a system and a state, with many kinds of political and cultural mediation, it was easy for the perception to diminish though the fact was increasing. Many modern ruralists, many urban conservationists, see 'the state' or 'the planners' as their essential enemy, when it is quite evident that what the state is administering and the planners serving is an economic system which is capitalist in all its main intentions, procedures and criteria. The motorway system, the housing clearance, the office-block and supermarket replacing streets of homes and shops, may materialize in the form of a social plan, but there is no case in which the priorities of a capitalist system have not, from the beginning, been built in. It may be simple industrial development or mining: the decision will have been made originally and will be finally determined by owners calculating profit. The road system will include their needs and preferences for modes of distribution and transport, and these are given priority, either as in the case of lorries against railways or as in the more general situation in which the land itself is looked on, abstractly, as a transport network, just as it is looked on elsewhere, again abstractly, as an opportunity for production. Housing clearance and housing shortage are alike related to the altered distribution of human settlement which has followed from a set of minority decisions about where work will be made available, by the criteria of profit and internal convenience. What are called regional policies are remedial efforts within these priorities rather than decisively against them. The industrial-agricultural balance, in all its physical forms of town-and-country relations, is the product, however mediated, of a set of decisions about capital investment made by the minority which controls capital and which determines its use by calculations of profit.

When we have lived long enough with such a system it is difficult not to mistake it for a necessary and practical reality, whatever elements of its process we may find objectionable. But it is not only that the specific histories of country and city, and of their immediate interrelations, have been determined, in Britain, by capitalism. It is that the total character of what we know as modern society has been similarly determined. The competitive indifference or the sense of isolation in the cities can be seen as bearing a profound relation to the kinds of social competition and alienation which just such a system promotes. These experiences are never exclusive, since within the pressures and limits people make other settlements and attachments and try to live by other values. But the central drive is still there.

Again, enough of us now, for a long enough period, have been living in cities for new kinds of communication to become necessary, and these in their turn reveal both the extension and mobility of the urban and industrial process and the appropriation and exploitation of the same media for capitalist purposes. I do not only mean advertising, though that is a specific deformation of the capitalist city. Nor do I mean only the minority ownership and purposes of the press. I mean the conversion of a necessary social mode into specific forms. It is very striking that in response to the city and to a more deeply interrelated society and world we have developed habitual responses to information, in an altered sense. The morning newspaper, the early radio programme, the evening television, are in this sense forms of orientation in which our central social sense is both sought and in specific and limited ways confirmed.

Wordsworth saw that when we become uncertain in a world of apparent strangers who yet, decisively, have a common effect on us, and when forces that will alter our lives are moving all around us in apparently external and unrecognizable forms, we can retreat, for security, into a deep subjectivity, or we can look around us for social pictures, social signs, social messages, to which, characteristically, we try to relate as individuals but so as to discover, in some form, community. Much of the content of modern communications is this kind of substitute for directly discoverable and transitive relations to the world. It can be properly related to the scale and complexity of modern society, of which the city is always the most evident example. But it has become general, reaching to the most remote rural regions. It is a form of shared consciousness rather than merely a set of techniques. And as a form of consciousness it is not to be understood by rhetorical analogies like the 'global village'. Nothing could be less like the experience of any kind of village or settled active community. For in its main uses it is a form of unevenly shared consciousness of persistently external events. It is what appears to happen, in these powerfully transmitted and mediated ways, in a world with which we have no other perceptible connections but which we feel is at once central and marginal to our lives. This paradoxical set of one-way relationships, in itself determining what we take to be relevant information and news, is then a specific form of consciousness which is inherent in the dominant mode of production, in which, in remarkably similar ways, our skills, our energies, our daily ordering of our lives, our perceptions of the shape of a lifetime, are to a critical extent defined and determined by external formulations of a necessary reality: that external, willed reality – external because its means are in minority hands – from which, in so much of our lives, we seem to have no option but to learn.

Underlying social relations often manifest themselves in these habitual and conventional ways. The communications system is not only the information network but also the transport network. The city, obviously, has always been associated with concentration of traffic. Notoriously, in modern transport systems, this is still the case, and the problem often seems insoluble. But traffic is not only a technique; it is a form of consciousness and a form of social relations. I do not mean only the obvious derivation of so many problems of traffic from a series of decisions about the location of work and the centralization of political power; decisions which were never, in any real sense, socially made, but which were imposed by the priorities of a mode of production. I mean also the forms of modern traffic. It is impossible to read the early descriptions of crowded metropolitan streets – the people as isolated atoms, flowing this way and that; a common stream of separated identities and directions – without seeing, past them, this mode of relationship embodied in the modern car: private, enclosed, an individual vehicle in a pressing and merely aggregated common flow; certain underlying conventions of external control but within them the passing of rapid signals of warning, avoidance, concession, irritation, as we pursue our ultimately separate ways but in a common mode. And this is no longer only a feature of the city, though it is most evident there. Over a whole network of the land this is how, at one level, we relate; indeed it is one form of settlement, intersecting and often deeply affecting what we think of as settlements – cities, towns, villages – in an older mode.

In all these actual social relations and forms of consciousness, ideas of the country and the city, often of an older kind, continue to act as partial interpreters. But we do not always see that in their main bearings they are forms of response to a social system as a whole. Most obviously since the Industrial Revolution, but in my view also since the beginning of the capitalist agrarian mode of production, our powerful images of country and city have been ways of responding to a whole social development. This is why, in the end, we must not limit ourselves to their contrast but go on to see their interrelations and through these the real shape of the underlying crisis.

It is significant, for example, that the common image of the country is now an image of the past, and the common image of the city an image of the future. That leaves, if we isolate them, an undefined present. The pull of the idea of the country is towards old ways, human ways, natural ways. The pull of the idea of the city is towards progress, modernization, development. In what is then a tension, a present experienced as tension, we use the contrast of country and city to ratify an unresolved division and conflict of impulses, which it might be better to face in its own terms.

Aspects of the history of the ideas can then help us. Often an idea of the country is an idea of childhood: not only the local memories, or the ideally shared communal memory, but the feel of childhood: of delighted absorption in our own world, from which, eventually, in the course of growing up, we are distanced and separated, so that it and the world become things we observe. In Wordsworth and Clare, and in many other writers, this structure of feeling is powerfully expressed, and we have seen how often it is then converted into illusory ideas of the rural past: those successive and endlessly recessive 'happy Englands of my boyhood'. But what is interesting now is that we have had enough stories and memories of urban childhoods to perceive the same pattern. The old urban working-class community; the delights of corner-shops, gas lamps, horsecabs, trams, piestalls: all gone, it seems, in successive generations. These urban ways and objects seem to have, in the literature, the same real emotional substance as the brooks, commons, hedges, cottages, festivals of the rural scene. And the point of saying this is not to disprove or devalue either kind of feeling. It is to see the real change that is being written about, as we discern its common process.

For what is at issue, in all these cases, is a growth and alteration of consciousness: a history repeated in many lives and many places which is fundamentally an alteration of perception and relationship. What was once close, absorbing, accepted, familiar, internally experienced becomes separate, distinguishable, critical, changing, externally observed. In common or backstreet, village or city quarter, this process happens. We can say, of course, that it is an inevitable process; that this growth of adult consciousness is profoundly necessary, if only to see that these valued worlds were and are being created by men. But we have to say also that the village or backstreet of a child is not and cannot be the village or backstreet of the contemporary working adult. Great confusion is caused if the real childhood memory is projected, unqualified, as history. Yet what we have finally to say is that we live in a world in which the dominant mode of production and social relationships teaches, impresses, offers to make normal and even rigid, modes of detached, separated, external perception and action: modes of using and consuming rather than accepting and enjoying people and things. The structure of feeling of the memoirs is then significant and indispensable as a response to this specific social deformation. Yet this importance can only be recognized when we have made the historical judgment: not only that these are childhood views, which contemporary adult experience contradicts or qualifies; but that a process of human growth has in itself been deformed, by these deep internal directions of what an adult consciousness must be, in this kind of using, consuming, abstracting world. It is not so much the old village or the old backstreet that is significant. It is the perception and affirmation of a world in which one is not necessarily a stranger and an agent, but can be a member, a discoverer, in a shared source of life. Taken alone, of course, this is never enough. Indeed its displacement to fantasies about old villages and old backstreets can diminish even its immediate significance. To make an adult, working world of that kind would involve sharp critical consciousness and long active agency. Yet we can see here, in a central example, the true aetiology of some of the powerful images of country and city, when unalienated experience is the rural past and realistic experience is the urban future. If we take only the images, we can swing from one to the other, but without illumination. For we have really to look, in country and city alike, at the real social processes of alienation, separation, externality, abstraction. And we have to do this not only critically, in the necessary history of rural and urban capitalism, but substantially, by affirming the experiences which in many millions of lives are discovered and rediscovered, very often under pressure: experiences of directness, connection, mutuality, sharing, which alone can define, in the end, what the real deformation may be.

1.3 The growth of the city

E.W. Burgess

The outstanding fact of modern society is the growth of great cities. Nowhere else have the enormous changes which the machine industry has made in our social life registered themselves with such obviousness as in the cities. In the United States the transition from a rural to an urban civilization, though beginning later than in Europe, has taken place, if not more rapidly and completely, at any rate more logically in its most characteristic forms.

All the manifestations of modern life which are peculiarly urban – the skyscraper, the subway, the department store, the daily newspaper and social work – are characteristically American. The more subtle changes in our social life, which in their cruder manifestations are termed 'social problems', problems that alarm and bewilder us, as divorce, delinquency, and social unrest, are to be found in their most acute forms in our largest American cities. The profound and 'subversive' forces which have wrought these changes are measured in the physical growth and expansion of cities. That is the significance of the comparative statistics of Weber, Bücher and other students.

These statistical studies, although dealing mainly with the effects of urban growth, brought out into clear relief certain distinctive characteristics of urban as compared with rural populations. The larger proportion of women to men in the cities than in the open country, the greater percentage of youth and middle-aged, the higher ratio of the foreign-born, the increased heterogeneity of occupation increase with the growth of the city and profoundly alter its social structure. These variations in the composition of population are indicative of all the changes going on in the social organization of the community. In fact, these changes are a

Source: R.E. Park *et al* (1925) *The City* University of Chicago Press. Reprinted in Murray Stewart (ed.) 1972 *The City: Problems of Planning* Penguin, pp. 117–29.

part of the growth of the city and suggest the nature of the processes of growth.

The only aspect of growth adequately described by Bücher and Weber was the rather obvious process of the *aggregation* of urban population. Almost as overt a process, that of *expansion*, has been investigated from a different and very practical point of view by groups interested in city planning, zoning and regional surveys. Even more significant than the increasing density of urban population is its correlative tendency to overflow, and so to extend over wider areas, and to incorporate these areas into a larger communal life. This paper, therefore, will treat first of the expansion of the city, and then of the lesser known processes of urban metabolism and mobility which are closely related to expansion.

Expansion as physical growth

The expansion of the city from the standpoint of the city plan, zoning and regional surveys is thought of almost wholly in terms of its physical growth. Traction studies have dealt with the development of transportation in its relation to the distribution of population throughout the city. The surveys made by the Bell Telephone Company and other public utilities have attempted to forecast the direction and the rate of growth of the city in order to anticipate the future demands for the extension of their services. In the city plan the location of parks and boulevards, the widening of traffic streets, the provision for a civic centre, are all in the interest of the future control of the physical development of the city.

This expansion in area of our largest cities is now being brought forcibly to our attention by the Plan for the Study of New York and Its Environs, and by the formation of the Chicago Regional Planning Association, which extends the metropolitan district of the city to a radius of fifty miles, embracing 4000 square miles of territory. Both are attempting to measure expansion in order to deal with the changes that accompany city growth. In England, where more than one-half of the inhabitants live in cities having a population of 100,000 and over, the lively appreciation of the bearing of urban expansion on social organization is thus expressed by C.B. Fawcett (1922):

> One of the most important and striking developments in the growth of the urban populations of the more advanced peoples of the world during the last few decades has been the appearance of a number of vast urban aggregates, or conurbations, far larger and more numerous than the great cities of any preceding age. These have usually been formed by the simultaneous expansion of a number of neighbouring towns, which have grown out toward each other until

they have reached a practical coalescence in one continuous urban area. Each such conurbation still has within it many nuclei of denser town growth, most of which represent the central areas of the various towns from which it has grown, and these nuclear patches are connected by the less densely urbanized areas which began as suburbs of these towns. The latter are still usually rather less continuously occupied by buildings, and often have many open spaces.

These great aggregates of town dwellers are a new feature in the distribution of man over the earth. At the present day there are from thirty to forty of them, each containing more than a million people, whereas only a hundred years ago there were, outside the great centres of population on the waterways of China, not more than two or three. Such aggregations of people are phenomena of great geographical and social importance; they give rise to new problems in the organization of the life and well-being of their inhabitants and in their varied activities. Few of them have yet developed a social consciousness at all proportionate to their magnitude, or fully realized themselves as definite groupings of people with many common interests, emotions and thoughts (pp. 111–12).

In Europe and America the tendency of the great city to expand has been recognized in the term 'the metropolitan area of the city', which far overruns its political limits, and in the case of New York and Chicago, even state lines. The metropolitan area may be taken to include urban territory that is physically contiguous, but it is coming to be defined by that facility of transportation that enables a businessman to live in a suburb of Chicago and to work in the loop, and his wife to shop at Marshall Field's and attend grand opera in the Auditorium.

Expansion as a process

No study of expansion as a process has yet been made, although the materials for such a study and intimations of different aspects of the process are contained in city planning, zoning and regional surveys. The typical processes of the expansion of the city can best be illustrated, perhaps, by a series of concentric circles, which may be numbered to designate both the successive zones of urban extension and the types of areas differentiated in the process of expansion (see Figure 1).

This represents an ideal construction of the tendencies of any town or city to expand radially from its central business district – on the map 'The Loop'. Encircling the downtown area there is normally an area in transition, which is being invaded by business and light manufacture. A third area is inhabited by the workers in industries who have escaped from the area of deterioration but who desire to live within easy access of their work. Beyond this zone is the 'residential area' of high-class apartment buildings or of exclusive 'restricted' districts of single family dwellings. Still farther, out beyond the city limits, is the commuters zone – suburban areas, or satellite cities – within a thirty- to sixty-minute ride of the central business district.

Figure 1   The growth of the city

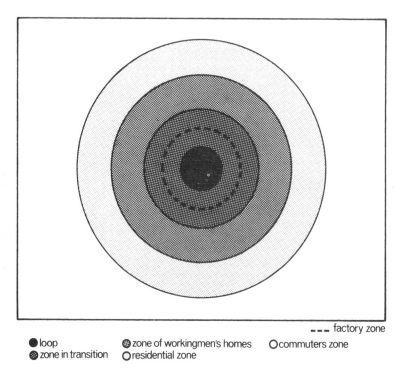

● loop   ⊕ zone of workingmen's homes   ○ commuters zone
⊛ zone in transition   ○ residential zone
--- factory zone

This chart brings out clearly the main fact of expansion, namely, the tendency of each inner zone to extend its area by the invasion of the next outer zone. This aspect of expansion may be called *succession*, a process which has been studied in detail in plant ecology. If this chart is applied to Chicago, all four of these zones were in its history included in the circumference of the inner zone, the present business district. The present boundaries of the area of deterioration were not many years ago those of the zone now inhabited by independent wage-earners, and within the memories of thousands of Chicagoans contained the residences of the 'best families'. It hardly needs to be added that neither Chicago nor any other city fits perfectly into this ideal scheme. Complications are introduced by the lake front, the Chicago River, railroad lines, historical factors in the location of industry, the relative degree of the resistance of communities to invasion, etc.

Besides extension and succession, the general process of expansion in urban growth involves the antagonistic and yet complementary process of concentration and decentralization. In all cities there is the natural tendency for local and outside transportation to converge in the central business district. In the downtown section of every large city we expect to find the department stores, the skyscraper office buildings, the railroad stations, the great hotels, the theatres, the art museum and the city hall. Quite naturally, almost inevitably, the economic, cultural and political life centres here. The relation of centralization to the other processes of city life may be roughly gauged by the fact that over half a million people daily enter and leave Chicago's 'loop'. More recently sub-business centres have grown up in outlying zones. These 'satellite loops' do not, it seems, represent the 'hoped for' revival of the neighbourhood, but rather a telescoping of several local communities into a larger economic unity. The Chicago of yesterday, an agglomeration of country towns and immigrant colonies, is undergoing a process of reorganization into a centralized decentralized system of local communities coalescing into sub-business areas visibly or invisibly dominated by the central business district. The actual processes of what may be called centralized decentralization are now being studied in the development of the chain store, which is only one illustration of the change in the basis of the urban organization.[1]

Expansion, as we have seen, deals with the physical growth of the city, and with the extension of the technical services that have made city life not only livable, but comfortable, even luxurious. Certain of these basic necessities of urban life are possible only through a tremendous development of communal existence. Three millions of people in Chicago are dependent upon one unified water system, one giant gas company, and one huge electric light plant. Yet, like most of the other aspects of our communal urban life, this economic cooperation is an example of cooperation without a shred of what the 'spirit of cooperation' is commonly thought to signify. The great public utilities are a part of the mechanization of life in great cities, and have little or no other meaning for social organization.

Yet the processes of expansion, and especially the rate of expansion, may be studied not only in the physical growth and business development, but also in the consequent changes in the social organization and in personality types. How far is the growth of the city, in its physical and technical aspects, matched by a natural but adequate readjustment in the social organization? What, for a city, is a normal rate of expansion, a rate of expansion with which controlled changes in the social organization might successfully keep pace?

Social organization and disorganization as processes of metabolism

These questions may best be answered, perhaps, by thinking of urban growth as a resultant of organization and disorganization analogous to the anabolic and katabolic processes of metabolism in the body. In what way are individuals incorporated into the life of a city? By what process does a person become an organic part of his society? The natural process of acquiring culture is by birth. A person is born into a family already adjusted to a social environment – in this case the modern city. The natural rate of increase of population most favourable for assimilation may then be taken as the excess of the birth-rate over the death-rate, but is this the normal rate of city growth? Certainly, modern cities have increased and are increasing in population at a far higher rate. However, the natural rate of growth may be used to measure the disturbances of metabolism caused by any excessive increase, as those which followed the great influx of southern Negroes into northern cities since the war. In a similar way all cities show deviations in composition by age and sex from a standard population such as that of Sweden, unaffected in recent years by any great emigration or immigration. Here again, marked variations, as any great excess of males over females, or of females over males, or in the proportion of children, or of grown men or women, are symptomatic of abnormalities in social metabolism.

Normally the processes of disorganization and organization may be thought of as in reciprocal relationship to each other, and as cooperating in a moving equilibrium of social order toward an end vaguely or definitely regarded as progressive. So far as disorganization points to reorganization and makes for more efficient adjustment, disorganization must be conceived not as pathological, but as normal. Disorganization as preliminary to reorganization of attitudes and conduct is almost invariably the lot of the newcomer to the city, and the discarding of the habitual, and often of what has been to him the moral, is not infrequently accompanied by sharp mental conflict and sense of personal loss. Oftener, perhaps, the change gives sooner or later a feeling of emancipation and an urge toward new goals.

In the expansion of the city a process of distribution takes place which sifts and sorts and relocates individuals and groups by residence and occupation. The resulting differentiation of the cosmopolitan American city into areas is typically all from one pattern, with only interesting minor modifications (Figure 2). Within the central business district or on an adjoining street is the 'main stem' of 'hobohemia', the teeming Rialto of the homeless migratory man of the Middle West.[2] In the zone of deterioration encircling the central business section are always to be found the so-called 'slums' and 'bad lands', with their submerged regions of poverty, degradation, and disease, and their underworlds of crime and vice. Within a deteriorating area are rooming-house districts, the purgatory of 'lost souls'. Near by is the Latin Quarter, where creative and rebellious spirits resort. The slums are also crowded to overflowing with immigrant colonies – the Ghetto, Little Sicily, Greektown, Chinatown – fascinatingly combining old world heritages and American adaptations. Wedging out from here is the Black Belt, with its free and disorderly life. The area of deterioration, while essentially one of decay, of stationary or declining population, is also one of regeneration, as witness the mission, the settlement, the artists' colony, radical centres – all obsessed with the vision of a new and better world.

The next zone is also inhabited predominatingly by factory and shop workers, but skilled and thrifty. This is an area of second immigrant settlement, generally of the second generation. It is the region of escape from the slum, the *Deutschland* of the aspiring Ghetto family. For *Deutschland* (literally 'Germany') is the name given, half in envy, half in derision, to that region beyond the Ghetto where successful neighbours appear to be imitating German Jewish standards of living. But the inhabitant of this area in turn looks to the 'Promised Land' beyond, to its residential hotels, its apartment-house region, its 'satellite loops', and its 'bright light' areas.

This differentiation into natural economic and cultural groupings gives form and character to the city. For segregation offers the group, and thereby the individuals who compose the group, a place and a role in the total organization of city life. Segregation limits development in certain directions, but releases it in others. These areas tend to accentuate certain traits, to attract and develop their kind of individuals, and so to become further differentiated.

The division of labour in the city likewise illustrates disorganization, reorganization and increasing differentiation. The immigrant from rural communities in Europe and America seldom brings with him economic skill of any great value in our industrial, commercial or professional life. Yet interesting occupational selection has taken place by nationality, explainable more by racial temperament or circumstance that by old-world economic background, as Irish policemen, Greek ice-cream parlours, Chinese laundries, Negro porters, Belgian janitors, etc.

Figure 2   Urban areas

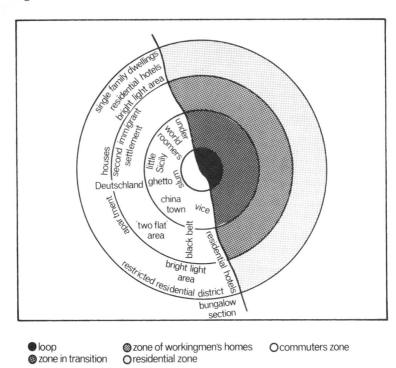

● loop   ⊛ zone of workingmen's homes   ○ commuters zone
⊕ zone in transition   ○ residential zone

The facts that in Chicago one million (996,589) individuals gainfully employed reported 509 occupations and that over 1,000 men and women in *Who's Who* gave 116 different vocations, give some notion of how in the city the minute differentiation of occupation 'analyzes and sifts the population, separating and classifying the diverse elements'.[3] These figures also afford some intimation of the complexity and complication of the modern industrial mechanism and the intricate segregation and isolation of divergent economic groups. Interrelated with this economic division of labour is a corresponding division into social classes and into cultural and recreational groups. From this multiplicity of groups, with their different patterns of life, the person finds his congenial social world and – what is not feasible in the narrow confines of a village – may move and live in widely separated, and perchance conflicting, worlds. Personal disorganization may be but the failure to harmonize the canons of conduct of two divergent groups.

If the phenomena of expansion and metabolism indicate that a moderate *expansion = disorganisation which lead must to soc. organisation*

degree of disorganization may and does facilitate social organization, they indicate as well that rapid urban expansion is accompanied by excessive increases in disease, crime, disorder, vice, insanity and suicide, rough indexes of social disorganization. But what are the indexes of the causes, rather than of the effects, of the disordered social metabolism of the city? The excess of the actual over the natural increase of population has already been suggested as a criterion. The significance of this increase consists in the immigration into a metropolitan city like New York and Chicago of tens of thousands of persons annually. Their invasion of the city has the effect of a tidal wave inundating first the immigrant colonies, the ports of first entry, dislodging thousands of inhabitants who overflow into the next zone, and so on and on until the momentum of the wave has spent its force on the last urban zone. The whole effect is to speed up expansion, to speed up industry, to speed up the 'junking' process in the area of deterioration. These internal movements of the population become the more significant for study. What movement is going on in the city, and how may this movement be measured? It is easier, of course, to classify movement within the city than to measure it. There is the movement from residence to residence, change of occupation, labour turnover, movement to and from work, movement for recreation and adventure. This leads to the question: What is the significant aspect of movement for the study of the changes in city life? The answer to this question leads directly to the important distinction between movement and mobility.

Mobility as the pulse of the community

Movement, *per se*, is not an evidence of change or of growth. In fact, movement may be a fixed and unchanging order of motion, designed to control a constant situation, as in routine movement. Movement that is significant for growth implies a change of movement in response to a new stimulus or situation. Change of movement of this type is called *mobility*. Movement of the nature of routine finds its typical expression in work. Change of movement, or mobility, is characteristically expressed in adventure. The great city, with its 'bright lights', its emporiums of novelties and bargains, its palaces of amusement, its underworld of vice and crime, its risks of life and property from accident, robbery, and homicide, has become the region of the most intense degree of adventure and danger, excitement and thrill.

Mobility, it is evident, involves change, new experience, stimulation. Stimulation induces a response of the person to those objects in his environment which afford expression for his wishes. For the person, as for the physical organism, stimulation is essential to growth. Response to stimulation is wholesome so long as it is a correlated *integral* reaction of the entire personality. When the reaction is *segmental*, that is, detached from, and uncontrolled by, the organization of personality, it tends to become disorganizing or pathological. That is why stimulation for the sake of stimulation, as in the restless pursuit of pleasure, partakes of the nature of vice.

The mobility of city life, with its increase in the number and intensity of stimulations, tends inevitably to confuse and to demoralize the person. For an essential element in the mores and in personal morality is consistency, consistency of the type that is natural in the social control of the primary group. Where mobility is the greatest, and where in consequence primary controls break down completely, as in the zone of deterioration in the modern city, there develop areas of demoralization, of promiscuity and of vice.

In our studies of the city it is found that areas of mobility are also the regions in which are found juvenile delinquency, boys' gangs, crime, poverty, wife desertion, divorce, abandoned infants and vice.

These concrete situations show why mobility is perhaps the best index of the state of metabolism of the city. Mobility may be thought of in more than a fanciful sense, as the 'pulse of the community'. Like the pulse of the human body, it is a process which reflects and is indicative of all the changes that are taking place in the community, and which is susceptible of analysis into elements which may be stated numerically.

The elements entering into mobility may be classified under two main heads : (1) the state of mutability of the person, and (2) the number and kind of contacts or stimulations in his environment. The mutability of city populations varies with sex and age composition, the degree of detachment of the person from the family and from other groups. All these factors may be expressed numerically. The new stimulations to which a population respond can be measured in terms of change of movement or of increasing contacts. Statistics on the movement of urban population may only measure routine, but an increase at a higher ratio than the increase of population measures mobility. In 1860 the horse-car lines of New York City carried about fifty million passengers; in 1890 the trolley-cars (and a few surviving horse-cars) transported about 500 million; in 1921, the elevated, subway, surface, and electric and steam suburban lines carried a total of more than 2500 million passengers.[4] In Chicago the total annual rides per capita on the surface and elevated lines were 164 in 1890; 215 in 1900; 320 in 1910; and 338 in 1921. In addition, the rides per capita on steam and electric suburban lines almost doubled between 1916 (23) and 1921 (41), and the increasing use of the automobile must not be overlooked.[5] For example, the number of automobiles in Illinois increased from 131,140 in 1915 to 833,920 in 1923.[6]

Mobility may be measured not only by these changes of movement, but also by increase of contacts. While the increase of population of Chicago in 1912–22 was less than 25 per cent (23.6 per cent), the increase of letters delivered to Chicagoans was double that (49.6 per cent) – (from 693,084,196 to 1,038,007,854).[7] In 1912 New York had 8.8 telephones; in 1922, 16.9 per 100 inhabitants. Boston had, in 1912, 10.1 telephones; ten years later, 19.5 telephones per 100 inhabitants. In the same decade the figures for Chicago increased from 12.3 to 21.6 per 100 population.[8] But increase of the use of the telephone is probably more significant than increase in the number of telephones. The number of telephone calls in Chicago increased from 606,131,928 in 1914 to 944,010,586 in 1922,[9] an increase of 55.7 per cent, while the population increased only 13.4 per cent.

Land values, since they reflect movement, afford one of the most sensitive indexes of mobility. The highest land values in Chicago are at the point of greatest mobility in the city, at the corner of State and Madison streets, in the Loop. A traffic count showed that at the rush period 31,000 people an hour, or 210,000 men and women in sixteen and one-half hours, passed the south-west corner. For over ten years land values in the Loop have been stationary, but in the same time they have doubled, quadrupled, and even sextupled in the strategic corners of the 'satellite loops', an accurate index of the changes which have occurred. Our investigations so far seem to indicate that variations in land values, expecially where correlated with differences in rents, offer perhaps the best single measure of mobility, and so of all the changes taking place in the expansion and growth of the city.

In general outline, I have attempted to present the point of view and methods of investigation which the department of sociology is employing in its studies in the growth of the city, namely, to describe urban expansion in terms of extension, succession, and concentration; to determine how expansion disturbs metabolism when disorganization is in excess of organization; and, finally, to define mobility and to propose it as a measure both of expansion and metabolism, susceptible to precise quantitative formulation, so that it may be regarded almost literally as the pulse of the community.

Notes

1 See E.H. Shideler *The Retail Business Organization as an Index of Community Organization.*

2 For a study of this cultural area of city life see Anderson (1923).

3 Weber (1899, p.442).

4 Adapted from W.B. Monro (1923, p. 377).
5 *Report of the Chicago Subway and Traction Commission* (p.81) and
   the *Report on a Physical Plan for a Unified Transportation System*
   (p.391).
6 Data compiled by automobile industries.
7 Statistics of mailing division, Chicago Post Office.
8 Determined from *Census Estimates for Intercensual Years.*
9 From statistics furnished by Mr R. Johnson, traffic supervisor, Illinois
   Bell Telephone Company.

References

ANDERSON, N. (1923) *The Hobo* Chicago
FAWCETT, C. B. (1922) 'British conurbations in 1921' *Sociology Review*
   14, pp. 111–12
MONRO, W.B. (1923) *Municipal Government and Administration*
   Macmillan
WEBER, A. (1899) *The Growth of Cities in the Nineteenth Century*
   Macmillan

1.4 Ideas for town planners

David Donnison

The more we learn about human settlements, the clearer it becomes that their development can only be understood, and urban policies can only be formulated, if both are conceived as integral parts of the development and policies of the whole society in which we live. Thus we should beware of consensus, for the main conflicts in that society – conflicts between development and conservation, between the drive for greater wealth and the attempt to distribute it more fairly, and between the competing interests of different groups – must all be reflected in debates about planning.

But since planning policies must grow out of a real understanding of cities, much of which can be verified in practical ways, it may be possible to identify some of the basic processes of urban development which most people would agree about. We can then focus more productively on the implications of these basic observations. But note, first, the objects of the whole exercise. Three, I suggest, are particularly important.

1 The most general aim of urban planning is to extend people's opportunities – their liberty, their effective choices, their access to everything that society can offer ... many different words can be used to describe these objectives. That is only to propose a way of talking about aims: such words do not tell us what to do when different people compete for the same opportunities, or when one opportunity can only be enlarged by restricting another. Yet the choice of language is not a trivial matter. The rhetoric of planning debate (Homes before roads! Subsidize people, not bricks and mortar! Protect the environment from the polluters!) too often conceals the fact that the argument is really about opportunities for people of different kinds, or for the same people considered as workers, residents, drivers, holiday-makers and so on.

Source: *Three Banks Review* December 1972, No. 96, pp. 10–27.

2   When choices have to be made between the opportunities of different people, we should normally give priority to those whose opportunities are most restricted. That egalitarian assertion can be explained and defended (it is not the sort of thing that can be 'proved'), but I shall not trouble to do so here[1] because governments of both Parties have so often committed themselves to egalitarian urban policies that the aim is not in *general* a controversial one (specifics are different). The previous Secretary of State for the Environment continued this tradition, introducing his most important legislation with a White Paper which pointed out that 'millions of our fellow citizens still face acute housing problems', and calling for 'a final assault on the slums, the overcrowding, the dilapidation and the injustice that still scar the housing scene'.[2] Since the days of Abercrombie the growing strength of economists within the planning professions has tended to reinforce this emphasis because their studies repeatedly show that the urban squalor which planners have traditionally battled against is due to poverty of one sort or another.

To pursue egalitarian policies in specific cases is often very difficult – not only in the political sense; it may even be difficult to decide what a truly egalitarian policy would be – but some practical principles are clear. Whenever decisions about priorities have to be made, their distributional consequences should be examined; it is never good enough to consider only their total benefits or total costs. Action which cannot be shown to exert an equalizing influence may have to be taken, but if compensating steps are not envisaged special reasons should always be given to justify it.

3   If we succeed in extending people's opportunities they will make changing and unpredicted use of their freedom. That's what it's for. So how do we discover what they really want? The market can help to guide us. But in a relatively affluent urban society a growing proportion of the opportunities to be expanded and equalized are not bought for cash. Education, medical care, clean air, law and order, peace and quiet are at least as important as the kinds of consumption that are covered in the Family Expenditure Survey.

It follows that when decisions are to be taken about any aspect of urban development, from a general improvement area to procedures for the allocation of children to secondary schools, we should ask whether the people concerned have been involved in the decision, or whether they have demonstrated by their behaviour that they want it. Although that rule – even the definition of 'the people concerned' – will often be difficult to interpret, it could have a salutary effect in many quarters.

If these rules had been followed in the past, they would have posed some good questions about policies which have had a pervasive influence: people would have recognized that the green belts were likely to enrich the

householders and farmers of suburban counties (by driving up the pric ...
housing land and holding down the price of farm land) and impoverish
tenants in the inner city who cannot escape to the suburbs. Before investing
35 million pounds a year of the taxpayers' money in grants to private
owners for the improvement of over 100,000 houses a year,[3] governments
would have taken the trouble to discover that those who benefit from these
grants are the richer and the younger sections of the population, and the
owners of obsolete housing which can be sold at enhanced prices.[4] It might
still be right to pursue these or similar policies, but more effective
proposals would have been urged to compensate for the unequalizing
impact.

Thus far I have argued that planners should try to extend people's
opportunities – particularly the opportunities of those who lead the most
impoverished and restricted lives – and should try to involve the people
most affected by their policies in decision-making. That much could be
said about policies in any field.

I want to turn more specifically now to urban planning. My subject is
'urban', not because it is 'non-rural', but because I deal mainly with
problems which arise at the *scale* of the city and its surrounding region,
rather than at the larger scales of the nation or economic planning region,
or the smaller scales of the neighbourhood or building site; it is 'planning',
not because policies for employment and other departments of government
are excluded, but to focus attention on the spatial implications of all
policies, the structure of urban-scale settlements, and the impact that
policies of all kinds make upon the city and the distribution of
opportunities among its citizens.

Urban structure and concepts

We should briefly recall the main elements in the urban system. It is with
jobs that most analyses begin – particularly the work going on in the
centres of cities. The central meeting place and market – usually a natural
one, alongside an important river crossing – is still a hub of intense activity
from which other activities flow outward along radial communications. The
American term, the 'central business district', does not exactly fit the
British central areas, where government, higher education and medical
care are often the most rapidly growing activities – as a glance at
Manchester, Sheffield, Liverpool, Edinburgh and other places will show.
The service industries which are growing in central areas recruit well-paid
executives and professionals, but more numerous by far are their
messengers, packers, cleaners and others – predominantly unskilled and
poorly paid, and many of them women.[5]

Manufacturing and warehousing, particularly of the older sorts, occupies flat land, alongside heavy transport facilities: rivers, railways and harbours. These plants, offering many jobs for skilled, male manual workers, are disappearing as manufacturers take a falling share of the nation's labour force, and as they move out of central areas towards the suburbs and beyond. A growing proportion of the labour force now produces goods and services for local residents, rather than for export to other communities. Where homes once clustered around the work, work now increasingly follows the resident population.

The distribution across the map of people and homes follows broadly similar patterns in many cities. Since the stock of houses grows slowly and the social character of a neighbourhood changes slowly, the structure of a city is a record of its history. The well-to-do, as they abandoned the grander houses in the centre to an expanding commerce, sought homes on the pleasant side of the town, giving easy access to the central area. Their houses spread outwards, often up a hill, and away from the smoke and the din towards attractive villages and parklands already being colonized by their own class. Their progress can be traced from the tramways and commuter railways and the services strung along the route − from art galleries and banks at the inward end, past medical schools, to the college which became a university, and out to well-apppointed pubs in the gin-and-tonic belt beyond.

As the city grew, other well-to-do quarters sprang up, forming crescents on its fringes, typically on high ground, as their names often suggest: Alderley Edge, Edgbaston, Richmond Hill, Harrow-on-the-Hill....

Meanwhile the poor lived close to their work where land was cheap, alongside the warehouses, and on the smoky side of the centre, typically in low-lying, marshy places or 'seas' as familiar names again suggest: Battersea, Bermondsey, the Isle of Dogs, the Bogside ... [6] The middle-income groups, into which the poor might climb, generally occupied the land between them and the rich, and the outer fringes of the poorer segments of the city.

As new building for the families of the rich and the middle-income groups spread outwards, older houses left behind in the path of the expanding centre tended to be subdivided or redeveloped and used more intensively by childless households and the elderly, and by families too poor to escape. The pattern is found in good housing (South Kensington and St Marylebone) as well as in bad (Stepney and Islington).

New households − newly arrived in the city or newly split off from their parents' homes − often settled in these inner zones of 'non-family housing' and later made their way outwards as they secured more income and started their own families. Firms, too, tended to move outwards, often in short steps, searching for larger premises while keeping in touch with their labour force, their suppliers and customers.[7]

These glacial, centrifugal flows shape people's perceptions of the city.[8] Working-class people use and perceive a smaller and more cramped urban world than the one to which wealthier and more educated people have access: they inhabit a smaller town. But the movements of rich and poor alike are strongly radial. Their paths may seldom cross those of people on the other side of town.

This attempt to identify the common factors of urban structure is inevitably confined to the simpler patterns imprinted by the market. But we should pause to note the varied character of cities, each unique and so complex. There are major economic differences between one city and another. Some, full of growth industries, suck in talent and enterprise. Having recruited and raised more than their share of young, mobile and successful people, they also throw out more emigrants.[9] Others move at a slower tempo.

There are signs that long-term economic and political changes have tipped the scales against the really big city. The world has too many places like Glasgow, Liverpool and Manchester, and they cannot all find prosperous roles for themselves. A few – in the UK, London alone – can aspire to become world cities. Others appreciably smaller – Bristol, Edinburgh and Southampton – thrive as regional centres, and at a smaller scale still there are the most rapidly growing towns of all – Leicester, Oxford and Swindon, for example.

Cities have many social characteristics which cannot be explained in purely economic terms, though they may have important economic effects. Dr Boal's maps of Belfast are rent by jagged sectarian barriers that utterly divide neighbourhoods of similar economic composition, sending people of the same age and class to different bus routes, schools, shops and recreations.[10] Dr Evans has shown that a curious distortion in London's journey-to-work patterns can only be explained by the evolution of the Jewish community, many of whose more successful families retained their working links with Stepney and the East End long after moving to areas of north London where journeys to work more often run to the city and the West End.[11]

My generalizations trace the social effects of the market. But society has made its own impact on the market, confining the outward spread of cities with green belts, encircling middle- and upper-income housing and arresting its outward growth with large Council estates for working people, reducing the highest densities and raising the lowest. The propositions derived from social area analyses from which urban sociologists sought to formulate a theory of 'residential differentiation' repeatedly break down in

British cities where the markets for land and housing have been so drastically modified by public intervention.[12]

Constraints

The interlocking character of the urban system I have so briefly outlined imposes constraints which must be understood by anyone who wants to change things. Three of them – all perfectly familiar to plain men – have too often been neglected by analysts who confine their attention to one aspect of the city or to one point in time.

1   Anyone who cares to find out knows that incomes and opportunities are very unequally distributed, and that taxes and social service benefits make only a modest impact on the dispersion of these distributions. Inequalities are pervasive, and difficult to modify in a peace-time parliamentary democracy.

But for the individual and his family the chief wage earner's income is often less important that the income available for each member of the household. Earnings generally reach a peak in mid-career – rather sooner for manual workers than for professional and executive workers. But income per head is highest for the young (when all the members of a childless household are at work) and for the middle-aged (when their children have started work and wives are working again); conversely, it is lowest in childhood, again when several children have to be supported by one earner, and finally in retirement. The 'poverty cycle' afflicts rich and poor alike at predictable stages of their lives. Since Seebohm Rowntree coined the phrase in 1899, reductions in family size, and the growth of pensions, tax allowances and family benefits of various kinds have eased the troughs of this cycle. But other changes which have taken place – the massive entry of women to the labour market, the prolongation of education, and the bringing forward of retirement – have tended to sharpen its amplitude again.

The chance of breaking through to new opportunities and lasting changes in life styles generally comes – and goes – early in life: earlier, perhaps, than ever before. Entry to occupations which go far to determine people's working responsibilities, and hence their earnings, credit and opportunities for personal development, depends increasingly on education and professional training which people complete in their early twenties or sooner.[13] The average age of people buying a house for the first time has fallen to twenty-four, as lenders try to reach successively lower income groups by extending periods for repayment. Very few start buying after the age of forty: building societies and insurance companies soon lose interest in the middle-aged.

Any analysis of the effects of income, wealth, class and race – important factors, all of them – which neglects these characteristics of the life cycle will be apt to mislead us.

2 Many activities and many demands for goods and services are closely linked to each other, and cannot be understood in isolation. The complementarities that bind some activities and demands, and the substitutions that separate others, together define people's life-styles. Their growing interest in 'the quality of life' has led economists to talk in terms of 'the consumption services of an environment', rather than confining their attention to individual goods which change hands for cash. This led to the view that 'experiential environments are analogous to "clubs" ... ' whose members have 'quasi-property rights in the environmental goods offered by the club ...'. Shelter and accessibility are two of the benefits wrapped within a larger package secured by members of such 'clubs'.[14]

Demands for shelter and for access to the opportunities which cities afford are linked in the choice of housing which provides both. How people trade off space against accessibility depends on their valuation of housing and their valuation of the time they spend in travelling – which depend, in turn, on their income, the size of their household, the number of people in it who must travel each day, and the speed and comfort of their journeys.

Thus in a free market, lodgers, single people and married couples who both go to work will tend to cluster in the inner parts of cities; so will the richest and the poorest. Married couples with one earner and no children will tend to concentrate in the inner suburbs; so will middle-income groups. Couples with several children and one earner will more often be found in the outer suburbs; so too, will the rich. Alan Evans, who analyses and explains these relationships, points out that when transport is fast, expensive and comfortable, the rich (for whom time is scarce and discomfort unacceptable) tend to flee to the suburbs, while the poor (for whom money is scarce) remain in the centre of the town. He suggests, 'not too seriously', that the quickest way to bring the rich back to live in central areas and encourage the poor to move out would be to make transport cheap, uncomfortable and slow.[15]

Many other links can be discerned in the urban system which have yet to be properly researched. What happens, for example, if the education system of a particular city or region enables students to attain higher qualifications than students in other places – as in Wales? Either more work demanding high qualifications must be done in the region, or more workers must take jobs elsewhere done by people less qualified than themselves, or more well qualified workers must emigrate from the region or commute outwards, or fewer must immigrate or commute inwards, or more must die, retire, become housewives or remain unemployed. If, on the other hand, a regional economy begins to develop faster than its neighbours – as in parts of the Highlands – then the educational system must grow too, or converse results will follow: less unemployment, fewer housewives, less emigration and so on. We need to know much more about these links and the ways in which they actually work if we are to talk sense about regional development or educational programmes, or plan effectively for either. Too often such problems and the policies for dealing with them are discussed in isolation from each other.

3   The constraints I have outlined arise from the links between different but simultaneous activities. A third pattern of constraints arises from the links between similar activities at different times.

In the housing market the process is called 'filtering'. Each year about 2 per cent is added to our stock of houses, and about 1 per cent subtracted from it. Since about 9 per cent of households move in a year, most of them go to second-hand houses, waiting on others to vacate them, while their successors wait to move into the houses they will vacate in turn. Once set in train, the 'flows' of households who follow each other through the housing market can be slowly diverted in one direction or another, but are exceedingly difficult to reverse.

This process of succession works, less clearly but equally powerfully, in many other parts of the urban system. Across the territory of urban neighbourhoods there passes a continuing flow of people and firms. The places where succession to land proceeds quickly (as in some densely occupied inner areas) permit a slower turnover elsewhere (as in many inter-war suburbs). Planners and redevelopers who freeze movement in the former are liable to hasten it in the latter.

The stock of places in schools and universities changes much more slowly than the population of students who pass through them. Education develops gradually, as each generation builds on the efforts of its predecessors and draws along its own well beaten route a continuing flow of successors. The job market too is largely 'second-hand' in the sense that someone else did most of the work it offers before the present holders of these jobs succeeded to them.

These processes, familiar to ordinary people, have been neglected by most urban research workers (which is why we know so little about them in detail) and hence by town planners. Both have too often assumed that we live in 'instant cities' without a history.

Implications for policy

I have space to explore only a few of the practical implications of these ideas. Campaigns to raise educational attainment or to improve housing in deprived areas often seem to be based on the assumption that people will change their behaviour if cajoled or bribed to do so. But most people already want better housing,[16] and most parents want their children to take their education much further than they themselves did.[17] The question is not 'how can we stimulate their aspirations?' but 'What stopped them?'

It would help people if the rungs in the ladders of opportunity were set close to each other, economically, spatially and culturally. People move most easily to a *slightly* more expensive house, *close* to their previous home. More important still, the different ladders which people mount must be set close to each other: it will be easier to get that more expensive house if there are better paid jobs within reach, and easier to get the jobs if there are opportunities for a better education and further training. Conversely, it will be easier for people to stick at their education (or persuade their children to do so) if it promises a better job, it will be easier to stick at the job if it offers more money, and the money will be worth more if it could secure a better home for the worker – or something else which his family really wants.

Unless urban resources grow faster than population it is very difficult to furnish these opportunities, let alone match them to each other. Everyone must wait for dead men's shoes. Zero growth transforms each market into a zero sum game in which one man's gain must be another's loss. Unless they are confident that there will be more and better opportunities of all kinds in future, the most vulnerable people find it difficult to spend an extra year at school, to leave a secure tenancy, to stand up for their rights, or to take risks of any kind. Politicians find it very difficult to improve the living conditions of the poor if that can only be done at the expense of others upon whose votes they depend: egalitarian policies are easier to adopt if everyone can be given something and the poor get a bit extra.

Planners must therefore take growth more seriously. They should ask whether their policies will enable a town to make new things which can be exported to other places, and familiar things which have now to be imported from elsewhere. If poorer people are to benefit from growth the town needs more than a general improvement in its balance of payments. Its economy must be permeated with expanding opportunities.

An outbreak of offices and hotels on London's South Bank would be more heartening to contemplate if we could be sure that many local residents would soon be running their own tourist shops, cafés, taxi firms, office cleaning and laundry services – not simply labouring for the big enterprises which are more likely to do so. That thought is unlikely to occur to governments whose favourite and fabulously subsidized investments in growth have more often been refineries or smelters, built by migrant construction workers and manned by managers and technologists who can only be succeeded by equally qualified outsiders. Such industrial monsters may scare off those who would build holiday and retirement cottages (put up by small local firms, maintained by local plumbers and painters, and served by the local grocers, newsagents and filling stations) which would diversify and strengthen the ladders of opportunity.

Discontinuities in the urban system frustrate opportunities. But often they cannot be avoided. If slums are to be cleared, their residents must be found good housing, not compelled to spend a generation or two climbing slowly through gradually brightening twilight areas. But people should not be rehoused far from their jobs; or, if that cannot be avoided, better jobs must be found for them within reach of their new homes, or their transport costs must be subsidized, or some combination of these steps must be taken to bridge the resulting discontinuities.

We should be suspicious of building programmes which purport to show that the housing problem will be 'solved', without considering economic and spatial discontinuities which may prevent people from getting the houses which are to be built. Encouragement for Council tenants to buy their own homes will have little effect on estates where the great majority of householders are over forty, unless special steps are taken to provide credit for people who are beyond the age at which building societies lend to first-time buyers. People in Tower Hamlets may move to Newham on the traditional escape routes from the East End, but they are unlikely to move to Milton Keynes and Northampton – distant expansion schemes on the wrong side of town. The community development projects, the educational priority areas and the new 'six cities' projects to be mounted by the Department of the Environment cannot greatly enlarge the opportunities of people in the impoverished inner areas if they are *confined* to inner areas, making no impact on the rest of the city.

People find it easier to try new things – under-educated children to prolong their schooling, immigrants to go to new towns where they have rarely been seen before, or gypsies to enter regular jobs which could give them a decent income – if they are accompanied by others of their own kind. Highly selective policies which offer opportunities only to those who are prepared to abandon their own class, family or friends, will only help a few rugged individualists.

Policies which are designed to enable large groups to pursue their aspirations together may produce destructive discontinuities of other kinds if they segregate the different elements in an urban society too completely from each other. Residents of suburbs built entirely to low densities and high prices have, wittingly or unwittingly, kicked down the ladders up which they themselves climbed. For every green-belted and improvement-granted commuter village which excludes all but the rich there must somewhere else be communities whose opportunities have been unnecessarily impoverished. Meanwhile, in urban belts of slum housing and Council estates from which anyone who wants to buy an adequate home or enter higher education must escape, the ladders of opportunity are cut short.

I have only touched on a dauntingly large subject – saying practically nothing, for example, about profoundly important aspects of urban life such as city government and politics. My speculative assertions will be amended at many points as we learn more about cities and the way they work. To do that we must study the relations between different activities in the urban economy, different points in urban space, and different phases in urban history. Such studies are likely to show, depressingly for radicals, that major and lasting changes in the distribution of opportunities will be difficult and slow. They will also show, disturbingly for conservatives, that we must change most things if we are to change anything much.

Notes

1 I have done a little better elsewhere – 'Liberty, equality and fraternity', *Three Banks Review* December 1970.

2 *Fair Deal for Housing* Cmnd. 4728, 1971; paragraphs 2 and 4.

3 The figures are for Great Britain in 1971; they were much higher in 1972. *Housing and Construction Statistics*, No. 1 HMSO, 1972.

4 For evidence supporting these assertions, see Richard Kirwan and D.B. Martin *The Economics of Urban Residential Renewal and Improvement* Centre for Environmental Studies Working Paper 77, 1972, p. 126.

5 Ray Pahl, 'Poverty and the urban system', this volume, pp. 109–20.

6 The influence of the physical structure of a city upon its social structure, too often neglected by urban sociologists, is stressed by Peter Willmott and Michael Young 'Social class and geography', in *London: Urban Patterns, Problems and Policies*, David Donnison and David Eversley (eds) Heinemann, 1973, from whom some of these examples come.

7 Evidence about the movement of firms within cities is scarce: mine comes from Professor Gordon Cameron, e.g. 'Intra-urban location and the new plant', *Urban and Regional Studies Discussion Papers No. 5* University of Glasgow, September 1972.

8 For some evidence on these points see Terence R. Lee 'Psychology and living space', *Transactions of the Bartlett Society* Vol. 2, 1963–4, p. 9.

9 A.J. Fielding 'Internal migration in England and Wales', Centre for Environmental Studies, *University Working Paper 14* 1972.

10 'Territoriality on the Shankill-Falls Divide, Belfast', *Irish Geography* Vol. 6, No. 1, 1969; p. 30.

11 Alan W. Evans *Residential Location in Cities* Macmillan, p. 302 *ff.*

12 'In the twentieth century,' Dr Robson points out, 'the development of council housing and of town planning and the effects of social changes have had profound effects upon the urban scene and have largely invalidated many of the bases on which the classical models have been built.' *Urban Analysis*, p. 240.

13 For some recent and revealing evidence on this point see Lester C. Thurow, 'Education and economic equality', *The Public Interest* No. 28, Summer 1972, p. 66.

14 The quotations come from Lowdon Wingo's Donald Robertson memorial lecture, 'The quality of life: towards a microeconomic definition', *Urban Studies* February 1973.

15 *Op. cit.* chapters 9, 10 and 11.

16 For a summary of some of the evidence on this, see *The Government of Housing*, p. 201 *ff.*

17 For one of many sources on this point, see *Children and Their Primary Schools* (The Plowden Report) HMSO, 1967, Vol. 2, Appendix 3, Table 27.

1.5 Urbanism and suburbanism as ways of life

H. J. Gans

The contemporary sociological conception of cities and of urban life is
based largely on the work of the Chicago School, and its summary
statement in Louis Wirth's essay, 'Urbanism as a Way of Life' (1957). In
that paper, Wirth developed a 'minimum sociological definition of the city'
as 'a relatively large, dense and permanent settlement of socially
heterogeneous individuals' (1957, p. 50). From these prerequisites, he
then deduced the major outlines of the urban way of life. As he saw it,
number, density, and heterogeneity created a social structure in which
primary-group relationships were inevitably replaced by secondary
contacts that were impersonal, segmental, superficial, transitory, and often
predatory in nature. As a result, the city dweller became anonymous,
isolated, secular, relativistic, rational, and sophisticated. In order to
function in the urban society, he was forced to combine with others to
organize corporations, voluntary associations, representative forms of
government, and the impersonal mass media of communications. These
replaced the primary groups and the integrated way of life found in rural
and other pre-industrial settlements....

Despite its title and intent, Wirth's paper deals with urban-industrial
society, rather than with the city. This is evident from his approach. Like
other urban sociologists, Wirth based his analysis on a comparison of
settlement types, but unlike his colleagues, who pursued urban–rural
comparisons, Wirth contrasted the city to the folk society. Thus, he
compared settlement types of pre-industrial and industrial society. This
allowed him to include in his theory of urbanism the entire range of
modern institutions which are not found in the folk society, even though

Source: Arnold M. Rose (ed) (1962) *Human Behaviour and Social Processes* Routledge
and Kegan Paul, pp.625–48; reprinted in John Raynor and Jane Harden (eds) (1973)
Cities, Communities and the Young Readings in Urban Education, Vol. 1, Routledge and
Kegan Paul, pp.21–40.

many such groups (e.g. voluntary associations) are by no means exclusively urban. Moreover, Wirth's conception of the city dweller as depersonalized, atomized, and susceptible to mass movements suggests that his paper is based on, and contributes to, the theory of the mass society.

Many of Wirth's conclusions may be relevant to the understanding of ways of life in modern society. However, since the theory argues that all of society is now urban, *his analysis does not distinguish ways of life in the city from those in other settlements within modern society.* In Wirth's time, the comparison of urban and pre-urban settlement types was still fruitful, but today, the primary task for urban (or community) sociology seems to me to be the analysis of the similarities and differences between contemporary settlement types.

This paper is an attempt at such an analysis; it limits itself to distinguishing ways of life in the modern city and the modern suburb. A re-analysis of Wirth's conclusions from this perspective suggests that his characterization of the urban way of life applies only – and not too accurately – to the residents of the inner city. The remaining city dwellers, as well as most suburbanites, pursue a different way of life, which I shall call 'quasi-primary'. This proposition raises some doubt about the mutual exclusiveness of the concepts of city and suburb and leads to a yet broader question: whether settlement concepts and other ecological concepts are useful for explaining ways of life.

The inner city

Wirth argued that number, density, and heterogeneity had two social consequences which explain the major features of urban life. On the one hand, the crowding of diverse types of people into a small area led to the segregation of homogeneous types of people into separate nieghbourhoods. On the other hand, the lack of physical distance between city dwellers resulted in social contact between them, which broke down existing social and cultural patterns and encouraged assimilation as well as acculturation – the melting pot effect. Wirth implied that the melting pot effect was far more powerful than the tendency toward segregation and concluded that, sooner or later, the pressures engendered by the dominant social, economic, and political institutions of the city would destroy the remaining pockets of primary-group relationships. Eventually, the social system of the city would resemble Tönnies' *Gesellschaft* – a way of life which Wirth considered undesirable.

Because Wirth had come to see the city as the prototype of mass society, and because he examined the city from the distant vantage point of the folk society – from the wrong end of the telescope, so to speak – his view of urban life is not surprising. In addition, Wirth found support for his theory in the empirical work of his Chicago colleagues. As Greer and Kube (1959, p. 112) and Wilensky and Lebeaux (1958, p. 121) have pointed out, the Chicago sociologists conducted their most intensive studies in the inner city.[1] At that time these were slums recently invaded by new waves of European immigrants and rooming house and skid row districts, as well as the habitat of Bohemians and well-to-do Gold Coast apartment dwellers. Wirth himself studied the Maxwell Street Ghetto, an inner-city Jewish neighbourhood then being dispersed by the acculturation and mobility of its inhabitants (1928). Some of the characteristics of urbanism which Wirth stressed in his essay abounded in these areas.

Wirth's diagnosis of the city as *Gesellschaft* must be questioned on three counts. First, the conclusions derived from a study of the inner city cannot be generalized to the entire urban area. Second, there is as yet not enough evidence to prove – nor, admittedly, to deny – that number, density, and heterogeneity result in the social consequences which Wirth proposed. Finally, even if the causal relationship could be verified, it can be shown that a significant proportion of the city's inhabitants were, and are, isolated from these consequences by social structures and cultural patterns which they either brought to the city, or developed by living in it. Wirth conceived the urban population as consisting of heterogeneous individuals, torn from past social systems, unable to develop new ones, and therefore prey to social anarchy in the city. While it is true that a not insignificant proportion of the inner city population was, and still is, made up of unattached individuals (Rose 1947), Wirth's formulation ignores the fact that this population consists mainly of relatively homogeneous groups, with social and cultural moorings that shield it fairly effectively from the suggested consequences of number, density, and heterogeneity. This applies even more to the residents of the outer city, who constitute a majority of the total city population.

The social and cultural moorings of the inner city population are best described by a brief analysis of the five types of inner city residents. These are:

1 the 'cosmopolites'
2 the unmarried or childless
3 the 'ethnic villagers'
4 the 'deprived', and
5 the 'trapped' and downward mobile.

The 'cosmopolites' include students, artists, writers, musicians, and entertainers, as well as other intellectuals and professionals. They live in the city in order to be near the special 'cultural' facilities that can only be located near the centre of the city. Many cosmopolites are unmarried or childless. Others rear children in the city, especially if they have the income to afford the aid of servants and governesses. The less affluent ones may move to the suburbs to raise their children, continuing to live as cosmopolites under considerable handicaps, especially in the lower-middle-class suburbs. Many of the very rich and powerful are also cosmopolities, although they are likely to have at least two residences, one of which is suburban or exurban.

The unmarried or childless must be divided into two subtypes, depending on the permanence or transience of their status. The temporarily unmarried or childless live in the inner city for only a limited time. Young adults may team up to rent an apartment away from their parents and close to job or entertainment opportunities. When they marry, they may move first to an apartment in a transient neighbourhood, but if they can afford to do so, they leave for the outer city or the suburbs with the arrival of the first or second child. The permanently unmarried may stay in the inner city for the remainder of their lives, their housing depending on their income.

The 'ethnic villagers' are ethnic groups, which are found in such inner city neighbourhoods as New York's Lower East Side, living in some ways as they did when they were peasants in European or Puerto Rican villages (Gans 1959). Although they reside in the city, they isolate themselves from significant contact with most city facilities, aside from workplaces. Their way of life differs sharply from Wirth's urbanism in its emphasis on kinship and the primary group, the lack of anonymity and secondary-group contacts, the weakness of formal organizations, and the suspicion of anything and anyone outside their neighbourhood.

The first two types live in the inner city by choice; the third is there partly because of necessity, partly because of tradition. The final two types are in the inner city because they have no other choice. One is the 'deprived' population: the very poor; the emotionally disturbed or otherwise handicapped; broken families; and, most important, the non-white population. These urban dwellers must take the dilapidated housing and blighted neighbourhoods to which the housing market relegates them, although among them are some for whom the slum is a hiding place, or a temporary stop-over to save money for a house in the outer city or the suburbs (Spectorsky 1955).

The 'trapped' are the people who stay behind when a neighbourhood is invaded by non-residential land users or lower-status immigrants, because they cannot afford to move, or are otherwise bound to their present location (Spectorsky 1955). The 'downward mobiles' are a related type;

they may have started life in a higher class position, but have been forced down in the socioeconomic hierarchy and in the quality of their accommodations. Many of them are old people, living out their existence on small pensions.

These five types all live in dense and heterogeneous surroundings, yet they have such diverse ways of life that it is hard to see how density and heterogeneity could exert a common influence. Moreover, all but the last two types are isolated or detached from their neighbourhood and thus from the social consequences which Wirth described.

When people who live together have social ties based on criteria other than mere common occupancy, they can set up social barriers regardless of the physical closeness or the heterogeneity of their neighbours. The ethnic villagers are the best illustration. While a number of ethnic groups are usually found living together in the same neighbourhood, they are able to *isolate* themselves from each other through a variety of social devices. Wirth himself recognized this when he wrote that 'two groups can occupy a given area without losing their separate identity because each side is permitted to live its own inner life and each somehow fears or idealizes the other' (1928, p. 283). Although it is true that the children in these areas were often oblivious to the social barriers set up by their parents, at least until adolescence, it is doubtful whether their acculturation can be traced to the melting pot effect as much as to the pervasive influence of the American culture that flowed into these areas from the outside.

The cosmopolites, the unmarried, and the childless are *detached*[2] from neighbourhood life. The cosmopolites possess a distant subculture which causes them to be disinterested in all but the most superficial contacts with their neighbours, somewhat like the ethnic villagers. The unmarried and childless are detached from neighbourhood because of their life-cycle stage, which frees them from the routine family responsibilities that entail some relationship to the local area. In their choice of residence, the two types are therefore not concerned about their neighbours, or the availability and quality of local community facilities. Even the well-to-do can choose expensive apartments in or near poor neighbourhoods because if they have children, these are sent to special schools and summer camps which effectively isolate them from neighbours. In addition, both types, but especially the childless and unmarried, are transient. Therefore, they tend to live in areas marked by high population turnover, where their own mobility and that of their neighbours creates a universal detachment from the neighbourhood.[3]

The deprived and the trapped do seem to be affected by some of the consequences of number, density, and heterogeneity. The deprived population suffers considerably from overcrowding, but this is a consequence of low income, racial discrimination, and other handicaps, and cannot be considered an inevitable result of the ecological make-up of the city.[4] Because the deprived have no residential choice, they are also forced to live amid neighbours not of their own choosing, with ways of life different and even contradictory to their own. If familial defences against the neighbourhood climate are weak, as is the case among broken families and downward mobile people, parents may lose their children to the culture of 'the street'. The trapped are the unhappy people who remain behind when their more advantaged neighbours move on; they must endure the heterogeneity which results from neighbourhood change.

Wirth's description of the urban way of life fits best the transient areas of the inner city. Such areas are typically heterogeneous in population, partly because they are inhabited by transient types who do not require homogeneous neighbours or by deprived people who have no choice, or may themselves be quite mobile. Under conditions of transience and heterogeneity, people interact only in terms of the segmental roles necessary for obtaining local services. Their social relationships thus display anonymity, impersonality, and superficiality.[5]

The social features of Wirth's concept of urbanism seem therefore to be a result of residential instability, rather than of number, density, or heterogeneity. In fact, heterogeneity is itself an effect of residential instability, resulting when the influx of transients causes landlords and realtors to stop acting as gatekeepers – that is, wardens of neighbourhood homogeneity.[6] Residential instability is found in all types of settlements and, presumably, its social consequences are everywhere similar. These consequences cannot therefore be identified with the ways of life of the city.

The outer city and the suburbs

The second effect which Wirth ascribed to number, density, and heterogeneity was the segregation of homogeneous people into distinct neighbourhoods,[7] on the basis of 'place and nature of work, income, racial and ethnic characteristics, social status, custom, habit, taste, preference and prejudice' (1957, p. 56). This description fits the residential districts of the *outer city*.[8] Although these districts contain the majority of the city's inhabitants, Wirth went into little detail about them. He made it clear, however, that the socio-psychological aspects of urbanism were prevalent there as well.

Because existing neighbourhood studies deal primarily with the exotic sections of the inner city, very little is known about the more typical residential neighbourhoods of the outer city. However, it is evident that the way of life in these areas bears little resemblance to Wirth's urbanism.

Both the studies which question Wirth's formulation and my own observations suggest that the common element in the ways of life of these neighbourhoods is best described as *quasi-primary*. I use this term to characterize relationships between neighbours. Whatever the intensity or frequency of these relationships, the interaction is more intimate than a secondary contact, but more guarded than a primary one.[9]

There are actually few secondary relationships, because of the isolation of residential neighbourhoods from economic institutions and workplaces. Even shopkeepers, store managers, and other local functionaries who live in the area are treated as acquaintances or friends, unless they are of a vastly different social status or are forced by their corporate employers to treat their customers as economic units (Stone 1954). Voluntary associations attract only a minority of the population. Moreover, much of the organizational activity is of a sociable nature, and it is often difficult to accomplish the association's 'business' because of the members' preference for sociability. Thus, it would appear that interactions in organizations, or between neighbours generally, do not fit the secondary relationship model of urban life. As anyone who has lived in these neighbourhoods knows, there is little anonymity, impersonality or privacy.[10] In fact, American cities have sometimes been described as collections of small towns.[11] There is some truth to this description, especially if the city is compared to the actual small town, rather than to the romantic construct of anti-urban critics (Vidich and Bensman 1958).

Postwar suburbia represents the most contemporary version of the quasi-primary way of life. Owing to increases in real income and the encouragement of home ownership provided by the FHA (Federal Housing Authority), families in the lower-middle class and upper-working class can now live in modern single-family homes in low-density sub-divisions, an opportunity previously available only to the upper and upper-middle classes (Wattell 1958).

The popular literature describes the new suburbs as communities in which conformity, homogeneity, and other-direction are unusually rampant (Berger 1960; Vernon 1959). The implication is that the move from city to suburb initiates a new way of life which causes considerable behaviour and personality change in previous urbanites. A preliminary analysis of data which I am now collecting in Levittown, New Jersey, suggests, however, that the move from the city to this predominantly lower-middle-class suburb does not result in any major behavioural changes for most people. Moreover, the changes which do occur reflect the move from the social isolation of a transient city or suburban apartment building to the quasi-primary life of a neighbourhood of single-family homes. Also, many of the people whose life has changed reported that the changes were intended. They existed as aspirations before the move, or as reasons for it. In other words, the suburb itself creates few changes in ways of life. Similar conclusions have been reported by Berger in his excellent study of a working-class population newly moved to a suburban subdivision (1960).

A comparison of city and suburb

If urban and suburban areas are similar in that the way of life in both is quasi-primary, and if urban residents who move out to the suburbs do not undergo any significant changes in behaviour, it would be fair to argue that the differences in ways of life between the two types of settlements have been overestimated. Yet the fact remains that a variety of physical and demographic differences exist between the city and the suburb. However, upon closer examination, many of these differences turn out to be either spurious or of little significance for the way of life of the inhabitants (Wattell 1958).[12]

The differences between the residential areas of cities and suburbs which have been cited most frequently are:

1 Suburbs are more likely to be dormitories.
2 They are further away from the work and play facilities of the central business districts.
3 They are newer and more modern than city residential areas and are designed for the automobile rather than for pedestrian and mass-transit forms of movement.
4 They are built up with single-family rather than multi-family structures and are therefore less dense.
5 Their populations are more homogeneous.
6 Their populations differ demographically: they are younger; more of them are married; they have higher incomes; and they hold proportionately more white collar jobs (Duncan and Reiss 1956, p. 131).

Most urban neighbourhoods are as much dormitories as the suburbs. Only in a few older inner city areas are factories and offices still located in the middle or residential blocks, and even here many of the employees do not live in the neighbourhood.

The fact that the suburbs are farther from the central business district is often true only in terms of distance, not travel time. Moreover, most people make relatively little use of downtown facilities, other than workplaces (Foley 1957; Jonassen 1955). The downtown stores seem to hold their greatest attraction for the upper-middle class (Jonassen 1955, pp. 91–2); the same is probably true of typically urban entertainment facilities. Teenagers and young adults may take their dates to first-run movie theatres, but the museums, concert halls, and lecture rooms attract mainly upper-middle-class ticket-buyers, many of them suburban.

The suburban reliance on the train and the automobile has given rise to an imaginative folklore about the consequences of commuting on alcohol consumption, sex life, and parental duties. Many of these conclusions are, however, drawn from selected high-income suburbs and exurbs, and reflect job tensions in such hectic occupations as advertising and show business more than the effects of residence (Spectorsky 1955). It is true that the upper-middle-class housewife must become a chauffeur in order to expose her children to the proper educational facilities, but such differences as walking to the corner drug store and driving to its suburban equivalent seem to me of little emotional, social, or cultural import.[13] In addition, the continuing shrinkage in the number of mass-transit users suggests that even in the city many younger people are now living a wholly auto-based way of life.

The fact that suburbs are smaller is primarily a function of political boundaries drawn long before the communities were suburban. This affects the kinds of political issues which develop, and provides somewhat greater opportunity for citizen participation. Even so, in the suburbs as in the city, the minority who participate are the professional politicians, the economically concerned businessmen, lawyers and salesmen, and the ideologically motivated middle- and upper-middle-class people with better than average education.

The social consequences of differences in density and house type also seem overrated. Single-family houses on quiet streets facilitate the supervision of children; this is one reason why middle-class women who want to keep an eye on their children move to the suburbs. House type also has some effects on relationships between neighbours, insofar as there are more opportunities for visual contact between adjacent homeowners than between people on different floors of an apartment house. However, if occupants' characteristics are also held constant, the differences in actual social contact are less marked. Homogeneity of residents turns out to be more important as a determinant of sociability than proximity. If the population is heterogeneous, there is little social contact between neighbours, either on apartment house floors or in single-family-house blocks; if people are homogeneous, there is likely to be considerable social contact in both house types. One need only contrast the apartment house located in a transient, heterogeneous neighbourhood, and exactly the same structure in a neighbourhood occupied by a single ethnic group. The former is a lonely, anonymous building; the latter, a bustling microsociety. I have observed similar patterns in suburban areas; on blocks where people are homogeneous, they socialize; where they are heterogeneous, they do little more than exchange polite greetings (Gans 1961).

Suburbs are usually described as being more homogeneous in house type than the city, but if they are compared to the outer city the differences are small. Most inhabitants of the outer city, other than well-to-do homeowners, live on blocks of uniform structures as well – for example, the endless streets of rowhouses in Philadelphia and Baltimore or of two-storey duplexes and six-flat apartment houses in Chicago. They differ from the new suburbs only in that they were erected through more primitive methods of mass production. Suburbs are of course more predominantly areas of owner-occupied single homes, though in the other districts of most American cities home-ownership is also extremely high.

Demographically, suburbs as a whole are clearly more homogeneous than cities as a whole, though probably not more so than outer cities. However, people do not live in cities or suburbs as a whole but in specific neighbourhoods. An analysis of ways of life would require a determination of the degree of population homogeneity within the boundaries of areas defined as neighbourhoods by residents' social contacts. Such an analysis would no doubt indicate that many neighbourhoods in the city as well as the suburbs are homogeneous. Neighbourhood homogeneity is actually a result of factors having little or nothing to do with the house type, density, or location of the area relative to the city limits. Brand new neighbourhoods are more homogeneous than older ones, because they have not yet experienced resident turnover, which frequently results in population heterogeneity. Neighbourhoods of low- and medium-priced housing are usually less homogeneous than those with expensive dwellings because they attract families who have reached the peak of occupational and residential mobility, as well as young families who are just starting their climb and will eventually move to neighbourhoods of higher status. The latter, being accessible only to high-income people, are therefore more homogeneous with respect to other resident characteristics as well. Moreover, such areas have the economic and political power to slow down or prevent invasion. Finally, neighbourhoods located in the path of ethnic or religious group movement are likely to be extremely homogeneous.

The demographic differences between cities and suburbs cannot be questioned, especially since the suburbs have attracted a large number of middle-class child-rearing families. The differences are, however, much reduced if suburbs are compared only to the outer city. In addition, a detailed comparison of suburban and outer city residential areas would show that neighbourhoods with the same kinds of people can be found in the city as well as the suburbs. Once again, the age of the area and the cost of housing are more important determinants of demographic characteristics than the location of the area with respect to the city limits.

Characteristics, social organization, and ecology

The preceding sections of the paper may be summarized in three propositions:

1 As concerns ways of life, the inner city must be distinguished from the outer city and the suburbs; and the latter two exhibit a way of life bearing little resemblance to Wirth's urbanism.

2 Even in the inner city, ways of life resemble Wirth's description only to a limited extent. Moreover, economic condition, cultural characteristics, life-cycle stage, and residential instability explain ways of life more satisfactorily than number, density, or heterogeneity.

3 Physical and other differences between city and suburb are often spurious or without much meaning for ways of life.

These propositions suggest that the concepts urban and suburban are neither mutually exclusive, nor especially relevant for understanding ways of life. They – and number, density, and heterogeneity as well – are ecological concepts which describe human adaptation to the environment. However, they are not sufficient to explain social phenomena, because these phenomena cannot be understood solely as the consequences of ecological processes. Therefore, other explanations must be considered.

Ecological explanations of social life are most applicable if the subjects under study lack the ability to *make choices*, be they plants, animals, or human beings. Thus, if there is a housing shortage, people will live almost anywhere, and under extreme conditions of no choice, as in a disaster, married and single, old and young, middle and working class, stable and transient will be found side by side in whatever accommodations are available. At that time, their ways of life represent an almost direct adaptation to the environment. If the supply of housing and of neighbourhoods is such that alternatives are available, however, people will make choices, and if the housing market is responsive, they can even make and satisfy explicit *demands*.

Choices and demands do not develop independently or at random; they are functions of the roles people play in the social system. These can best be understood in terms of the *characteristics* of the people involved; that is, characteristics can be used as indices to choices and demands made in the roles that constitute ways of life. Although many characteristics affect the choices and demands people make with respect to housing and neighbourhoods, the most important ones seem to be *class* – in all its economic, social and cultural ramifications – and *life-cycle stage*.[14] If people have an opportunity to choose, these two characteristics will go far in explaining the kinds of housing and neighbourhoods they will occupy and the ways of life they will try to establish within them.

Many of the previous assertions about ways of life in cities and suburbs can be analysed in terms of class and life-cycle characteristics. Thus, in the inner city, the unmarried and childless live as they do, detached from neighbourhood, because of their life-cycle stage; the cosmopolites, because of a combination of life-cycle stage and a distinctive but class-based subculture. The way of life of the deprived and trapped can be explained by low socioeconomic level and related handicaps. The quasi-primary way of life is associated with the family stage of the life-cycle, and the norms of child-rearing and parental role found in the upper-working class, the lower-middle class, and the non-cosmopolite portions of the upper-middle and upper classes.

The attributes of the so-called suburban way of life can also be understood largely in terms of these characteristics. The new suburbia is nothing more than a highly visible showcase for the ways of life of young, upper-working-class and lower-middle-class people. Ktsanes and Reissman have aptly described it as 'new homes for old values' (Ktsanes and Reissman 1959–60). Much of the descriptive and critical writing about suburbia assumes that as long as the new suburbanites lived in the city, they behaved like upper-middle-class cosmopolites and that suburban living has mysteriously transformed them (Duhl 1955; Fromm 1955, pp. 154–62; Riesman 1958; Whyte 1956). The critics fail to see that the behaviour and personality patterns ascribed to suburbia are in reality those of class and age (Dobriner 1958). These patterns could have been found among the new suburbanite when they still lived in the city and could now be observed among their peers who still reside there – if the latter were as visible to critics and researchers as are the suburbanites.

Needless to say, the concept of 'characteristics' cannot explain all aspects of ways of life, either among urban or suburban residents. Some aspects must be explained by concepts of social organization that are independent of characteristics. For example, some features of the quasi-primary way of life are independent of class and age, because they evolve from the roles and situations created by joint and adjacent occupancy of land and dwellings. Likewise, residential instability is a universal process which has a number of invariate consequences. In each case, however, the way in which people react varies with their characteristics. So it is with ecological processes. Thus, there are undoubtedly differences between ways of life in urban and suburban settlements which remain after behaviour patterns based on residents' characteristics have been analysed, and which must therefore be attributed to features of the settlement (Fava 1958).

Characteristics do not explain the causes of behaviour; rather, they are clues to socially created and culturally defined roles, choices and demands. A causal analysis must trace them back to the larger, social, economic, and political systems which determine the situations in which roles are played and the cultural content of choices and demands, as well as the opportunities for their achievement. These systems determine income distributions, educational and occupational opportunities, and in turn, fertility patterns, child-rearing methods, as well as the entire range of consumer behaviour. Thus, a complete analysis of the way of life of the deprived residents of the inner city cannot stop by indicating the influence of low income, lack of education, or family instability. These must be related to such conditions as the urban economy's 'need' for low-wage workers, and the housing market practices which restrict residential choice. The urban economy is in turn shaped by national economic and social systems, as well as by local and regional ecological processes. Some phenomena can be explained exclusively by reference to these ecological processes. However, it must also be recognized that as man gains greater control over the natural environment, he has been able to free himself from many of the determining and limiting effects of that environment. Thus, changes in local transportation technology, the ability of industries to be footloose, and the relative affluence of American society have given ever larger numbers of people increasing amounts of residential choice. The greater the amount of choice available, the more important does the concept of characteristics become in understanding behaviour.

Consequently, the study of ways of life in communities must begin with an analysis of characteristics. If characteristics are dealt with first and held constant, we may be able to discover which behaviour patterns can be attributed to features of the settlement and its natural environment. Only then will it be possible to discover to what extent city and suburb are independent — rather than dependent or intervening — variables in the explanation of ways of life.

This kind of analysis might help to reconcile the ecological point of view with the behavioural and cultural one, and possibly put an end to the conflict between conceptual positions which insist on one explanation or the other (Duncan and Schnore 1959). Both explanations have some relevance, and future research and theory must clarify the role of each in the analysis of ways of life in various types of settlement (Dobriner 1958, p. xxii). Another important rationale for this approach is its usefulness for applied sociology — for example, city planning. The planner can recommend changes in the spatial and physical arrangements of the city. Frequently, he seeks to achieve social goals or to change social conditions through physical solutions. He has been attracted to ecological explanations because these relate behaviour to phenomena which he can affect. For example, most planners tend to agree with Wirth's formulations, because they stress number and density, over which the planner has some control. If the undesirable social conditions of the inner city could be traced to these two factors, the planner could propose large-scale clearance projects which would reduce the size of the urban population, and lower residential densities. Experience with public housing projects has, however, made it apparent that low densities, new buildings, or modern site plans do not eliminate anti-social or self-destructive behaviour. The analysis of characteristics will call attention to the fact that this behaviour is lodged in the deprivations of low socioeconomic status and racial discrimination, and that it can be changed only through the removal of these deprivations. Conversely, if such an analysis suggests residues of behaviour that can be attributed to ecological processes or physical aspects of housing and neighbourhoods, the planner can recommend physical changes that can really affect behaviour....

Conclusion

Many of the descriptive statements made here are as timebound as Wirth's.[15] Twenty years ago, Wirth concluded that some form of urbanism would eventually predominate in all settlement types. He was, however, writing during a time of immigrant acculturation and at the end of a serious depression, an era of minimal choice. Today, it is apparent that high-density, heterogeneous surroundings are for most people a temporary place of residence; other than for the Park Avenue or Greenwich Village cosmopolites, they are a result of necessity rather than choice. As soon as they can afford to do so, most Americans head for the single-family house and the quasi-primary array of life of the low-density neighbourhood, in the outer city or the suburbs.[16]

Changes in the national economy and in government housing policy can affect many of the variables that make up housing supply and demand. For example, urban sprawl may eventually outdistance the ability of present and proposed transportation systems to move workers into the city; further industrial decentralization can forestall it and alter the entire relationship between work and residence. The expansion of present urban renewal activities can perhaps lure a significant number of cosmopolites back from the suburbs, while a drastic change in renewal policy might begin to ameliorate the housing conditions of the deprived population. A serious depression could once again make America a nation of doubled-up tenants.

These events will affect housing supply and residential choice; they will frustrate but not suppress demands for the quasi-primary way of life. However, changes in the national economy, society, and culture can affect people's characteristics – family size, educational level, and various other concomitants of life-cycle stage and class. These in turn will stimulate changes in demands and choices. The rising number of college graduates, for example, is likely to increase the cosmopolite ranks. This might in turn create a new set of city dwellers, although it will probably do no more than encourage the development of cosmopolite facilities in some suburban areas....

Notes

1 By the *inner city*, I mean the transient residential areas, the Gold Coasts and the slums that generally surround the central business district, although in some communities they may continue for miles beyond that district. The *outer city* includes the stable residential areas that house the working- and middle-class tenant and owner. The *suburbs* I conceive as the latest and most modern ring of the outer city, distinguished from it only by yet lower densities, and by the often irrelevant fact of the ring's location outside the city limits.

2 If the melting pot has resulted from propinquity and high density, one would have expected second-generation Italians, Irish, Jews, Greeks, Slavs, etc. to have developed a single 'pan-ethnic culture', consisting of a synthesis of the cultural patterns of the propinquitous national groups.

3 The corporation transients (Whyte 1956; Wilensky and Lebeaux 1958) who provide a new source of residential instability to the suburb, differ from city transients. Since they are raising families, they want to integrate themselves into neighbourhood life, and are usually able to do so, mainly because they tend to move into similar types of communities wherever they go.

4 The negative social consequences of overcrowding are a result of high room and floor density, not of the land coverage of population density which Wirth discussed. Park Avenue residents live under conditions of high land density, but do not seem to suffer visibly from overcrowding.

5 Whether or not these social phenomena have the psychological consequences Wirth suggested depends on the people who live in the area. Those who are detached from the neighbourhood by choice are probably immune, but those who depend on the neighbourhood for

their social relationships – the unattached individuals, for example – may suffer greatly from loneliness.

6 Needless to say, residential instability must ultimately be traced back to the fact that, as Wirth pointed out, the city and its economy attract transient – and, depending on the sources of outmigration, heterogeneous – people. However, this is a characteristic of urban-industrial society, not of the city specifically.

7 By neighbourhoods or residential districts I mean areas demarcated from others by distinctive physical boundaries or by social characteristics, some of which may be perceived only by the residents. However, these areas are not necessarily socially self-sufficient or culturally distinctive.

8 For the definition of *outer city*, see note 1.

9 Because neighbourly relations are not quite primary, and not quite secondary, they can also become *pseudo-primary*; that is, secondary ones disguised with false effect to make them appear primary. Critics have often described suburban life in this fashion, although the actual prevalence of pseudo-primary relationships has not been studied systematically in cities or suburbs.

10 These neighbourhoods cannot, however, be considered as urban folk societies. People go out of the area for many of their friendships, and their allegiance to neighbourhood is neither intense nor all-encompassing. Janowitz has aptly described the relationship between resident and neighbourhood as one of 'limited liability' (1952, chapter 7).

11 Were I not arguing that ecological concepts cannot double as sociological ones, this way of life might best be described as small-townish.

12 They may, of course, be significant for the welfare of the total metropolitan area.

13 I am thinking here of adults; teen-agers do suffer from the lack of informal meeting places within walking or bicycling distance.

14 These must be defined in dynamic terms. Thus, class includes also the process of social mobility, stage in the life-cycle, and the processes of socialization and ageing.

15 Even more than Wirth's they are based on data and impressions gathered in the large Eastern and Midwestern cities of the United States.

16 Personal discussions with European planners and sociologists suggest that many European apartment dwellers have similar preferences, although economic conditions, high building costs, and the scarcity of land make it impossible for them to achieve their desires.

References

BERGER, Bennett (1960) *Working Class Suburb: A Study of Auto Workers in Suburbia* Berkeley: University of California Press

DOBRINER, William M. (1958) 'Introduction: theory and research in the sociology of the suburbs', in W. Dobriner (ed) *The Suburban Community* New York: Putnam, pp. xiii–xxviii

DUHL, Leonard J. (1956) 'Mental health and community planning' in *Planning 1955* pp. 31–9, Chicago: American Society of Planning Officials

DUNCAN, Otis Dudley and REISS, Albert J. Jr (1956) *Social Characteristics of Rural and Urban Communities* New York: Wiley

DUNCAN, Otis Dudley and SCHNORE, Leo F. (1959) 'Cultural behavioral and ecological perspectives in the study of social organization' *American Journal of Sociology* 65, September, pp. 132–55

FAVA, Sylvia Fleis (1958) 'Contrasts in neighboring: New York City and a suburban community' in William M. Dobriner (ed) *The Suburban Community* New York: Putnam, pp. 122–31

FOLEY, Donald L. (1957) 'The use of local facilities in a metropolis' in Paul Hatt and Albert J. Reiss, Jr. (eds) *Cities and Society* Chicago: Free Press, pp. 237–47

FROMM, Erich (1955) *The Sane Society* Routledge and Kegan Paul: New York: Rinehart

GANS, Herbert J. (1959) 'The urban villager: A study of the second generation Italians in the West End of Boston' Boston: Center for Community Studies (mimeographed)

GANS, Herbert J. (1961) 'Planning and social life: An evaluation of friendship and neighbor relations in suburban communities' *Journal of the American Institute of Planners* 27, May, pp. 134–40

GREER, Scott and KUBE, Ella (1959) 'Urbanism and social structure: A Los Angeles study' in Marvin B. Sussman (ed) *Community Structure and Analysis* New York: Crowell, pp. 93–112

JANOWITZ, Morris (1952) *The Community Press in an Urban Setting* Chicago: Free Press

JONASSEN, Christen T. (1955) 'The shopping center versus downtown' Columbus, Ohio: Bureau of Business Research, Ohio State University

KTSANES, Thomas and REISSMAN, Leonard (1959–60) 'Suburbia: New homes for old values' *Social Problems* 7, winter, pp. 187–94

RIESMAN, David (1958) 'The suburban sadness', in William M. Dobriner (ed) *The Suburban Community* New York: Putnam, pp. 375–408

ROSE, Arnold M. (1947) 'Living arrangements of unattached persons' *American Sociological Review* 12, August, pp. 429–35

SPECTORSKY, A. G. (1955) *The Exurbanites* Philadelphia: Lippincott

STONE, Gregory P. (1954) 'City shoppers and urban identification: Observations on the social psychology of city life' *American Journal of Sociology* 60, July, pp. 36–45

VERNON, Raymond (1959) 'The changing economic function of the central city' New York: Committee on Economic Development, Supplementary Paper No. 1

VIDICH, Arthur J. and BENSMAN, Joseph (1958) *Small Town in Mass Society: Class, Power and Religion in a Rural Community* Princeton University Press

WATTELL, Harold (1958) 'Levittown: A suburban community', in William M. Dobriner (ed) *The Suburban Community* New York:Putnam, pp. 287–313

WHYTE, William F., Jr. (1956) *The Organization Man* New York: Simon and Schuster

WILENSKY, Harold L. and LEBEAUX, Charles (1958) *Industrial Society and Social Welfare* New York: Russell Sage Foundation

WIRTH, Louis (1928) *The Ghetto* University of Chicago Press

WIRTH, Louis (1938 and 1957) 'Urbanism as a way of life' *American Journal of Sociology* 44 (July 1938), pp. 1–24. Reprinted in Paul Hatt and Albert J. Reiss, Jr. (eds) *Cities and Society* Chicago: Free Press, 1957, pp. 46–64 (all page references are to this reprinting of the article)

1.6   The origins: urban growth in Britian 1801–1939

Peter Hall

Introduction

The British are so conscious of being an urban nation that they treat the fact as self evident: it does not normally occur to them to question it, or to ask themselves what they mean by it. But we can start, by looking at how other observers have categorized the English population into urban or rural.

The obvious starting point is Adna Ferrin Weber. A young American scholar, Weber, in 1899 produced a book which is the true beginning of comparative urban analysis.[1] He was the first to document the fact that the British were the most urbanized nation in the world, and that they had been highly urbanized for a longer period than any other. In reaching this conclusion, he was also the first to treat comprehensively the problems of defining what an urban population was. He found that already in 1801, 16.9 per cent of the population of England and Wales lived in cities of 20,000 and more; by 1851 this figure was 35 per cent, and by 1891 it was 53.6 per cent. But this figure excluded the very large aggregate of population within the smaller urban settlements, and fuller figures, available only for the second half of the nineteenth century, showed that the entire urban population was already 50.1 per cent in 1851, and had reached 72.1 per cent in 1891. No other nation, at that date, had anything like a comparable percentage. France had 37.4 per cent, Prussia 40.7 per cent, and the United States only 27.6 per cent.

Since then the other countries have all caught up to a large degree, but England and Wales are remarkable for their degree of urbanization. The official Census statistics take up Weber's series, and show that the urban

Source: Peter Hall *et al* (1973) *The Containment of Urban England*, Vol. 1, George Allen and Unwin, pp. 59–90.

population was already 77.0 per cent of the whole in 1901. Thereafter it rose only marginally, to 80.8 per cent in 1951; and thence it fell, to 80 per cent in the 1961 Census and to 78.3 per cent in 1971 (Table 1). Meanwhile, the urban percentage for Germany had risen to 76.8 per cent (in 1961), and in the United States to 69.9 per cent (in 1960).[2] In these countries, transfers of population from the countryside to the towns were still taking place as a result of the growing efficiency of agriculture and the continuing demands of the towns for manufacturing and servicing labour. But in Britain the process seems to have been about as complete, by the beginning of the twentieth century, as it could possibly be.

The difficulty with this analysis, and this conclusion, is that it is based on a very arbitrary definition of what is urban and what is not. According to the English Census an urban area is an adminstrative area described as urban; that is, a county borough, a municipal or metropolitan or London borough, or an urban district. These areas came into existence as the result of a series of local government reforms made between 1835 and 1901, with an additional term, the London borough, introduced as late as 1963. They may bear only a very distant relationship to urban areas defined in other, narrower ways. Thus an urban district or a borough may be overbounded so that it contains large tracts of open farmland, occupied by a population engaged chiefly in farming and in providing services to farmers; most people would probably agree that this land was not urban in a meaningful sense. To take the opposite and perhaps commoner case, rural districts may be increasingly invaded by suburban development as the growth of towns washes across administrative boundaries. They may be covered largely by houses with gardens, and by services for these houses such as shops and schools, while the great majority of the inhabitants do not earn their living from agriculture or from services rendered to agriculturalists. Most people would probably agree that in some sense, this type of area would fall in the category of urban land. This indeed is the only possible explanation of a paradox: in the decade 1951–61, the rural districts of England and Wales were increasing in population more than twice as fast as the urban areas; in the decade 1961–71, they were increasing seven times as fast. Clearly, some more firmly-based definition of an urban area is needed.

People and land: a basis for definition?

One elementary approach to this question is to say that urban areas are areas with a special relationship between people and land; in other words, to try to forge a *physical* definition of urbanization. [There are two different sorts of physical definitions: urban clusters are based on a density criterion; but the conurbations are essentially based on a bricks and

Table 1 The urban population of England and Wales, 1851–1971

Population (thousands)

	1851	1861	1871	1881	1891	1901	1911	1921
Urban	8,990.9	10,961.0	14,041.4	17,636.6	20,895.5	25,058.4	28,162.9	30,035.4
Rural	8,936.8	9,105.2	8,670.9	8,337.8	8,107.0	7,469.5	7,907.6	7,851.3

	1931	1951	1961	1966	1971*
Urban	31,951.9	35,335.7	36,872.0	37,213.3	38,025.4
Rural	8,000.5	8,422.2	9,233.0	9,922.3	10,568.3

Percentages of total

	1851	1861	1871	1881	1891	1901	1911	1921
Urban	50.1	54.6	61.8	67.9	72.0	77.0	78.1	79.3
Rural	49.9	44.4	38.2	32.1	28.0	23.0	21.9	20.7

	1931	1951	1961	1966	1971*
Urban	80.0	80.0	80.0	78.9	78.3
Rural	20.0	20.0	20.0	21.1	21.7

Percentage growth

	1851–61	1861–71	1871–81	1881–91	1891–1901	1901–11	1911–21	1921–31
Urban	21.9	28.1	25.6	18.5	19.9	12.4	6.5	6.5
Rural	1.9	−5.9	−3.8	−2.8	−7.9	5.9	−0.7	1.9

	1931–51	1951–61	1961–66	1961–71*
Urban	15.2†	4.3	1.8†	2.4
Rural	2.6†	9.2	15.0†	18.0

Source: Adna F. Weber, *The Growth of Cities in the Nineteenth Century*, op. cit., Tables p. 44, 18 (p. 46), 19 (p. 47). Census 1951, *General Tables*, Tables 3 (p. 3), 4 (p. 5), 5 (p. 7). Census 1961, *General Tables*, Tables 3 (p. 3), 4 (p. 5), 5 (p. 7). Census 1966, unpublished data.

* Preliminary results.
† Per decade.

mortar, or land use, criterion.] ...

Up to now, the most extensive and careful work done on land use changes in Britain has come from Dr Robin Best, in an ongoing research project at Wye College in the University of London. Best's starting point is an attempt to compare the reliability of the agricultural returns and the Land Use Surveys. Already in the 1930s two separate estimates of the urban acreage had been produced for Great Britain by Sir George Stapeldon, on the basis of the agricultural returns, and by Dudley Stamp, on the basis of his own survey. The discrepancy is very great; 4,685,000 acres in England and Wales according to Stapeldon, to 2,748,000 acres according to Stamp.[3] Best discovered from his analysis that the total urban acreage in England and Wales in 1950 was about 3,602,200 acres,[4] and bearing in mind the amount of urban growth that had taken place since the early 1930s, he concluded that the Stamp estimate was validated.

Table 2   The urban acreage, England and Wales, 1900–1960, with projections to 1980 and 2000

Year	Population (millions)	Urban area million acres	Urban land provision acres per thousand population	Urban area as percentage of total land area
1900–1	32.5	2.0	61.5	5.4
1920–1	37.9	2.2	58.0	5.9
1930–1	40.0	2.6	65.0	7.0
1939	41.5	3.2	77.1	8.6
1950–1	43.8	3.6	82.2	9.7
1960–1	46.1	4.0	86.8	10.8
1970–1	50.1	4.4	87.8	11.9
1980–1	53.8	4.9	91.1	13.2
1990–1	58.2	5.4	92.8	14.5
2000–1	63.7	6.0	94.2	16.2

Source: Robin Best, *Town and Country Planning*, Vol. 32 (1964), Table 1 (p. 352).

On this basis, Best could proceed with some confidence to analyse changes in time from the agricultural returns from 1900 onwards, correcting them by references to better sources wherever this proved possible. The main results are set out in Table 2. They show that in 1900 only 2 million acres, or just over 5 per cent of the total land area of Britian, could be regarded as urban; this figure advanced very slowly indeed to only 2.2 million acres, or 5.9 per cent, by 1920. But then , during the 1920s and 1930s, the urban acreage of Britain increased almost 50 per cent, to 3.2 million, or 8.6 per cent, in 1939. Since then the increase has been more modest, to a total of 4 million acres, or 10.8 per cent, in 1960. Best predicted that on the most realistic estimates of likely planning policies for the future this figure would have increased to only 6 million acres, or 16.2 per cent of the total area, by the year 2000.[5]

In fact, Best demonstrates conclusively that the loss of land to urban uses was much greater between the two world wars, than after the Second World War. The period 1927–34 witnessed the early growth of new suburbs around the nineteenth-century towns with the acceptance of higher space standards for housing, somewhat countered by economic depression, and the annual loss averaged 46,800 acres a year. Between 1934 and 1939, when mass surburban development was coupled with economic revival, the annual rate of loss accelerated to 60,600 acres a year. In the decade 1950–60, in contrast, the annual loss averaged only 36,300 acres a year, a fact mainly ascribable to the more effective physical planning controls introduced by the 1947 Town and Country Planning Act.[6] This compares with an official estimate (recently disputed) for over 1 million acres a year loss in the United States of America.

This overall picture, though, conceals very great localized pressures in the major urban regions. Here, Best's closer analysis demonstrated that the main transfers of agricultural land to all other uses have taken place in a definite belt of the country, the area which used to be known in the 1930s as the coffin, later as the hourglass, and which [we call] Megalopolis England. Through this belt, in the period 1955–60, losses of 1 per cent or more of the rural area were common and in places, as in the Midlands and. also west of London, the losses exceeded 1.5 per cent, compared with an average national loss of only 0.7 per cent.[7] Indeed, Best's study shows that invariably the losses of land were greatest in the areas which are already heavily urbanized. Thus in the South-East, around London, more than one-third of the land is already urbanized and the rate of urbanization (considered as a percentage of the total regional area) is double the national average. However, in terms of the percentage growth of the urban area in relation to the 1951 urban area, the highly urbanized regions score rather low; this is because they have not got the room for rapid expansion. Here it is not surprising that the highest percentage rates of growth are marked up in regions with moderate degrees of urbanization, notably the Eastern region (25.9 per cent), Southern region (20.9 per cent), North Midland region (12.6 per cent) and Midlands region (12.4 per cent). These happen to be the parts of Megalopolis England, or the coffin, where land is still available.

Subsequently, Best and Champion obtained more reliable offical land use data which allowed them to make a detailed county by county study of urban growth in five-year periods since the Second World War. Their analysis shows that urban growth between 1945 and 1965 was again concentrated along the main axial belt from London to Lancashire and Yorkshire. However, the areas of most rapid transfer of land to urban use do not form a continuous zone. Rather, they form two clearly separated areas. One is around London; the other embraces the West and East Midlands, Lancashire and Yorkshire, and can be called for simplicity the central urban zone. Between these two areas runs a clear divide formed by rather rural counties with rates of urban growth that are below the national average. Best and Champion's other significant finding is that while both areas have consistently displayed above average rates of urban growth, the conversion rates for the central urban zone have speeded up over the period 1945–65, while those for the London region have actually slowed down.[8] The reason, the authors suggest, is that demands for space resulting from redevelopment and rising space standards are greater than are often recognized, and they have been particularly concentrated in the Midlands and North during the 1960s.

Structures and functions

Even a physical definition of urbanization, then, may be approached in more than one way, with different results. But there is quite another way of looking at urbanization: in terms of functions or activities. It could be argued that to define cities and towns in terms of physical structures, or of densities, or of land uses, is to miss the point; that cities are essentially places with rather special sorts of interrelated activities, and that these should be the main focus of our study, rather than the structures or shells that happen to contain them at any time.

But looking at the problem more widely, it is possible to integrate the two approaches, and this is the objective of modern systems planning. In this approach, *activities* are central: they are broken up by coarser or finer categories, of which the most basic are work, residence, social and travel. Some of these activities are described as *within-place activities*: that is, they occur in a fixed place. Others are described as *between-place activities*: these are activities requiring motion, such as travelling or communicating across geographical space. The within-place activities are housed in *structures*: factories, offices, shops (for work activities), houses, flats and other dwellings (for residence activities), and so on. The between-place activities are carried on via *networks* of roads, railways, telephone lines, water mains and similar channels; and these in turn can be viewed as being housed in *structures* of a particular type. In this broad view a critical question is obviously going to be the relationship between activities on the one hand, and between the networks and structures (invariably of a physical character) on the other.

This analysis gives us several alternative ways of looking at cities and towns from a functional point of view. We have already seen that in a physical sense we could define urban areas in terms of densities of people or of structures (for instance houses) per unit of land area, or in terms of the coverage of land uses (representing coverage by certain sorts of structure, or the absence of structures). Similarly, in a functional sense we could define urban areas in terms of a certain density of a defined activity or activities per unit of land area: for instance, the density of industrial workers per square kilometre or square mile. Or we could define urbanization in terms of network linkages with activities: for instance, the percentage of residents who travel daily to work into areas that have already been defined as urban, on the basis of density of activities per unit of land area. All this depends, of course, on the availability of reliable and fairly sophisticated statistics, which provides a major limitation until fairly recent times.

Without benefit of such statistics, we can make one generalization about the growth of urban areas in Britain since the Industrial Revolution. It is that over the course of time urban growth has been accompanied by increasing complexity of the urban structure, and in particular by growing complexity in the relationship between the physical definitions of urbanization and the functional ones. At the beginning of the nineteenth century, urban areas were compact and tightly packed; they ended sharply against open countryside. Physical definitions corresponded with functional ones: the town looked different from the countryside, and it performed different functions. Internally, the structure was also simple. Workplaces and residential areas tended to be intermingled, because of an almost total lack of mechanical transport for the journey to work. Where there was an element of differentiation, for instance in the formation of a central business district in the largest cities, residential areas gathered tightly round it, so as to minimize the walk to work.

The modern urban area presents just the opposite picture. More extremely so in North America or in Australia than in Britain or in Europe generally, the tidy division between town and country tends to disappear: suburban growth penetrates far into the countryside, sometimes leapfrogging open areas to land on others further from the city. Even when an attempt is made through planning to preserve a tidy physical demarcation, there is still an almost complete lack of relation between physical forms and functional realities: the old villages may be occupied almost completely by commuters to the city, and even the jobs performed in the countryside are likely to have little to do with agriculture, directly or indirectly. Within the urban areas as functionally defined, the patterns of within-place activities and between-place activities are extremely complex, with a wide scatter (modified by local concentration) of employment opportunities, and criss-cross patterns of movement in all directions between home and workplace.

In the paragraphs that follow we try to show how this process of increasing complexity affected British cities between about 1800, the time of the early Industrial Revolution, and about 1939, when the continued growth of urban areas was just beginning to be viewed as a subject for public concern. The account essentially covers that period when cities and towns grew through uncoordinated private actions, modified by elementary planning provisions of a local and regulatory kind, and in the case of some cities by broader coordinated action in the sphere of municipal housing and municipal transport. It is a period in which the broad philosophy of British town and country planning developed.

Urban growth in England, 1801–1939

Even up to the middle nineteenth century, it is a surprising fact that in England there were relatively few cities of any size; even they were relatively small in population by the standards we have become accustomed to in the twentieth century, and they were occupied at relatively high densities, so that by modern standards they occupied very small areas. In 1801 London had about a million people; no other town had as many as 100,000. The biggest were Liverpool with 82,000, Manchester with 75,000, Birmingham with 71,000, and Bristol with 61,000. By 1851 the population of London was up to 2,491,000 (or 2,685,000 if the area of Greater London is considered); three other great provincial cities had over 200,000: Liverpool with 376,000, Manchester with 303,000 and Birmingham with 233,000. Four other cities had more than 100,000: Leeds with 172,000, Bristol with 137,000, Sheffield with 135,000 and Bradford with 104,000.

Furthermore, these populations were often crowded on to very small areas. London provides the extreme example; because of its relatively large population, the lack of urban transportation caused extremely high densities close to the workplaces in the centre. In 1801, the most crowded districts of central London, totalling in all only 2,852 acres of $4^1/_2$ square miles, held some 425,000 people (44 per cent of the total population of London) at an average density of 149 to the acre. By 1851, this most crowded area had extended somewhat, to include 5,797 acres (9 square miles); it then housed 945,000 people (40 per cent of the population of London) living at an average density of 165 to the acre. Statistics are not available on an equally fine grain for most provincial cities, but Manchester provides an illustration. In 1851, with 303,000 people, it was the third city of England. It had a roughly circular form with an average radius of about 2 miles from the centre; that is, an area of about 12 square miles. But five innermost statistical areas covering only 1,480 acres (2.5 square miles) contained 187,000 of these, or about 60 per cent of the total, at a density of 126 to the acre.[9] This was the typical situation in a city without any developed form of mass transportation; it reached its extreme point around 1851 or 1861.

Such a degree of crowding could be relieved only by cheap and efficient mass transportation; and this arrived only slowly, during the second half of the nineteenth century. Then the innermost areas, which had suffered the most intense overcrowding, lost population quite rapidly as they were taken over by offices, warehouses and factories, and the suburbs began to spread at moderate densities. As a result, the internal distribution of the urban population changed rapidly. Colin Clark, Brian Berry and others have observed that in almost all cities at all times, population densities decline from the centre to the rural edge according to a negative exponential law,[10] but that in the century since 1860 the slope of the line in the advanced Western cities has become steadily less steep, due to the liberating effects of urban mass-transportation. For London detailed statistics allow the process to be very precisely documented; it began after the 1861 Census, when cheap suburban trains allowed first the middle class, then the working class, to seek homes at progressively greater distances from the centre. By the end of the nineteenth century this had produced a radical change in the form of most British cities. The available forms of urban transportation, the steam train, or the electric tram, both demanded appreciable investment in basic infrastructure. They therefore tended to be concentrated along certain radial routes, and the growth of the city tended to a tentacular form alongside these routes and within walking distance of them. Homer Hoyt, for Chicago in 1933, was probably the first to demonstrate this effect in detail, [11] it could be repeated for most British cities about 1900.

This process was recorded by contemporaries. 'Every year London grows, stretching out into the country long and generally unlovely arms', wrote Henrietta Barnett in 1905;[12] between 1881 and 1901, most of the inner area within seven miles of the centre had been losing population by migration, while an outer area had been growing at the rate of more than 50 per cent each decade. Simultaneously, redevelopment was eating into the old slum area near the centre; land near the Bank of England was costing up to £1 million an acre and, 'Even a mile or two away the commercial value is so great that the residential population is steadily and rapidly vanishing'. In the West Midlands, 'A very large scheme is gradually being developed for covering practically the whole of the Midlands with a network of tram lines, electrically equipped', and already 'it might be said that the continuous roads and houses from Aston on the east to Wolverhampton on the west, covering as they do various municipalities and urban districts, are quite as much entitled to a single name as is Greater London'. Around Manchester the 'conglomeration of people spreads over an unusual space, the working class here preferring small self-contained houses to barrack-like tenements', and the houses 'extend long tentacles along the roads leading to the neighbouring towns, which often seemed to be joined to the central mass'. In West Yorkshire the towns had grown into 'one vast manufacturing hive, in which city verges on city, and one village merges into another, so that a person travelling by night from Kildwick on the north to Holmfirth on the south would never be out of sight of the gas lamps'.

This tentacular growth and coalescence of towns depended on the characteristics of the steam train and the electric tram. But already, in 1890, the first electric tube line in London had been opened; by 1907 the earlier Underground lines had been electrified and London had a dense network of new Tube lines; by 1908 the electrification of the surface lines south of the river was beginning to take place. In Manchester the line to Bury had been electrified in 1913–16 and the line to Altrincham was electrified in 1931; in Liverpool the Mersey Railway was electrified in 1903 and the line to Southport in 1904.[13] The number of electric trams continued to rise rapidly during the period up to the First World War, from 6,783 (in all Britain) in 1904 to 12,518 in 1914. Thence the total rose slowly to a peak of 14,413 in 1927. It fell slowly up to about 1935, then much more rapidly.[14]

Already, long before this time, new extensions of the urban network in many cities had been by bus; Sheffield contemplated this step in 1905, and opened its first bus service in 1913, though it was building new stretches of tramway as late as 1928.[15] Manchester from the start served its new housing estate in Wythenshawe by buses in the early 1930s,[16] and started abandoning trams after 1930.[17]

The result of this change is almost dramatically illustrated in the case of London. Between 1919 and 1939 Greater London expanded in population from 6 million to 8 million; but it expanded in area about five times. Furthermore, the form of the growth changed; the electric railway network, with its relatively frequent stops at half-mile intervals, and the new motor bus feeder services into the stations, permitted a much freer spread of development, which assumed a circular rather than a tentacular form. It is almost certain that in the 1920s and 1930s the real cost of housing plus transportation in the London suburbs fell to an unprecedentedly low level.[18] The result was a much wider spread of rather low-density suburban housing, built at a generally uniform standard of about twelve to the net residential acre, than had ever been possible with previous transportation technologies. There was a parallel extension in the major provincial cities, though in general it was less dramatic because of their lower total rate of growth in the interwar period, and in some of the northern cities, notably Manchester and Liverpool, the pattern of extensions was dominated to a much greater degree by local authority housing schemes.[19]

Between about 1880 and 1939, therefore, almost all major British urban areas witnessed a rapid and pronounced decentralization of their residential populations. But work activities showed a much greater inertia. It was about 1880 that the real growth of central business districts first came about in British cities. Sometimes this happened spontaneously, as in Manchester where warehouses gave way to offices in the 1880s; sometimes, as in Joseph Chamberlain's Birmingham, the process was accelerated and guided by the city itself. By the 1930s, all major British cities had well-differentiated central areas, which occupied an appreciable percentage of their entire employed population. Factory industry, in contrast, had shown a much greater willingness to disperse on its own initiative. Up to about 1880, in the bigger cities there was a characteristic belt or collar of small workshop industry just outside the central area; good examples are the furniture and clothing quarters of the East End of London, or the jewellery and gun quarters of Birmingham.[20] But between 1880 and 1914, there was a marked outward movement of bigger plants to green field sites in the suburbs of both cities: Cadbury at Bournville and General Electric at Witton Park in the case of Birmingham, Lebus and others in the Lea Valley in the case of London, and the whole Trafford Park development in Manchester. However, in this process factory industry still remained tightly concentrated in certain belts or zones. To its existing industrial areas in the East End and along the river, London added new zones in the Lea Valley and then in West Middlesex; to its older industrial quarters and the canal and railway-based industry of the inner suburbs, Birmingham added concentrations in places like Longbridge and the Tame Valley; soon after the coming of the Manchester Ship Canal made it a major port, Manchester built one of the greatest industrial concentrations in Europe at Trafford Park.

The result for transportation was interesting. To a large degree, up to 1939 mass transportation in most British cities remained largely radial.

The Tube lines and Southern Electric lines in London, the bus routes in Birmingham and Manchester, ran from the city centres to the new housing estates and on their way they passed the factory zones. In the mornings they brought large flows of commuters into the centres; they took commuters in both directions to the industrial estates, outwards from the older areas of the city, inwards from the newer housing estates. In the evenings, the reverse happened. The public transport systems were efficient, and they were well adapted to the job they had to do; they attracted heavy flows of traffic, in an age when car ownership was still the privilege of the minority, and they thus managed to combine a high level of service with impressive financial results.

For most municipal councillors, and most city treasurers, this seemed to be a beneficial and desirable form of development, which could long continue. They asked merely for freedom from economic depression for their city, coupled with sufficient prosperity in the country generally to keep their housing and slum clearance programmes rolling. But especially in relation to London, a growing vocal minority viewed the whole process with alarm, and in the aftermath of the Great Depression of 1929–32 their views began to command much respect.

The axial belt
The Great Depression marked a fundamental divide. Up until then the few reformers who had been interested in city planning had mainly concerned themselves with the individual city; only a very few men of insight, like Howard and Geddes, had grasped the significance of the broader geographical patterns of urban growth. But in Britain, throughout the Great Depression and afterwards, there came the growing realization of strong and enduring regional differences between one industrial area and another. While areas like Central Scotland, the North-East and South Wales seemed to be unable to share in the gradual climb out of the trough, other areas like London, Birmingham and Leicester never seemed to have gone through it. Seeking to generalize about this distinction, the geographers and planners of the time seized on the notion of the axial belt. Under the alternative names of the hourglass and the coffin, it became a main theme of public controversy in the late 1930s.

In a sense, the notion of the axial belt is implicit in Geddes' classic description of the conurbations, written as long ago as 1910. But it became explicit only in 1931, with Fawcett's redefinition of the conurbations. His map of the seven major conurbations, and thirty other minor ones, made it clear that the great majority (five out of the seven; fifteen out of the thirty) were concentrated into a single axial belt running from Lancashire and Yorkshire, down through the Midlands and London, to the south coast of

Kent, Sussex and Hampshire (Figure 1a). Fawcett himself drew attention to the fact that:

> An observer in an airship hovering above one of these conurbations on a clear dark evening, when all its lamps are lit, would see beneath him a large area covered by a continuous network of lights, glowing here and there in brighter patches where the main roads meet in its nodal shopping districts and elsewhere shading into the darker patches of its less fully urbanized areas − parks, water surfaces, or enclaves of rural land. To such an observer the continuity of the conurbation would be the most salient fact about it. If he were high above the Pennines between Leeds and Manchester he could see at least four great conurbations. Near him to the north-east is the one formed by the confluent industrial towns of West Yorkshire; westward he would see the still larger one which is focused on Manchester and beyond it the lights of the seaport on Merseyside; while to the south-east lies Sheffield. If he were at a sufficient height he might be able to see the haze of light over Birmingham, 75 miles to the south and over Tyneside, 90 miles away to the north. Amongst and around the nearer conurbations he would see the many smaller scattered patches of light which mark the lesser towns. And it would be easy to imagine an outspreading of all these towards coalescence in one vast urban region covering the whole of this industrialized central area of Great Britain.[21]

Incipiently, then, Fawcett had recognized the idea of what came to be known as an axial belt of industry and people, or Megalopolis England. But he was careful to notice that the pattern of population growth gave a different picture: a concentration into two relatively small areas, one in the South-East, one in the Midlands. This difference was subsequently to be the source of much confusion and much controversy; and it still exists.

Fawcett wrote:

> There is an area of marked concentration of population in the form of a zone extending diagonally across England from south-east to north-west ... In the last inter-Censal period (1921−31), three-fourths of the increase of population in Great Britain was in this zone ... This zone across England covers approximately 18,000 square miles, or about a fifth of the area of Great Britain. And it had in 1921, 56 per cent of the total population, a proportion which rose to 58 per cent in 1931, when its population numbered 25,805,915.[22]

Figure 1   The Coffin or Axial Belt (a) as defined by C. B. Fawcett, (b) as defined by E. G. R. Taylor

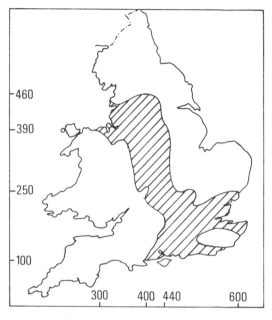

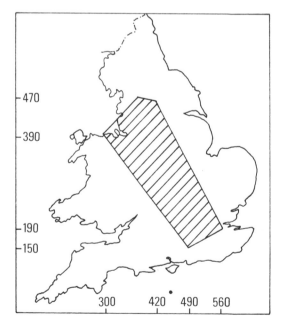

But by this time, the notion was exciting politicians and administrators as well as geographers. In 1934 Sir Malcolm Stewart was appointed Special Commissioner for the Special Areas; these were the areas which had shown exceptionally high unemployment rates during the Great Depression, and exceptional difficulty in recovering subsequently. His second report, in 1936, made this comment on London:

> The macrocosm of London grows with a rapidity which is beginning to cause alarm ... There is a considerable portion of industrial production not dependent on considerations which are absolutely essential to its location in London. It is this part of the industrial flow which might reasonably be directed elsewhere.[23]

Stewart was criticized by some observers, but the point was a politically sensitive one; in 1937, the government set up the Royal Commission on the Geographical Distribution of the Industrial Population, under the chairmanship of Sir Anderson Montague-Barlow. The terms of reference were threefold:

> To inquire into the causes which have influenced the present geographical distribution of the industrial population of Great Britain and the probable direction of any change in that distribution in the future; to consider what social, economic or strategical disadvantages arise from the concentration of industries or of the industrial population in large towns or in particular areas of the country; and to report what remedial measures if any should be taken in the national interest.[24]

The geographers responded warmly to the Barlow Commission's call for expert evidence, and at a discussion at the Royal Geographical Society in May 1938, Professor E. G. R. Taylor further refined the notion of Megalopolis. In a discussion on the geographical location of industry she said:

> ... there is a belt of such high concentration, following an axis aligned from south-east or north-west, and broadening as it gets farther from Greater London. At either extremity of this belt are the sea-entries which dominate England's external trade relations; the Port of London, and Liverpool-Manchester, together handling two-thirds of the total imports and exports. Southampton and Hull, though they exist mainly to serve this axial belt, are separated from it by forty to fifty miles of non-industrial farming country.[25]

As Baker and Gilbert noted in 1941,[26] there is a change in emphasis here; the south coast area disappears, and there is a suggestion that the area is dominated by areas of dense population, defined by the rather low minimum limit of 200 persons per square mile or roughly one-third of a person to each acre. Nevertheless, the notion of the axial belt was blessed by the Royal Geographical Society and was passed on in the form of a memorandum to the Royal Commission (Figure 1b). There, it is described as a belt covering approximately 14,500 square miles, or 39 per cent of the area of England and Wales, stretching from Greater London up to South Lancashire and the West Riding.[27] This evidence was referred to in the Barlow Commission report when it appeared in 1940,[28] and in the subsequent report of the Scott Committee on Land Use in Rural Areas.

After this general acceptance of the notion, in 1941, J. N. L. Baker and E. W. Gilbert delivered a weighty attack on it in a talk to the Royal Geographical Society. They based their criticism on two main grounds: first, that there was no continuous belt of dense population from London up to the North, because the belt was in fact intersected at right angles by a low density from the Severn to the Wash; secondly, that in terms of population growth the real contrast was between the South and the Midlands on one hand, and the North on the other.[29] In fact, the Barlow Commission had already recognized this fact, by stressing the regional differences rather than the common identity of Megalopolis. Their analysis showed that while in England and Wales as a whole employment had risen by 22.3 per cent from 1923–37, for London and the Home Counties the figure was 42.7 per cent. The same figure, 42.7 per cent, represented the share of London and the Home Counties, in the national growth. At the same time, as Table 3 shows, other parts of Megalopolis were stagnant or in decline. The growth of London was the outstanding feature of the economic geography of Britain in the interwar years; and if anything, the concept of an axial belt only tended to obscure it.

Therefore, though the Barlow Commission recognized the existence of the Megalopolis, they put the main weight of their analysis elsewhere.[30] First, they analysed the conurbations, and reached their celebrated conclusion:

> It is not possible from the evidence submitted to us to avoid the conclusion that the disadvantages in many, if not in most of the great industrial concentrations, alike on the strategical, the social, and the economic side, do constitute serious handicaps and even in some respects dangers to the nation's life and development, and we are of the opinion that definite action should be taken by the Government towards remedying them.[31]

Table 3 The development of the regions of the Axial Belt and regions outside it, up to 1937

A *Percentage distribution of total population*

	1801	1901	1921	1931	1937
London and Home Counties	18.0	23.4	23.5	24.8	25.7
Lancashire	6.4	11.9	11.6	11.2	10.9
West Riding, Notts and Derbyshire	8.5	10.7	10.9	11.0	10.8
Midlands	8.1	9.2	9.5	9.6	9.7
Total axial belt	**41.0**	**55.2**	**55.5**	**56.6**	**57.1**
Northumberland and Durham	3.0	4.8	5.2	5.0	4.8
Mid-Scotland	3.7	6.2	6.2	5.9	6.0
Glamorgan and Monmouth	1.1	3.1	4.0	3.7	3.4
Peripheral industrial areas	**7.8**	**14.1**	**15.4**	**14.6**	**14.2**
Rest of Great Britain	**51.2**	**30.7**	**29.1**	**28.8**	**28.7**
Total Great Britain	100.0	100.0	100.0	100.0	100.0

B *Percentage distribution of the insured (employed) population*

	1923	1937
London and Home Counties	22.4	26.0
Lancashire	15.7	13.8
West Riding, Notts and Derbyshire	13.0	12.2
Midlands	11.2	11.7
Total axial belt	**62.3**	**63.7**
Northumberland and Durham	5.7	4.9
Mid-Scotland	7.3	6.6
Glamorgan and Monmouth	4.2	3.3
Peripheral industrial areas	**17.2**	**14.8**
Rest of Great Britain	**20.5**	**21.5**
Total Great Britain	100.0	100.0

Then they analysed the related problem: the growth of one of these great industrial concentrations, the London area. They concluded:

> The continued drift of the industrial population to London and the Home Counties constitutes a social, economic and strategical problem which demands immediate attention.[32]

These conclusions were backed by an impressive weight of evidence, much of it statistical, to the effect that industrial and urban areas suffered grave social and economic disadvantages including poor housing, overcrowding, poor public health (especially child health), high land and property values, long journeys to work, and traffic congestion; in addition there were strategic disadvantages (on which the Commission heard evidence in camera) through liability to mass destruction from the air. They culminated in recommendations for the state to take an active role in influencing the future distribution of industry. Here the Commission split, the majority recommending a fairly modest control on new industrial location in the London area, a minority (including the influential planner Patrick Abercrombie) preferring a comprehensive system of state control of industrial location. These arguments and these recommendations may be read in the pages of the report itself, and in many commentaries; they need not be repeated again here. But it is important to try to bring out some general points about the essential historical basis of the idea of the Barlow Commissioners and their contemporaries.

Notes

1 Adna Ferrin Weber (1899) *The Growth of Cities in the Nineteenth Century* Macmillan, New York, Table 18, p.46.

2 Peter Hall (1966) *The World Cities* World University Library, London, Table 3, p. 18, quoting *United Nations Demographic Yearbook* (1960).

3 Robin Best (1959) *The Major Land Uses of Great Britain* Wye College, Wye, Table 5, p.30; Table 6, p.32.

4 *Ibid.*, Table 8, p.34.

5 Best has presented this analysis in various articles. The most convenient is probably Robin Best (1964) The future urban acreage *Town and Country Planning*, Vol.32, pp.350–5.

6 Again the estimate is available in various of Best's publications. This is from Robin Best (1965) Recent changes and future prospects of land use in England and Wales *Geographical Journal*, Vol.131, Table 1, p.3.

7 Best, *op. cit.* (1965) Table 3, pp.8–9.

8 R. H. Best and A. G. Champion (1970) Regional conversions of agricultural land to urban use in England and Wales, 1945–67 *Institute of British Geographers, Transactions*, Vol. 49, pp.15–32.

9 Direct calculation from 1851 Census *Population Tables*. For a more detailed analysis of London population in the nineteenth century see Karl Gustav Grytzell, *County of London: Population Changes*

1801–1901. Lund Studies in Geography, Ser. B, No. 26, Gleerup, Lund (1969), *passim*.

10 Colin Clark (1967) *Population Growth and Land Use* Macmillan, Chapter 8, *passim*. Colin Clark (1951) Urban population densities *Journal of the Royal Statistical Society*, A, Vol.114, pp.490–6. Colin Clark (1957) Urban population densities *Bulletin of the International Statistical Society*, Vol.36, pp.60–8. Brian J. L. Berry, James W. Simmons, Robert J. Tennant (1963) Urban population densities: structure and change *Geographical Review*, Vol.53, pp.389–405.

11 Homer Hoyt (1933) *One Hundred Years of Land Values in Chicago* University of Chicago Press, Chicago, *passim*.

12 Henrietta Barnett (1905) A garden suburb at Hampstead *Contemporary Review*, Vol.87, p.231. This and all other quotations in this paragraph are from Peter Hall (1973) 'England in 1900' in H. C. Derby (ed) *An Historical Geography of England to the Year 1900* Cambridge University Press.

13 H. W. A. Linecar (1949) *British Electric Trains* Ian Allen, *passim*.

14 British Road Federation, *Basic Road Statistics, 1969*, and information from BRF staff.

15 Sheffield Transport Department (1960) *The Tramway Era in Sheffield*.

16 A. Redford (1940) *The History of Local Government in Manchester*, Vol.3, *The Last Half Century* Longman, p.283.

17 *Ibid.*, p.285

18 Mary Waugh (1968) *The Suburban Development of North-West Kent 1861–1961*. Unpublished Ph.D. thesis, University of London. In the 1930s, £800 houses could be bought around London for as little as £25 down, and then between 1931 and 1939 745,000 houses were built by private builders in the Home Counties, out of a total of 1,810,000 in all England and Wales.

19 Between 1920 and 1938, the Manchester City Corporation built 27,447 houses while private enterprise built 8,315 houses with City assistance, and 15,845 houses unassisted. Redford, *op.cit.*, Table following p.246. Between 1919 and 1939 in Birmingham the totals were: 50,268 by the City, 54,536 by private enterprise, Asa Briggs (1952) *The History of Birmingham*, Vol.2, *Borough and City 1865–1938* Oxford University Press, p.229.

20 Peter Hall (1962) *The Industries of London since 1861* Hutchinson.

21 C. B. Fawcett (1932) Distribution of the urban population in Great Britain *Geographical Journal*, Vol.79, p.101.

22 C. B. Fawcett (1934) Areas of concentration of population in the

English-speaking countries *Population*, p.10. Also C. B. Fawcett (1937) The changing distribution of population *Scottish Geographical Magazine*, Vol.53, pp.361–73.

23 *Third Report of the Commissioner for the Special Areas (England and Wales)* (1936) Cmd 5303, HMSO, para.21.

24 *Report of the Royal Commission on the Distribution of the Industrial Population* (1940) Cmd 6153, HMSO, pp.vii-viii.

25 E. G. R. Taylor (1938) Discussion on the geographical distribution of industry *Geographical Journal*, Vol.92, p.23.

26 J. N. L. Baker and E. W. Gilbert (1944) The doctrine of an axial belt of industry in England *Geographical Journal*, Vol.103, p.51.

27 Memorandum on the geographical factors relevant to the location of industry (1938) *Geographical Journal*, Vol.92, p.502.

28 Royal Commission on the Industrial Population, *op.cit.*, p.152.

29 Robin Best's analysis, published twenty-six years later, supports the contention that Baker and Gilbert's analysis is still true; on the basis of urban growth. Best concludes, 'Megalopolis still does not exist as a single continuous area.' *Cf.* Best and Champion, *op.cit.*, (1970), pp.17–19, 26.

30 They advocated an attempt to drive the growth of activity in London into other parts of the belt. *Ibid.*, para.319.

31 *Ibid.*, para.413.

32 *Ibid.*, para.428.

1.7 The good uses of the city

Richard Sennett

In the stages of adolescent growth, most young people seem faced with an imbalance between what they are ready to experience and what they have experienced. This imbalance leads to a shortcut for experience – the creating of imaginary myths of what the world outside is like. Getting to the stages beyond this point in adolescence is now, however, very difficult for most young people. The two stages beyond are the playing out of some vision of coherent, painless life in a social environment responsive to the young person, followed by a change in concern and in the capacity for caring when the complexities of life defeat the painless myths. What happens now is that the patterns of coherence in earlier points of growth either meet no social resistance or are confined to a peculiar limbo. Where modern community life can be said to fail the young is in its inability to lead them into a social matrix where they will have to learn to deal with other people. Thus the young, whether they are radical, centrist, or conservative, can pass, and have passed, into physical adulthood with fixed pictures of themselves and a deep fear of exposing those pictures to social tests. Emotionally, then, they have failed to become adults.

What I envisage is a restructuring of city life so that these adolescent patterns have a challenging social matrix. There are definite and workable means, I believe, by which cities can become human settlements that *force* these coherence drives to be tested and challenged. These same city structures could confront as well older persons who have regressed to childish or adolescent indifference about the effect of their acts on the people around them.

Cities organized along these lines would not simply be places where the inhabitants encountered dissimilar people; the critical need is for men to have to deal with the dissimilarities. The outside world has to feel

Source: *The Uses of Disorder* (1971) Allan Lane, pp. 113–38.

D

important for the dreams from within to be touched. Thus the first problem in the design of such human communities is how to plug people into each other's lives without making everyone feel the same.

Survival communities: the idea

The most direct way to knit people's social lives together is through necessity, by making men need to know about each other in order to survive. What should emerge in city life is the occurrence of social relations, and especially relations involving social conflict, through face-to-face encounters. For experiencing the friction of differences and conflicts makes men personally aware of the milieu around their own lives; the need is for men to recognize conflicts, not to try to purify them away in a solidarity myth, in order to survive. A social forum that encourages the move into adulthood thus first depends on making sure there is no escape from situations of confrontation and conflict. The city can provide a unique meeting ground for these encounters.

The present use of affluent community life in cities is to make it possible for men to hide together from being adults. Building a survival community where men must confront differences around them will require two changes in the structuring of city life. One will be a change in the scope of bureaucratic power in the city; the other will be a change in the concept of order in the planning of the city.

It has become standard in modern governments, though not in modern business, for bureaucracies to become pyramids of power, with the most control exercised by a few individuals at the top of the organization and increasingly less control over basic decisions exercised by the many workers below. This pyramid shape is the basis of centralized educational systems such as that of France or legislative welfare systems like that of the United States. Businesses, on the other hand, are finding that this pyramid shape is often counterproductive. General Motors, as Peter Drucker describes it, was one of the early innovators in creating a more complex pattern of bureaucracy, and many of the businesses involved in large-scale merger or holding operations also have had to evolve similar new forms.

In the field of urban planning, the pyramid form remains endemic, despite some notable attempts to restructure it in the United States, attempts that have failed prematurely for lack of funds. Yet in order to make cities survival communities, where the affluent as well as the poor will have to deal directly with each other to survive, the bureaucracies of control in these cities must change their form.

For certain city functions, a pyramid-shaped central organization is necessary for economies of scale. One police dispatch system is more productive than ten, one central department to control fires or to deal with sanitation better than many small ones. The problem with such central organizations is not whether they should exist, but what they should do. People today are imbued with the technological belief that the larger the structure the more inclusive should be its scope, an idea derived, again, from the nature of machine productivity; thus it is difficult to accept the idea that a strong central control apparatus can exist in the city and yet do very limited, defined tasks. Part of the difficulty in imagining this curb is that those who traditionally have wanted to limit central authority have wanted the result to be a public power vacuum, so that in the place of public power there is substituted the power of a few individuals who control the private enterprises of the city. Almost all advanced countries, with the exception of the United States, have come to understand this fallacy of 'decentralization'. The removal of central authority, following libertarian lines of the nineteenth century, all too often means the passing of central authority to a few private individuals who cannot be touched by the public at large.

What is needed in order to create cities where people are forced to confront each other is a reconstituting of public power, not a destruction of it. As a rule of change, the situations creating survival encounters would be as follows: there would be no policing, nor any other form of central control, of schooling, zoning, renewal, or city activities that could be performed through common community action, or, even more importantly, through direct, nonviolent conflict in the city itself. This abstract idea comes clearer by examining a second change needed in city structure.

To make the experience of conflict a maturing one requires the destruction of an assumption regnant since the work of Baron Haussmann in Paris, an assumption that the planning of cities should be directed to bring order and clarity to the city as a whole. Instead of this idea, whose basis is found in mechanical ideas of production, the city must be conceived as a social order of parts without a coherent, controllable whole form. The planning of functional divisions, of processes, of land use in advance of the habitation of the land should be abolished. Rather, the creations of city spaces should be for varied, changeable use. Areas, for example, that during one period serve as commercial places should be able in another era to serve as living places. The creation of neighbourhood areas must not mean that the socioeconomic level of activities of the area are frozen by predetermined zoning specifications and the like.

The prohibition on preplanned, functional space is important because it permits great diversity to arise in city neighbourhoods, and because it permits whatever social encounters and conflicts exist in the neighbourhood to 'take hold' in the character of the neighbourhood itself.

Once preplanned city space is removed, the actual use of the space becomes much more important in the lives of its users. For when predetermined use through zoning is eliminated, the character of a neighbourhood will depend on the specific bonds and alliances of the people within it; its nature will be determined by social acts and the burden of those acts over time as a community's history. The preplanned 'image' of city neighbourhoods would not be definable on a planner's map; it would depend on how the individuals of the neighbourhood dealt with each other.

Encouraging unzoned urban places, no longer centrally controlled, would thus promote visual and functional disorder in the city. My belief is that this disorder is *better* than dead, predetermined planning, which restricts effective social exploration. It is better for men to be makers of historical change than for the functional design of a pre-experiential plan to be 'carried out'. If the element of history in city places is allowed to re-emerge in this way, if functional dislocation and a jumble of concurrent events and peoples inhabiting common ground is permitted, then the desires for purified identity can have a testing ground of the strongest sort. This would occur in the following way.

Survival communities: some examples

Let us imagine a community free to create its own patterns of life, in this case a neighbourhood where cheap rents were to be found, thus likely to attract young people. Here also, if the functional divisions that now operate in city life were erased, would be found whites and blacks who were blue-collar labourers, old people living in reduced circumstances, perhaps some immigrant clusters, perhaps a few small shopkeepers. Because the land use had not been rigidly zoned, all kinds of activities appropriate to cheap rents would be found – some light manufacturing, perhaps a brothel or two, many small stores, bars, and inexpensive family restaurants.

The outstanding characteristic of this area, for the young people who move into it, would be the high level of tension and unease between the people living there. It would be a vital place, to be sure – and this is what draws urbanists like Jane Jacobs to it – but a part of the vitality would be a great deal of conflict between dissimilar groups of people. And because metropolitan-wide controls would be lessened, the threat, or the assurance, of police control would be gone, for the police would have the responsibility not of keeping peace in the community by repressing deviance but rather of dealing with organized crime or other similar problems.

Precisely because the community was on its own, because the people had to deal with each other in order to survive at all, some kind of uneasy truce between these hostile camps, those conflicting interests, would have to be arranged by the people themselves. And the act of participating in some sort of truce would force people to look at each other, if only to find areas in which some bond, tenuous and unloving as it would be, could be forged.

How would a young person feel in such a place? He would be as much a part of its life as anyone else, since controls apart from the people living there would have been lessened, especially police controls; he couldn't escape the Irish factory workers who hate the 'spoiled' kids who go to college, nor the blacks who want no part of adolescent white sympathy. Yet he, and all the people around him, would have only each other; that would be the undeniable fact of life for them all. If the kids were playing records loudly, late at night, no cop would come to make them turn the record player off – the police would no longer see to that kind of thing. If a bar down the street were too noisy for the children of the neighbourhood to sleep, the parents would have to squeeze the bar owner themselves, by picketing or informal pressure, for no zoning laws would apply throughout the city. Whatever happens in this city place, whatever shape the community acquires, would occur because of either the direct control or the sufferance of the people there.

Such a community would probably stimulate a young person, and yet scare him, make him want to hide, as it would everyone else, to find some nice, safe, untroubled place. But the very diversity of the neighbourhood has built into it the obligation of responsibility; there would be no way to avoid self-destruction in the community other than to deal with the people who live around the place. The feeling that 'I live here and I count in this community's life' would consist, not of a feeling of companionship, but of a feeling that something must be done in common to make this conflict bearable, to survive together.

Thus the impulse to hide from pain, which is at the heart of the adolescent desire for a purified identity, would have a concrete social matrix, one in which the impulse would become untenable if the person were to survive. It is hard to imagine an eighteen-year-old who suddenly has to do something to make peace with white labourers who don't like college kids and Negroes who don't like whites making a snap decision about what he will do and be in the world; he can't help seeing everything around him, he can't help having to understand differences in other people whom he may not like, and who may not like him, in order to survive. In such a complex city, a young person must become an active being, a man, and not an abstract thinker discoursing on the evils of society at large. Confronted with the need to act, to deal with human differences in order to survive, it seems plausible that the desire for a mythic solidarity would be defeated by this very necessity for survival, this need for enough knowledge of disparate people to establish a common truce.

In this way a young person could come to feel dissatisfied with his own powers for making coherent world- and self-pictures. Survival communities could give him a field, resistant to purification by him or those around him, in which he could act on his desires for secure order and in which these desires would be defeated.

But these survival communities would lead men into adult concerns as well; they would be not merely a corrective to adolescence but a field for a richer life beyond it. The reasons for this can be understood by examining why survival communities would not escalate the expressions of social conflict into violence.

Survival communities and violence

Since the common pattern in the relations between men is a reversion to the wilfully blind selfishness of the child, the materials for conflict are innate to social life. There are few areas in which it should be expected that men would want to work actively together. But, as in any intimate relationship, there are group relationships that can be sustaining and productive for all concerned as a result of letting conflicts of interests, emotional jealousies, class hatreds, and racial fears express themselves. These conflicts are after all as much, if not much more, a part of every human being's life as brotherly love, yet we make our children feel these are terrible, guilty secrets that should never see the light of public display. These conflicts and fears especially now racial fears, can only be socialized if they are allowed to be expressed and play themselves out. I have never been able to understand how white liberals think they are realists when they tell their children there are no differences between blacks and whites but cultural prejudices, as if this meant nothing in the end. It is these cultural differences, exactly, that must be allowed to show themselves in all their crudity and vulgarity among both whites and blacks. Again, if the experience of meaningful conflict were possible in cities, the young would be led to a realization of the blindness of talking about non-negotiable demands, as the more rigid among them do now. It is in the essence of experiences of conflict, when the conflict matters for survival, that men learn to talk to their enemies, learn to see the dimensions of that which they oppose.

It is one of the terrible simplicities of modern city life that we believe the expression of these hostile feelings will lead to violence. Perhaps the reason this belief is so widely held is that it justifies repression of our feelings, and so lets us hide from them, as we assume that once they are out in the open, only chaos can be the result. This is similar to that adolescent metaphor by which guilt over a specific transgression is transformed into a much broader self-definition – that 'I am a sinner' – so that the act or feeling itself can be denied as a reality to be dealt with.

Yet if men do not grow out of this denial, if men continue to believe that hostility between groups should be muted, not encouraged in its social expression, the cities will continue to burn, for nothing exists socially now to mediate hostility, to force people to look beyond their images of threatening outsiders to the actual outsiders themselves. By restructuring the power of city bureaucracies so that they leave to the hostile groups themselves the *need* to create some truce, in order for chaos to be prevented, hostility can take on more open and less violent forms.

Certainly, this is to gamble with social life itself. Yet it is of the essence of adult lives that chance and chance situations should provide the medium for new insight and a new understanding of discrete, other beings. To assure tranquillity in advance is to revert to a dream of painless immunity, and ultimately, if we are to judge from some social revolutions of our own time, to bring on a totalitarian rigidity for the sake of the dream.

Releasing conflict between groups in survival communities is not as great a gamble as it might seem. Certain processes, connected with the final stage of transition from adolescence to adulthood, ensure at least some measure of social peace, I believe, because of changes wrought in the individual involved in the web of social conflict between diverse urban groups.

Survival communities and adulthood

In any large central city, there remain today many differences in life styles that could be used to distribute conflict, or at least fragment it. Ethnicity, social class, and race are not simple conditions of life, but complex factors that tend to interpenetrate and become diffused. For instance, it is a popular error to suppose that the violence of recent summers in American cities is a 'race' phenomenon, for most middle-class blacks are not only uninvolved but also hostile to the Negro militants; however, given the structure of community life and police control in American cities, middle-class blacks and poor blacks never have to deal with each other about their common ties or differences; each can sink back into a comfortable disgust over what the other group does. Yet if they had to confront each other, if the police stopped their blanket repression and gave the segments of the black community the responsibility to control themselves, these hostilities could be expressed, and both groups, in order to survive, would find that they could go no further to achieve their own ends without finding out something about each other. Let us imagine added to this situation a refusal of the police to intervene between any black group and the whites who now feel threatened by them. I believe that, instead of massive violence erupting, the people involved would learn that there is too much complex feeling involved to be taken care of by the burning of stores. When people have to come face to face in order to survive, the death instinct does not prevail; it is only when men are alienated from using their own power, from being real men, that they burn themselves out and invite massive repression from the outside.

In other words, if we could increase the complexity of confrontation and conflict in the city, not polarize it, the aggression, still there, would channel itself into paths that allow at least mutual survival. This, I believe, is not as grim a prospect as it might seem. For when a man fails to achieve coherent ends, when there is too much complexity impinging on him for him to advocate something 'pure and simple', the failure that results leads not to dissolution of his social resolve, but to exactly that state of mind now open only to a few among those who have experienced revolutionary conflict. As a consequence of this failure, one wants to understand the complexity that defeated one; the sense of curiosity can be awakened, has to be awakened, if a man is going to know enough in order to survive.

This is how the adult's kind of care, independent of some painless order in which he is safe, comes into being. It is a caring based on the curiosity and commitment to the immediate, impinging social world rather than an otherwordly love or an urge towards purity. The French psychologist Georges Lapassade has said that adulthood is a stage in which pleasure and pain are no longer separable, because the individual is engaged by choice in situations without an end, situations that are 'unachieved'. It is exactly the character of these survival communities to create 'unachieved' situations that have no clear form or definition in advance of the experience of social interaction. By wilfully making the question of social survival depend on the confused impure actions men take, these adult capacities to care and to wonder about the unknown will be generated. By a fundamental paradox of psycho-social development, the primitive questions of intergroup survival must resurface for a more civilized and mature life to exist.

The question may be posed as to what is particularly 'urban' about such communities of survival. What role does the city as a special human settlement play in this communal movement to adulthood?

Survival communities as cities
The structural conditions under which survival communities could work are, first, those of heavy population density and, second, those of multiple contact points. Both of these structures are brought to a high point in urban settlements.

The first of these conditions seems readily apparent. If people are to deal with an environment too complex to control, a small village or a suburb, with its intimacy and isolation, will hardly suffice. There needs to be an enormous number of people packed together for a truly uncontrollable environment to exist. But what if this mass simply acted as a little group enlarged? It is here that the real promise of city life begins, for as the number of people concentrated together in one place grows very large, the quality of human relations changes.

This appears more obvious than it is. In fact, those writers of the past two decades who have confused a 'mass-culture' society with an increasingly urban one have ignored the fact that cities of the postwar era have become less dense and their population dispersed over a wide area even as the numbers in the megalopolis, as Jean Gottman calls it, have increased. There are definite reasons why a massive, dense city society is opposed to a mass-culture society.

The first of these is the possibility, indeed the encouragement, of deviance in urban places. The first great American urban sociologist, Robert Park, wrote of the dense cities of his time that exactly because so many people were packed together it was hard for central agencies of control like the police to see all those who were different, or to control them through coercive means. Numbers provided, he said, a kind of screen for deviations or idiosyncrasies; a man will not be noticed or forced into a community-wide mould with anything like the pressure found in a small town or suburb. Researchers since Park's time bear this idea out in many ways. It is known that sexual deviations are much more easily expressed in dense urban areas than in the careful watching of the suburb or small town. Historically, deviant subcultures, be they bohemian, ethnic, or, today, youth and student, survive much longer in dense urban areas than in sparsely populated, easily controlled areas.

The second reason large dense communities are freed from the controls inherent in small ones concerns the instability of their populations. Jane Jacobs and other popular writers are greatly at fault for looking at the dense ethnic inner-city areas as traditionally stable places where people got to know their neighbours through years and years of common association. Historically and demographically this has not been true. There has been and is a great deal of movement from place to place within dense cities and between them. The warm associations Jacobs found are due to factors other than population stability. (I do not wish to quarrel with the ethnical values she sees in dense city places; she simply ascribes them to the wrong factual base.)

The effect of this population movement in cities, so much greater than the intra-communal movement found in suburbs, is to destroy the power of tight-knit structures or local rules on the citizenry. The popular stereotype of Italian or Jewish urban communities as closed and impenetrable is flawed, because the people in them are continually moving around. That kind of tightness more likely occurs in the white, middle-class suburb, for the rate of household movement is lesser there when compared to the second generation in any of the inner-city groups.

Large numbers of people living densely packed together thus provide the medium of diversity and instability necessary for these survival communities to operate. But one may object that this instability makes it impossible for people to be able to face each other, to become involved with those around them. It *is* impossible as long as we understand coming together in community action along the old lines of common endeavour and a sharing of similarity. But the kinds of contacts that once existed in these ethnic ghettos suggest how direct, face-to-face associations might actually be encouraged under conditions of instability and diversity.

In the old ghetto order, multiple contact points with diverse people and groups in the city were necessary, since none of the institutions in that era of scarcity had the power to be self-sustaining. By removing centralized bureaucracies of social control and by eliminating preplanning with restrictive zoning, the same effect could be reproduced today; the intimate institutions of city life would not be able to be self-sustaining, and the individual or family would have to look beyond their own borders in order to survive. Decentralization, as the idea is used here, would have the effect of necessitating multiple social contacts for survival, without leading to community cohesion.

This process can be illustrated as follows. Let us suppose that a city university were deprived of its special zoning and centralized controls. Like Columbia, Harvard, or the University of Chicago, its students and faculty would live in a heterogeneous area with many hostile non-university people intermixed among the school population. But unlike these three schools, the city university we envisage would not possess the power of eminent domain, nor police protection for students as well as faculty, and would be forbidden to use its money for coherent territorial acquisition. I believe such an arrangement would force a communal confrontation of the diverse elements that necessitate exploration of the 'otherness' of all sides. An attempt would have to be made to survive together in the midst of great tension through finding out something about each other. In this way people would begin to think beyond the convenient fictions of the 'administration', the 'student movement', or the 'community'. When men and women must deal with each other as people, in a community where there is no overriding control to ensure survival, the flight into abstraction becomes unreal. The complexities of conducting a community life together are going to make the generalized pictures *dysfunctional*, because concrete men and women simply will not act in the predictable ways generalized pictures would indicate. Acting on the level of mythic 'we' and 'they', there is no contact between the concrete beings who must work out some arrangements in order to survive each day. If power were decentralized in this way, a multiple chain of contacts, between people living in the same block, or working in the same area, would be necessary. Since the people would be diverse, the web of affiliation for sheer survival would become particularized, not abstracted into 'us' against the outside.

In fact, just such a mutual adjustment process occurred in New York's much maligned school district I.S. 201. During the few weeks that this project had to operate on its own, conditions *within* the affected schools were remarkably nonviolent between Jewish white teachers, black teachers, and their black, Puerto Rican, and poor white students. Paths of real accommodation were beginning to emerge. Once the strike forced a we–they confrontation with a central authority – the teacher's union – the level of violence and the easy images of 'us and them' behind violent encounters again became dominant.

Multiple contacts necessitated by dense, decentralized social conditions such as those occurring within this school district, illustrate a process well thought out in Lewis Coser's *The Functions of Social Conflict*. This is the binding power of face-to-face tension and conflict, as opposed to the destructive power of conflict between bureaucratic institutions. For the experience of expressing hostility or simply an alternative to the acts or the feelings of someone else creates a certain kind of mutual commitment. People are dealing with each other, willing to express themselves, rather than storing up their grievances in private, where the character of their enemies and themselves becomes black-and-white clear. Multiple points of contact with different elements in a city diffuse hostility to the point where an individual will despair of defining some safe, secure attributes of his own identity and social space. This sense of failure is precisely the point at which he begins to become an adult and to feel that his identity instead turns on his very power to reach out and explore.

In these dense, diverse communities, the process of making multiple contacts for survival would burst the boundaries of thinking couched in homogeneous small-group terms. Since urban space would not be preplanned into separate units, as it now is, but would be free for all manner of incursions and combinations, the neat categories of spatial experience in cities, such as home, school, work, shopping, parks, and playgrounds, could not be maintained. They would come to interpenetrate, as Jane Jacobs observed in the dense inner-city community of New York where she lived, or as Robert Park once observed in Chicago. However, now such interpenetration would not just be part of the local colour of the ethnic working class but a part of the life of more affluent people as well. Men would find in the places where they worked community problems and community experiences, as well as community conflicts, not limited to the sphere of their own small jobs, just as the region where a man lived would not be immune to a diverse circle of influences and modes of life. If an increased density in the planning of cities was connected to a limiting of central bureaucratic authority, spheres of multiple contact like this in the opportunities for city-wide action would emerge, as would the necessity to act in a direct and personal way.

The kind of urban community life I have in mind has specific as well as general guidelines. What I should like to explore now is the techniques by which this kind of community life might actually be realized in the future planning of cities.

Some suggestions for action

It might seem that the tone of this essay would preclude a discussion of planning: isn't an uncontrolled environment innately an unplanned one? Yet I disagree with some community thinkers who believe that diverse communities can arise naturally and spontaneously, once 'the system' is destroyed. I believe diverse communities do not arise spontaneously, nor are spontaneously maintained, but instead have to be created and urged into being. Let me try to show why this is so.

The suburbanization and increasing organization of city spaces into functional compartments is not a process arbitrarily imposed on city people but one responsive to their human desires, the desires to hide from pain and disorder. The idea that the 'people' are straining at the bit against the 'system' is much too naive, requires that all these dark elements of fear and cowardice in the process of growing be denied. More realistically, the people and the system are in conspiracy with each other to establish a comfortable slavery to the known and the routine.

Furthermore, the social dimensions of affluence in city life show themselves easily put to the service of such voluntary slavery. For affluence weakens the need for sharing of scarce goods and services, and lends each man the power to buy or control the survival necessities for his everyday activities.

Given this disposition, both in the development of men and in the immediate past history of city communities, there seems to be little reason to think that creating a power vacuum, by simply abolishing the present 'system', is going to lead to a millennial flowering. People have an innate impulse to recapitulate under different names the slaveries they have known in the past. This is what revolutionary thinkers like Fanon have understood so well, and what the 'community revolutionaries' have yet to learn. Some positive directions towards change are necessary.

The first of these directions is to increase the visible density of urban areas. Unfortunately, high-density living space is now planned only along the lines of a suburban model. The large housing projects, like Lefrak City in New York, have all their functions neatly prelabelled and separated, so that although many people live together they seldom come into unknown, unplanned contact. If these parts were jumbled together, the density of these housing projects would serve a social purpose. This can be done in a number of ways.

High-rise buildings should be thought of, Frank Lloyd Wright once said, as vertical streets. Instead of putting all the common meeting places on the ground or on the top storeys, the public places should be distributed throughout the buildings. Wright's 'Mile-High City' contained some of these ideas in embryo.

But a more direct and perhaps more practical way of establishing visible density in cities has already been developed historically. In the great squares of such cities as Paris or Florence, unlike those of London, the arrangement of town houses around a common space provided a superb mingling ground for the residents. The density of these areas, as portrayed in Arnold Zucker's *Town and Square* was very high, even in modern terms. We do know, for example, that townhouse blocks with spacious quarters have been designed to provide a density almost approaching that of the high-rise towers which are isolated on their plots of land, the open space walled by chain-link fencing. In contrast, the square surrounded by townhouses makes human density count socially. Such density permits the expression of personal deviation or idiosyncracy in a milieu where there are too many people thrown together to discipline everyone to the same norm. The visible density of such places, if past patterns are a guide, increases the mobility and flow of the population.

This mixing together of dense numbers of people requires in its turn a second direction of change: a concerted effort to effect socioeconomic integration of living, working, and recreational spaces. In the United States, this would extend to trying to push integration racially. Since this idea is anathema to sectors of both the Left and the Right, I should spell out first how it is practicable, and second why it is absolutely necessary to restore a truly civilized city life.

In the rebuilding of Paris by Baron Haussmann, socioeconomic integration of housing units was in some cases attempted. The new apartment units contained the rich, the middle class, and the poor. As David Pinckney points out in his book on the subject, the rich occupied the lower floors, the middle classes the middle floors, and the poor the roof garrets. The system worked for a long time, and contributed, Pinckney points, to the sense of diversity and vitality in central-city Paris. Since Haussmann's time, only sporadic and halfhearted efforts have been made to continue this form of residential building. In the United States, there have been a few such attempts within government housing, but the mixing of rich and middle class or middle class and poor has always been radically weighted at one end or the other, and the actual apartment groups kept separate socioeconomically. Real estate interests have said over and again that in private apartments or housing developments this homogeneity is a necessity imposed on the builder, because people feel uncomfortable unless they know that their neighbours are mostly like themselves.

True enough, but the point is that it would be *better* in the end if they did feel uncomfortable, and began to experience a sense of dislocation in their lives. If it takes government money to assist in this socioeconomic mixing, then the money ought to be spent. Again, the spontaneous character of people's desires is no guide to social virtue. The government has subsidized some integration, but hardly enough, and hardly in the kind of living space where people would have to come to terms with each other's presence.

Certain US planners have objected that this mixing of classes, which would result in the mixing of races as well, has brought only unbearable racial conflict, and is inhumane to enforce when both sides don't want it. The public housing projects these people point to certainly have been miserable failures. But this is a very biased picture. The sociologist Thomas Pettigrew has estimated that there are a large number of communities in the United States outside the South that are integrated house by house rather than with a Negro 'sector', and that at least passable relations have been achieved. There are also, despite the current stereotype of anti-black feeling among white workers, a large number of inner-city communities that are racially integrated areas containing white working class and black working class. The levels of violence, as measured by the incidence of high school violence and the like, is *lower* in these communities than in either homogeneously white or black working-class neighbourhoods. There is tension to be sure, but it isn't escalated to violence. The difficulty is that as long as people keep thinking of the majority of blacks as unemployed misfits and the white working class as authoritarian haters, this comfortable sense of the impossibility of racial integration can be maintained.

A more serious challenge to the practicality of racial integration in cities is that offered by such writers as Norman Podhoretz. In his essay 'My Negro Problem, and Ours' Podhoretz describes the strong anti-Negro feeling of Jews, and the anti-Semitic feeling of blacks, in an integrated situation where both groups are enmeshed in poverty. It may be that, for blacks and whites in poverty, socioeconomic integration of housing and schools would be only an inhuman and brutalizing experience, being thrust among those who have made it or are about to rise. However, all the popular stereotypes treating 'the urban problem' as essentially one of poverty ignore the fact that the majority of urban blacks are not destitute but are working class and lower middle class. They, like their white working-class compeers, have been dealt out of the *qualitative* opportunities wealthier people in the city can have. Once one gets above the poverty line, racial integration is practicable, and has, in the cases where it has been permitted to take hold, proved to be a viable community structure. It is also, I would argue, qualitatively necessary, for the same reasons that socioeconomic integration is.

It is the mixing of such diverse elements that provides the materials for the 'otherness' of visibly different life styles in a city; these materials of otherness are exactly what men need to learn about in order to become adults. Unfortunately, now these diverse city groups are each drawn into themselves, nursing their anger against the others without forums of expression. By bringing them together, we will increase the conflicts expressed and decrease the possibility of an eventful explosion of violence.

It has been said over and over by black community organizers that integration attempts only fragment further the sense of selfhood and self-dignity of ghetto residents. This may be true below the lines of poverty. But for the large segment of the urban black population that has become or is becoming middle class, I am convinced that this cultural insularity will lead in the end to the same kind of dullness and routine experienced by white ethnic groups that have become both prosperous and self-enclosed. Class and wealth *do* make a difference in people's lives. What we need to find are community forms that are affirmative and growth-producing for men freed from the boundaries of poverty, and such communities seem to me possible only when diverse and ineradicably different kinds of people are thrown together and forced to deal with each other for mutual survival.

It may be that ethnic and racial differences would eventually be weakened in such communities. The point is that concord would not therefore be reached; the inevitable disruptions caused by regression to childhood selfishness would still be present. But in dense, visibly diverse communities where people would have to deal with each other, these regressions would provide a constant starting point for conflict and conciliation. The racial, ethnic, and economic shadings that now exist in city life are places to begin in forming communities where this confrontation occurs.

Diversifying the community through such integration raises the third, and most important, direction of replanning cities for such adult growth: the removal of central bureaucracies from their present directive power.

The closest that community workers in the last decades came to a theory of community control was the belief that functions carried on in city hall ought to be 'decentralized', turned over to local community groups. When this kind of decentralization has been practised, which is rarely, and is limited to the black ghetto, it has produced some results. Hostile white school or government administrators have been replaced by less hostile black administrators. In a very few cases, the change actually meant the man on the street could begin to grapple with the environment around him and worry about changing it. But the problem with this view of decentralization, especially where it applies to the broader, non-poverty society outside the ghetto, is that no changes of power in *essence* are involved. In other words, localism doesn't bring a change in the seat of power, so that the individual has to act for himself. Suburbs, after all, are decentralized, local units of power, and yet the only community-control exercises at this level which grip the inhabitants are acts of repressing deviates: i.e., fights about open housing, gerrymandering of school districts, and the like.

Really 'decentralized' power, so that the individual has to deal with those around him, in a milieu of diversity, involves a change in the essence of communal control, that is, in the refusal to regulate conflict. For example, police control of much civil disorder ought to be sharply curbed; the responsibility for making peace in neighbourhood affairs ought to fall to the people involved. Because men are now so innocent and unskilled in the expression of conflict, they can only view these disorders as spiralling into violence. Until they learn through experience that the handling of conflict is something they have to deal with, something that cannot be passed on to police, this polarization and escalation of conflict into violence will be the only end they can frame for themselves. This is as true of those who expect police reprisals against themselves, like the small group of militant students, as those who call in the police 'on their side'.

In a less extreme dimension, the spending of money for neighbourhood schools or civic improvements is meaningless when the neighbourhood school or committee is merely spending money along lines sent down from a central authority. How and why the money is to be spent needs to be the responsibility of the people who will feel its impact. In the first case, central authority is retained under the guise of 'decentralization'; in the second case the nature of the power truly changes.

We also need to explore how a centralized state apparatus can be made compatible with decentralized ends. There is no reason why centralized resources, like taxes, fire and police services, health and welfare benefits, have to be destroyed in order to decentralize power in essence. The community leaders who advocate this make a mistake: it is not the existence of centralized structures which is *per se* the evil, but the machine-like uses to which these structures are so easily directed. Conceivably through social experiment we can learn how to distribute centralized resources to create decentralized, uncontrolled social situations. The essence of bureaucracies, Simmel wrote, is the use to which they are put; these impersonal structures are corrupting only when they are taken as ends in themselves, when the processes by which they work most efficiently are taken to be an image of how society itself ought to function. By breaking this machine image, and removing from massive bureaucracies the power to regulate conflict, we may be able to invent new activities for them in which they help create diversity and disorder rather than stifle it.

These suggestions for a greater density, diversity, and power relations in city communities would create in general a high level of tension. They would not create a stifling sense of localism, of 'urban villages' in Herbert Gans's term; instead, they would create a sense of the need to deal with shifting combinations of people and shifting issues over the course of time in order to keep daily life ongoing. I don't imagine any sort of joyous communion in these encounters but rather a feeling of needing to keep in touch, a feeling of having to be involved in a social world.

A disordered, unstable, direct social life of this kind would lead to structural changes in the city itself as well as to the individuals in the social milieu.

2   Urban processes

Introduction
In this short section we have chosen to focus on two interrelated issues. The first of these is concerned with the distribution of justice across urban space and attendant on that is the extent to which the city, or the urban system, helps to generate poverty, working against principles of equity and social justice. The second theme is related to the physical planning of the city and considers some of the assumptions that are said to lie behind the decisions and the plans drawn up for the development of our cities. All the articles in this section supplement material discussed in the first three units of the Education in the Urban Environment course.

The paper by Harvey (2.2) develops the theme which he discusses more fully in his book *Social Justice and the City* (1973). Harvey sets out to introduce normative thinking into geographical analysis by introducing the concept of distribution into discussions of location theory and by asking questions such as 'what are we distributing?' and 'to whom?'; from this he arrives at a theory of *territorial* distributive justice. This is not merely an attempt to replace the criterion of efficiency by one of justice, but a plea for an acknowledgment that the efficiency factors in the end may prove inefficient unless justice and social cost factors are considered at the same time. Pahl's article (2.1) considers the way in which the urban system operates and considers the likelihood that it is working to pauperize considerable numbers in our cities, thereby generating greater inequality and injustice.

The two articles on planning are, in a way, an exemplification of this process. Sarkissian (2.4) reviews the development of the idea of social mix in planning with its belief that if people are socially mixed territorially certain results will follow – the raising of the standards of the lower classes, the production of social harmony and increased equality of opportunity. Certainly, it has proved a belief that is long standing and is still persuasive. Simmie's paper (2.3), echoing other criticisms of urban planners, attacks their assumptions, lack of clarity, narrowness and élitism.

2.1   Poverty and the urban system

Raymond Pahl

The redistribution of real income and the equitable distribution of public services and facilities

It has been stated that there may be a process of pauperization engendered by changes in the country's industrial and occupational structure. It is necessary to consider, therefore, other sources of real income apart from the labour market.

The orthodox view that life chances are directly related to income gained from the work situation alone is perhaps too limited.Thus, for example, wage differentials might have been decreasing but the poor could still be getting relatively poorer if their greater income were relatively less valuable as a means for getting scarce urban resources and facilities. Differentials in *real* income could increase, as differentials in wages decrease. Hence the operation of 'the urban system' could lead to a process of pauperization independently of the situation in the job market. In Eastern Europe, attempts to redistribute resources in favour of less-skilled workers were frustrated by the distributional effects of an urban system which appeared to be creating new or deeper patterns of inequality (Konrád and Szelényi 1969). It is evident that even in a socialist economy the inability to understand urban distributive mechanisms can inhibit the move to greater equality, based on earned income alone. It is evident also that the availability of some of the more important urban resources and facilities is not dependent solely on the ability to pay. Those provisions which are administered by local or national government are critical determinants of life chances. Such facilities may be compulsory – such as primary or secondary education – or may be provided upon request as a right or may be granted as a privilege. One strand in the ideology of the

Source: *Spatial Policy Problems of the British Economy*, ed. Michael Chisholm and Gerald Manners, Cambridge University Press (1971), pp.133–45.

Welfare State as a type of society was that need should be a more important criterion than wealth to determine access to facilities. If this ideology had been comprehensively pursued and supported, we might have expected a considerable redistribution of real income within and between localities. Thus, to take the example of the physical distribution of primary schools, the state attempts to provide schools in relation to the age structure of the population, the pattern of residential development and the distance a small child can be expected to walk. This contrasts with schools in the private sector which need not bear any relation to catchment areas but which rely on the wealth of their clients to transport pupils, often to inconveniently situated converted mansions.

If the provision of public services followed such a principle systematically, we would expect to find a positive correlation between the need for public services and facilities and their provision. Thus, the Welfare State and notions of citizenship would be a reality and the inequalities following from wage differentials would be compensated for, so that the poor would not be doubly penalized. However, it is a commonplace to observe that this does not happen, although detailed documentation presents many complicated methodological problems (Davies 1968). The provision of public services and facilities has its own pattern of inequalities. It can be argued that the exploration of the systematic structuring of such inequalities provides a useful focus to students of stratification working in urban areas (Pahl 1969). The pattern of territorial injustice exemplified in the work of Davies for Britain can be found in every industrial society (e.g. Scardigli 1970) and the elimination of such inequalities could well be extremely difficult, even in a post-revolutionary situation. The hidden mechanisms of redistribution operate in socialist as well as in capitalist societies; one of the tasks of a radical sociology might be to expose such mechanisms and to consider how an understanding of the urban redistributive system can be used to develop new theories of stratification in industrial society.

Regard should not simply be paid to those services which are traditionally discussed by students of social administration and social policy – what might be called the Seebohm services (Seebohm Committee 1968). It is also important to consider all other aspects of public policy which have a redistributive effect. The siting of power stations, hospitals or motorways all help to redistribute real income. Externality effects, as economists call them, are an important element in the system. And the central problem is to understand how policies and programmes designed to reduce inequalities may actually increase them. It is a matter of exploring the distribution of 'fringe benefits generated by changes in the urban system', to take Harvey's phrase (Harvey 1971).

The public provision of health and welfare services, roads, public transport, fire and police protection, libraries, schools, swimming pools, parks and so on, is financed out of public rates and taxes 'for the community at large'. No one openly denies that the poorest man has as much right to walk in the park, use the public library, call out a fire engine or have domestic help under certain circumstances, as the richest man. If this does not happen we must ask whether the public sector generates its own system of inequality, or whether it simply reflects the economic system within which it is encapsulated.

Unfortunately, a systematic sociology of public provision has hardly started, despite the contention of one urban economist that 'local public services bid fair to become the chief means of income *re*distribution in our economy' (Thompson 1965, p.118; present author's emphasis). Only educational provision has been systematically studied, although something of a start in the sociology of the Health Service and the physical planning process has been made. If we compare the amount of effort and energy that has been devoted to the sociology of industry (mainly private) with that devoted to the sociology of public services, the contrast is striking. Certainly something is known of *The Faith of the Counsellors* (Halmos 1965), the ideologies of teachers, planners and social workers; but it is not very helpful to talk of 'bourgeois' values in these professions if very similar values are found in socialistic societies. Thus, for example, planners in both socialist and capitalist societies may share similar goals and values, even if the means at their disposal are different. The same applies to many other caretaking professions and to the managers of the public sector. To some extent, their power and ideology derive from the political party or council that employs them. However, it would surely be naive to assume that managers of the urban system are merely tools of their political masters, ready to shift policies and programmes according to political fashion. Clearly, there is a considerable tension between administrator, professional and politician which the Fulton (1968) and Maud (1967) Reports document for National and Local Government respectively. Such managerial tensions are likely to produce different patterns of resource allocation in different localities as the distribution of power shifts between the three contending groups. This point is made by Davies (1968, pp.114–15):

> The power of a Committee over the Council may be the result of many factors. The authority may always have prided itself on the performance of one service – perhaps having been a pioneer in this field – and be generous in its allocation of funds to it. A chief officer may have built up a distinguished team and have a distinguished

successor who may ensure the continuation of the department's status in the authority.... Members may be particularly sensitive to the needs of some services because of local pressure groups' activity, because of the political ideology of dominating members or because the needs of the area, as perceived by almost anyone, suggest that an above-average development of the service in question is appropriate. Such factors may vary greatly in strength between authorities, but there can be no doubt that they have a major effect on the extent and manner of provision of services.

There appears to be no systematic relationship between the level of provision of public resources and facilities and the political party in power. Old people, for example, do not necessarily receive better care under a Labour than under a Conservative local authority. There exists a need for a typology of allocative structures based upon a number of dimensions. At present it is known that territorial inequality is substantial and that men with the same occupation, income and family characteristics have substantially different life chances in different localities. The systematic portrayal of such inequalities remains to be undertaken. The range of territorial inequality is probably greater in many instances than the range of inequality between certain positions in the occupational structure; moreover, the former inequalities are widening more rapidly than the latter. Authorities differ in the rules they adopt for the allocation of public services and facilities; they differ in wealth; they differ in the number and the degree of skills of the professional gatekeepers they employ; they differ in the system of administration and organization which they adopt and the degree of cooperation and coordination which may exist between 'chief officers' and the rest of their managerial staff. Max Weber was surely wrong when he described the end of the political autonomy of the medieval city as the end of a distinctive urban sociology (Weber 1960). There is still a considerable concentration of power over the allocation of scarce resources in localities. Although there may be, as it were, conflicts between the line and staff managers and the shareholders (i.e. the Council), there is a united and common ideology of the need to control, plan and provide for the lower participants or clients in the urban system. There is a vested interest in maintaining the Local Authority (a title with significant Dahrendorfian implications) (Dahrendorf 1959) which pays the managers good salaries and provides the context for the expansion of various professions. To some extent, each professional group in an Authority's management structure is an interest group, which gains power by increasing the number of its own clients or lower participants. Since few Authorities have an overall programme or policy, such as may occur at the national level, the cumulative effect of *ad hoc* policies, reflecting a fluctuating power situation, may provide greater 'diswelfare' and increasing inequality for the majority of an Authority's lower participants.

Managers and professionals in the urban distributive system
Harvey suggests that 'it is tempting to hypothesize that any activity that generates strong external costs will be undercontrolled or undercompensated for' and that small, but well-mobilized pressure groups will be able to influence disproportionately allocational and locational decisions (Harvey 1971). As an example he cites 'Central Business District Imperialism' in which the well-organized business interests of the central city (with their small-group oligopolistic structure) effectively dominate the looser and weaker coalitions found in the rest of the city. This view of the city is very clearly exemplified by the nature and style of objections to the Greater London Development Plan, which formed the basis of an Inquiry which began in 1970. Individual London Boroughs engaged counsel to argue for more resources (floorspace allocations or population totals) and one of the longest and most elaborate cases for more resources was made by the institution which already had most – the City. Whatever the particular merits of the cases put forward, it is evident that the poorer areas and populations have less resources to compete for more resources. They are dependent on the advocacy of others.

Conflict, then, is a necessary condition of urban life (Meltzer and Whitley 1968, pp. 173–4):

> In the most general terms, therefore, the city is composed of groupings of residents, clearly identified within a spatial location, who are competing for the resources that the city offers. Whether organized or not, they are competing for good jobs, good houses, good education, and all the other 'goodies' available in the urban milieu.

The same authors go on to argue that slums exist and are maintained because the people living there have insufficient influence or control over the allocation of resources.

The argument so far is that scarce urban resources and facilities are distributed by the managers of the urban system (elaborated in Pahl 1969), and that those professionals who, directly or indirectly, manage these resources are concerned individually to advance as professionals and collectively to maintain the boundaries between themselves and other professional interest groups. The important question which now emerges is the degree of independent and autonomous control which can be exercised by the urban managers as distinct from industrial managers or national and local politicians. How far, in terms of the main theme of this chapter, can urban managers work within the existing economic and political system to make their limited urban system operate more equitably? Furthermore, what indicators would be appropriate to measure the effects of the redistribution of real income within urban systems?

This is a difficult issue and all that one can say with certainty is that it is easier to find examples where the differentials between the poorest and the richest social groups have increased, rather than the reverse. Some interesting material is presented in *The Property Boom* by Oliver Marriott, who was financial editor of *The Times* from 1945 to 1965. Discussing the development of provincial town centres between 1948 and 1955 Marriott (1967, pp.61–5) notes:

> Building licences were only granted for replacing bombed shops or shops on new housing estates. Each local authority was given permission by the Ministry of Housing for a certain amount to be spent in its area, and if the allocation was not taken up by the year end, it lapsed. This spurred the local authorities to busy on with redevelopment and quickened the flow of work into Ravenseft's eager hands between 1950 and 1955. In these crucial years Freedman and Maynard had virtually no opposition. One reason was that they were opening up a type of redevelopment which had previously been unknown. This was large-scale cooperation between municipal authorities and private enterprise....

> The grapevine of local officials also helped Freedman and Maynard; at their annual conferences the town clerks or the surveyors or the borough architects would discuss the developer, which for a few years meant a word of mouth advertisement for Ravenseft....

> Towards the end of 1953 Freedman and Maynard saw that before long they would be running out of blitzed cities. They began to look at the New Towns ... the multiple shops flocked in to the New Towns' centres – and so did the New Townspeople....

> In 1953 Harold Samuel's land securities bought out Freedman and Maynard and friends and took its holding in Ravenseft from 50 per cent to 100 per cent. This deal valued Ravenseft at £2,100,000....

> ... by the summer of 1967, after the property share boom had cooled, Harold Samuel's holding in land securities was worth £12,400,000, Louis Freedman's £1,850,000 and Fred Maynard's £845,000. The entire company, including the much bigger stake of

the public and the insurance companies, was valued by the stock market at £62,000,000.

And that is how we got our nice new shops and Louis Freedman made a personal fortune of nearly £2 million. Certainly it was government policy to redevelop town centres with the profit and benefit of private developers in mind and local authorities could do little else than pass the best central sites to commercial organizations. Sites for public services and facilities had to be found away from the most accessible locations. There was little scope for policies for a more equitable distribution of real income.

The current interest in cost-benefit analysis as a managerial tool in urban resource allocation may also lead to a widening of real income differentials, since it has an inevitable bias towards the values of property and capital. In the Roskill Commission's study of amenity costs at a new international airport, it was found that the depreciation of property values near Heathrow and Gatwick was highly sensitive to the class of property. On average, for all noise levels, the percentage depreciation of high-class property was four times the depreciation of low-class property. Simply because their property values were so little affected, the poor were assumed to be little bothered by noise, and small or nil values were attached to their loss of amenity for the purposes of the cost-benefit quantification (Adams 1970). Again, although there are techniques for determining the cost of, say, an urban motorway to the owners of property in its path, other costs, less easily quantified, are not taken into account. In a working-class area of rented housing, kin links and supporting patterns of social relationships may have created a form of social capital which, on one system of accounting, is more valuable to those who have it than the gardens of the middle class. The problem is how to quantify such a value. Since the middle class are more likely to be compensated and may also suffer less from forced mobility – they normally have the means to overcome distance and to maintain close social distance where this has been established – they are much less likely to lose from changes in the physical structure of cities. And not only would they suffer less if they were to be disturbed (because of capital compensation and so forth), but they are less likely to be disturbed, simply because their costs are more easily quantified and because they are more articulate and knowledgeable about proposals that may affect them. Sections of the working class are much more likely to be at risk, partly because of their lack of property and partly because of their ecological position in the city. The relationship between ecology and equality is relatively unexplored.

An interesting study by Ornati, *The Transportation Needs of the Poor* (1969), demonstrates that the developing ecological structure of a city – in this case New York – has built into it certain constraints which lead to an increasing disjunction between poor people's homes and their workplaces. Public transport routes, originally developed to link middle-class residences to middle-class workplaces, greatly inconvenience the poor who move into old middle-class areas and have different transport needs. A consumer-oriented society is more concerned with transporting the poor to spend their money in central shopping centres, Ornati implies, than to opening up a wider range of employment opportunities. Even the cost of getting to shops may be considerable, and is well illustrated in this country by the case of Glasgow, where new flats on the urban periphery have few local shops and the people not only have to pay higher rents but are obliged to travel back to the area where they used to live, now redeveloped as a shopping centre. Such examples illustrate how differentials in real income may increase as a result, in this case, of the increased cost of physical access to urban resources such as employment or shops.

Spatial policy and social policy

A further theme which has been a focus of controversy in relation to Birmingham, Glasgow, London and many other cities concerns the decentralization of manufacturing industry. The suburbanization of manufacturing industry is a well-established trend in the United States: in Britain the development of New Towns, specifically planned to ease the pressures on the main conurbations, has accentuated the trend. Those growth industries which are expanding the most rapidly tend to be those which have a high demand for skills, a high ratio of managers to managed and a favourable ratio of floorspace to worker. Space and skilled workers are the crucial locational factors and the peripheries of city regions appear to be ideal sites. Thus, in the case of the London Region, the most rapidly expanding area economically is in the Outer Metropolitan Region, immediately beyond the Green Belt (Pahl 1965; South East Joint Planning Team 1970). The effect of this peripheral expansion may be to limit the opportunities for social mobility by those in the central cities, hemmed in by middle-class suburbs and offered employment either in old-established, and possibly declining, manufacturing industries, where the wages are often low (e.g. the textile industry), or the service sector, where opportunities for training and advancement may be less good. This point links back to the occupational structure of the expanding functions of the City of London. In the past large cities were more likely to have higher rates of social mobility (Lipset and Bendix 1959). Such a conclusion must now be severely questioned as urban diffusion 'decentralizes opportunity'.

This possibility that cities, which are continuing to concentrate a particular type of activity at the centre, may cause blockages in social mobility for the offspring of sections of the population now working in the service industries, is a very serious issue. It is the main theme of 'Social Structure and Social Change', a chapter in *Studies Volume 2* of the South East Joint Planning Team's Report (1971a). Certain of the points touched on in this chapter are also discussed in that chapter. Of particular interest are the positive policy proposals for a *Sector City* which are elaborated at length in Chapter 6 of *Studies Volume 4* (1971b). Here some attempt is being made to understand the social and economic forces at work in the urban system and to manage and organize the system so that resources may be reallocated to those at present most deprived and also to create the conditions under which rates of social mobility may increase. The interplay between social, physical (land use) and economic planning is innovatory and much more detailed research and experience are needed. It seems clear, however, that management of housing and employment needs to be phased together and that arranging the amount of coordination required seems beyond the scope of the market. If it is hard to imagine the activities of a New Town Development Corporation being undertaken by private agencies, it is even harder to imagine the coordination of urban redevelopment, renewal and industrial re-location within a city being done for private profit alone.

In a society where so much of the urban fabric was created over a century ago, during a period of rapid industrial and urban growth, it is inevitable that some people will be living in conditions defined by the rest of society as intolerable. What does not have to be inevitable is that such populations also have limited access to job opportunities, schools, health services and other facilities, which are differentially distributed within the city. If those with low wages have to bear a disproportionate amount of the costs of noise, pollution and renewal of the urban fabric then they will be doubly penalized. As Harvey (1971, p.273) aptly notes, 'almost all of this extensive literature has focused on the allocation problems posed by externalities and very little attention has been paid to the distributional effects'. He goes on to remark that the 'best' distribution of incomes involves problems of equity not easy to resolve and hence frequently avoided. That there is frequently 'a quite substantial regressive redistribution of income in a rapidly changing urban system' (Harvey 1971, p.277) should be a matter for serious concern and one would expect this to be reflected in the political arena.

Spatial inequality and political consciousness
Until now lower participants in the urban system have not developed much consciousness of their common deprivations. There are, however, some signs of change (Miller and Roby 1970, p.143):

For generations, the arena of action was more narrowly the workplace, the setting of production. Recently in the United States, low income persons have been organizing to affect their rights to welfare ar.d other forms of government services rather than to affect the economic market.

Political consciousness may be slow to develop in the urban system because the mechanisms of redistribution are hidden. However, it may be that well-organized squatting and sporadic demonstrations against high rents, or intolerable noise from motorways, are the forerunners of more organized locality-based associations concerned with the basic issues of urban equity. Attempts to assess the relative costs and benefits of various locational decisions have had the unintended consequence of making explicit the fact that some people benefit and some lose. When it is manifest that the *same* category tends to benefit in a variety of circumstances and situations a more conscious pressure for an equitable distribution of urban resources and facilities may emerge.

Urban analysis may help us to reformulate our notions of the nature of our distributive system and to redefine lines of conflict based on constraints and limitations of life chances, which restrict the *use* of income and the access to rights and benefits rather than access to income alone in the labour market. It is possible that, in terms of access to urban facilities, the division between the skilled manual workers and the less-skilled manual workers may be becoming more significant than the division between the skilled manual workers and the routine non-manual workers. This might lead us to revise our notions of the conventional cutting points in the class structure.

The inequalities and possible pauperization generated by the operation of the urban system are extremely hard to document precisely. Although Harvey may well be right that the hidden mechanisms governing the redistribution of income 'seem to be moving us towards a state of greater inequality and greater injustice', such an assertion is extremely hard to substantiate. And even if the assertion were to be accepted it would be extraordinarily difficult to incorporate into a political programme policies that would ensure greater equity. It is hard to envisage a society which would accept such clear goals of equity and few would consider it legitimate to coerce, even without the use of armed force, to achieve a given pattern of distribution. We are left with arguments based on a sense of justice which assume that multiple deprivation is not part of a good society. The same people should not be at the bottom of all the hierarchies and receive the worst of all the public services and private markets. Yet even given a willingness to achieve such a measure of social justice, the means to that end are not easy to determine. Questions of costs and benefits involve value judgments as well as calculations, and conflicts, even between those who agree on the ends, are likely to increase.

References

ADAMS, J. (1970) 'Westminster: the fourth London airport?' *Area* 2, 1–9

DAHRENDORF, R. (1959) *Class and Class Conflict in an Industrial Society* Routledge and Kegan Paul

DAVIES, B. (1968) *Social Needs and Resources in Local Services* Joseph

FULTON Committee (1968) *Report on the Civil Service (Cmnd 3638)* HMSO

HALMOS, P. (1965) *The Faith of the Counsellors* Constable

HARVEY, D. (1971) 'Social processes, spatial form and the redistribution of real income in an urban system' in M. Chisholm, A. E. Frey and P. Haggett (eds) *Regional Forecasting* Butterworths

KONRAD, G. and SZELENYI, I. (1969) *Sociological Aspects of the Allocation of Housing: Experiences from a Socialist non-Market Economy* Budapest: Hungarian Academy of Sciences Sociological Research Group

LIPSET, S. M. and BENDIX, R. (1959) *Social Mobility in Industrial Society* University of California Press

MARRIOTT, O. (1967) *The Property Boom* Hamilton

MAUD COMMITTEE (1967) *Report and Papers on the Management of Local Government* HMSO

MELTZER, J. and WHITLEY, J. (1968) 'Planning for the urban slum' in T. D. Sharrard (ed) *Social Welfare and Urban Problems*

MILLER, S. M. and ROBY, P. (1970) *The Future of Inequality* Basic Books

ORNATI, Oscar A. (1969) *The Transportation Needs of the Poor* Praeger

PAHL, R. E. (1965) *Urbs in Rure. The Metropolitan Fringe in Hertfordshire* LSE, Geographical Paper No. 2, Weidenfeld and Nicolson

PAHL, R. E. (1969) 'Urban social theory and research' *Environment and Planning* 1, 143–53

PAHL, R. E. (1970) 'The sociologist's role in regional planning' chapter 14 in *Whose City?* Longman

SCARDIGLI, V. (1970) 'La fréquentation des équipment collectifs' *Consommation*, Annales du CREDOC, 1, 1–27

SEEBOHM COMMITTEE (1968) *Report on Local Authority and Allied Personal Social Services* (Cmnd 3703) HMSO

SHARRARD, T. D. (ed) (1968) *Social Welfare and Urban Problems* Columbia University Press

South East Joint Planning Team (1970) *Strategic Plan for the South East* HMSO, for Ministry of Housing and Local Government

South East Joint Planning Team (1971a) 'Social structure and social change' in *Studies Volume 2* HMSO for the Department of the Environment

South East Joint Planning Team (1971b) 'The social, employment and housing problems of London' in *Studies Volume 4* HMSO for the Department of the Environment

THOMPSON, W. (1965) *A Preface to Urban Economics* Johns Hopkins Press

WEBER, M. (1960) *The City* Heinemann

2.2 Social justice and spatial systems

David Harvey

Normative thinking has an important role to play in geographical analysis. Social justice is a normative concept and it is surprising, therefore, to find that considerations of social justice have not been incorporated into geographical methods of analysis. The reason is not far to seek. The normative tools characteristically used by geographers to examine location problems are derived from classical location theory. Such theories are generally Pareto-optimal since they define an optimal location pattern as one in which no one individual can move without the advantages gained from such a move being offset by some loss to another individual. Location theory has therefore characteristically relied upon the criterion of *efficiency* for its specification. Efficiency may be defined in a variety of ways, of course, but in location theory it usually amounts to minimizing the aggregate costs of movement (subject to demand and supply constraints) within a particular spatial system. Models of this type pay no attention to the consequences of location decisions for the distribution of income. Geographers have thus followed economists into a style of thinking in which questions of distribution are laid aside (mainly because they involve unwelcome ethical and political judgments), while efficient 'optimal' location patterns are determined with a particular income distribution assumed. This approach obviously lacks something. In part the reaction away from normative thinking towards behavioural and empirical formulations may be attributed to the search for a more satisfying approach to location problems. This reaction has been healthy, of course, but partly misplaced. It is not normative modelling which is at fault but the *kind* of norms built into such models. In this chapter, therefore, I want to diverge from the usual mode of normative analysis and look at the possibility of constructing a normative theory of spatial or territorial allocation based on

Source: *Antipode Monographs in Social Geography*, No.1 (1972); reprinted in David Harvey *Social Justice and the City* (1973) Edward Arnold, pp. 96–118.

principles of social justice. I do not propose this as an alternative framework to that of efficiency. In the long run it will be most beneficial if efficiency and distribution are explored jointly. The reasons for so doing are evident. If, in the short run, we simply pursue efficiency and ignore the social cost, then those individuals or groups who bear the brunt of that cost are likely to be a source of long-run inefficiency either through decline in what Liebenstein (1966) calls 'x-efficiency' (those intangibles that motivate people to cooperate and participate in the social process of production) or through forms of antisocial behaviour (such as crime and drug addiction) which will necessitate the diversion of productive investment towards their correction. The same comment can be made about the single-minded pursuit of social justice. It is counter-productive in the long run to devise a socially just distribution if the size of the product to be distributed shrinks markedly through the inefficient use of scarce resources. In the long-long-run, therefore, social justice and efficiency are very much the same thing. But since questions of social justice have been neglected (except in political rhetoric) and there is a persistent tendency to lay them aside in short-run analysis, I shall do the opposite and lay aside questions of efficiency. This should not be taken to imply, however, that efficiency is irrelevant or unimportant.

The concept of social justice is not an all-inclusive one in which we encapsulate our vision of the good society. It is rather more limited. Justice is essentially to be thought of as a principle (or set of principles) for resolving conflicting claims. These conflicts may arise in many ways. Social justice is a particular application of just principles to conflicts which arise out of the necessity for social cooperation in seeking individual advancement. Through the division of labour it is possible to increase production: the question then arises as to how the fruits of that production shall be distributed among those who cooperate in the process. The principle of social justice therefore applies to the division of benefits and the allocation of burdens arising out of the process of undertaking joint labour. The principle also relates to the social and institutional arrangements associated with the activity of production and distribution. It may thus be extended to consider conflicts over the locus of power and decision-making authority, the distribution of influence, the bestowal of social status, the institutions set up to regulate and control activity, and so on. The essential characteristic in all such cases, however, is that we are seeking a principle which will allow us to evaluate the distributions arrived at as they apply to individuals, groups, organizations, and territories, as well as to evaluate the mechanisms which are used to accomplish this distribution. We are seeking, in short, a specification of a just distribution justly arrived at.

Unfortunately there is no one generally accepted principle of social justice to which we can appeal. Yet the notion of social justice underpins social philosophical thought from Aristotle's *Ethics* onwards. Its two most important forms are derivative of the social contract (initially formulated by Hume and Rousseau) and utilitarianism (initially formulated by Bentham and Mill). Recently, there has been a resurgence of interest in these principles resulting in modern versions of them which seem much more acceptable for a number of reasons – the work of Rawls (1969; 1971), Rescher (1966) and Runciman (1966), being outstanding in this respect. There are other strands to this thinking of course. The detailed discussion of the concept of equality by writers such as Tawney (1931), and the now voluminous literature on the question of the proper distribution of income in society have added their weight to the argument. I do not wish to review this literature here, however, and I shall confine myself to one possible argument concerning social justice and endeavour to show how it can be formulated in a manner that is geographically relevant and useful.

The principle of social justice which I shall explore starts with the skeleton concept of 'a just distribution justly arrived at'. The main task of this chapter is to put flesh on this skeleton and to formulate its geographic variant. Two preliminary questions may be asked about it:

What are we distributing?
It is easy enough to say that we are distributing the benefits to be had from social cooperation but it is very much more difficult to specify what those benefits are, particularly as they relate to individual preferences and values. For the purpose of this paper I shall leave this question unanswered and merely call whatever it is that we are distributing 'income'. This indicates a very general definition of income – such as Titmuss's (1962) 'command over society's scarce resources' or an even more general one such as that proposed by Miller and Roby (1970). I shall assume here that we can devise a socially just definition of income – for it would indeed be a net injustice to devise a socially just distribution of something defined in an unjust manner!

Among whom or what are we distributing it?
There is general agreement that the ultimate unit with which we should be concerned is the human individual. For convenience it will often be necessary to discuss distribution as it occurs among groups, organizations, territories, and so on. Geographers are particularly interested in the territorial or regional organization of society and it will be convenient to work at that level of aggregation. But we know enough about the various

forms of ecological fallacy (see Alker 1969) to know that a just distribution across a set of territories defined at one scale does not necessarily mean a just distribution achieved at another scale •or a just distribution among individuals. This scale or aggregation problem poses some thorny methodological difficulties. In principle, we may hold that distribution made at any scale or across any aggregates should be accountable to distribution as it occurs at the individual level of analysis. This is difficult to do, but for present purposes I shall assume that justice achieved at a territorial level of analysis implies justice achieved for the individual, even though I am too aware that this is not necessarily the case.

'A just distribution'

Having assumed away two rather important questions, I shall now undertake an analysis of the principle of social justice. This can be split into two parts and here I shall seek an understanding of what is meant by 'a just distribution'. To do this I must first establish a basis for that distribution. This is, of course, an ethical problem which cannot be resolved without making important moral decisions. These decisions essentially concern what it is that justifies individuals making claims upon the product of the society in which they live, work, and have their being. Several criteria have been suggested (see Rawls 1969, 1971; Rescher 1966):

1   *Inherent equality* – all individuals have equal claims on benefits irrespective of their contribution.

2   *Valuation of services in terms of supply and demand* – individuals who command scarce and needed resources have a greater claim than do others. It is perhaps important to differentiate here between situations in which scarcity arises naturally (inherent brain and muscle power) and situations in which it is artificially created (through the inheritance of resources or through socially organized restrictions on entry into certain occupations).

3   *Need* – individuals have rights to equal levels of benefit which means that there is an unequal allocation according to need.

4   *Inherited rights* – individuals have claims to the property or other rights which have been passed on to them from preceding generations.

5   *Merit* – claims may be based on the degree of difficulty to be overcome in contributing to production (those who undertake dangerous or unpleasant tasks – such as mining – and those who undertake long periods of training – such as surgeons – have greater claims than do others).

6   *Contribution to common good* – those individuals whose activities

benefit most people have a higher claim than do those whose activities benefit few people.

7 *Actual productive contribution* – individuals who produce more output – measured in some appropriate way – have a greater claim than do those who produce a lesser output.

8 *Efforts and sacrifices* – individuals who make a greater effort or incur a greater sacrifice relative to their innate capacity should be rewarded more than those who make little effort and incur few sacrifices.

These eight criteria are not mutually exlusive and they obviously require much more detailed interpretation and analysis. I shall follow Runciman (1966) and suggest that the essence of social justice can be embodied in a weak ordering of three of these criteria so that *need* is the most important, *contribution to common good* is the second and *merit* is the third. I shall not argue the case for this decision. It necessarily rests, however, on an appeal to certain controversial and ethical arguments. But as will become apparent in what follows, the issues raised in the detailed examination of these three criteria are sufficiently comprehensive to subsume many of the issues which could legitimately be raised under the other headings. These three criteria could be examined in detail in a variety of contexts. I choose at this juncture to introduce the geographic aspect to the argument and examine how they might be formulated in the context of a set of territories or regions. For purposes of exposition I shall mainly consider the problem as one of a central authority allocating scarce resources over a set of territories in such a way that social justice is maximized. As I have already stated, I shall assume that territorial distributive justice automatically implies individual justice.

Territorial distributive justice

The first step in formulating a principle of territorial distributive justice lies in determining what each of the three criteria – need, contribution to common good, and merit – means in the context of a set of territories or regions. Procedures may then be devised to evaluate and measure distribution according to each criterion. The combination of the three measures (presumably weighted in some way) provides a hypothetical figure for the allocation of resources to regions. This figure can then be used, as happens in most normative analysis, to evaluate existing distributions or to devise policies which improve existing allocations. A measure of territorial justice can be devised by correlating the actual allocation of resources with the hypothetical allocations. Such a procedure allows the identification of those territories which depart most from the norms suggested by standards of social justice: but this is not, of course, easy. Bleddyn Davies (1968), who first coined the term 'territorial justice' has published a pioneering work on the subject, which indicates some of the problems involved.

1   Need

Need is a relative concept. Needs are not constant for they are categories of human consciousness and as society is transformed so the consciousness of need is transformed. The problem is to define exactly what it is that need is relative to and to obtain an understanding of how needs arise. Needs can be defined with respect to a number of different categories of activity — these remain fairly constant over time and we can list nine of them:

1   food
2   housing
3   medical care
4   education
5   social and environmental service
6   consumer goods
7   recreational opportunities
8   neighbourhood amenities
9   transport facilities.

Within each of these categories we can set about defining those minimum quantities and qualities which we would equate with needs. This minimum will vary according to the social norms at a given time. There will also be a variety of ways of fulfilling such needs. The need for housing can be met in a number of ways but at this time these would presumably not include living in shacks, mud-huts, tents, crumbling houses, and the like. This raises a whole host of issues which I can best examine in the context of a particular category — medical services.

Nobody, presumably, would deny that medical care is a legitimate form of need. Yet that need is not easily defined and measured. If we are to obtain a normative measure of social justice we have first to define and measure need in a socially just way. For example, the category 'health services' comprises a multitude of subcategories some of which, such as cosmetic surgery and back massages, can reasonably be regarded (in our present society at least) as non-essential. An initial decision has to be made, therefore, on which subcategories should be regarded as 'needs' and which should not. Decisions then have to be made as to what are reasonable standards of need within each subcategory. Let us consider some of the methods for doing this:

1 Need can be determined through looking at *market demand*. Wherever facilities are working very close to capacity we may take it that there is an unfulfilled need in the population and thereby justify the allocation of more resources to expand medical services. This procedure is only acceptable if we can reasonably assume that nothing is inhibiting demand (such as lack of money or lack of access to facilities). To accept market demand as a socially just measure of need requires that the other conditions prevailing in society (affecting both demand and supply) are themselves socially just. This is usually not the case and this method of determining need is therefore likely to be socially unjust.

2 *Latent demand* may be assessed through an investigation of relative deprivation as it exists among individuals in a set of regions. Individuals would be relatively deprived if (a) they do not receive a service (b) they see other people (including themselves at a previous or an expected time) receiving it (c) they want it, and (d) they regard it as feasible that they should receive it (Runciman 1966, p. 10). The concept of relative deprivation (basically similar to perceived or felt need) has been associated in the literature with the concept of a reference group (a group against which an individual measures his or her own expectations). The reference group may be socially determined – i.e. all blacks or all blue-collar workers – or spatially determined – i.e. everybody in a neighbourhood or even in a large region. The difference between the expectations of the group for health care and actual services received provides a measure of relative deprivation. This measure can be obtained either by direct survey data, or if we know something about reference groups we can calculate likely relative deprivation by looking at variance in provision within different groups. The advantages of the latter approach are that it incorporates a behavioural element so that legitimate differences in group preferences can be expressed, while also providing a measure of dissatisfaction and therefore an indicator of likely political pressure. Its disadvantage is that it assumes that 'real' needs are reflected by felt needs. This is often not the case. Very poorly served groups often have very low standards of felt need. Also, all kinds of social inequities are likely to be incorporated into the measure of need if, as is usually the case in class differentiated and (or) segregated societies, the reference group structure is itself a response to conditions of social injustice.

3 *Potential demand* can be evaluated by an analysis of the factors which generate particular kinds of health problem. Population totals and characteristics will have an important impact on territorial needs. Health problems can be related to age, life-cycle, amount of migration, and so on.

In addition there are special problems which may relate to occupational characteristics (such as mining), to sociological and cultural circumstances, as well as to income levels. Health problems can also be related to local environmental conditions (density of population, local ecology, air and water quality, and so on). If we knew enough about all of these relationships we should be able to predict the volume and incidence of health care problems across a set of territories. This requires, however, a far more sophisticated understanding of relationships than we currently possess; even so, various attempts have been made to employ this method. Its attraction, of course, is that it does provide a reasonably objective method for measuring potential demand for health care. Unfortunately, we are still left with the problem of converting this demand into a measure of need, which in this case requires that we determine appropriate forms and levels of response to these statistically determined potential demands. The response usually amounts to setting standards, which is usually done with a given quantity of resources in mind.

4   We could also seek to determine needs through *consultation* with experts in the field. Experts tend to determine need with one eye on available resources. But those who have lived and worked in a community for a long period of time can often draw upon their experience to provide subjective assessments which are nevertheless good indicators of need. The resolution of opinions provided by judiciously selected experts in the health field (health planners, hospital administrators, physicians, community groups, social workers, welfare rights groups, and so on) may provide a socially just determination of need. The method relies upon the subjective judgments of a selected set of individuals, but it has the considerable benefit of drawing directly upon the experience of those who have been most concerned with the health care problem. The disadvantage, of course, lies in the possibility that the experts are selected on the basis of socially unjust criteria – for example, to place the determination of need in the hands of a committee of the American Medical Association would at present be disastrous from the point of view of social justice.

We must select among the various methods for determining need in such a way that we maximize on the social justice of the result. In the current circumstances I would discard (1) altogether in the health field and I would only accept (2) if I felt that legitimate variations in preference were being expressed rather than variations in a felt need arising out of a socially unjust social situation or out of ignorance or false consciousness. Both (3) and (4) provide possible methods for establishing needs in the health field, but neither is easy to employ and both contain within them the possibility of a socially unjust determination of need.

If need is a primary criterion for assessing the social justice of a distribution of resources across a set of territories, then we are first obliged to establish a socially just definition and measurement system for it. The various methods (and their attendant difficulties) outlined in the medical care case can be applied to each of the categories – education, recreation, housing, consumer goods, and so on. It is not easy to decide upon a socially just definition of need within each category. The appropriate method may also vary from category to category – it may be best to determine consumer need through conventional supply and demand analysis, recreational needs through relative deprivation analysis, housing needs through statistical analysis, and medical care needs through resolution of expert opinion. These, however, are open questions. Defining social justice in terms of need thrusts onto us the whole uncomfortable question of what is meant by need and how it should be measured. It is imperative that we make socially just decisions on these issues. Otherwise our pursuit of a principle of social justice for evaluating geographic distributions will be worthless.

2 Contribution to common good

The concept of contribution to common good can be translated into existing geographic concepts with relative ease. We are here concerned with how an allocation of resources to one territory affects conditions in another. A technology exists to handle some of these questions in the work on interregional multiplier analysis, growth poles and externalities. The spread effects may be good or bad – pollution being an example of the latter. The notion of contribution to common good (or common 'bad' in the case of pollution) suggests that our existing technology should be used to extend our understanding of interregional income transfers, interregional linkages, spatial spread effects and so on, insofar as these have actual or potential consequences for the distribution of income in society. This is not an easy task, as is demonstrated by the problems which have plagued the attempt to evaluate the benefits of urban renewal (Rothenberg 1967). There are two rather different aspects to this problem. We can seek to improve on existing allocations given the existing pattern of interregional multipliers or we can take a more radical approach and seek to restructure the pattern of interregional multipliers by reorganizing the spatial system itself. If we take the latter approach we seek a form of spatial organization which will make the greatest contribution to fulfilling needs through the multiplier and spread effects generated by a particular pattern of regional investment. Common good may have a second component to it, that of increasing the total aggregate product. In this case contribution to common good comes close to the usual efficiency and growth criteria with externalities and side-effects incorporated into the analysis. In the search for social justice this sense of contributing to the common good should remain subsidiary to the concern for distributive consequences.

3   Merit

I shall translate the concept of 'merit' into a geographical concept which relates to the degree of environmental difficulty. Such difficulties may arise out of circumstances in the physical environment. Certain hazards, such as drought, flood, earthquakes and so on, pose extra difficulty to human activity. If there is a need for a facility (say a port in an area subject to hurricane damage) then extra resources should be allocated to counter this hazard. In terms of the weak ordering that I have imposed on the criteria for social justice, this means that if a facility is needed, if it contributes to the common good in some way, *then and only then* would we be justified in allocating extra resources for its support. If people live in flood plains when they have no need to live in flood plains and if they contribute nothing to the common good by living there, then under the principle of social justice they ought not to be compensated for damage incurred by living there. If, however, individuals are forced by circumstances (such as lack of alternative choice) to live there then the primary criterion of need may be used to justify compensation. The same remarks apply to problems which arise in the social environment. Hazards posed by crimes against property, fire and riot damage, and the like, vary according to the social circumstances. Individuals need adequate security if they are to be able to contribute meaningfully to the common good and if they are to be able to allocate their productive capacity to fulfil needs. Under a principle of social justice it can therefore be argued that society at large should underwrite the higher costs of insurance in areas of high social risk. To do so would be socially just. The same argument can be applied to the allocation of extra resources to reach groups who are particularly difficult to service – as Davies (1968, p. 18) points out 'it may be desirable to over-provide needy groups with services since they have not had access to them in the past and have not formed the habit of consuming them'. This issue arises particularly with respect to the education and health care facilities extended to very poor groups, recent immigrants, and the like. Merit can therefore be translated in a geographical context as an allocation of extra resources to compensate for the degree of social and natural environmental difficulty.

The principles of social justice as they apply to geographical situations can be summarized as follows:

1 The spatial organization and the pattern of regional investment should be such as to fulfil the needs of the population. This requires that we first establish socially just methods for determining and measuring needs. The difference between needs and actual allocations provides us with an initial evaluation of the degree of territorial injustice in an existing system.

2 A spatial organization and pattern of territorial resource allocation which provides extra benefits in the form of need fulfilment (primarily) and aggregate output (secondarily) in other territories through spillover effects, multiplier effects, and the like, is a 'better' form of spatial organization and allocation.

3 Deviations in the pattern of territorial investment may be tolerated if they are designed to overcome specific environmental difficulties which would otherwise prevent the evolution of a system which would meet need or contribute to the common good.

These principles can be used to evaluate existing spatial distributions. They provide the beginnings of a normative theory of spatial organization based on territorial distributive justice. There will be enormous difficulties in elaborating them in detail and there will be even greater difficulties in translating them into concrete situations. We have some of the technology at hand to do this. It needs to be directed towards an understanding of just distributions in spatial systems.

To achieve a distribution justly

There are those who claim that a necessary and sufficient condition for attaining a just distribution of income lies in devising socially just means for arriving at that distribution. Curiously enough this view prevails at both ends of the political spectrum. Buchanan and Tullock (1965) – conservative libertarians in viewpoint – thus suggest that in a properly organized constitutional democracy the most efficient way to organize redistribution is to do nothing about it. Marx (*A Critique of the Gotha Programme*, 11) attacked those 'vulgar socialists' who thought that questions of distribution could be considered and resolved independent of the prevailing mechanisms governing production and distribution. Marx and constitutional democrats have a basic assumption in common – that if socially just mechanisms can be devised then questions of achieving social justice in distribution will look after themselves. In the literature on social justice (and in the arena of practical policy determination) there is a varied emphasis on 'means' or 'ends' with liberal and some socialist opinion apparently believing that social justice in the latter can be achieved without necessarily tampering with the former. But most writers indicate that it is foolhardy to expect socially just ends to be achieved by socially unjust means. It is instructive to follow Rawls's (1969) argument in this respect:

> ... the basic structure of the social system affects the life prospects of typical individuals according to their initial places in society.... The fundamental problem of distributive justice concerns the differences in life-prospects which come about in this way. We ... hold that these differences are just if and only if the greater expectations of the more advantaged, when playing a part in the working of the social system, improve the expectations of the least advantaged. The basic structure is just throughout when the advantages of the more fortunate promote the well-being of the least fortunate.... *The basic structure is perfectly just when the prospects of the least fortunate are as great as they can be.* (Emphasis mine)

The problem, then, is to find a social, economic and political organization in which this condition is attained and maintained. Marxists would claim, with considerable justification, that the only hope for achieving Rawls's objective would be to ensure the least fortunate always has the final say. From Rawls's initial position it is not difficult by a fairly simple logical argument to arrive at a 'dictatorship of the proletariat' type of solution. Rawls tries to construct a path towards a different solution:

> ... if law and government act effectively to keep markets competitive, resources fully employed, property and wealth widely distributed over time, and to maintain the appropriate social minimum, then if there is equality of opportunity underwritten by education for all, the resulting distribution will be just.

To achieve this Rawls proposes a fourfold division in government in which an allocation branch acts to keep the market working competitively while correcting for market failure where necessary; a stabilization branch maintains full employment and prevents waste in the use of resources; a transfer branch sees to it that individual needs are met; and a distribution branch looks after the provision of public goods and prevents (by proper taxation) any undue concentration of power or wealth over time. From Rawls's initial position it is possible to arrive, therefore, at a Marx or a Milton Friedman, but in no way can we arrive at the liberal or socialist solutions. That this is a sensible conclusion is attested by the fact that the socialist programmes of post-war Britain appear to have had little or no impact upon the distribution of real income in society, while the liberal anti-poverty programmes in the United States have been conspicuous for their lack of success. The reason should be obvious: programmes which seek to alter distribution without altering the capitalist market structure within which income and wealth are generated and distributed, are doomed to failure.

Most of the evidence we have on group decision-making, bargaining, the control of central government, democracy, bureaucracy, and the like, also indicates that *any* social, economic and political organization which attains any permanence is liable to cooptation and subversion by special interest groups. In a constitutional democracy this is usually accomplished by small well-organized interest groups who have accumulated the necessary resources to influence decision-making. A dictatorship of the proletariat solution is likewise subject to bureaucratic subversion as the Russian experience all too readily demonstrates. An awareness of this problem has led good constitutional democrats, such as Jefferson, to look favourably on an occasional revolution to keep the body politic healthy. One of the practical effects of the sequence of revolutions in China since 1949 (and some have attributed this to Mao's conscious design) has been to prevent what Max Weber (1947) long ago called the 'routinization of charisma'. The question of the appropriate form of social, economic and political organization and its maintenance for the purpose of achieving social justice is beyond the scope of this essay. Yet the way in which it is resolved effectively determines both the mode and likelihood of achieving territorial justice. I shall therefore confine myself to considering how considerations of the means of achieving distribution take on a specific form in the territorial context.

The geographical problem is to design a form of spatial organization which maximizes the prospects of the least fortunate region. A necessary initial condition, for example, is that we have a socially just way of determining the boundaries of territories and a just way of allocating resources among them. The former problem lies in the traditional field of 'regionalizing' in geography, but in this case with the criterion of social justice put foremost. The experience of gerrymandering indicates only too well that territorial aggregates can be determined in a socially unjust way. Boundaries can be placed so that the least advantaged groups are so distributed with respect to the more advantaged groups in a set of territorial aggregates that whatever the formula devised for allocation of resources the latter always benefit more than the former. It should be possible to devise territorial boundaries to favour the least advantaged groups – in which case social justice in allocation becomes the normative criterion for regionalization. In the actual allocation of resources we may take Rawls's objective to mean that the prospects for the least advantaged territory should be as great as they can be. How to determine when this condition exists is itself an intriguing problem, but the prospects for its achievement are presumably contingent upon the way in which a central authority decides on the territorial disposition of the resources under its control. Since poor areas are often politically weak, we are forced to rely on the sense of social justice prevailing in *all* territories (and it takes an assumption of only mild self-interest to counter that hope), upon the existence of a benevolent dictator or a benevolent bureaucracy at the centre (the latter perhaps prevails in Scandinavia), or upon a constitutional mechanism in which the least advantaged territories have the power of veto over all decisions. Exactly what arrangements are made for arbitrating among the demands of political territories (demands which do not necessarily reflect need) and for negotiating between a central authority and its constituent territories are obviously crucial for the prospect of achieving territorial justice. It is arguable, for example, whether a greater centralization of decision-making (which has the potential for ironing out differences between territories) should prevail over a greater decentralization (which has the merit of being able to prevent the exploitation of disadvantaged territories by the richer territories). The answer to this probably depends upon the initial conditions. When they are characterized by exploitation (as they appear to be in the United States), a tactical decentralization may be called for as an initial step; when exploitation is not so important (as in Scandinavia), centralization may be more appropriate. Advocacy of metropolitan control or neighbourhood government should be seen in this light.

Similar kinds of problem arise if we examine the impact of the highly decentralized decisions over capital investment characteristic of a freely working capitalist economy. Leaving aside the problems inherent in the tendency for modern capital to congeal into monopoly forms of control, it is useful to examine how an individualistic capitalist system typically operates with respect to territorial justice. Under such a system it is accepted as rational and good for capital to flow to wherever the rate of return is highest. Some (Borts and Stein 1964) argue that this process will continue until rates of return are equalized over all territories, while others (Myrdal 1957) suggest that circular and cumulative causation will lead to growing imbalances. Whatever the long-term implications of this process are for growth, capital clearly will flow in a way which bears little relationship to need or to the condition of the least advantaged territory. The result will be the creation of localized pockets of high unfulfilled need, such as those now found in Appalachia or many inner city areas. Most societies accept some responsibility for diverting the natural stream of capital flow to deal with these problems. To do so without basically altering the *whole* capital flow process seems impossible however. Consider, as an example, the problems arising out of the housing situation in inner city areas of British and American cities. It is no longer profitable for private capital to flow into the inner city rental housing market. In London in 1965 a return of 9 per cent or more would have been necessary to encourage private investment and conditions were such that there was no hope of obtaining such a return by reasonable or legal means (Milner-Holland Report 1965). In Baltimore in 1969 a rate of 12 to 15 per cent would be required but actual rates were probably nearer 6 to 9 per cent (Grigsby *et al* 1971). It is hardly surprising that the private inner city rental housing market has collapsed in most cities as capital is withdrawn, buildings have depreciated, and capital has been transferred to other sectors or out to the much more profitable private building market in the suburban ring. Thus arises the paradox of capital withdrawing from areas of greatest need to provide for the demands of relatively affluent suburban communities. Under capitalism this is good and rational behaviour – it is what the market requires for the 'optimal' allocation of resources.

Is it possible to reverse this flow using capitalist tools? Government can (and often does) intervene to make up the difference between what is now earned in the inner city and what could be earned elsewhere. It can do this in a number of ways (rent supplements to tenants, negative income taxes, direct grants to financial institutions, etc.). But whatever the means chosen the effect is to bribe financial institutions back into the inner city rental market where the government would otherwise have to take over responsibility for provision (through public housing). The first solution initially appears attractive, but it has certain flaws. If we bribe financial institutions, one effect will be to create a greater relative scarcity of capital funds for (say) suburban development. The more advantaged suburbs will adjust the rate of return they offer upwards to bring back the capital flow. The net effect of this process will be a rise in the overall rates of return which is obviously to the advantage of financial institutions – most of which are owned, operated and managed by people who live in the suburbs anyway! Thus there appears to be a built-in tendency for the capitalist market system to counteract any attempt to divert the flow of funds away from the most profitable territories. More specifically, it is impossible to induce action in one sector or territory without restricting it at the same time in other sectors and territories. Nothing short of comprehensive government control can do this effectively.

What this suggests is that 'capitalist means invariably serve their own, capitalist, ends' (Huberman and Sweezy 1969), and that these capitalist ends are not consistent with the objectives of social justice. An argument can be formulated in support of this contention. The market system functions on the basis of exchange values and exchange values can exist only if there is relative scarcity of the goods and services being exchanged. The concept of scarcity is not an easy one to comprehend although we are constantly making reference to it when we talk of the allocation of scarce resources. It is questionable, for example, whether there is any such thing as a naturally arising scarcity. Pearson thus writes (1957, p. 320):

> ... the concept of scarcity will be fruitful only if the natural fact of limited means leads to a sequence of choices regarding the use of these means, and this situation is possible only if there is alternativity to the uses of means and there are preferentially graded ends. But these latter conditions are socially determined; they do not depend in any simple way upon the facts of nature. To postulate scarcity as an absolute condition from which all economic institutions derive is therefore to employ an abstraction which serves only to obscure the question of how economic activity is organized.

The concept of scarcity, like the concept of a resource, only takes on meaning in a particular social and cultural context. It is erroneous to think that markets simply arise to deal with scarcity. In sophisticated economies scarcity is socially organized in order to permit the market to function. We say that jobs are scarce when there is plenty of work to do, that space is restricted when land lies empty, that food is scarce when farmers are being paid not to produce. Scarcity must be produced and controlled in society because without it price fixing markets could not function. This takes place through a fairly strict control over access to the means of production and a control over the flow of resources into the productive process. The distribution of the output has likewise to be controlled in order for scarcity to be maintained. This is achieved by appropriative arrangements which prevent the elimination of scarcity and preserve the integrity of exchange values in the market place. If it is accepted that the maintenance of scarcity is essential for the functioning of the market system, then it follows that deprivation, appropriation and exploitation are also necessary concomitants of the market system. In a spatial system this implies (the ecological fallacy permitting) that there will be a series of appropriative movements between territories which leads some territories to exploit and some to be exploited. This phenomenon is most clearly present in urban systems, since urbanism, as any historian of the phenomenon will tell us, is founded on the appropriation of surplus product.

Certain benefits stem from the operation of the market mechanism. The price system can successfully coordinate a vast number of decentralized decisions and it can consequently integrate a vast array of activities into a coherent social and spatial system. The competition for access to scarce resources, on which the capitalistic market system rests, also encourages and facilitates technological innovation. The market system therefore helps to increase, immeasurably, the total product available to society. It is also expert at promoting overall growth, and this has led some to argue that, since the market mechanism successfully promotes growth, it follows as a matter of course that the prospects for the least fortunate territory are naturally as great as they possibly can be. Appropriation obviously takes place but this appropriation, it is held, should not be characterized as exploitation because the appropriated product is put to good use and is the source of benefits which flow back into the territories from which it was initially exacted. Appropriative movements which occur under the price system are therefore justified because of the long-term benefits which they generate. This argument cannot be rejected out of hand. But to concede that appropriation is justifiable under certain conditions is not to concede that the appropriation achieved under the market mechanism is socially just. In any economy appropriation and the creation of a social surplus product is necessary, but the pattern achieved under the market economy is not in many respects a necessary one unless the internal logic of the market economy itself is regarded as a form of justification. In a capitalist market economy an enormous concentration of surplus product (at the present time this is mainly located in large corporations) has to be absorbed in ways which do not threaten the continuance of that scarcity upon which the market economy is itself based. Hence the surplus product is consumed in socially undesirable ways (conspicuous consumption, conspicuous construction in urban areas, militarism, waste): the market system cannot dispose of the socially won surplus product in socially just ways. It therefore seems necessary, from the point of view of social justice, to increase total social product without the use of the price-fixing market mechanism. In this regard the Chinese and Cuban efforts to promote growth with social justice are probably the most significant so far undertaken. The third world is otherwise presumably doomed to repeat the experience of individual or state capitalism in which growth is achieved at huge social and human cost.

In contemporary 'advanced' societies the problem is to devise alternatives to the market mechanism which allow the transference of productive power and the distribution of surplus to sectors and territories where the social necessities are so patently obvious. Thus we need to move to a new pattern of organization in which the market is replaced (probably by a decentralized planning process), scarcity and deprivation systematically eliminated wherever possible, and a degrading wage system steadily reduced as an incentive to work, without in any way diminishing the total productive power available to society. To find such a form of organization is a great challenge, but unfortunately the enormous vested interest associated with the patterns of exploitation and privilege built up through the operation of the market mechanism, wields all of its influence to prevent the replacement of the market and even to preclude a reasoned discussion of the possible alternatives to it. Under conditions of social justice, for example, an unequal allocation of resources to territories and appropriative movements would be permissible if (and only if) those territories favoured were able, through their physical and social circumstances and through their connections with other territories, to contribute to the common good of all territories. This pattern of appropriation will obviously be different to that achieved under the market mechanism for the latter is institutionally bound to maintain patterns of appropriation, deprivation, and scarcity, and institutionally incapable of distributing according to need or of contribution to common good. The social organization of scarcity and deprivation associated with price-fixing markets makes the market mechanism automatically antagonistic to any principle of social justice. Whether the market mechanism can be justified on grounds of efficiency and growth depends on how it compares with those alternatives which most are not prepared even to discuss.

A just distribution justly achieved: territorial social justice
From this examination of the principles of social justice we can arrive at the sense of *territorial social justice* as follows:

1   The distribution of income should be such that (a) the needs of the population within each territory are met, (b) resources are so allocated to maximize interterritorial multiplier effects, and (c) extra resources are allocated to help overcome special difficulties stemming from the physical and social environment.
2   The mechanisms (institutional, organizational, political and economic) should be such that the prospects of the least advantaged territory are as great as they possibly can be.

If these conditions are fulfilled there will be a just distribution justly arrived at.

I recognize that this general characterization of the principles of territorial social justice leaves much to be desired and that it will take a much more detailed examination of these principles before we are in a position to build some kind of theory of location and regional allocation around them. It took many years and an incredible application of intellectual resources to get to even a satisfactory beginning point for specifying a location theory based on efficiency and there is still no general

David Harvey

theory of location – indeed we do not even known what it means to say that we are 'maximizing the spatial organization of the city' for there is no way to maximize on the multiplicity of objectives contained in potential city forms. In the examination of distribution, therefore, we can anticipate breaking down the objectives into component parts. The component parts are as follows:

1 How do we specify need in a set of territories in accord with socially just principles, and how do we calculate the degree of need fulfilment in an existing system with an existing allocation of resources?
2 How can we identify interregional multipliers and spread effects (a topic which has already some theoretical base)?
3 How do we assess social and physical environment difficulty and when is it socially just to respond to it in some way?
4 How do we regionalize to maximize social justice?
5 What kinds of allocative mechanisms are there to ensure that the prospects of the poorest region are maximized and how do the various existing mechanisms perform in this respect?
6 What kinds of rules should govern the pattern of interterritorial negotiation, the pattern of territorial political power, and so on, so that the prospects of the poorest area are as great as they can be?

These are the sorts of questions which we can begin to work on in some kind of single-minded way. To work on them will undoubtedly involve us in making difficult ethical and moral decisions concerning the rights and wrongs of certain principles for justifying claims upon the scarce product of society. We cannot afford to ignore these questions for to do so amounts to one of those strategic non-decisions, so prevalent in politics, by which we achieve a tacit endorsement of the *status quo*. Not to decide on these issues is to decide. The single-minded exploration of efficiency has at best amounted to a tacit endorsement of the *status quo* in distribution. To criticize those who have pursued efficiency for this reason is not to deny that importance of analysis based on efficiency itself. As I indicated at the beginning of this chapter, we need to explore efficiency and distribution jointly. But to do so we first need a detailed exploration of those questions of distribution which have for so long been left in limbo.

References

ALKER, H. (1969) 'A typology of ecological fallacies' in M. Dogan and S. Rokan (eds) *Quantitative Ecological Analysis in the Social Sciences* Cambridge, Mass: MIT Press

BORTS, G. H. and STEIN, J. L. (1964) *Economic Growth in a Free Market* New York: Columbia University Press

BUCHANAN, J. M. and TULLOCK, G. (1965) *The Calculus of Consent* Ann Arbor: University of Michigan Press

DAVIES, B. (1968) *Social Needs and Resources in Local Services* London

GRIGSBY, W. C., ROSENBERG, L., STEGMAN, M., and TAYLOR, J. (1971) *Housing and Poverty* Philadelphia: University of Pennsylvania, Institute of Environmental Studies

HUBERMAN, L. and SWEEZY, P. (1969) *Socialism in Cuba* New York: Monthly Review Press

LIEBENSTEIN, H. (1966) Allocative efficiency versus x-efficiency *American Economic Review* 61, 392–415

MARX, K. (1938) *A Critique of the Gotha Programme* New York: International Publishers Edition

MILLER, S. M. and ROBY, P. (1970) *The Future of Inequality* New York: Basic Books

MILNER-HOLLAND REPORT (1965) *Report of the Committee on Housing in Greater London* Cmnd. 2605 HMSO

MYRDAL, G. (1957) *Economic Theory and Under-developed Regions* London

PEARSON, H. (1957) 'The economy has no surplus: A critique of a theory of development' in K. Polanyi, C. M. Arensberg and H. W. Pearson (eds) *Trade and Market in Early Empires* New York: The Free Press

RAWLS, J. (1969) 'Distributive justice' in P. Laslett and W. G. Runciman (eds) *Philosophy, Politics, and Society*

RAWLS, J. (1971) *A Theory of Justice* Cambridge, Mass: Harvard University Press

RESCHER, N. (1966) *Distributive Justice* Indianapolis: Bobbs Merrill

ROTHENBERG, J. (1967) *Economic Evaluation of Urban Renewal* Washington, D.C: Brookings Institution

RUNCIMAN, W. G. (1966) *Relative Deprivation and Social Justice* Los Angeles: University of California Press

TAWNEY, R. H. (1931) *Equality* London

TITMUSS, R. M. (1962) *Income Distribution and Social Change* London

WEBER, M. (1947) *The Theory of Economic and Social Organization* New York: Oxford University Press

2.3   Physical planning and social policy

J. M. Simmie

Statutory physical planning in Britain emerged during the first half of the twentieth century in response to the social issues of heavy mortality, poverty, poor housing, unemployment and regional discrepancies between population and employment opportunities. After nearly a quarter of a century of extensive power, authority and responsibility for the environmental aspects of these problems, the time has come to assess the achievements of physical planning in these areas.

Public health

It may be reasonably claimed that the first social problem to be tackled by physical planners was that of public health. The start of the effective campaign to reduce mortality was signalled by the Public Health Act of 1875. The results of these efforts have been felt during the twentieth century. Thus, between 1910 and 1968 infant mortality per 1,000 live births in England and Wales dropped from 105 to 18. Male expectation of life at birth in England and Wales rose from 52 in 1910–12 to 69 in 1964–66 and female from 55 to 75. Furthermore, the differences in, for example, the neonatal death rate (i.e. deaths at birth and during the first week of life) between social classes have become less significant than those between the regions since 1960. Only in the Northern region does the traditional type of social class gradient exist showing statistically significant differences between each of the social class groups. Thus, great strides have been made in public health but the difference in mortality rates between the regions is one indicator that both central and local government have not sufficiently redressed the balance of power and resources between those regions and the people who live in them, and are relatively deprived,

Source: *Journal of the Royal Town Planning Institute* (1971), 57 (10), pp. 450–3.

and those who are not. As long as mortality rates between the regions are significantly different then the life-chances of people living in different regions are not equal. Therefore equality of opportunity has not been created nor has distributive justice been done.

Income distribution

Equality of opportunity and distributive justice are also conspicuously absent in the field of income distribution. Between 1938 and 1958 the authors of the Crowther Report (1959) estimated that the real standard of living per head of the population increased by about 10 per cent. If the rate of increase in real standards of living averages only about 0.5 per cent a year then a given generation must rely primarily on income redistribution for significant short-term improvements in its living standards. Thus, the questions of income redistribution and poverty are inextricably linked. There is persistent inequality in income distribution between occupational groups in Britain. For example, Ryder and Silver (1970) say that:

> While unskilled workers received approximately 19 per cent of the average earnings of higher professional workers in 1913–14, in 1960 they earned 26 per cent. They earned 31 per cent of the average income of managers in the earlier period but only 29 per cent in 1960.

Furthermore:

> Less than 10 per cent of the population owns 80 per cent of all private wealth in Britain, the richest 1 per cent of these receiving 12 per cent of total incomes. At the other end of the scale, one third of all income units have no liquid assets at all.

Although the proportion of the population living in poverty has halved since the time of Booth (1906), Townsend (1965), using the standard of 40 per cent above National Assistance rates as a measure of minimum subsistence, estimated that in 1961 three million members of families whose head was in full-time work, two and a half million persons of pensionable age, three quarters of a million chronically sick or disabled and over half a million families of unemployed fathers were in poverty. This represents about 14 per cent of the total population. Ryder and Silver (1970) comment that:

> Only a very small proportion of families entitled to rent rebates actually obtain them, and nearly half of the children eligible for free

school meals in fact pay for them. These families make fewer demands on the National Health Service and derive fewer returns from the state educational system.

Although poverty and inequalities in income distribution were among the fundamental causes of the environmental conditions that physical planning emerged to deal with, in its statutory terms of reference its day-to-day practice and its aims for social reform it has singularly failed to attack this problem in a comprehensive or realistic fashion. In practice, physical planning has largely evaded its responsibilities in this field on the grounds that poverty is not a central element of the physical environment. It might just as well be argued that foundations are not part of visible buildings and may therefore be left to the chance that someone else will provide them.

Although poverty may not be seen as a central concern of physical planning, housing certainly is. Nevertheless, the problem of insufficient and inadequate housing has been a persistent characteristic of urban settlements in Britain throughout the duration of statutory town planning. In England and Wales alone, there are some two million houses containing about five and a half million occupants which have officially been declared unfit for human habitation. A quarter of the country's entire housing stock is over eighty years old and has thus exceeded the officially defined period of its useful life. In 1964, 22 per cent of householders either had to share a bath or had no fixed bath at all. Six per cent shared a lavatory and 11 per cent were without one altogether. Despite this, in 1960, for example, a greater exchequer subsidy was granted to owner-occupiers in the private sector in the form of tax reliefs in respect of payments of mortgage interest, ground rent, and insurance premiums related to house purchase. They received some £210–220 million while the public sector received £155 million for National Assistance allowances attributable to rent, exchequer subsidies on local authority housing, and rate-borne subsidies on local authority housing. Furthermore, while Cullingworth (1960) has estimated that Britain requires an annual building programme of 485,000, this figure has never been reached during the entire period of statutory town planning. Since 1955 the shortfall has almost invariably been in excess of 100,000 houses per annum. Not surprisingly, and particularly in the metropolis, the number of homeless people in Britian is increasing.

Unemployment

Such problems were characteristic of Victorian Britain, were directly responsible for the institution of statutory town planning and, therefore, should have been dealt with more adequately by physical planners. Massive unemployment, however, was new to those in planning between the two World Wars. It took two decades for offical recognition, by the Barlow Commission on the Distribution of the Industrial Population (1940) in 1940, that regional differences between the numbers of people and the employment available required significant interference with market forces by government economic and physical planners. Despite this recognition out of a total labour force of 22.6 millions in 1951, some 0.3 million were unemployed, and out of a work force of 25.3 millions in 1967 some 0.6 million were unemployed. It is possible that one million people will find themselves without work in 1972.

More significant for physical planners than the total unemployment is its distribution. A persistent problem since the early post-war Acts concerned with the distribution of industry has been the discrepancy between the rates of growth, in the different regions, of employment and population. Thus, for example, between 1949 and 1957, Eastern, Southern, London and South-Eastern areas experienced half the total increase in employment. A further one-fifth of the total growth took place in Scotland, Northern and North-Western areas and Wales, all of which had been scheduled as Development Areas in 1945. This means that out of every ten insured persons added to these two major groups, seven went to the Midlands and South-East and three went to the rest. Similarly over the same period, out of every ten net change in the distribution of population between the regions, nine were added to the Midlands and the South-East, and one to the rest. In practice, this meant that Scotland actually lost population during the period. Thus, the movement and growth of population and employment after the war faced planners with different problems in different regions. In some regions employment opportunities attracted more people than could adequately be housed, while in other regions changes in employment structure left numbers of people impoverished and local authorities unable or unwilling to sustain sufficient redevelopment or development to house or employ them in the prevailing economic climate.

Failures of physical planning

There can be no doubt that physical planning has played a part in the inadequate efforts of central and local government to create equal life chances, combat poverty, provide adequate housing for those who are relatively deprived and to prevent unemployment. This is a particularly severe indictment of physical planning because aspects of these four problems are central to its *raison d'être*. Three of the reasons why it has not contributed more to the solutions of these problems are:

1   its narrow outlook
2   lack of competence

3   its predominantly upper class and paternalistic ideology.

In many ways physical planning has a narrow professional outlook reminiscent of a medieval guild. In 1904 Geddes was recommending wide-ranging surveys of the social origins and conditions of towns as a basis for planning, but his proposals were considered too drastic for those times. When the Town Planning Institute was founded in 1914 by members of the existing architects', engineers' and surveyors' institutes there was, not surprisingly, some ignorance of all but the most superficial social aspects of the growth of cities. Unfortunately this led to a narrowing of the focus of physical planning from its social *raison d'être* and the broad conception of Geddes, to a small sector of town planning concerned with the physical manifestations of town life and confined within a very limited and restricted legalistic framework. Consequently, few plans have matched or seriously considered the diversity and complexity of the issues with which they are dealing. Nevertheless, a common defence of plans is that they must be confined within the range of current powers. But, as Westergaard (1970) points out in his comments on the Greater London Development Plan, 'If such powers are inadequate, it is an essential function of planning to say so; to set out the alternatives; and thus, to demonstrate the consequences if new powers are not made available.'

Not only is physical planning confined within a legalistic strait-jacket, but its focus is often further narrowed by planning for trends. Trend planning usually starts with projections of current situations into the future and the plan consists in harmonizing public and private development with these trends. Thus, if poverty, bad housing and unemployment exist when the plan is formulated it is likely that these features will be unconsciously projected into the future and not greatly ameliorated as the plan is implemented. Such planning, as Westergaard (1970) again points out, assumes that many factors are fixed 'and not ranges of alternative figures within which the choice of particular value is, in part or whole, a matter of policy judgment'.

Very often plans purport to be normative in so far as they start with goals and then define the means for achieving these goals. On closer examination, however, it is usually found that these goals are not seriously referred to throughout the plan and that there is a continual tendency to revert to trend planning. Westergaard also   complains of just this procedure in the Greater London Development Plan. He says that:

There is an initial statement of aims ... but these are couched in such vague and general terms as neither to constitute, nor to be capable of translation into, specific objectives and targets. They do not include, or even suggest, any criteria by which priorities could be assessed.

Thus, while the two main objectives of the Plan are 'to eradicate slums, overcrowding and the evils of congested and lamentable domestic environments from London' and secondly, to preserve London's special commercial position, 'Neither of these objectives is translated into terms that can make them operational as criteria for an appropriate allocation-and-reallocation of resources' (Westergaard, 1970).

Thus, much physical planning pays only lip service to the establishment of goals and their reduction to means. This, of course, would be an extremely complex political and technical process. Nevertheless, Gans (1968) has suggested that goals might be achieved in the following way:

1 Values must be specified to refer to the individual in various social rôles ... a given value will have a different priority for the rôles people play.
2 Values must be restated also to refer to collectivities, for example interest groups, subcultures, society.
3 Values must be translated into operational goal statements; these would take the form of normative statements.
4 The list must include priority values.

These are values which allow planners and decision makers to determine which values and resulting goals have priority. He goes on to say that priority values might include:

1 universal benefits – the most desirable goals are those producing the greatest benefits for the largest number of people.
2 incremental benefits – those people who now have the least of any value should have the highest priority in benefiting from government programmes.
3 economizing – resources should be allocated to maximize universal and incremental benefits at least cost, especially of the scarcest resources, and with the fewest undesirable consequences for other values and goals.

As far as the Greater London Development Plan is concerned, Westergaard has suggested a series of priority changes which might be placed within Gans' framework of priority values. Thus, in Greater London, it could be argued that universal benefits would be increased by the allocation of more land and other resources to housing, and the appropriation of development values in the land or of the land itself. Certainly incremental benefits would be increased by increasing residential densities in inner London, a shift of resources towards public housing, reducing the interest rates on public housing and replacing rates by a local, progressive income tax. It might be possible to show that such shifts in priorities lead to economies in, for example, the use of welfare services and transportation over and above the social benefits they would provide.

A second reason for the relative failure of physical planning in social terms has been the lack of competence of many of its practitioners. This may be seen primarily as the result of planning methodology generated from an unspecified belief in physical determinism and over-simplifications of the problems to be dealt with. This has resulted in the failure to produce plans adequate to urban social problems. Among the instances of this process at work was the uncritical adoption, by planners devoted to change in the physical environment, of the neighbourhood concept. Thus, while housing shortages are concentrated in the inner areas of the conurbations and manifested most acutely in obsolete housing and shortages of small self-contained accommodation, physical planners have been busily planning outer ring or, further out, new towns with neighbourhoods full of accommodation unrelated to the demographic structure of the population or the location of the most poorly paid employment. Such planning effectively imposes a tax on the poor by requiring them either to move into a decreasing supply of therefore increasingly expensive inner residential areas or incurring increased and unnecessary journey-to-work and housing costs.

Another example of the problems that planning has failed to deal with is the speed and magnitude of urban change. Thus, while statutory planning was approached gradually, some of the conurbations and other large towns grew rapidly. Between 1901 and 1968 Greater London grew from 6.6 to 7.8 million, and West Midlands from 1.5 to 2.4 million people. In 1923, motor car production was 17,000, in 1968 it was 1.8 million. By these and other means the population was on the move. Each year, some 10 per cent of the population of England and Wales move house, the overwhelming majority of these moves being less than ten miles but quite sufficient continually to change the social composition of individual parts of urban areas. It was left, however, to transportation planners to unravel the resulting urban congestion and change, formulating new kinds of master plan, and introducing electronic data processing to physical planners. Despite the introduction of this new tool, many planners have been content to take replacement decisions in a data vacuum. In Dennis's case-study of planning in Sunderland (1970), some planners even saw no need for data and were content to condemn whole areas on the basis of a cursory visit from a moving car.

This lack of understanding of the complexity of the social problems with which planners were dealing is manifested in the policy of controlled decentralization clarified in the 1920s and implemented by suburbanization and the New Towns. The latter in particular represent a platonic, static view of planning, not adapted to continuous change, too small and too close to major urban settlements.

Another characteristic of physical planning which has contributed to its failure to support radical social reform is its political neutrality. Unlike the other local government functions of education and housing, the two main political parties have no distinguishable differences in planning policy.

This may be partly the result of planners' efforts to invest their activities with the cloak of science. This has involved developing unnecessary and meaningless jargon to baffle politicians and public alike, and the resistance to public participation in planning in the shape of community forums suggested by the Skeffington Committee (1970). Participation in general has been handled in a paternalistic, public-relations way with no opportunity to debate the goals and priorities of plans or, as in one case, reweighting the goals defined by the public to give them priorities defined by the planners. So far, nobody has taken a radical political view of physical planning. This is critical if an effective attack is to be made on urban poverty, bad housing, unemployment, pollution and congestion.

Need for a political impetus
Such a political impetus is also needed in physical planning if the third reason for its relative failure is to be combated. Since its inception, it has developed an essentially upper-class ideology. The results have been that planning costs have fallen more heavily on the poor and its benefits accrued more directly to those who can already compete in a market economy. Secondly, although planning demands interference with the market in favour of changing market distribution of the social product and establishing alternative goals, physical planning has conspicuously failed to do this, and private interests and private appropriation of community increased land values have continued to flourish. Thirdly, physical planning has in no way shared its power with its clients as behoves any institution in a democratic society.

Upper-class ideology in planning is exemplified by the garden suburb, new-town thinking of the twentieth century. The fundamental social problems of poverty and bad housing have been largely evaded by these movements. The belief that the best aspects of town and country could be combined in the garden city represented an erroneous and idealized notion of country social life and increased the costs of housing and journey to work for those who could least afford to bear them.

Not only have costs been increased for the poor but also the paternalistic and vague concept of balanced communities has, in practice, increased the social and physical segregation of the population. As Westergaard (1970) points out:

> It is no accident that both the 'social gaps' and 'housing gaps' between Inner and Outer London have widened since 1951. Just as housing conditions have improved least in the inner areas where the need is greatest, so the contrast between 'working class Inner London' and the 'middle class suburbs' has sharpened. Furthermore, reliance by planners on private provision of housing has accentuated the character of public housing as housing for those who cannot help themselves.

Thus, the population is being re-sorted into increasingly divided camps by the implementation of plans.

Planners v. clients

Conflict between the goals of planners and their clients is greatest in inner residential areas. There, housing conditions are worst, incomes are largely the lowest and alternative accommodation is often more expensive. Nevertheless, planners are decreasing the choices open to such groups by demolition and thereby forcing them either into adjacent slums or into distant estates. Either way costs are increased. Whatever else planners do, they should rehouse the residents of slums without increasing costs of accommodation or journey-to-work. This is not likely to be achieved by current policies of rehabilitation relying on filtering to provide vacated properties for the poor. As experience in Islington shows, rehabilitation is used most effectively by the middle classes and again decreases the amount of accommodation available to the poor. Again as Westergaard (1970) says, filtering 'is designed to perpetuate a hierarchy of housing conditions corresponding to the hierarchy of income, wealth influence and opportunity in society at large'.

A second aspect of upper-class ideology in physical planning is the failure to recognize that to be in favour of planning is to be in favour of either ensuring that market forces produce a specified set of results or of interfering with those forces so that those goals are obtained. This, physical planning has conspicuously failed to do. There are three examples of this failure:

1   over-reliance on the private sector in housing
2   insufficient resistance to development lobbies
3   the failure to appropriate communally increased land values.

2 Urban processes

As a result of the distribution of incomes, the availability of credit, land values and interest rates, owner-occupation is beyond the means of most of those in greatest need in Britain. Reliance by planners on private housing and rehabilitation is therefore an abrogation of their responsibilities to the poor. Under present conditions, heavy subsidies must be given to poor tenants, the private renting sector, and a much increased and more heavily subsidized public building programme must be instituted. Either requires greater interference with market forces than is presently the case.

Frequently, however, physical planning is a deliberately vague exercise so that as many options as possible are kept open to the planners while private-interest groups lobby in semi-secrecy. Examples of this process are to be found particularly among developers who devote much time to persuading planners to alter allocated land uses. In this way developers are able to supplant planning goals with their own profit-motivated objectives. Three reasons why special-interest lobbying is often successful are:

1 the lack of clear goals if one object of the exercise is to keep as many options open to planners as possible
2 the absence of clear political positions over planning
3 because private interests provide a great deal of highly selective information to policy makers.

As information is a scarce and expensive commodity, neither planners nor public can readily afford the costs of counter-evaluation. In the absence of clear political attitudes to planning activities the pursuit of special class interests is often helped by public ignorance about the significance of policies, or by the pursuit of policies which are asserted to be in the public interest without any clear definition of what that interest is. Also, without goals, only those who have a clear understanding of what their objectives are, know what they want to get out of planning.

Thirdly, physical planning has failed to appropriate communally increased land values. These have been greatly increased by administrative decisions such as the green-belt policy and yet the resulting benefits have been almost exclusively reaped by private interests. It would be paradoxical indeed if even the values preserved in the countryside and the national parks for the general public are converted to the private interests of mining companies.

The upper-class attitudes of physical planners also manifest themselves in the way clients are treated. Participation in planning is seen largely as a public relations exercise in which ruffled clients should be passive recipients of the services handed out by planners after plans have been 'explained' to them. This upper-class authoritarian and paternalistic attitude is in the tradition of British democracy and successfully prevents the public from discussing the crucial fundamental goal of physical planning. Decision making would, of course, become increasingly uncomfortable if the ends of physical planning were continuously examined in public debate and found not to correspond with those of the public.

Conclusions

Nevertheless, physical planning is a matter of establishing priorities for the future and ensuring that these are achieved. This is essentially a political debate and, therefore, one immediate requirement is that physical planning should become politicized. Debate on poverty, housing, unemployment and pollution is essential if the urban settlements of Britain are to provide equality of opportunity, distributive justice and adequate human environment for all citizens of the United Kingdom during the twentieth century.

References

BARLOW, M. (1940) *Report of the Royal Commission on the Distribution of the Industrial Population* Cmd 6153 HMSO

BOOTH, C. (1906) *Life and Labour of the People of London* Macmillan

CROWTHER, Sir Geoffrey (1959) *15 to 18* Report of the Central Advisory Council for Education HMSO

CULLINGWORTH, J. B. (1960) *Housing Needs and Planning Policy* Routledge and Kegan Paul

DENNIS, N. (1970) *People and Planning in the Sociology of Housing in Sunderland* Faber

GANS, H. J. (1968) *People and Plans* New York: Basic Books

GEDDES, P. (1904) *City Development: A Study of Parks, Gardens and Culture Institutes* Edinburgh

RYDER, J. and SILVER, H. (1970) *Modern English Society* Methuen

SKEFFINGTON, A. M. (1970) *People and Planning* Report of the Ministry of Housing and Local Government HMSO

TOWNSEND, P. and ABEL-SMITH, B. (1965) *The Poor and the Poorest* Bell

WESTERGAARD, J. (1970) Paper submitted to GLDP inquiry, B. 600, London School of Economics and Political Science

2.4 The idea of social mix in town planning: an historical review

Wendy Sarkissian

The postwar revival of interest in social mix

Interest in social mix was revived on a very large scale at the end of World War 2 for reasons that had more to do with the problems of postwar society and the world at large than with the desultory discussion hitherto carried on by planners. Although the impact of these problems varied in Britain and America, their effects tended to be similar.

A desire to extend to the postwar, reconstructed society, the 'togetherness and lack of social barriers exhibited during the War years' in the armed forces and the civil defence services, led to a renewed interest in the concept of 'social balance' at the neighbourhood level as the end of the war approached (Thorns 1972, p. 13). Accepting that in Britain national service would 'tend to become a permanent feature' of life in peacetime, the National Council of Social Service recommended in 1943 that physical planning should 'encourage and facilitate the growth of that spirit of fellowship without which true community life is impossible' (Mann 1958, p. 92). This postwar interest in revitalizing communal life was not confined to Britain. Comparing the utopian writings of the early postwar period with the 'sodden intellectual air' of the late 'fifties, David Riesman observed that 'it is easy to forget how much enthusiasm there was, during and immediately after World War 2, for creative planning and reorganization of communal life, both here [the USA] and in Europe' (Riesman in Dobriner 1958, p. 393).

For many planners the material expression of the postwar 'spirit of fellowship' was the 'neighbourhood unit', which Americans had invested with the character of the garden city and its precursors, the ideal English village of memory, the New England village and the American small town. (Clarence Perry's ideal neighbourhood was built around a square as a

Source: *Urban Studies*, Vol. 13, No. 3, October 1976, pp. 231–47.

'visible sign of unity … an appropriate location for a flag-pole, a memorial monument, a bandstand … the place for local celebrations': Perry, quoted in Dewey 1950, p. 502.) It was in the immediate postwar period that the 'socially balanced' neighbourhood was given a specifically sanctified place in planning texts, although neither the degree of mix nor the means of achieving mix was spelled out very clearly (Foley 1960, p. 223).

The physical and ideological challenge of Soviet and Chinese communism after the war gave the Western democracies cause to re-examine, defensively, the justice of their own economic system. Social mix, by removing impediments to educational and other opportunities, was seen as a way 'to demonstrate that under its new welfare economy the lengthening arm of [US] government will now be employed to secure a decent family life in neighbourhoods which afford equal access to all, regardless of race, creed, or colour'. Likening the demonstration that freedom of opportunity existed in America's neighbourhoods to the Declaration of Independence, Charles Abrams claimed that 'it will awaken all minorities who now suspect the West to a new faith in the democratic principle' (Abrams 1955, pp. 388–9).

Abrams's main aim, however, was the rapid destruction of racial segregation. His *Forbidden Neighbors* (1955) argued the case for residential social mix from every conceivable angle, in order to prove the more important case for racial justice. As such, it was part of a movement dating from the early 1940s when a group of NAACP lawyers began painstakingly to gather evidence to challenge school segregation in America. The burden of their argument was that separate facilities for an underprivileged minority were inherently inferior facilities: an argument with implications that went beyond purely racial questions. It thus happened that, *en route* to the Supreme Court's ruling that segregation was unconstitutional (1954), America's civil libertarians were drawn into discussions on housing and planning as champions of social mix to promote equality of opportunity.

The arguments used in the desegregation battle are well known: homogeneous areas promote bias and group conflicts which may lead to violence; segregation blocks communication between different racial groups, imposes upon individuals a distorted sense of reality, and perpetuates rigid stereotypes; above all, totally homogeneous areas limit choice (Abrams 1955, pp. 279–85; Gans 1968, p. 293; Gans 1961, p. 182). It is true that some sociologists have questioned whether school integration (and, by analogy, housing mix) would lead to increased tolerance and understanding, but most continue to support heterogeneous schools.

American housing and planning legislation since 1954 has

understandably (if inefficiently) emphasized social mix at the neighbourhood level. The Rent Supplement Program in the 1964 Housing Act, the New Communities Act of 1968, for example, are attempts to increase opportunities for low-income and black families to live in neighbourhoods which would otherwise have been racially or socially homogeneous. Although schools were not segregated by race in Britain, the painful process of decolonization and the rise in non-white immigration gave the American campaign for civil rights through residential social mix a British dimension. Furthermore, most of the arguments developed to prove the damaging effects of segregated communities on underprivileged blacks could be readily adapted to attack segregation according to class (Foley 1960, p. 225; Grier and Grier 1966, pp. 19–23). It could be said that the battle for the comprehensive school was fought largely on lines already laid down across the Atlantic.

Housing shortage and suburban boom

Britain and America both suffered from unprecedented housing shortages after the war. Long before government action tackled the problem in America, the private developer had stepped into the breach with mass-produced suburban subdivisions (Dobriner 1963, pp. 86–7), frequently as a part of federal housing policy, which sought to meet the pressing demand for housing through a 'public decision' to use the private enterprise system (Grier and Grier 1966; Warner 1972, p. 240). Although suburban expansion was a well-established (and abused) feature of urban life (Mumford 1961, p. 496), the newness, lack of amenity, homogeneity and size of the new postwar suburbs were profoundly disturbing (Berger 1961, pp. 38–49). And although postwar suburbs in Britain and America differed in many ways, the 'myths of suburbia' in each country were similar enough to permit a few generalizations – Westchester County and 'the stockbroker belt' convey almost identical stereotypes (Thorns 1972, pp. 150–1).

Suburbia-watching became one of journalism's favourite pastimes during the 'fifties, and high on every list of suburbia's deficiences was homogeneity (Dobriner 1963, p. 5). The picture framed by the picture window was thought to be uniformly monotonous. 'Suburbia,' it was said, 'is not classless (i.e. it is all middle-class) it has been homogenized: social and personal differences are submerged beneath a great wet blanket of conformity' (Dobriner 1963, pp. 5–6). 'Mass-produced, standardized housing' was alleged to breed 'standardized inhabitants, too, especially among youngsters' (Gruenberg 1954, p. 14). 'Scientists' like David Riesman seemed to agree with the journalists' indictment. Likening the limitations of the suburb to those of a 'fraternity house at a small college',

Riesman argued that the homogeneity of suburbia was anathema to intellectual and cultural advance (Dobriner 1958, p. 385). A forum of 'citizens and professionals' which met in the late 'fifties to 'reconsider' the neighbourhood, voted unanimously for neighbourhood heterogeneity and attacked one-class, one-race suburban developments as 'stultifying' and 'undemocratic', despite the fact that less than half the members of the forum lived in mixed neighbourhoods (Hallman 1959, p. 123).

An odd result of the postwar campaign against the new suburbia was that the chosen domain of the middle-class family was declared underpriviliged. Children of the station-wagon and the semi-detached became the object of a commiseration previously reserved for ghetto hoodlums and street urchins. This gave the case for social mix a double potency which it had been lacking since Octavia Hill's discovery that the well-off could learn much from the poor.

The impact of urban renewal

Even before the war, the continuing decay of inner-city residential areas and the flight of better-off residents to the urban fringe had been matters of concern in both countries. After the war, national housing shortages and the loss through bombing of inner-area housing again drew the attention of planners to the central city's residential areas. Services had deteriorated, housing standards had fallen, crime was rife, and many areas were officially pronounced 'slums' by urban renewal authorities. In response to the physical problems of the 'decaying core' and the social problems which were seen as the product of high residential mobility and racial and class homogeneity, many planners advocated residential social mix.

American urban renewal programmes in the 'fifties were decidedly pro-mix on the assumption that mix contributed to community stability and would stem the movement of the upper classes to the suburbs. This emphasis on mix to encourage community stability, which Glazer sees as a traditional American goal (1959, p. 195), was soon applied to residential areas outside the inner city. Furthermore, the argument that services suffered in central areas as they tended toward homogeneity was extended to all neighbourhoods. Poor inner-city neighbourhoods were unable to support good school systems, public transit systems, welfare services; therefore, planners argued, '*a unit that consists of workers, without the middle-class and rich groups ... is unable to support even the elementary civic equipment*, of roads, sewers, fire department, police services, and schools', whether the 'unit' is in the centre, at the fringe, or in a new town (Mumford 1938, p. 459, his italics).

Public reaction to the effects of early urban renewal programmes (which featured 'slum clearance' and 'comprehensive redevelopment') finally significantly changed the direction of thinking about social mix, and is responsible in part for the present re-evaluation of the concept. When the dust from demolition and new construction settled, the remaining or 'relocated' poor residents discovered that the mix of housing in redeveloped neighbourhoods distinctly favoured the middle class.

Careful researchers like Herbert Gans and Bennett Berger set about to demolish the myth of suburbia almost as quickly as it was raised. Nevertheless, the myth was remarkably resilient, and it lingered on long enough to spark off a search for communities full of the vibrant diversity which the suburbs supposedly lacked (Clark 1964, p. 5). A surprising number of searchers purported to find it in neighbourhoods deep inside the old city: '... it is now the city rather than the rural area that is the repository of all virtue and the suburb has now been cast in the role vacated by the city of the promoter of an inferior way of life' (Thorns 1972, p. 14). Jane Jacobs, most articulate and vehement of the downtown champions, bitterly attacked the suburban 'neighbourhood' and the 'nauseating' suburban ideal of 'togetherness' (Jacobs 1961, pp. 62–4, 112). She celebrated instead the unplanned vitality of the heterogeneous urban neighbourhood with its special mix of buildings, densities, functions and schedules contained in a complex order known only to its regulars.

Although she was mistaken by Mumford for an anti-planner who wanted a 'random' and 'hit-and-miss' community (Mumford 1968, p. 197), and although some of her enthusiastic disciples (and critics) ignored her warning against trying to enshrine her 'exuberant diversity' in contemporary suburban planning, Jacobs's view of social mix was remarkably in tune with traditional notions. The safety, the sense of community, the pleasing diversity, the services and amenities which she found downtown closely resemble the features which nineteenth-century essayists imagined to exist in the ideal village and many Americans felt had existed in the Puritan village. Charles Abrams (1955, p. 6), another convert to the inner city, unwittingly makes the same point when he harks back nostalgically to the turn-of-the-century 'downtown' where 'employer and employee, mistress and servant, tradesman and customer lived in the same neighbourhoods'.

Re-evaluating social mix
The simultaneous alignment of so many favourable forces made the idea (though not the reality) of social mix nearly irresistible to postwar planners. Beginning with the Reith Committee report of 1946, British planners committed themselves vaguely but practically unanimously to some degree of social mix in decentralization, new-town planning and education (Heraud 1966, p. 9).

Postwar concern for mix in Britain can be traced from the identification of the problems of one-class council estates to the need for rebuilding war-damaged cities and the publication of the Barlow, Scott and Uthwatt reports. Finally, a consensus developed that 'segregation was bad and that town planning schemes should be designed so that some degree of mixing occurred'. Class mixing became 'a feature of the neighbourhood unit concept which was accepted at this time as the theoretical basis for the planning of residential areas ...' (Collison 1963, pp. 26–7).

Although the degree to which a community should be balanced was rarely specified for the British new towns, and the most desirable levels and kinds of social heterogeneity still remain questionable, 'the goal of social balance ... [was] continuously maintained as a central tenet of urban development policy in Britain', especially for the new towns (Popenoe 1973, pp. 311–5). Americans followed suit with FHA policy changes, urban renewal, school desegregation and new-town financing policies.

It was inevitable that reappraisals of mix would begin when the external forces nurturing the idea retreated. The replacement of wartime mobilization by peacetime competition, the Cold War by detente, the ideal of integration by the idea of black power, and the image of the 'plastic' suburb by the plainer and tamer reality, all led to a questioning of the exaggerated claims that had been made for social mix. Most notable among the reappraisers was Herbert Gans (1968). A great many planners were caught out by the simple requests he made for evidence; others were embarrassed by the conflict between social mix and democratic choice which Gans insisted would have to be faced head-on. It has become increasingly common in recent years for professional planners to express scepticism about the feasibility and 'desirability of intervention to foster socio-economic mixing in residential areas' (*Freedom of Choice in Housing* 1972, p. 36).

A second group of reappraisers has attacked social mix from the left. Black militants insisted that integration threatened the solidarity of the ghetto, that it was a device to divide and rule.[1] Analogous charges have been heard on the left in Britain, where social mix has been variously attacked as an ineffectual liberal alternative to social change, as an attack on working-class values, and as an attack on working-class solidarity (see Glass 1955, p. 14–19 and Simmie 1974). On the other hand, the idea of social mix continues to command a great deal of respect. Support comes not only from institutions and parties committed by the force of inertia, but from thoughtful critics like Richard Sennett (1970; 1973). For Sennett, modern man is trying vainly to fly from urban pluralism, chaos, and disorder because he has lost the ability to handle conflict. Sennett denies Gans's claim that 'in a democracy people themselves are in the best position to know what they want and need'. Reviving the belief in the 'vitalizing challenge of dissonance', Sennett would defy estate agents, sociologists and politicians to administer the medicinal residential mixing that people need but do not want.

Conclusions

This review of the idea of social mix in town planning has not attempted to discover the benefits and disadvantages of mix for local residents or the wider community. It has, however, raised certain issues which could help inform the planning process and can help to establish an agenda for further research. Some tentative conclusions merit special emphasis.

First, the idea that residential areas should be mixed is not new. Moreover, it was not invented by architects or physical planners. The Quaker industrialist, George Cadbury, appears to have been the first person to translate the liberal reformist views of his time into a physical reality at Bournville, when he moved his factory from Birmingham in 1879. Cadbury was absolutely inflexible on the subject of the Estate's mix and insisted that his policies be continued. It is clear that Bournville has significantly influenced residential planning in the ensuing century.

It is important that planners should be aware of the long history of planning ideas which they frequently treat as modern phenomena. Perhaps a greater sense of humility and an historical perspective might deter planners from adopting simplistic solutions to complicated problems, or making mis-statements about current policies.

Second, since the idea of the mixed neighbourhood became an accepted part of town planning (particularly new-town planning), architects, planners and legislators have shown that they rarely understand the complexity of the issues involved. Legislation has frequently defined as goals planning strategies that can at best be means for achieving social goals and at worst meaningless exercises in the physical arrangement of parts of urban areas. Without ever being precise about the way they would like to see people live, many planners have relied on *physical* solutions to solve social problems. It is dangerous to recommend that all politicians and town planners should study sociology (the study of history, on the other hand, can do no one harm). But those who educate planners might at least consider how they could help them distinguish between means and ends in planning.

Third, no one of much consequence has suggested that social mix is the way to equality in capitalist societies. At most, it has been argued that socially mixed communities offer more opportunities to the least privileged sections of society than do unmixed urban ghettos. It follows that attempts to prove that social mix will not rid us of fundamental equalities are assaults upon a straw person. By the same token, the proponents of mix as a means of improving the life of the poor would do well to avoid the hyperbole of Charles Abrams's Cold War statements on the subject.

Fourth, there is no evidence that the supporters of the idea of social mix have consciously or unconsciously sought to divide and rule the British working class or black Americans. Nor have they notably set out to attack working-class values or Afro-American culture. For Octavia Hill, the Barnetts, Geddes, Mumford, Abrams and Richard Sennett, the mixed community is an educational two-way street; it is if anything, the middle class which is most in need of education. Further, even if social mix could somehow be proved to be a middle-class plot, the failure of planners, developers and legislators to achieve truly mixed communities suggests that it was a very unsuccessful plot.

Fifth, throughout decades of discussion on social mix, remarkably little attention has been paid to the vital question of scale. What is the unit which the mixers propose to mix? The scale of proposed mix has shrunk more by accident than by design. Wakefield proposed a mixed colony in New Zealand; Howard reduced Wakefield's colony to the garden city; the Hampstead Garden Suburb effected a further reduction. The American neighbourhood unit, a reduction of the New England village and the small country town, finally found itself injected back into Howard's garden city as 'the balanced neighbourhood' after the war. The whole process took place without a single attempt to establish experimentally the effects of mix upon residential units of differing size.

Sixth, the review of the current state of the debate indicates that planners will not find the sociological profession united in their views if they turn to them for help. Some, like Sennett, clearly operate on a 'conflict model' of society. A planner who believes that his client wishes to help urban man regain the skills of handling conflict creatively might design residential areas to promote interaction among very different types of people. If, however, a client seems to value urban peace highly, a planner may agree with Gans that heterogeneity should not threaten residents to the degree that irreconcilable conflict results. The residential areas in the latter development may be much more homogeneous than in the former one. A planner will have to be aware of the political and ideological framework within which a sociologist operates before she can expect to find a simple answer to her questions. In any case, there are no simple answers.

Seventh, very little empirical evidence exists to support the claims of those who favour residential mix. Many 'community studies' discuss the subject, but very few come to grips with the issues raised in this paper.[2]

Eighth, we need more careful research studies designed to prove or disprove the modest claims on which the case for social mix ultimately rests. We need better answers, for example, to the following questions:

1   Are individuals in mixed communities moved to improve their condition by a 'spirit of emulation'?
2   Do people (as opposed to planners) regard diversity in their area as a positive element in their standard of living? If people in mixed areas are more satisfied than those in unmixed areas, is mix the reason for their satisfaction?
3   Do people in mixed areas engage in common cultural and social pursuits? To what extent? Do they regard these common activities as preferable to the traditional communal life of homogeneous areas?
4   What real additional opportunities are provided for underprivileged individuals and groups in residentially mixed areas? Do some important opportunities exist in unmixed areas that would be destroyed by mix?
5   Does residential propinquity actually lead to greater interaction among dissimilar people and greater tolerance for social differences?
6   Does middle-class leadership in mixed areas produce any positive benefits for other residents?
7   Are services more efficient, less costly, and more available to underprivileged groups in mixed areas than in unmixed areas?
8   Which groups tolerate mix best? Under what conditions can people mix safely and happily?

We need more studies of the effects of social mix and homogeneity in established areas to determine the characteristics of these areas which have led to the existing pattern, and their effects on residents.

Finally, although the advantages of the mixed area are hard to measure, it is probably safe to say that diverse areas should be encouraged simply because they are not homogeneous. The sense of stigma and lack of opportunity of one-class areas should be avoided. This view is supported by a number of aesthetic and philosophical arguments which have been advanced on behalf of residential mix. Many of these are neither quantifiable nor testable. Such arguments, however, are still worth considering in the final reckoning.

Notes
1   Even Mumford recognized in 1962 that 'the policy of dispersal now quietly favoured by educated middle-class Negroes ... would leave the metropolitan ghettos without leadership ...' (1968, pp. 249–50; see also Hughes (ed) 1971, p. 439).

2 See Durand and Eckart, 1973 and Ryan *et al*, 1974, for two recent empirical studies.

References

ABRAMS, C. (1955) *Forbidden Neighbors* New York: Harpers

BERGER, B. M. (1960) *Working-Class Suburb: A Study of Auto Workers in Suburbia* Los Angeles: University of California

BERGER, B.M. (1961) The myth of suburbia *Journal of Social Issues*, Vol. 17, pp. 38–49

CLARK, S.D. (1964) *The Suburban Society* Toronto: University of Toronto

COLLISON, P. (1963) *The Cutteslowe Walls: A Study in Social Class* Faber

DEWEY, R. (1950) The neighborhood, urban ecology, and city planners *American Institute of Planners Journal*, Vol. 15, No. 4, pp. 502–6

DOBRINER, W.M. (ed) (1958) *The Suburban Community* New York: Putnam's

DOBRINER, W.M. (1963) *Class in Suburbia* Englewood Cliffs, New Jersey: Prentice-Hall

DURAND, R. and ECKART, D. R. (1973) Social rank, residential effects and community satisfaction *Social Forces*, Vol. 52, No. 4, pp. 74–85

FOLEY, D.L. (1960) British town planning: one ideology or three? *British Journal of Sociology*, Vol. 2, pp. 211–31

GANS, H.J. (1961) The balanced community: homogeneity or heterogeneity in residential areas? *American Institute of Planners Journal*, Vol. 27, No. 3, pp. 176–84

GANS, H.J. (1968) *People and Plans: Essays on Urban Problems and Solutions* New York: Basic Books

GLASS, R. (1955) Urban sociology in Great Britain: a trend report *Current Sociology*, Vol. 4, pp. 5–76

GLAZER, N. (1959) The school as an instrument in planning *American Institute of Planners Journal*, Vol. 25, No. 4, pp. 191–9

GRIER, G. and GRIER, E. (1966) *Equality and Beyond: Housing Segregation and the Goals of the Great Society* Chicago: Quadrangle Books

GRUENBERG, S. (1954) Homogenized children of new suburbia *New York Times Magazine* September, p. 14

HALLMAN, H.W. (1959) Citizens and professionals reconsider the neighborhood *American Institute of Planners Journal*, Vol. 25, pp. 121–7

HERAUD, B. J. (1966) The new towns and London's housing problem

Urban Studies, Vol. 3, No. 1, pp. 8–21

HUGHES, M. R. (ed) (1971) *The Letters of Lewis Mumford and Frederic J. Osborn: A Transatlantic Dialogue 1938–70* Bath, Adams and Dart

JACOBS, J. (1961) *The Death and Life of Great American Cities* New York: Vintage

MANN, P. (1958) The socially balanced neighbourhood *Town Planning Review*, Vol. 29, pp. 91–8

MUMFORD, L. (1938) *The Culture of Cities* Secker and Warburg

MUMFORD, L. (1961) *The City in History* Secker and Warburg

MUMFORD, L. (1968) *The Urban Prospect* Secker and Warburg

POPENOE, D. (1973) A brief social evaluation of British new towns *Town and Country Planning*, Vol. 41, No. 6, pp. 311–15

SENNETT, R. (1970) *Families Against the City: Middle-Class Homes of Industrial Chicago, 1872–1890* Cambridge, Massachusetts: Harvard

SENNETT, R. (1973) *The Uses of Disorder: Personal Identity and City Life* Penguin

SIMMIE, J. (1974) *Inequality and Social Mix* Seminar paper. Centre for Environmental Studies

THORNS, D.C. (1972) *Suburbia* MacGibbon and Kee

UNITED STATES, DEPARTMENT OF HOUSING AND URBAN DEVELOPMENT (1972) *Freedom of Choice in Housing: Report of the Social Science Panel to the Advisory Committee* Washington: National Academy of Science

WARNER, J.B. Jr (1972) *The Urban Wilderness: A History of The American City* New York: Harper-Row

3   Community and neighbourhood

Introduction
The concept of 'community' has acquired an important place in the
vocabularies of politicians, planners, social workers and educationists
within recent years. It is an attractive concept but an ambiguous one. It is
difficult to define (indeed Hillery (1955) identified ninety-four different
definitions) and is used frequently almost as a humanizing additive sprayed
on whatever subject is under discussion. But however difficult it is to define
'community', and despite the generosity with which it is applied, it does
encompass at least three broad and related uses. The first of these is that of
social relations within a defined geographic area – the community of
residence, if you like. The second is that of belonging to a group which
shares beliefs and holds certain values in common. The third is that usage
which sees community as a worthwhile goal to be pursued because it
implies control over our major institutions and services, as opposed to the
large-scale, distant and supposedly unaccountable organization of them on
a societal basis.

The four essays here are ones which lie within the sociological
imagination rather than the geographical. Buttimer's (3.1) article, while
still very much concerned with the physical implications of the concept of
community, nevertheless demonstrates that cities contain communities
within them, each with varying levels of local interaction. He also shows
how the varying interpretations of community overlap in spatial and
physical planning. The article by Jane Jacobs (3.2) is included for its
powerful critique of the way in which neighbourhoods succeed or fail. All
city dwellers witness from time to time the decline or the rise of
neighbourhoods, as some previously stable fragment and others start to
regain coherence. As Jacobs describes it, successful neighbourhoods keep
abreast of the problems they face and are not destroyed by them. She
interestingly casts a sceptical eye on the belief that schools can ever be

dependable institutions for the creation of good neighbourhoods or for rescuing the bad. The article by Willmott (3.3) is included for its analysis of population movements within London and the believed consequences for community life. Finally, Benington's paper (3.4) rounds off this section with a critical look at community development projects in our cities and the danger built into the basic pluralist assumptions of these projects which divert attention away from the more fundamental, structural, economic and political inequities within our social system.

Reference
HILLERY, G. (1955) Definitions of community *Rural Sociology* page 20

3.1 Community

A. Buttimer

The demise of socially autonomous and spatially-circumscribable social groups has raised questions about the viability of 'community' as a conceptual framework. Social change and geographical mobility have tended to splinter social groups and disaggregate their impact on, and relationship to, a particular physical environment. The logical direction for sociological investigation has thus been to explore individual dimensions of 'community' for example, changes in working-class life styles, the emergence of suburban 'communities' and the changing significance of the neighbourhood. Generalizations about these dimensions of community can provide useful practical guidelines for planning policy.

The 'community studies' tradition
The literature

In Britain and the USA, two predominant parent streams of research in community studies can be discerned. On the one hand there are the studies which tried to grasp the total institutional structure and behavioural systems of whole communities within their environmental context; on the other hand there are the problem-inspired analyses of urban sub-communities which endeavoured to place a specific set of behavioural problems within a community context. While the latter naturally appear to have more direct relevance to planning, the former also have yielded important insights into the nature of social behaviour and social change.

These distinct and contrasting sources help to explain the different approaches used in Britain and their different degrees of relevance to planning. ⌈Studies of whole communities,⌉ often modelled on anthropological research procedures, ⌈tended to select identifiable and

Source: Extract from 'Sociology and planning' *Town Planning Review*, Vol. 42, No. 2, 1971, pp. 154–68.

spatially-circumscribed [settlement groups at various stages of socio-economic development and analyse their nature, internal dynamics and life styles. The micro-sociological orientation, on the other hand, tended to focus on specific problem areas, for example, poverty-stricken sections of industrial cities, and examine these areas as far as possible from the perspective of the occupants.] The former in general are intellectually exciting explorations done in detached academic fashion with little or no references to planning implications; the latter tended to be *postfacto* evaluations or critiques of planned or unplanned urban situations.

While various charges regarding *raison d'être*, methodological efficacy, and scientific accuracy can be and have been raised against community studies, there are certain strengths evident in the approach which appear to be particularly relevant for planners.[1] The comprehensive perspective on social life taken in a community study parallels the comprehensive perspective on physical planning for social life which a planner has to adopt. Community sociologists usually look at the full range of institutional participation as each aspect of it affects every other aspect. The individual's total life space – his modes of participating in major institutional areas – is usually the main focus of attention.

Generalizations about 'community'
What conclusions seem to emerge from this rich body of substantive research? What insights or generalizations can the planner glean as guidelines for practical policy? The evidence falls naturally into sociological categories, that is, generalizations have been reached about sociologically defined aspects of community, rather than directly about planning implications. The literature yields generalizations about people's relationships to their social rather than physical environment. However, since these two kinds of environmental web are intricately interwoven, insights about one provide valuable guidelines for shaping the other. In an attempt to reduce such generalizations to operationally testable propositions, Margaret Stacey has recently outlined the 'state of the arts' on community studies (1969). Her propositions deal primarily with the necessary preconditions for the development of local social systems, the implications of adding or subtracting certain local institutions, the interplay of roles and 'power points' within the system, and the complex interweaving of local and non-local systems within one area.

The central implication for planning concerns the relationship (if any) between people's differential participations in social systems and the kind of physical organization of space which would facilitate such participations. People's subjective perceptions and attitudes toward distance often distort the 'objective' (geodesic) measures of distances; their participation in various kinds of social subsystems reflects the interplay of local and non-local influences on their lives. The critical point is that no one physical organization of space, no one kind of community service provision could satisfy all these varying needs. The locally-orientated type will demand different kinds of services and institutions close to his residence; the non-locally-orientated may prefer *not* to have the same facilities close to his home. The implication then is to provide for both types, and for as many variations in between as possible.

The social composition of population in a planned residential area also poses questions for which community studies have some insights to offer. The ratio of host to migrant population may well determine the probability that a local social system could develop. The planner cannot add or subtract institutions (such as employment) from an area without expecting certain predictable social concomitants. Finally, the scale of development, that is, the size of the area to be taken as a whole for redevelopment, should reflect the scale and degree of development within and among local social systems.

In general, community studies indicate two contrasting kinds of social participation in space which have significance for planning. First, there is the spatially-circumscribed 'home area' type of identity, as ghettoes, 'urban villagers' and ethnic neighbourhoods, and secondly, the nodally-organized network of spatial influences radiating from key institutions like work, school, recreation centre and others. While the former tends to orientate people primarily toward local loyalties and a degree of local independence, the latter tends to expand spatial horizons and produce outward orientations and interdependence. Both types of influence probably co-exist within every locality. Physical planning can influence the balance of these two kinds of force, and the investment of effort should reflect the socio-cultural characteristics of the people being planned for. As John Rex suggests (1968, pp. 28–33):

> It is the task of the planner and the sociologist to work out what kinds of community the economic circumstances will allow in each particular case and, having done this, to provide for the kind of physical facilities which will make it possible.

Working-class life styles

The nature of the working class and the dynamics of social life within working-class areas have considerably evoked the intellectual curiosity of community sociologists and social anthropologists.[2] To the urban planner, the working class has become more than an object of intellectual curiosity. In many senses, working class communities have become the 'fly in the ointment' for many of his idealistic redevelopment renewal plans. Assumptions about human behaviour which stemmed either from models of middle-class life styles or stereo-typical models of the working class have continually been called into question because of the limited success and often failure of efforts to design for the social needs and tastes of working-class people.[3]

A two-fold motivation, then – frustrated idealism on the part of the planner, heightened intellectual curiosity on the part of the sociologist – underlies the growing interest in working-class behaviour evident in post-war Britain. Dennis's *Coal is Our Life* (1956), Firth's *Studies of Kinship in London* (1956), Young and Willmott's *Family and Kinship in East London* (1957) and *The Evolution of a Community* (1963) and a host of evaluative studies of planning endeavours within 'twilight' areas all constitute a mine of information on the nature of working-class life styles.

There are certain obvious processes of secular social change which have deeply affected working-class life styles and values in recent times. Most of these processes would seem to point to a general demise of a monolithic cohesive working-class stratum within or opposed to society. These changes could be subsumed roughly under three major headings:

1 *Economic*: rising income and living standards which appear to give workers an *entrée* to middle-class consumption patterns.
2 *Technological*: changes in industrial technology which alter the nature of work and the salaries paid for labour, and are associated with changing attitudes toward work and restructuring of social relationships at shop floor level.
3 *Ecological*: the movement of workers from rural to urban and from urban to suburban residential environments with the consequent dilution of old life styles and place-orientated ties.

Individuals are thus freed from traditional social networks and exposed to a wide variety of choices and influences, so working-class consciousness is reduced from internal and external influences. Changes in employment, the break-up of traditional work-based communities, geographical mobility, bureaucratization of trade unions and the institutionalization of conflict have all tended to reduce the solidary nature of communal attachments and the feeling of working-class consciousness. As old attachments and values are gradually eroded, they tend to be replaced by a more individualistic outlook in terms of expenditure, use of leisure time and aspiration level (Goldthorpe *et al* 1969, pp. 1–29). A similar set of forces has influenced white-collar groups, but in different ways. Bureaucratization of the white-collar worker situation, for instance, has led to more depersonalized working conditions and lowered chances of upward mobility. As a result some white-collar groups have tended to lose faith in the virtues of 'individualism' and have turned to collective trade union action of an apolitical or instrumental kind.

Marxist interpretations of these changes stress the enduring alienation of workers despite superficial changes in life styles. Other interpretations include the *embourgeoisement* thesis, for example, which suggests that changes in the economic situation of workers (increased earnings, increased ownership of consumer durables, etc.) have led to the adoption of a middle-class outlook and way of life among large sections of the working class.[4] Primary emphasis is focused on the economic aspects of class, that is, they have taken that similarity of income and living standards among members of the working class and the middle class would automatically lead to similar attitudes and behaviour. A contrasting thesis suggests a convergence between certain 'affluent workers' and lower-middle-class workers. Goldthorpe and Lockwood's critique of the *embourgeoisement* thesis, for example, holds that the economic situation is presumably only a necessary, not sufficient condition in class membership (Goldthorpe 1969). Equally important in their view are the normative (what is valued and how it is to be achieved) and relational (the pattern of social life, acceptance or rejection by middle class) aspects of class. In their empirical research they found little evidence that the working class was actually becoming 'middle class' either in terms of their values or their patterns of social participation. They found directions of change in working-class life styles which seemed to be leading away from the traditional pattern, but *not* towards assimilation with the middle class. Rather they were leading to what they called convergence in the normative orientations of certain sections of the working class and some white-collar groups. Changes away from traditional working-class and middle-class patterns of life were leading certain groups (on the margins of both classes) in the same direction in terms of similarity of outlook and aspiration.[5]

Certain social characteristics of middle-class people, family and home-centredness, may not mean an adoption of middle-class ways, but rather an adaptation of traditional patterns to accommodate changing situations (such as movement to new estates and separation from traditional ties). More important still – in view of planning implications – changes in standards and styles of living may not mean there has been a concomitant change in the nature of social relationships between workers and other groups within society. Finally, there is still insufficient evidence as to whether in fact working-class people actually wish to be associated with middle-class groups in social relationships.[6]

Young and Willmott's studies of kinship systems among rehoused working-class people in East London provide a uniquely valuable set of insights into these differential rates of change in working-class life styles. Family and kin continued to play a highly significant rôle in the behaviour and life aspirations of working-class communities. In a sense, the East London case epitomizes the rather consistent syndrome of behaviour and attitudes found among working-class communities in several industrial cities through Britain, Continental Europe and North America, where ties of kinship and neighbourhood traditionally provided a warmth and security which seemed to compensate for the dreariness of the physical environment.[7]

Urban renewal and relocation of working-class families, it appears, involve more than a potential rupture of social networks; they also involve a rupture with a particular place – a home ground which has become invested with previous social memories and associations.[8] This two-fold link – physical and social – helps explain the traumatic effects of relocation on some working-class families. In urban renewal, a rupture with physical location may be inevitable, but the break-up of social networks need not be. In Young and Willmott's Bethnal Green study, for example, a plea was made that whole communities or at least substantial blocks of a social network be relocated together rather than be allocated houses according to their positions on a waiting list. However, after a period of time, people can adjust to the process of urban renewal, though this adjustment does not necessarily have to lead to the adoption of middle-class values. Willmott's Dagenham study showed that after forty years within their new housing environment, the residents showed remarkable social ease and identity with their environment, and traditional social patterns showed a remarkable resiliency and vitality (Young and Willmott 1963).

Studies of working-class communities in the USA reiterate this general finding, which lends empirical support to Goldthorpe and Lockwood's theoretical critique of the *embourgeoisement* thesis. Berger's *Working-Class Suburb* (1960) provided significant evidence that working-class suburbanites do not adopt the behaviour patterns and beliefs characteristic of middle-class suburbs. However, several studies of relocated slum families in some Eastern cities point to a rather different conclusion. Where relocation corresponded with an improvement in the physical surroundings, and an increase in cultural and educational opportunities, significant change in life style and aspiration took place among certain black families.[9]

Two clear sets of conclusions emerge from the empirical evidence: working-class communities have a more resilient type of life style than was previously believed. First, their behaviour patterns are changing at different rates and in different directions, but certainly not all tending toward the model of middle class. Secondly, the two-fold attachments of working-class people to (a) neighbourhood, and (b) social networks, are intricately interwoven, and changes in one, as the removal from traditional home area, may cause a temporary rupture of the other, but over time these can again be repeated or substituted for.

What are some of the planning implications of these studies for working-class communities? These are best considered in the context of some of the major problems posed by the older 'slum' areas and by the new housing estates to which working-class people have been relocated. Problems associated with older working-class areas have been fairly well documented: problems of health, crime, poverty and others; problems of the rehoused populations are not yet thoroughly known, but the commonly held lore includes such social problems as *anomie*, delinquency, 'unbalanced' age structure and lack of facilities (MHLG 1967). Since the planner is presumably more in a position to influence the latter, the focus of discussion will rest on these. Basically, four sets of problems have been encountered in the planning of working-class housing estates:

1 problems of social composition
2 problems of control and decision-making
3 problems associated with the provision of employment, social services and other facilities
4 problems of physical design and layout.

The problems of class homogeneity and 'unbalanced' age-structure in housing estates have been well documented. Typically the first wave of migrants includes young families sometimes accompanied by older relatives. The associated needs for schools, recreational facilities and other amenities for young children have often been lacking. The provision of such facilities from the outset appears extremely important since they could provide opportunities for social interaction in an environment which lacks the traditionally established foci for social contact characteristic of the older areas from which these people have come. After some time, other needs develop: facilities for teenage and young adult populations and other kinds of provision arising out of the natural development of the population. Even if the housing estates are carefully designed to fit the social requirements of the first generation of residents, the initial programme cannot be considered as a *fait accompli*; as the population matures, social provision must also develop and expand to meet the normal concomitants of such evolution. Such provision involves primarily (a) job opportunities, namely, accessibility to suitable employment; (b) adequate range of choice in housing to fit the demands of households of varying age and class composition; (c) provision of transport, educational, recreational and other cultural facilities. In Dagenham, for example, an exodus of the 'second generation' became inevitable because of the lack of housing and other provision. This left a high proportion of older people often living alone in large houses which could have been occupied by young couples. This led to the curious anomaly of young people leaving the area because of a housing shortage while actually several houses were 'under-occupied' (Young and Willmott 1963, pp. 118–22).

While questions relating to demographic structure are reasonably predictable, however, the question of class composition poses greater problems. Despite a continuing ideological predilection for 'social balance', and 'integration' there is considerable empirical evidence on the wishes of people to live with people of their own class. The advantages of being socially at ease with one's neighbours appear more important to many people – particularly working-class communities – than the loss of such social and cultural opportunities which might come as a result of class heterogeneity. Willmott therefore suggests that one should perhaps plan for one-class 'neighbourhoods' within mixed-class communities – the neighbourhood being large enough to give the residents a sense of social ease, but not so large that they isolate people from those in other social classes. A similar recommendation also stems from American experience. Gans (1961) has argued for block homogeneity and community heterogeneity as one solution to the question of social integration in residential areas.

The political question of coordinating the control and allocation of houses also poses serious problems. From the viewpoint of planning, it is difficult to design physical provision for a population whose characteristics are not specifically known; from the viewpoint of some residents too, it is frustrating not to be consulted by the authorities who make decisions about their residential environment. Reforms of local government may well reduce or eliminate this problem; but there is a case for unifying or at least coordinating the control of housing estates. It would appear desirable that the same authority should handle the allocation of houses and the eventual administration of the estate. This leads to the question of community participation in the process of urban renewal and redevelopment.

To what extent do working-class people know, or have any interest in knowing, the mechanisms through which the planning process affects or determines their environment? There is little evidence of active public participation by working-class people either in Britain or North America. Various case studies have revealed rather their passivity in the face of questions regarding environmental planning. The renewal/redevelopment process may appear clearly as a 'We-They' issue, and working-class people may continue to be unwilling or incapable of participating actively in planning. This is not an argument for dismissing community participation; on the contrary it argues of a deliberate cultivation of the proper dispositions which would make such participation possible.[10]

Finally, there remains the question of physical design and the nature of social relationships. Willmott suggests that street layout can influence the extent to which people have neighbourly relations with each other in three ways:

1 the physical 'framing' of the housing unit: if this has a clear physical unity, people find it easier to feel a sense of identity with it and with their fellow residents
2 the actual arrangement of the dwellings in relation to each other and to the transport lines
3 the general housing density: the closer homes are to each other, other things being equal, the more likely it is that people become acquainted with their fellow residents.

The Dagenham study illustrated how the first two formulae affected social life. The Plan for a new town at Hook argued strongly for density control as a mechanism for promoting more social interaction among residents.[11] Several plans echoed a similar argument for higher densities, for example, the new town of Cumbernauld, but the effectiveness of such policy has not yet been fully proven.[12] It appears probable that communities like working-class communities, which have always been used to high density in their traditional home areas, may wish comparatively higher densities in their new housing environment than others. However, the philosophical problem of how much and what kind of sociability is desirable in a residential area remains an open question. The general recommendation would be to provide for a choice; housing arrangements which facilitate frequent social interaction should co-exist on the same estate with arrangements for more privacy if such should be desired.

This leads finally to the question of location and distribution of local services and public amenities. Zoning of land uses has become such an entrenched policy among town planners that it is difficult to argue for scattered and diffuse types of distributions. However, if the social functions of shops, public houses, schools and other facilities were considered, a strong argument for wide dispersal could be made. Willmott's Dagenham study showed that corner shops and pubs can help to foster and maintain acquaintances among local people. Two kinds of locational network could presumably be designed: a spatially clustered set of major services and facilities where considerations of scale economies must enter, and a spatially diffuse set of minor services and facilities justified largely by their social functions.

Studies of working-class communities in the context of urban renewal have thus two important messages for the planners. First, an explosion of the 'architectural determinism' myth, and secondly, an orientation to new dimensions in the traditional theories of working-class behaviour.

How can the planner best apply these lessons in practical terms? To what extent can these aspirations of working-class families be accommodated in redevelopment plans, and to what extent are they changing, changeable, and finally, how desirable or feasible is it to attempt to satisfy them? It is in the discussion and resolution of such issues that dialogue with sociology should be most beneficial. Sociological considerations should be part of the planner's argument in his effort to implement plans which must ultimately be justified in terms of cost/benefit to society at large. But urban renewal is rarely if ever justifiable on grounds of purely economic cost/benefit; in the USA, for example, the federal government grants up to two-thirds of the cost of redevelopment, and the criteria on which such subsidies are granted, are invariably social rather than economic (McConnell 1969b).

Suburbia

Generalizations regarding the life styles of particular social groups rank among the most important contributions which sociologists have made to the planning enterprise. The declining importance of place-orientated communities and the increasingly ambiguous significance of class in the determination of particular or unique types of social behaviour became evident in the discussion of working class. Suburbia, however, has occasioned a reversal of many behavioural trends observable in urban society. To a certain extent, class-related life styles – diluted and transformed in the process of urbanization – are reappearing in the suburbs; attachments to particular neighbourhoods are often consciously or unconsciously fostered by escapees from the anonymity of city life and by profit-seeking development agencies.[13]

Images of suburbia, and the research on which such images are based, reflect the socio-cultural context within which these studies have been done. In America, for example, there is a marked contrast between the old suburbs of the twenties and thirties and the privately-developed suburban tracts of post Second World War metropolitan areas. Similarly, a contrast appears between British public (local authority) suburban estates, privately built suburban estates, and new towns. It is difficult to derive generalizations which would cover the social characteristics of all suburbs.[14] In general, the British estates have been studied in terms of how they contrast and compare with old areas from which suburban residents come; whereas in America the standard polar types were 'urban' versus 'suburban' with some speculations on the rural-urban fringe. A contrast exists, too, between those sociologists who take a predominantly ecological view of the suburbs and those who explore suburban behaviour from the viewpoint of specific social characteristics. To the ecologist, for example, the two 'definitive' features of suburbia are, first, its physical location outside the political limits of the city; and secondly, its economic dependence on the city which generates commuting patterns (Martin 1952). Examining the impact of these situational factors upon the structure of suburban communities, the ecologist hypothesizes that participation in downtown activities will decrease, and community participation in the residential area will also be curtailed because of the time spent in travelling to work. In practice, however, the relatively small scale and low densities of suburban residential communities have been conducive to certain types of association: neighbourhood and informal association.[15]

Besides, it has been questioned whether commuting is in fact a peculiarly suburban pattern at all. Hoover and Vernon's analysis (1959, p. 145) of commuting patterns between the various 'rings' of the New York Metropolitan region discovered that 'over 80 per cent work in the zone in which they live, while the remaining 15 per cent or so commute to a more central zone'. In America generally, more suburban commuters travel within the suburban zone than between zones; similarly, more core workers commute within the core than between zones. Suburbanization of manufacturing, the growth of suburban shopping centres, the continued expansion of employing satellites have created many jobs within the suburban zone, and thus suburbanites find employment within the suburban area itself. Implications for the planning of transport routes and traffic flows are rather obvious – more intrasuburban lateral routes may be needed than direct urban–suburban ones.

But the consequences of a commuting work force are seen mainly in the nature of social life among the non-employed members of suburban families. 'Women,' the stereo-typical model suggests, 'are the force behind suburban organizations, indeed, behind the entire suburban ethic.' Several studies suggest that commuters participate less in the local community, but this may reflect age, recency of arrival and other characteristics rather than commuting *per se*. The relationship between commuting and participation in suburbia remains rather ambiguous. In general, the key to social participation can be found in the age and type of suburb and the social characteristics of the population.

To the sociologist, at least prior to the Second World War, the striking fact about the suburbs was their remarkably classless and homogeneous character; a peculiarly monolithic model of suburban personality types and ways of life had emerged. The suburbanite, according to Douglas in 1925, is typically an escapee from the noise and congestion of city life to the open spaces and quiet pace of life on the fringe. In a comparative study done during the thirties, Lundberg (1934) concluded that suburbanities differed psychologically from those who remained in the city: they had a great attachment to nature and the outdoor life, the neighbourhood, domestic and family life. In the fifties, Fava demonstrated that suburbia selectively attracted individuals who seek informal contacts and relationships which were not available in the city (1958b). The low-density and openness of suburban tracts also means a high degree of mutual visibility; as in the older working-class districts, suburban neighbours know each other's life styles far better than apartment-living urbanities ever could. This 'visibility' principle indirectly promotes standardization: one could almost speak of the 'formalized informality' of suburban life styles.

But the apparent uniformity of the early suburbs may well have been a temporary phase in the process of further differentiation.[16] Gans's studies in Park Forest (1966) and Levittown (1967) suggest that the physical uniformity of suburbia does not necessarily reflect any social homogeneity.

In fact, Gans supplied ample empirical evidence to illustrate the transfer of urban and suburban life styles and class heterogeneity into a suburban context. The behavioural characteristics now manifest in suburbia, he postulates, have always been at least latently present in the urban context, just as the social patterns of some new working-class housing estates in Britain reflect traditional patterns of the older areas (1966, pp. 549–620).

But contrasts between suburbs are also evident and enduring. Industrial suburbs or 'satellite cities' have little in common with residential suburbs. Dobriner (1963) shows how suburbs differ greatly in the circumstances of their creation, in the price and use of their real estate, their degree of transiency, their size and institutional complexity, and the income, life style, occupation and educational level of their residents. Sociological reflection on the class structure of suburbs, he points out, has been based largely on a few case studies of middle-class suburbs of the late forties, and in fact recent studies by Lazerwitz and Gans also show that the traditional middle-class monopoly of suburban living is being broken by the out-migration of semi-skilled workers to the suburbs.[17] In fact, the life styles, ideologies, folk-ways, values, aspirations and child-rearing practices of suburbanites in general defy generalization to 'homogeneity'.

The American experience, in many ways a foreshadowing of what is appearing embryonically in Britain, reveals another important facet of suburban life. The role of real estate private development companies in designing residential suburbs has assumed increasing importance even in

Britain. Craven and Pahl's study (1967) of residential expansion in south-east England, for example, is currently investigating the private builder/developer as a major agent of suburban expansion. Within the limits imposed by planning and other authorities the private developer, through his choice of sites, is seen as a major controller of residential growth patterns. Three important implications emerge from these general trends:

1　The changing and often convergent trends in social characteristics of suburban life, particularly the re-emergence of class and stage in the life-cycle as the predominant determinants of social life.
2　The appearance of new 'factors' and forces in shaping suburbia such as private development interests, suburbanization of industry and growing autonomy of suburban, commercial and retail activities.
3　The expanding scale in which the analysis and planning of suburbia must be placed. It makes little sense to design plans for suburbs without placing them within the broader metropolitan-economic, social and cultural context.

Before considering the planning implications of these social characteristics, it is instructive to look at the kinds of problem which frequently occur in suburbia. Gans has specified six major types of problem which the planner should keep in mind (1968b):

1　*Social isolation*, particularly prevalent among young mothers, recent arrivals and those who find it difficult to make friends in their new home.
2　*Physical isolation*, particularly for those who do not own a car, or are not mobile.
3　*Financial problems* where incomes are inadequate to cover the costs of living in suburbia where new kinds of expenditure become necessary.
4　*Adolescents' problems*, particularly if recreational and other facilities are not available.
5　*Community conflicts* – block conflicts between neighbours, economic conflict between the 'haves' and 'have-nots', conflicting interests of old and new residents, political conflicts between residents and builders and between residents and government.
6　*Persistent individual and family problems.*

How is the planner to address himself to these problems? As in the case of working-class communities, it appears that physical layout can significantly affect the nature of social life within a suburb. Here, however, the varying aspirations and life styles of individual family members assume perhaps more importance than the needs of the family unit. Each member participates in a network of social contacts which sometimes is quite distinct from the networks of other members. For all, however, accessibility ranks perhaps the highest priority: for men, access to work and to other men with shared interests; for the women, accessibility to friends, relatives and other women of shared interests; for youth, cultural and entertainment facilities with their contemporaries; for the elderly, an opportunity to interact with one another and to contribute in some way in the life of the community. For those whose feelings of isolation are related to the loss of frequent contact with kin and relatives, access to telephone and good public transportation should be provided; for the cultural minority group, adequate information on community organizations and activities should be available; for the elderly relatives, perhaps housing close to young families could be provided. The local social services, clinics, counselling agencies, churches and schools, could have a very valuable contribution to make in the resolution and prevention of problems related to social isolation. If planning could screen and supervise the kinds of personnel employed in these local institutions, perhaps suburbanites who normally do not attend could be attracted. Training in psychiatry and social psychology might sensitize the doctor, welfare worker, counsellor and others to the problems experienced by their clients and could thus be more effective agents in reducing the problems associated with social isolation.

Site planning and house design can also affect neighbouring and the evolution of neighbourhood life. A balance between involvement in the neighbourhood and privacy in family life has somehow to be realized. In general the house design should be such that household work routines are minimized, and people are free to interact with their neighbours as much or as little as they wish. Gans has argued for social homogeneity at the block level so as to reduce or eliminate conflicts and optimize the conditions for the development of neighbourly relations. The more homogeneous the block, he argues, the greater the opportunity for heterogeneity in neighbourhood and community life. On site planning specifically, he goes on to suggest:

1   A compromise between privacy and accessibility is necessary at the block-level; houses cannot be sited so as to put people on top of each other socially and visually. Small courts and narrow culs-de-sac are undesirable.

2   Social contact is determined to some extent by accessibility and, if the area is occupied by young families, by where children play; therefore, areas with young children should be well serviced with play areas, parks and meeting places.

3   Higher-priced houses should be socially and physically separated from lower-priced houses.

4   To prevent 'slum' development, strict performance standards on building need to be imposed.
5   Segregation of blocks by population characteristics might be feasible – groups of houses for families with small children separate from other groups for retired couples.
6   Neighbourhood shopping areas should include cafés and other meeting places for youth and other special interest groups.

Financial problems are less amenable to 'planning' solutions, but certain measures could be taken: selection of tenants according to income right from the beginning; subsidies for those who are forced to commute to work; careful and restrained taxation policies. While conflict resolution may be beyond the control of the planner, careful site planning may, however, help to remove some of the sources of conflict, and careful coordination of responsibilities may clarify certain issues over which conflicts often arise. In general the availability of adequate information about the estate is highly important.

The specific planning implications of the suburban literature also vary according to the context. The British situation is still quite different from the American one, and planning guidelines designed for Columbia, Maryland, cannot be transposed *en bloc* to the Cumbernaulds and Milton Keynes of Britain. Several of Gans's recommendations, however, are still applicable in the British context. The need for a wider choice of housing, possibly including a range of sizes in dwelling units seems particularly appropriate in new estates designed for relocated communities within British cities so that if necessary extended families could live together. Measures to counteract or prevent social isolation may have to be quite different from those recommended for American suburbs and here is an area where sociological research is necessary; however, community centres and other loci for social interaction should be considered everywhere.

Notes
1   See Vidich *et al* (1964); Stacey (1969); Anderson (1971).
2   See Goldthorpe *et al* (1969); Dennis (1956); Stacey (1960).
3   See Young and Willmott (1957); Blair (1969); Dennis (1970).
4   See Marshall (1950); Bendix (1964, 1965); Geiger (1949).
5   See Kerr *et al* (1960); Lipset (1964); Goldthorpe (1964).
6   See Abrams (1960); Butler and Rose (1960).
7   See Mogey (1956); Kerr (1958).
8   See Bakke (1953); Ferguson and Pettigrew (1954); Schorr (1963); Gans (1959); Fried and Gleicher (1961); Hole (1959); Mogey (1955); HMSO (1967).

9 See Millspaugh and Breckenfeld (1958).
10 See Dennis (1970); Ministry of Housing and Local Government (1969).
11 See London County Council (1961).
12 See McConnell (1969a).
13 See Martin (1952, 1958); Douglas (1925); Fava (1958a, 1958b); Duncan and Reiss (1956); Harris (1943).
14 See Dobriner (1963); Wood (1958); Martin (1953); Spectorsky (1955); Schnore (1957); Whyte (1956).
15 See Schaff (1952).
16 See Ktsanes and Reissman (1959–60).
17 See Lazerwitz (1960); Gans (1968a).

References

ABRAMS, M. (1960) New roots or working class conservatism *Encounter* May

ANDERSON, N. (1971) Diverse perspectives of community *International Review of Community Development* No. 7, 15–53

BAKKE, E. W. (1953) *The Unemployed Man* Nisbet

BENDIX, R. (1964) 'Transformations of Western European societies since the eighteenth century' in *National Building and Citizenship* Wiley

BENDIX, R. (1965) *Work and Authority in Industry* Wiley

BERGER, B. M. (1960) *Working-Class Suburb* University of California Press

BUTLER, D. E. and ROSE, R. (1960) *The British General Election of 1959* Macmillan

CRAVEN, E. A., and PAHL, R. E. (1967) Residential expansion; a preliminary assessment of the role of the developer in the South-East *Journal of Town Planning Institutes* 53, 137–43

DENNIS, N. (1956) *Coal is OUR Life* Tavistock

DENNIS, N. (1970) *People and Planning: The Sociology of Housing in Sunderland* Faber and Faber

DOBRINER, W. M. (1963) *Class in Suburbia* Prentice-Hall

DOUGLAS, H. (1925) *The Suburban Trend* Appleton-Century Crofts

DUNCAN, O. D. and REISS, A. J. Jr (1956) *Social Characteristics of Urban and Rural Communities* Wiley

FAVA, F. (1958a) 'Contrasts in neighboring: New York City and a suburban community' in W. M. Dobriner (ed) *The Suburban Community* Putnam

FAVA, F. (1958b) Suburbanism as a way of life *American Sociological Review* 25, 347

FERGUSON, T. and PETTIGREW, M. G. (1954) Study of 718 slum families rehoused for upwards of ten years *Glasgow Medical Journal* 38, 183–201

FIRTH, R. (1956) *Studies of Kinship in London* Athlone Press

FRIED, M. and GLEICHER, P. (1961) Some sources of residential satisfaction in an urban slum *Journal of the American Institute of Planners* 27, 305–15

GANS, H. J. (1959) The human implications of current redevelopment and relocation planning *Journal of the American Institute of Planners* 25, 15–25

GANS, H. J. (1961) The balanced community: homogeneity or heterogeneity in residential areas *Journal of the American Institute of Planners* 27, 176–84

GANS, H. J. (1966) 'Popular culture in America' in H. S. Becker (ed), *Social Problems: A Modern Approach* Wiley

GANS, H. J. (1968a) 'The suburban community and its way of life' in *People and Plans: Essays on Urban Problems and Solutions* Basic Books, reprinted in Penguin 1972

GANS, H. J. (1968b) 'Planning for the everyday life and problems of suburban and New Town residents' in *People and Plans: Essays on Urban Problems and Solutions* Basic Books, reprinted in Penguin 1972

GEIGER, T. (1949) *Die Klasse Gesellschaft im Schmelztiegel* Cologne

GOLDTHORPE, J. H. (1964) 'Social stratification in industrial society' in P. Halmos (ed) *The Development of Industrial Societies, Keele Sociological Review* monograph No. 8

GOLDTHORPE, J. H. *et al* (eds) (1969) *The Affluent Worker in the Class Struggle* Cambridge University Press

HARRIS, C. D. (1943) Suburbs *American Journal of Sociology* 49, 1–13

HOLE, V. (1959) Social effects of planned rehousing *Town Planning Review* 30, 161–73

HOOVER, E. and VERNON, R. (1959) *Anatomy of a Metropolis* Harvard University Press

KERR, C. *et al* (eds) (1960) *Industrialism and Industrial Man* Harvard University Press

KERR, M. (1958) *The People of Ship Street* Routledge and Kegan Paul

KTSANES, T. and REISSMAN, L. (1959–60) Suburbia, new homes for old values *Social Problems* 7, 187–94

LAZERWITZ, B. (1960) Metropolitan residential belts *American Sociological Review* 25, 245–52

LIPSET, S. M. (1964) The changing class structure of contemporary European politics *Daedalus* 60, p. 1

LONDON COUNTY COUNCIL (1961) *The Planning of a New Town* LCC

3 Community and neighbourhood

LUNDBERG, G. et al (1934) Leisure: A Suburban Study Columbia University Press

MARSHALL, T. H. (1950) Citizenship and Social Class Cambridge Univeristy Press

MARTIN, W. T. (1952) A consideration of differences in the extent and location of the formal associational activities of rural-urban fringe residents American Sociological Review 17, April

MARTIN, W. T. (1953) The Rural-Urban Fringe University of Oregon

MARTIN, W. T. (1958) 'The structuring of social relationships engendered by suburban residence' in W. M. Dobriner (ed) The Suburban Community Putnam

McCONNELL, S. (1969a) Residential density Official Architecture and Planning April 410–15

McCONNELL, S. (1969b) Urban renewal Official Architecture and Planning March 309–21

MILLSPAUGH, M. and BRECKENFELD, C. (1958) The Human Side of Urban Renewal (ed) M. Colean, Baltimore

MINISTRY OF HOUSING AND LOCAL GOVERNMENT (1967) The Needs of New Communities HMSO

MINISTRY OF HOUSING AND LOCAL GOVERNMENT (1969) People and Planning HMSO

MOGEY, J. M. (1955) Changes in family life experienced by English workers moving from slums to housing estates Marriage and Family Living 17, 123–8

MOGEY, J. M. (1956) Family and Neighbourhood Oxford University Press

REX, J. (1968) Economic growth and decline – their consequences for the sociology of planning Town and Country Planning Summer School September, 28–33

SCHAFF, A. H. (1952) The effect of commuting on participation in community organization American Sociological Review 17, 215–20

SCHNORE, L. F. (1957) The growth of metropolitan suburbs American Sociological Review 22, 165–73

SCHORR, A. L. (1963) Slums and Social Insecurity US Department of Health, Education and Welfare

SPECTORSKY, A. C. (1955) The Exurbanites Lippincott

STACEY, M. (1960) Tradition and Change Oxford University Press

STACEY, M. L. (1969) The myth of community studies British Journal of Sociology 20, 134–46

VIDICH, A. J. et al (1964) Reflections on Community Studies Wiley

WHYTE, W. H. Jr (1956) The Organization Man Cape

WOOD, R. C. (1958) Suburbia Houghton Mifflin

YOUNG, M. and WILLMOTT, P. (1957) *Family and Kinship in East London* Routledge and Kegan Paul Pelican edition 1967

YOUNG, M. and WILLMOTT, P. (1963) *The Evolution of a Community; Dagenham after Forty Years* Routledge and Kegan Paul

3.2   The uses of city neighbourhoods

Jane Jacobs

Neighbourhood is a word that has come to sound like a valentine. As a sentimental concept, 'neighbourhood' is harmful to city planning. It leads to attempts at warping city life into imitations of town or suburban life. Sentimentality plays with sweet intentions in place of good sense.

A successful city neighbourhood is a place that keeps sufficiently abreast of its problems so it is not detroyed by them. An unsuccessful neighbourhood is a place that is overwhelmed by its defects and problems and is progressively more helpless before them. Our cities contain all degrees of success and failure. But on the whole we Americans are poor at handling city neighbourhoods, as can be seen by the long accumulations of failures in our great grey belts on the one hand, and by the Turfs of rebuilt city on the other hand.

It is fashionable to suppose that certain touchstones of the good life will create good neighbourhoods – schools, parks, clean housing, and the like. How easy life would be if this were so! How charming to control a complicated and ornery society by bestowing upon it rather simple physical goodies. In real life, cause and effect are not so simple. Thus a Pittsburgh study, undertaken to show the supposed clear correlation between better housing and improved social conditions, compared delinquency records in still uncleared slums to delinquency records in new housing projects, and came to the embarrassing discovery that the delinquency was higher in the improved housing. Does this mean improved shelter increases delinquency? Not at all. It means, however, that other things may be more important than housing, and it means also that there is no direct, simple relationship between good housing and good behaviour, a fact which the whole tale of the Western world's history, the whole collection of our

Source: *Death and Life of Great American Cities*, 1961, Random House; 1962, Jonathan Cape; 1965, Pelican Books, pp. 122–39.

literature, and the whole fund of observation open to any of us should long since have made evident. Good shelter is a useful good in itself, as shelter. When we try to justify good shelter instead on the pretentious grounds that it will work social or family miracles we fool ourselves. Reinhold Niebuhr has called this particular self-deception, 'The doctrine of salvation by bricks'.

It is even the same with schools. Important as good schools are, they prove totally undependable at rescuing bad neighbourhoods and at creating good neighbourhoods. Nor does a good school building guarantee a good education. Schools, like parks, are apt to be volatile creatures of their neighbourhoods (as well as being creatures of larger policy). In bad neighbourhoods, schools are brought to ruination, physically and socially; while successful neighbourhoods improve their schools by fighting for them.

Nor can we conclude either that middle-class families or upper-class families build good neighbourhoods, and poor families fail to. For example, within the poverty of the North End in Boston, within the poverty of the West Greenwich Village waterfront neighbourhoods, within the poverty of the slaughterhouse district in Chicago (three areas, incidentally, that were all written off as hopeless by their cities' planners), good neighbourhoods were created: neighbourhoods whose internal problems have grown less with time instead of greater. Meantime, within the once upper-class grace and serenity of Baltimore's beautiful Eutaw Place, within the one-time upper-class solidity of Boston's South End, within the culturally privileged purlieus of New York's Morningside Heights, within miles upon miles of dull, respectable middle-class grey area, bad neighbourhoods were created, neighbourhoods whose apathy and internal failure grew greater with time instead of less.

To hunt for city neighbourhood touchstones of success in high standards of physical facilities, or in supposedly competent non-problem populations, or in nostalgic memories of town life, is a waste of time. It evades the meat of the question, which is the problem of what city neighbourhoods do, if anything, that may be socially and economically useful in cities themselves, and how they do it.

We shall have something solid to chew on if we think of city neighbourhoods as mundane organs of self-government. Our failures with city neighbourhoods are ultimately failures in localized self-government. And our successes are successes at localized self-government. I am using self-government in its broadest sense, meaning both the informal and formal self-management of society.

Both the demands on self-government and the techniques for it differ in big cities from the demands and techniques in smaller places. For instance, there is the problem of all those strangers. To think of city neighbourhoods as organs of city self-government or self-management, we must first jettison some orthodox but irrelevant notions about neighbourhoods which may apply to communities in smaller settlements but not in cities. We must first of all drop any ideal of neighbourhoods as self-contained or introverted units.

Unfortunately, orthodox planning theory is deeply committed to the ideal of supposedly cozy, inward-turned city neighbourhoods. In its pure form, the ideal is a neighbourhood composed of about seven thousand persons, a unit supposedly of sufficient size to populate an elementary school and to support convenience shopping and a community centre. This unit is then further rationalized into smaller groupings of a size scaled to the play and supposed management of children and the chit-chat of housewives. Although the 'ideal' is seldom literally reproduced, it is the point of departure for nearly all neighbourhood renewal plans, for all project building, for much modern zoning, and also for the practice work done by today's architectural-planning students, who will be inflicting their adaptations of it on cities tomorrow. In New York City alone, by 1959, more than half a million people were already living in adaptations of this vision of planned neighbourhoods. This 'ideal' of the city neighbourhood as an island, turned inward on itself, is an important factor in our lives nowadays.

To see why it is a silly and even harmful 'ideal' for cities, we must recognize a basic difference between these concoctions grafted into cities, and town life. In a town of five or ten thousand population, if you go to Main Street (analogous to the consolidated commercial facilities or community centre for a planned neighbourhood), you run into people you also know at work, or went to school with, or see at church, or people who are your children's teachers, or who have sold or given you professional or artisan's services, or whom you know to be friends of your casual acquaintances, or whom you know by reputation. Within the limits of a town or village, the connections among its people keep crossing and recrossing and this can make workable and essentially cohesive communities out of even larger towns than those of seven thousand population, and to some extent out of little cities.

But a population of five or ten thousand residents in a big city has no such innate degree of natural cross-connections within itself, except under the most extraordinary circumstances. Nor can city neighbourhood planning, no matter how cozy in intent, change this fact. If it could, the price would be destruction of a city by converting it into a parcel of towns. As it is, the price of trying, and not even succeeding at a misguided aim is conversion of a city into a parcel of mutually suspicious and hostile Turfs.

There are many other flaws in this 'ideal' of the planned neighbourhood and its various adaptations.

Lately, a few planners, notably Reginald Isaacs of Harvard, have daringly begun to question whether the conception of neighbourhood in big cities has any meaning at all. Isaacs points out that city people are mobile. They can and do pick and choose from the entire city (and beyond) for everything from a job, a dentist, recreation, or friends, to shops, entertainment, or even in some cases their children's schools. City people, says Isaacs, are not stuck with the provincialism of a neighbourhood, and why should they be? Isn't wide choice and rich opportunity the point of cities?

This is indeed the point of cities. Furthermore, this very fluidity of use and choice among city people is precisely the foundation underlying most city cultural activities and special enterprises of all kinds. Because these can draw skills, materials, customers, or clienteles from a great pool, they can exist in extraordinary variety, and not only downtown but in other city districts that develop specialities and characters of their own. And in drawing upon the great pool of the city in this way, city enterprises increase, in turn, the choices available to city people for jobs, goods, entertainment, ideas, contacts, services.

Whatever city neighbourhoods may be, or may not be, and whatever usefulness they may have, or may be coaxed into having, their qualities cannot work at cross-purposes to thoroughgoing city mobility and fluidity of *use*, without economically weakening the city of which they are a part. The lack of either economic or social self-containment is natural and necessary to city neighbourhoods – simply because they are parts of cities. Isaacs is right when he implies that the conception of neigbourhood in cities is meaningless – so long as we think of neighbourhoods as being self-contained units to any significant degree, modelled upon town neighbourhoods.

But for all the innate extroversion of city neighbourhoods, it fails to follow that city people can therefore get along magically without neighbourhoods. Even the most urbane citizen does care about the atmosphere of the street and district where he lives, no matter how much choice he has of pursuits outside it; and the common run of city people do depend greatly on their neighbourhoods for the kind of everyday lives they lead.

Let us assume (as is often the case) that city neighbours have nothing more fundamental in common with each other than that they share a fragment of geography. Even so, if they fail at managing that fragment decently, the fragment will fail. There exists no inconceivably energetic and all-wise 'They' to take over and substitute for localized self-management. Neighbourhoods in cities need not supply for their people an artificial town or village life, and to aim at this is both silly and destructive. But neighbourhoods in cities do need to supply some means for civilized self-goverment. This is the problem.

Looking at city neighbourhoods as organs of self-government, I can see evidence that only three kinds of neighbourhoods are useful: (1) the city as a whole; (2) street neighbourhoods; and (3) districts of large, sub-city size, composed of one hundred thousand people or more in the case of the largest cities.

Each of these kinds of neighbourhoods has different functions, but the three supplement each other in complex fashion. It is impossible to say that one is more important than the others. For success with staying power at any spot, all three are necessary. But I think that other neighbourhoods than these three kinds just get in the way, and make successful self-government difficult or impossible.

The most obvious of the three, although it is seldom called a neighbourhood, is the city as a whole. We must never forget or minimize this parent community while thinking of a city's smaller parts. This is the source from which most public money flows, even when it comes ultimately from the federal or state coffers. This is where most administrative and policy decisions are made, for good or ill. This is where general welfare often comes into direct conflict, open or hidden, with illegal or other destructive interests.

Moreover, up on this plane we find vital special-interest communities and pressure groups. The neighbourhood of the entire city is where people especially interested in the theatre or in music or in other arts find one another and get together, no matter where they may live. This is where people immersed in specific professions or businesses or concerned about particular problems exchange ideas and sometimes start action. Professor P. Sargant Florence, a British specialist on urban economics, has written, 'My own experience is that, apart from the special habitat of intellectuals like Oxford or Cambridge, a city of a million is required to give me, say, the twenty or thirty congenial friends I require!' This sounds rather snooty, to be sure, but Professor Florence has an important truth here. Presumably he likes his friends to know what he is talking about. When William Kirk of Union Settlement and Helen Hall of Henry Street Settlement, miles apart in New York City, get together with *Consumers' Union*, a magazine located still other miles away, and with researchers from Columbia University, and with the trustees of a foundation, to consider the personal and community ruin wrought by loan-shark instalment pedlars in low-income projects, they know what each is talking about and, what is more, can put their peculiar kinds of knowledge together with a special kind of money to learn about the trouble and find ways to fight it. When my sister, Betty, a housewife, helps devise a scheme in the Manhattan public school which one of her children attends, whereby parents who know English give homework help to the children of parents who do not, and the scheme works, this knowledge filters into a special-interest neighbourhood of the city as a whole; as a result, one evening Betty finds herself away over in the Bedford-Stuyvesant section of Brooklyn, telling a district group of ten Parent-Teacher Association presidents there how the scheme works, and learning some new things herself.

A city's very wholeness in bringing together people with communities of interest is one of its greatest assets, possibly the greatest. And, in turn, one of the assets a city district needs is people with access to the political, the administrative, and the special-interest communities of the city as a whole.

In most big cities, we Americans do reasonably well at creating useful neighbourhoods belonging to the whole city. People with similar and supplementing interests do find each other fairly well. Indeed, they usually do so most efficiently in the largest cities (except for Los Angeles which does miserably at this, and Boston which is pretty pathetic). Moreover, big-city governments, as Seymour Freedgood of *Fortune* magazine so well documented in *The Exploding Metropolis*, are able and energetic at the top in many instances, more so than one would surmise from looking at social and economic affairs in the endless failed neighbourhoods of the same cities. Whatever our disastrous weakness may be, it is hardly sheer incapability for forming neighbourhoods at the top, out of cities as a whole.

At the other end of the scale are a city's streets, and the minuscule neighbourhoods they form, like our neighbourhood of Hudson Street, for example.

[City streets have] self-government functions: to weave webs of public surveillance and thus to protect strangers as well as themselves; to grow networks of small-scale, everyday public life and thus of trust and social control; and to help assimilate children into reasonably responsible and tolerant city life.

The street neighbourhoods of a city have still another function in self-government, however, and a vital one: they must draw effectively on help when trouble comes along that is too big for the street to handle. This help must sometimes come from the city as a whole, at the other end of the scale. This is a loose end I shall leave hanging, but ask you to remember.

The self-government functions of streets are all humble, but they are indispensable. In spite of much experiment, planned and unplanned, there exists no substitute for lively streets.

How large is a city-street neighbourhood that functions capably? If we look at successful street-neighbourhood networks in real life, we find this is a meaningless question, because wherever they work best, street neighbourhoods have no beginnings and ends setting them apart as distinct units. The size even differs for different people from the same spot, because some people range farther, or hang around more, or extend their street acquaintance farther than others. Indeed, a great part of the success of these neighbourhoods of the streets depends on their overlapping and interweaving, turning the corners. This is one means by which they become capable of economic and visual variation for their users. Residential Park Avenue in New York appears to be an extreme example of neighbourhood monotony, and so it would be if it were an isolated strip of street neighbourhood. But the street neighbourhood of a Park Avenue resident only begins on Park, quickly turns a corner off it, and then another corner. It is part of a set of interweaving neighbourhoods containing great diversity, not a strip.

Isolated street neighbourhoods that do have definite boundaries can be found in plenty, to be sure. They are typically associated with long blocks (and hence with infrequent streets), because long blocks tend almost always to be physically self-isolating. Distinctly separate street neighbourhoods are nothing to aim for; they are generally characteristic of failure. Describing the troubles of an area of long, monotonous, self-isolating blocks on Manhattan's West Side, Dr Dan W. Dodson of New York University's Center for Human Relations Studies, notes:

Each [street] appears to be a separate world of its own with a separate culture. Many of those interviewed had no conception of the neighbourhood other than the street on which they resided.

Summing up the incompetence of the area, Dr Dodson comments, 'The present state of the neighbourhood indicates that the people there have lost the capacity for collective action, or else they would long since have pressured the city government and the social agencies into correcting some of the problems of community living.' These two observations by Dr Dodson on street isolation and incompetence are closely related.

Successful street neighbourhoods, in short, are not discrete units. They are physical, social, and economic continuities – small scale to be sure, but small scale in the sense that the lengths of fibres making up a rope are small scale.

Where our city streets do have sufficient frequency of commerce, general liveliness, use, and interest to cultivate continuities of public street life, we Americans do prove fairly capable of street self-government. This capability is most often noticed and commented on in districts of poor or one-time poor people. But casual street neighbourhoods, good at their functions, are also characteristic of high-income areas that maintain a persistent popularity – rather than ephemeral fashion – such as Manhattan's East Side from the fifties to the eighties, or the Rittenhouse Square district in Philadelphia, for example.

To be sure, our cities lack sufficient streets equipped for city life. We have too much area afflicted with the great blight of dullness instead. But many, many city streets perform their humble jobs well and command loyalty too, unless and until they are destroyed by the impingement of city problems too big for them, or by neglect for too long a time of facilities that can be supplied only from the city as a whole, or by deliberate planning policies that the people of the neighbourhood are too weak to defeat.

And here we come to the third kind of city neighbourhood that is useful for self-government: the district. This, I think, is where we are typically most weak and fail most disastrously. We have plenty of city districts in name. We have few that function.

The chief function of a successful district is to mediate between the indispensable, but inherently politically powerless street neighbourhoods, and the inherently powerful city as a whole.

Among those responsible for cities at the top, there is much ignorance. This is inescapable, because big cities are just too big and too complex to be comprehended in detail from any vantage point – even if this vantage point is at the top – or to be comprehended by any human; yet detail is of the essence. A district citizens' group from East Harlem, in anticipation of a meeting it had arranged with the Mayor and his commissioners, prepared a document recounting the devastation wrought in the district by remote decisions (most of them well meant, of course), and they added this comment: 'We must state how often we find that those of us who live or work in East Harlem, coming into daily contact with it, see it quite differently from ... the people who only ride through on their way to work, or read about it in their daily papers or, too often, we believe, make decisions about it from desks downtown.' I have heard almost these same words in Boston, in Chicago, in Cincinnati, in St Louis. It is a complaint that echoes and re-echoes in all our big cities.

Districts have to help bring the resources of a city down to where they are needed by street neighbourhoods, and they have to help translate the experiences of real life, in street neighbourhoods, into policies and purposes of their city as a whole. And they have to help maintain an area that is usable, in a civilized way, not only for its own residents but for other users – workers, customers, visitors – from the city as a whole.

To accomplish these functions, an effective district has to be large enough to count as a force in the life of the city as a whole. The 'ideal' neighbourhood of planning theory is useless for such a role. A district has to be big and powerful enough to fight city hall. Nothing less is to any purpose. To be sure, fighting city hall is not a district's only function, or necessarily the most important. Nevertheless, this is a good definition of size, in functional terms, because sometimes a district has to do exactly this, and also because a district lacking the power and will to fight city hall – and to win – when its people feel deeply threatened, is unlikely to possess the power and will to contend with other serious problems.

Let us go back to the street neighbourhoods for a moment, and pick up a loose end I left dangling: the job, incumbent upon good street neighbourhoods, to get help when too big a problem comes along.

Nothing is more helpless than a city street alone, when its problems exceed its powers. Consider, as an illustration, what happened with respect to a case of narcotics pushing on a street in uptown West Side Manhattan in 1955. The street on which this case occurred had residents who worked all over the city and had friends and acquaintances outside the street as well as on it. On the street itself they had a reasonably flourishing public life centred around the stoops, but they had no neighbourhood stores and no regular public characters. They also had no connection with a district neighbourhood; indeed, their area has no such thing, except in name.

When heroin began to be sold from one of the apartments, a stream of drug addicts filtered into the street – not to live, but to make their connections. They needed money to buy the drugs. An epidemic of hold-ups and robberies on the street was one answer. People became afraid to come home with their pay on Fridays. Sometimes at night terrible screaming terrorized the residents. They were ashamed to have friends visit them. Some of the adolescents on the street were addicts, and more were becoming so.

The residents, most of whom were conscientious and respectable, did what they could. They called the police many times. Some individuals took the initiative of finding that the responsible outfit to talk with was the Narcotics Squad. They told the detectives of the squad where the heroin was being sold, and by whom, and when, and what days supplies seemed to come.

Nothing happened – except that things continued to get worse.

Nothing much ever happens when one helpless little street fights alone some of the most serious problems of a great city.

Had the police been bribed? How is anybody to know?

Lacking a district neighbourhood, lacking knowledge of any other persons who cared about this problem in this place and could bring weight to bear on it, the residents had gone as far as they knew how to go. Why didn't they at least call their local assemblyman, or get in touch with the political club? Nobody on the street knew those people (an assemblyman has about 115,000 constituents) or knew anybody, who did know them. In short, this street simply had no connections of any kind with a district neighbourhood, let alone effective connections with an effective district neighbourhood. Those on the street who could possibly manage it moved away when they saw that the street's situation was evidently hopeless. The street plunged into thorough chaos and barbarism.

New York had an able and energetic police commissioner during these events, but he could not be reached by everyone. Without effective intelligence from the streets and pressure from districts, he too must become to a degree helpless. Because of this gap, so much good intent at the top comes to so little purpose at the bottom, and vice versa.

Sometimes the city is not the potential helper, but the antagonist of a street, and again, unless the street contains extraordinarily influential citizens, it is usually helpless alone. On Hudson Street we recently had this problem. The Manhattan borough engineers decided to cut ten feet off our sidewalks. This was part of a mindless, routinized city programme of vehicular road widening.

We people on the street did what we could. The job printer stopped his press, took off it work on which he had an urgent deadline, and printed emergency petitions on a Saturday morning so the children, out of school, could help get them around. People from overlapping street neighbourhoods took petitions and spread them farther. The two parochial schools, Episcopal and Catholic, sent petitions home with their children. We gathered about a thousand signatures from the street and the tributaries off it; these signatures must have represented most of the adults directly affected. Many businessmen and residents wrote letters, and a representative group formed a delegation to visit the Borough President, the elected official responsible.

But by ourselves, we would still hardly have had a chance. We were up against a sanctified general policy on street treatment, and were opposing a construction job that would mean a lot of money for somebody, on which arrangements were already far advanced. We had learned of the plan in advance of the demolition purely by luck. No public hearing was required, for technically this was merely an adjustment in the curb line.

We were told at first that the plans would not be changed; the sidewalk must go. We needed power to back up our pip-squeak protest. This power came from our district − Greenwich Village. Indeed, a main purpose of our petitions, although not an ostensible purpose, was to dramatize to the district at large that an issue had erupted. The swift resolutions passed by district-wide organizations counted more for us than the street-neighbourhood expressions of opinion. The man who got our delegation its appointment, Anthony Dapolito, the president of the citizens' Greenwich Village Association, and the people on our delegation who swung the most weight were from other streets than ours entirely; some from the other side of the district. They swung weight precisely because they represented opinion, and opinion makers, at district scale. With their help, we won.

Without the possibility of such support, most city streets hardly try to fight back – whether their troubles emanate from city hall or from other drawbacks of the human condition. Nobody likes to practise futility.

The help we got puts some individuals on our street under obligation, of course, to help other streets or aid more general district causes when help is wanted. If we neglect this, we may not get help next time we need it.

Districts effective at carrying the intelligence from the streets upward sometimes help translate it into city policy. There is no end to such examples, but this will do for illustration: As this is written, New York City is supposedly somewhat reforming its treatment of drug-addicts, simultaneously city hall is pressuring the federal government to expand and reform its treatment work, and to increase its efforts at blocking narcotics smuggling from abroad. The study and agitation that have helped push these moves did not originate with some mysterious 'They'. The first public agitation for reform and expansion of treatment was stirred not by officials at all, but by district pressure groups from districts like East Harlem and Greenwich Village. The disgraceful way in which arrest rolls are padded with victims while sellers operate openly and untouched is exposed and publicized by just these pressure groups, not by officials and least of all by the police. These pressure groups studied the problem and have pressed for changes and will continue to, precisely because they are in direct touch with experiences in street neighbourhoods. The experience of an orphaned street like that on the Upper West Side, on the other hand, never teaches anybody anything – except to get the hell out.

It is tempting to suppose that districts can be formed federally out of distinct separate neighbourhoods. The Lower East Side of New York is attempting to form an effective district today, on this pattern, and has received large philanthropic grants for the purpose. The formalized federation system seems to work fairly well for purposes on which virtually everyone is agreed, such as applying pressure for a new hospital. But many vital questions in local city life turn out to be controversial. In the Lower East Side, for example, the federated district organizational structure includes, as this is written, people trying to defend their homes and neighbourhoods from obliteration by the bulldozers; and it also contains the developers of cooperative projects and various other business interests who wish the governmental powers of condemnation to be used to wipe out these residents. These are genuine conflicts of interest – in this case, the ancient conflict between predator and prey. The people trying to save themselves spend much of their effort, futilely, trying to get resolutions adopted and letters approved by boards of directors that contain their chief enemies!

Both sides in hot fights on important local questions need to bring their full, consolidated, district-scale strength (nothing less is effective) to bear on the city policy they want to shape or the decisions they want to influence. They have to fight it out with each other, and with officials, on the plane where the effective decisions are made, because this is what counts in winning. Anything that diverts such contenders into fragmenting their power and watering their efforts by going through 'decision-making' motions with hierarchies and boards at inneffectual levels where no responsible government powers of decision reside, vitiates political life, citizen effectiveness, and self-government. This becomes play at self-goverment, not the real thing.

When Greenwich Village fought to prevent its park, Washinton Square, from being bisected by a highway, for example, majority opinion was overwhelmingly against the highway. But not unanimous opinion; among those for the highway were numerous people of prominence, with leadership positions in smaller sections of the district. Naturally they tried to keep the battle on a level of sectional organization, and so did the city government. Majority opinion would have frittered itself away in these tactics, instead of winning. Indeed, it was frittering itself away until this truth was pointed out by Raymond Rubinow, a man who happened to work in the district, but did not live there. Rubinow helped form a *Joint* Emergency Committee, a true district organization cutting through other organizational lines. Effective districts operate as Things in their own right, and most particularly must their citizens who are in agreement with each other on controversial questions act together at district scale, or they get nowhere. Districts are not groups of petty principalities, working in federation. If they work, they work as integral units of power and opinion, large enough to count.

Our cities possess many island-like neighbourhoods too small to work as districts, and these include not only the project neighbourhoods inflicted by planning, but also many unplanned neighbourhoods. These unplanned, too small units have grown up historically, and often are enclaves of distinctive ethnic groups. They frequently perform well and strongly the neighbourhood functions of streets and thus keep marvellously in hand the kinds of neighbourhood social problems and rot that develop from within.

But also, just such too small neighbourhoods are helpless, in the same way streets are helpless, against the problems and rot that develop from without. They are short-changed on public improvements and services because they lack power to get them. They are helpless to reverse the slow death warrants of area credit-blacklisting by mortgage lenders, a problem terribly difficult to fight even with impressive district power. If they develop conflicts with people in adjoining neighbourhoods, both they and the adjoining people are apt to be helpless at improving relationships. Indeed, insularity makes these relationships deteriorate further.

Sometimes, to be sure, a neighbourhood too small to function as a district gets the benefit of power through possessing an exceptionally influential citizen or an important institution. But the citizens of such a neighbourhood pay for their 'free' gift of power when the day comes that their interests run counter to those of Papa Bigwheel or Papa Institution. They are helpless to defeat Papa in the government offices, up where the decisions are made, *and therefore they are helpless also to teach him or influence him.* Citizens of neighbourhoods that include a university, for example, are often in this helpless fix.

Whether a district of sufficient potential power does become effective and useful as an organ of democratic self-government depends much on whether the insularity of too small neighbourhoods within it is overcome. This is principally a social and political problem for a district and the contenders within it, but it is also a physical problem. To plan deliberately, and physically, on the premise that separated city neighbourhoods of less than district size are a worthy ideal, is to subvert self-government; that the motives are sentimental or paternalistic is no help. When the physical isolation of too small neighbourhoods is abetted by blatant social distinctions, as in projects whose populations are price-tagged, the policy is savagely destructive to effective self-government and self-management in cities.

The value of city districts that swing real power (but in which street neighbourhoods are not lost as infinitesimal units) is no discovery of mine. Their value is rediscovered and demonstrated empirically over and over. Nearly every large city has at least one such effective district. Many more areas struggle sporadically to function like districts in time of crisis.

Not surprisingly, a reasonably effective district usually accrues to itself, with time, considerable political power. It eventually generates, too, whole series of individuals able to operate simultaneously at street scale and district scale, and on district scale and in neighbourhoods of the city as a whole.

To correct our general disastrous failure to develop functional districts is in great part a problem of city administrative change, which we need not go into at this point. But we also need, among other things, to abandon conventional planning ideas about city neighbourhoods. The 'ideal' neighbourhood of planning and zoning theory, too large in scale to possess any competence or meaning as a street neighbourhood, is at the same time too small in scale to operate as a district. It is unfit for anything. It will not serve as even a point of departure. Like the belief in medical blood-letting, it was a wrong turn in the search for understanding.

3.3 Population and community in London

Peter Wilmott

The population of greater London has been declining over the last twenty years or so. This decline has been more than matched by an increase in the Outer Metropolitan Area, the country ring within about forty miles of Charing Cross. In fact, of course, for nearly a century the population of inner London in particular has been falling, as people have flooded out to the suburbs and beyond. For a long time after this centrifugal process started, London remained an expanding employment market even though people were moving further out to live. But more recently jobs have been moving out as well as residents. Between 1961 and 1971, the total number of jobs in greater London fell by nearly 10 per cent, the biggest reduction being in manufacturing, where it was 25 per cent.

The main change in housing tenure has been the decline of the privately rented sector as against new council housing, and to a lesser extent more owner-occupation of houses both old and new. By 1971 there were already three London boroughs – Tower Hamlets, Barking and Southwark – where a majority of households were council tenants. In the future, the municipalization of older properties will accelerate the process already generated by the council's building programmes. More and more people will be local authority tenants, fewer and fewer the tenants of private landlords.

Owner-occupation has steadily increased in greater London as elsewhere. But in the last four or five years, because of the steep increase in house prices and in the cost of mortgages, the characteristics of house-purchasers in London have changed. The wealthy have, of course, still been able to buy inside London, but many of the kinds of people who in the past could do so – white-collar employees, for instance, and some of

Source: *New Society* 24 October 1974, pp. 206–10.

the higher-paid skilled manual workers — have found it beyond their means.

All this is familiar enough. But how have changes like these — in total population, in the employment structure and in housing — altered what might be called the social class geography of London? This is an issue about which there has been a good deal of discussion — and some disagreement, partly because such figures as there are can be interpreted in more than one way. My view of what seems to have happened over about the last ten years is based mainly on an analysis of 1966 and 1971 census data, using areas smaller than London boroughs.

For a geographical analysis of this kind, a city like London can be seen as a series of concentric zones. Our own studies at the Institute of Community Studies (most recently in Lambeth, in collaboration with Shankland/Cox) suggest that the central zone ought to be thought of as including not just what is sometimes called the 'central business district' but — mixed up with that and extending outwards to the west and north — what we have termed the 'central residential district'. This contains, in areas like Chelsea, South Kensington and St John's Wood, a high proportion of wealthy and high-status people. Immediately outside this centre is the 'inner city', with outer boundaries somewhat different from those of 'inner London' (whether that is defined as the ILEA area or as what the GLC calls 'A' boroughs, as distinct from the 'B'). Next would come the suburban ring. If one wanted to take the analysis further out, one could distinguish the Outer Metropolitan Area. On this way of looking at London, the central residential district, the suburban ring and the Outer Metropolitan Area have for a long time been relatively high in social class; and the inner city relatively low.

This remains the general pattern. But there have been some recent changes. One is 'gentrification' — the suggestion that the middle class, the so-called 'gentry', have invaded what were formerly largely working-class districts, buying up Georgian — or, as the demand increased, Victorian — houses. This process has, of course, contributed to the reduction of private rented property: in a sample survey in the part of Lambeth we are now studying for the Department of the Environment's Inner Area Study (around Stockwell), we found that a third of the owner-occupied houses had been rented immediately before the present owners moved in.

The kinds of London district in which this process has been particularly common are those in the inner city, nearest to the centre. When one allows for the fact that there has been a general upgrading in occupational class anyway, the percentage increases and the absolute increases among the people in professional and managerial jobs have been relatively small. But the figures do bear out the evidence of one's eyes. Gentrification *has* been taking place in districts like Barnsbury, Camden Town, Fulham, Hammersmith and Wandsworth. The result has been, as one could put it, that the higher-status central residential district has been expanding outwards, particularly to the north and west.

As it has done so, the inner city – the ring immediately around the centre – has moved further out. What seems to be happening is that the takeover of what was once privately rented housing, either by the invading 'gentry' or for large-scale redevelopment by the councils, has reduced the stock of housing accessible to some kinds of poor or immigrant families, and thus, in effect, pushed them further out. As well as the voluntary outflow of population that has been going on for a century, in which people have been 'pulled' out, it now seems that there are others who are being 'pushed'.

These changes have been part of a more general movement of population inside London and its region; some people moving because they wanted to, some because they had to, some with mixed motives and mixed feelings. Most of them have moved out of older privately rented property, becoming owner-occupiers or going into other private tenancies (where they could find them) or into council estates. In the first postwar years, the new council tenants were mainly rehoused off housing waiting lists. Later, most of them were caught up in council redevelopment schemes. Whatever their reasons, in the last twenty-five years many hundreds of thousands of Londoners have moved home, and probably in the process moved to another district. These and other changes have had important consequences for community life. What has happened over the past twenty years could be described – without too much exaggeration – as the breakdown of community. London has often been described as a collection of villages and, in the study of Bethnal Green that Michael Young and I carried out twenty years ago, we discovered and described the family and community life in one of those villages. The picture was of a predominantly working-class community where, because of stability of residence, a strong pattern of kinship and neighbourhood relationships had grown up. Bethnal Green may have been an extreme case, but the evidence of other studies in London and elsewhere suggested that it was not as extreme as all that. We concluded that most working-class Londoners belonged to similar kinds of locally-based networks and had a similar sense of local pride and attachment.

The main argument of our book, *Family and Kinship in East London*, was that housing and planning policies were, in the process of improving London's housing and its general physical environment, helping to destroy all this. I say 'helping to destroy' because we recognized that much of the migration was spontaneous, a private outflow on the part of families who wanted to get out; or at least wanted the new homes and gardens they could only find further out, more than they wanted to stay. Nevertheless, the planning policy was, as we saw it, accelerating the trend – pushing out of their settled communities some people who would have preferred to stay. I would now add the argument that over many decades national policy, again with the best motives, has, through rent controls and subsidies to owner-occupation, made it more and more attractive to private owners to get rid of their tenants where they could, and to deny tenancies to married sons and daughters, and that this again has encouraged the trend. As well as the pull outwards, public policies have clearly added to the push, not necessarily outwards but certainly out of the established community.

The irony is that, apart from a few traditional districts, in the East End in particular, the very places where community spirit is now strongest are the pockets of handsome low-density housing where the middle classes have either lived all along or have taken over. It is there that one finds in full swing the residents' associations, the conservation societies, the help-your-neighbour schemes, the wine and cheese parties to welcome new residents.

The reason for this class difference lies in the differences in background, in social skills, and in the relative weight traditionally given by the middle classes to occupational and geographical mobility as against the working-class attachment to kinship and to long-standing social relationships. Of course, since the eighteenth century, manual workers and their families have been moving into London in search of work, from the rural hinterland or from more distant depressed areas; just as, for a century at least, hundreds of thousands of Londoners have moved out to the new suburbs. But, for most of this time, those who moved in to inner areas entered relatively settled communities, where most of the other residents knew one another. Now most working-class neighbours are strangers to each other – partly because of the continued spontaneous movement out, but also because of the limited opportunities for continuity in the privately rented sector and because of the break-up of established communities that almost always results from council redevelopment.

It could be argued that, in the long run, this does not matter, since most people will either stay in their new districts or will eventually learn the middle-class skills of striking up friendships with people they do not already know. But such a long-term prospect is not much comfort to people who currently miss neighbourhood contacts and a sense of community identity.

It is perfectly true that most people, if you asked them what they felt about 'community spirit' or a 'sense of neighbourhood', would not know what you were talking about; or, if they did, would probably deny that they minded much about the lack of them. Places where these qualities are not missing include not only the middle-class pockets and what is left of the traditional working-class communities in the East End and elsewhere, but also, if any impression is right, some areas dominated by one or other of the immigrant groups − something of a paradox. These exceptions apart, our studies suggest that most people in most inner-city districts no longer have much pride of place or sense of community. This contrasts with the often-despised suburbs − yet another paradox. There, people are home-centred, but they use their home as a base from which to build bridges to other people and other institutions outside. My impression is that most working-class inner-city residents are now home-centred in the narrower sense that they have few outside loyalties, contacts or interests.

The social hostility seems specially marked in some of the prewar local-authority estates. There, the established residents complain about the sorts of people who have recently been moving in. Sometimes the criticism is in terms of class: skilled workers and the like who think of themselves as 'respectable working class', complain about an influx of 'problem families', or of 'roughs' with what they see as different standards from themselves. A study of some of these older estates shows that the proportions of low-skill − and presumably, therefore, low-income − families did indeed increase between 1961 and 1971. Sometimes the target is colour, the criticism that the estate is being swamped with black families. Again, research shows that the proportion of coloured people has increased in older council estates: in our survey in our Lambeth study area last year, we found that as many as 40 per cent of all people (children as well as adults) in the prewar council estates were black, compared with 26 per cent in the study area as a whole. Thus, it seems clear that there is a growing concentration in some of the older (and therefore less desirable) council estates of problem, low-income and black families. (This is not to suggest that they are the same; presumably what they have in common is strong claims on the council for rehousing but relatively weak bargaining power.) Because these families tend to have more children, the same estates also have high concentrations of children and young people. And these high child densities lead to the problems that residents in the older estates most often complain about − the dirt, the noise, the hooliganism and the vandalism.

These new concentrations of relatively large families who are seen, rightly or wrongly, as outsiders with different standards reinforce the trends described earlier. Add the turnover of population that has resulted from gentrification, from the decline in private renting and from the large-scale redevelopment programmes of the councils. Add the general weakening of community that has followed that population upheaval. And it then becomes relatively easy to explain the growth in social hostility, vandalism and crime in some parts of inner London.

These problems are being increasingly recognized. And what is the response? It is to bring in 'community development workers', 'neighbourhood workers', 'unattached youth workers', and the like. This seems ironic. This kind of work is obviously valuable and there needs to be more of it. But it does seem rather like closing the stable door after the horses have not only been let out but encouraged to run all over the field. If we wanted mutual aid and community spirit, why did we not try to nurture, instead of destroying them?

What, now, can we do, besides send in the community workers? I would suggest three initial policy objectives.

First, when the council moves in, existing residents should have the option of getting decent new or rehabilitated housing near their old home, if it is at all possible and if that is what they want to do. The corollary is that in council estates, the sons and daughters of tenants should have some chance of being rehoused nearby; again if it is possible and if they want to.

Secondly, the main emphasis should be (as it is now said to be) on rehabilitation rather than redevelopment.

Thirdly, high-rise and other high-density flats should be virtually stopped; and what there are should not be used for families with young children.

It could be argued, quite reasonably, that these aims might well come into conflict with each other. For instance, if rehabilitation or redevelopment was being carried out, and most people wanted to stay, the density would need to be impossibly high to accommodate them. This answer to that is twofold. The objectives are for guidance; they are not intended to be absolutes. It may well be that, in a particular situation, one objective would have to give way to another. The preservation of community ties, for instance, should not in my view be an absolute or overriding policy objective: it just ought to be given more weight than it has so far. The second answer is that there will, in any case, not necessarily be a sharp conflict of this kind. Many people have to move who would prefer to stay. But there are many others who would genuinely prefer to move out, but cannot do so at present. So I would add a fourth objective: every family who wants to move out of inner London should be encouraged and helped to move. I would like to say a little more about these four objectives.

The first is straightforward enough. Like the fourth, it rests on the proposition that people should, as far as possible, be allowed to choose what they do. Unlike the fourth, it has the additional argument that there are positive social advantages in allowing people to stay near their old homes, and the generations to keep together. In stable communities, there is more informal mutual aid which, as well as reducing the demands on social services, may help them to work more effectively. In stable communities, too, there are likely to be less social conflicts, less vandalism, less violence.

As for the second suggestion – emphasis on rehabilitation instead of renewal – that has now been accepted at least on an intellectual level. Yet all over inner London, local authorities are pushing ahead with schemes for so-called comprehensive redevelopment. Some of the planners will even admit that the houses themselves are not in too bad a shape. They agree the case in terms of prospective housing gain – i.e., they hope to be able to house more people on the site than at present.

All the evidence suggests that this is a will-of-the-wisp. For one thing, the whole process of redevelopment, from the first decision by the council to the last family moving in, can take as long as ten years – several years in which people are upset and worried about their future, several years of blight, and, later, several more years in which building work is going on and nobody lives there at all. But, in any case, because of the movement out of inner London by those who *do* want to go, there may well be no need of those extra homes in ten years' time.

If the housing gain case is a shaky one, there are other powerful arguments against redevelopment. In general, the whole comprehensive redevelopment ideology – which has held sway for so long – was almost certainly wrong. I can remember, twenty years ago, the gleam in planners' eyes as they argued that 'piecemeal development' was inadequate, that only the large new broom of 'comprehensive redevelopment' would enable them to sweep things clean and rebuild the urban fabric, freed from the outdated street pattern. It seemed a fairly persuasive argument at the time, and there have been some notable successes, like Lansbury. But Lansbury succeeded partly because it reproduced something like the old East End scale, and partly because most of its residents were people who had formerly lived nearby.

For the most part, what is wrong with comprehensiveness is its very effectiveness in obliterating the past. Of course, we need comprehensive *planning* but, as the architect-planner, Graeme Shankland, has recently put it, too often 'comprehensive redevelopment' has been synonymous with 'total destruction'. A city's old houses and streets are, as one might put it, part of its memory. When they are flattened, some of the city's past is wiped out with them. A rather more important argument, though, is the social one. Obliterate all the landmarks and, for established residents and regular visitors alike, the district loses its distinctive character: it looks just like everywhere else. This kind of boring anonymity has, I believe, helped to accelerate the breakdown of community identity and community spirit.

As for high-rise housing, it was clear in the early 1950s that most East Enders did not want it. It took fifteen years and the Ronan Point disaster to shift informed opinion in the same direction. Admittedly, in certain sites and for certain sorts of tenants, there is something to be said for tall blocks of flats. In theory, of course, tower blocks were never intended for families with children. In practice, however, there are often families with children living in them. This is partly because other homes are not readily available, and partly because many married couples who move in without children – not surprisingly – have them later. The result is horrifyingly high child densities in some towers; and all the problems and complaints that go with these concentrations of pattering feet. The new schemes that aim for high density (something more than about 100 people to the acre) without high buildings may be less universally disliked. But most of them are probably open to many of the same objections.

The fourth aim was helping people to move out of inner London if they wanted to go. It is clear that a sizeable minority of inner-city residents want the kind of house-with-garden style of life that, for all except the rich, can only be found in the suburbs outside greater London altogether. At present, these families are trapped in inner London. Most of them can see no real prospect of getting out, either as house-purchasers or as local-authority tenants. The conventional answer since 1945 has been the new and expanded towns. Several hundreds of thousands of Londoners have successfully moved under that scheme. By creating publicly rented housing, it has offered a way out for people who could not manage to buy. But it has on the whole, as recent research has confirmed, done little to ease the plight of those worst-off and worst-housed in London – the unskilled, the low-paid, the immigrants. They have not been able to get to the new towns because they lacked the skills in demand.

It is, in any case, clear from our own recent interviews that most people do not want to go as far as Stevenage or Basingstoke. Most of the potential emigrants want to go to a suburb in greater London, or somewhere just outside it. I realize that even to mention this raises two familiar political arguments – about building council housing for inner London in outer London boroughs and about breaching the Green Belt. The Action Group on London Housing has sounded the warning that firm action will be needed if voluntary cooperation fails. Since several years of attempted cooperation have made little headway, it very much looks as if the government will have to intervene.

I see no logical contradiction between advocating one set of policies to enable people to stay who want to stay, and another to enable those to go who want to go. The consequences would be a generally higher level of contentment (since more would be doing what they chose to do), a greater stability of population in inner London (since some people at least would be staying in their own district) and a general lowering of density and pressure (since the total population in inner areas would continue to decline). The problems are much more difficult than this neat equation suggests, especially in the areas of housing stress and as long as there is still homelessness. But in my view the general argument remains sound.

Apart from the suggestions already made, my main conclusion is about the importance of housing management, which is the key to most of these issues. The task is to make management, particularly the arrangements for allocation and transfer, more sensitive than at present to people's needs, and to the social consequences of whatever is done. One aspect of this is to recognize that there are a number of conflicting interests and that a balance has to be struck between them. To adapt a suggestion that was recently put forward by David Eversley, we need to take account of the following four criteria:

1 The familiar case on grounds of social justice: housing should go to people in housing need.
2 The functional case: certain sorts of workers, such as teachers, social workers, public health inspectors and bus drivers, need to live in inner London, and should be helped to do so.
3 The case for 'social balance': the argument that in some areas – dockland, for instance – there would be advantages to everybody if some relatively wealthy people moved in.
4 The 'community' case that I have been emphasizing in this article: the argument for allowing social groups to keep together, and the generations to keep together, if they want to.

The last of these four criteria – together with the growth, past and prospective, in local authority housing – supports the case for much greater tenant participation in management, and giving each estate the right to nominate tenants for a specified proportion or number of the tenancies that become available. Such a system of local tenant participation would be more likely to work effectively if much of housing management was devolved to a more localized level than at present. This would also humanize and personalize the relationship between the authority and the tenant, encouraging a greater sensitivity to the needs of particular families.

Two specific examples can be given. One is under-occupation. At present, there is a great wastage of housing in London, with small households, mainly of old people, occupying more space than they need. A more localized management network, closer to the circumstances of individual families, would, with support from above, be more able to juggle around tenancies so as to enable people to move to smaller homes without uprooting themselves from their familiar community.

The second example is another sort of under-use. All too often, a council flat remains vacant for three to six months after the tenant has left, on the argument that the walls need repapering or a broken window latch has to be replaced. Local management, with local tenant participation, could get such work done quickly; perhaps by the tenants doing it themselves, perhaps with the help of a small council-provided grant to cover the costs of this kind of small-scale day-to-day work.

All this is easily said. To change housing management along these lines would be expensive and difficult. In the stress areas, in particular, it would be far beyond present resources. The problems are immense. The staff are few; and those there are keep changing. The turnover of staff in inner London in local-authority housing departments, as in other departments, reflects both the special pressures of the work and the familiar problem that the workers have in finding homes for themselves as well as the people they serve. Yet if we are to avoid too monolithic a system and too sharp a distinction between the two great tenure blocs of the future – council tenants and owner-occupiers – we also need to do other things, too. We should experiment with new forms of public and semi-public housing. We need to think about new forms of tenure, including what is sometimes called 'equity sharing' – some kind of scheme in which the public authority and the tenant-cum-owner both have a financial stake in the value of the property.

All these proposals are directed to the same end; greater choice for people in their housing and in their district of residence, and a nurturing of stable community life. None of this will come easily. But we could make a start now.

References

DEAKIN, N. and UNGERSON, C. (1973) The non-movers *Town and Country Planning*, January

EVERSLEY, D. and HOLMES, C. (1974) Contributions to seminar organized by Central London Planning Conference, March

SHANKLAND, G. (1974) 'London planning now: precedent or warning' Address to Royal Town Planning Institute summer school, September

SHANKLAND COX PARTNERSHIP/INSTITUTE OF COMMUNITY STUDIES (1975) *People, Housing and District* and *Changes in Socio-Economic Structure* Reports on Lambeth Inner Area Study DOE

3   Community and neighbourhood

WILLMOTT, P. (1963) *The Evolution of a Community: a study of Dagenham after forty years* Routledge and Kegan Paul

YOUNG, M. and WILLMOTT, P. (1962) *Family and Kinship in East London* Penguin

3.4 The flaw in the pluralist heaven

John Benington

The original model for the national CDP was based on a belief that there were in our cities small concentrations of people with special problems which demanded special treatment. The Home Secretary in his 1969 speech in Parliament, when he announced the CDP, defined that category of people like this:

> Although the social services cater reasonably well for the majority they are much less effective for a minority who are caught up in a chain reaction of related social problems. An example of the kind of vicious circle in which this kind of family could be trapped is ill-health, financial difficulty, children suffering from deprivation, consequent delinquency, inability of the children to adjust to adult life, unstable marriages, emotional problems, ill-health – and the cycle begins again.

So it is clear that he had a precise view of the kind of people towards whom CDP was to be directed.

The Home Office in its original prescription clearly believed that one solution to these assumed concentrations of people with special pathology was to tighten coordination in the delivery of welfare support services to them. The original job description for my appointment to Coventry CDP in January 1970 was as the leader of a team which was to include a psychiatric social worker, a child care officer, education welfare officer, disablement resettlement officer, and mental welfare officer. It is clear that the problems are seen as those of social cripples and lame ducks. They are to be helped to make better use of the welfare state first by closer

Source: Lees, R. and Smith, G. (eds) *Action Research in Community Development* (1975) Routledge and Kegan Paul, pp. 174-87.

coordination in the delivery of personal services and second by self-help. In announcing the project in Coventry in February 1969, Richard Crossman perhaps unwittingly revealed one of the underlying paradoxes in these early views of the experiment:

> It is not just a matter of helping to get these people back on their feet by gearing up the social services for them in a fully coordinated way but of helping them to stand more on their own in the future by their own efforts without having to rely so much on external support.

Greater coordination should increase take-up of services and therefore costs, while self-help is designed to reduce demands on the welfare state and therefore limit costs. That is a paradox that was never resolved, or even really acknowledged.

Experience in the first two exploratory years of the project forced us to challenge and reject those initial assumptions. First, it became clear that in spite of its reputation, Hillfields did not have an abnormal share of families with personal social handicaps. The most obvious and blatant problems that people experienced were not internal and pathological but were external. They arose from the very low incomes people were having to live on and the very poor housing and environment in the district. These problems were not peculiar to that neighbourhood; they were the same as the problems which were afflicting large sections of the working-class population throughout Coventry. They were more acute in their degree but they were not different in kind. The major factor that was specific to the Hillfields neighbourhood was the council's intervention with a comprehensive plan for redevelopment. This again was not a problem which arose within the community; it was a problem which arose from the policies of the city towards that neighbourhood. It was clear that the issues did not just concern a deviant minority within the welfare state, but large sections of the population as a whole. We were looking as it were at a microcosm of processes that were part of the whole city's dynamics and were not peculiar to that neighbourhood.

Second, there was little evidence that the problems people experienced resulted from any obvious deterioration in the patterns or values of community life. When we arrived to start work in Coventry at the beginning of 1970, we found that the planners had identified a grid of twenty-six streets which was to be the target area for CDP. This had been selected on the basis of certain assumptions about social pathology. Different agencies had been asked to identify where their heaviest problems lay. Some departments had done this in detail and had plotted their caseloads by marking black dots on a street map of the city. Others were much more cavalier and just drew a circle around the area which they believed to have the worst reputation. The planners brought all this information together on base maps, overlaid with census information, and eventually chose a core of twenty-six streets which they saw to be the black spot of the area. As it happened, we arrived to find that a change in the redevelopment timetable meant that a large part of this core area was to be demolished within a matter of months. Ironically this gave us the opportunity to stand back and ask a lot more questions about the ways in which the area's reputation as a blackspot had arisen. We came to see that this was less a reflection of deteriorating standards of local community behaviour, than of processes external to the locality. The area's reputation for prostitution is a good illustration. Statistics of court convictions for 'loiter prostitution' would certainly show a heavy preponderance in Hillfields. But levels of surveillance by the vice squad are also greatest in Hillfields. A self-fulfilling prophecy seemed to be at work, whereby the police were more alert to this phenomenon in Hillfields than in other districts and so their levels of detection and hence conviction were also greater. In fact, it seems that the prostitution in the district is almost entirely a commuter business. It is not local women but women from the West Midlands who come from as far away as Nottingham to solicit in Hillfields. Their clients are not Hillfields men either but commuters from other parts of Coventry or the city region. So the 'malaise' statistics record a number of phenomena which have little connection with any deterioration of community values in Hillfields.

The third thing that became clear was that local people did not see more communication leading to better solutions to their problems at all. On the contrary, they were in direct dispute with the authorities about the nature of their needs and their aspirations. They saw the problem as their difficulty in influencing decisions which affected their lives in the directions which they wanted. It was not a consensual situation. It was a situation where residents believed they had a different interest from that represented by the public authorities. Communication was there in plenty; communication that was only sometimes vocal or articulate, expressed mostly in informal social settings, but sometimes through the traditional means of petitions and public meetings and at times of exceptional frustration, even in minor acts of insurrection. One local resident was prepared to barricade himself in his house and put live electric cables around to keep the bulldozers at bay. That seemed to be a fairly clear message.

So it became clear to us that the initial prescriptions of CDP were inadequate to the actual situation. The diagnosis was incorrect. The solution for Hillfields could not be looked for in stronger doses of the medicine that the welfare state had been serving up, or in a better mixing of ingredients in that dose, or even in a better bedside manner in the administering of the dose. We were in fact confronted by problems of politics, the problem of conflicts of interests in the city, and the problem of powerlessness in influencing political decisions.

This led us into our second phase of work. We felt at that stage that it was important to shift exclusive focus away from the neighbourhood as the source of problems and to concentrate research and action on the government agencies that appeared to be controlling the destinies of the people in that area. I say 'appeared' because later experience led us to see that this was not necessarily where effective control of all the processes lay. However, we felt at that time that a local CDP on its own was not in a position to tackle the ultimate causes of disadvantage which have their sources nationally in the economy and in government policy. So we began to map out a series of studies of the agencies which we believed to be mediating the distribution of public resources at the local level. We were aware that local government was not the only controller of people's destinies but we felt that it was at that level that we could best hope to contribute. So we began programmes of work which attempted to analyse and modify the processes within government agencies which sustain and reinforce disadvantage at the local level. We concentrated on the following main fields: income maintenance, housing and environment, community education, the transition from school to work, and services for the elderly. We were aware that this ran the danger of breaking the phenomenon of multiple-deprivation down into isolated parts. We therefore had another programme, which we called social priority planning, which tried to take some account of the structures within which the separate functional services operated. (At this stage we concentrated rather narrowly on organizational and managerial structures, and were too little aware of the wider political and economic structures.)

We approached this goal in a number of ways and at different levels. Our strategies have included research, promotion of change within the corporation's management system, and direct involvement with particular interest groups in the neighbourhood. They have ranged across the following kinds of intervention:

1   identifying those whose circumstances or conditions make them eligible for existing service provision and helping them to press their claims upon those services
2   attempting to make agencies more receptive to needs for which they are responsible and to argue for changes in the mechanisms for identifying and categorizing those in need

3 pressing agencies and institutions to consider alternative structures and methods of responding to need

4 experimentally developing innovatory structures for dealing with problems as a demonstration of alternatives to existing institutional patterns

5 presenting ways of redefining the problems themselves which may lead to more relevant ways of dealing with them

6 critically appraising the functioning of institutions and agencies to identify elements of their practices which may act to compound the problems they seek to resolve

I will try to share some of the general conclusions we have drawn from this experience, first in terms of the functioning of some of these agencies within the urban system and then in terms of our attempts to bring about change. The first thing that became clear to us was that government programmes were not benefiting everyone in the city equally. Even those programmes which purported to be universal were giving benefits to certain sections of the population often at the expense of others. The most obvious example is the ring road in the city. As in many cities this was assumed to contribute to the well-being of the city as a whole, enhancing mobility and tackling a general problem of traffic thrombosis. Car owners certainly benefited. But certain sections of the population actually lost out. It was the inner-city areas that were carved up to make way for the ring road. A few people lost their houses and many more were blighted. Furthermore, these were the very areas which had the least proportion of cars so the least number of people that could take advantage of the benefits.

Second, it became clear that even those programmes that were designed to tackle particular problems or to compensate for disadvantage very often had side-effects that outweighed the benefits. Redevelopment is a familiar example. Our observation and experience confirms much other research that on any kind of cost benefit calculation the advantages to be gained by residents of older housing areas through comprehensive redevelopment are very doubtful. First of all, it is not often the original residents of the depressed area who stay to enjoy the benefits of the redeveloped area. Second, redevelopment brings new physical capital into an area (houses, schools, roads, play areas) but often destroys the social capital which residents have invested in their neighbourhood over a long period of time. This is not easily quantifiable, as it is embodied in networks of informal relationships rather than in any formal institution. However, it can pay a tangible dividend towards the quality of life.

The third thing that came home to us was that even those programmes which were designed to offer support and help to the so-called disadvantaged groups, sometimes seemed to 'come over' in quite an opposite way to those on the receiving end. This has been well documented in the field of social security but less in the field of the 'caring' services where we have come to believe that the battery of community care provision for the elderly (meals on wheels, home helps) in practice may have very different effects from that which is often claimed. It seems possible that old people may find it a threat to their sense of status and their independence to be in receipt of meals on wheels and home helps. If this is so, then these services, in their current form, may reduce rather than enhance a person's capacity to maintain themselves in the community. A study we commissioned on the role of the schools, the youth employment service and employers in helping young people make the transition from school-life to work-life, led us to a similar kind of conclusion. It appears that many young people feel that the careers advisory system in practice serves to sort and file them into pre-ordained pigeon-holes.

With these kinds of perspectives on the functioning of local agencies, we began to try to negotiate with them for the development and testing of programmes which would discriminate positively towards those who had lost out most and begin to provide services more relevant to their values and interests. Our experience of trying to work for organizational change can be summarized crudely like this. We did gain a positive response from the education and social services and were able to design substantial joint programmes. We do not think that the responses from these two agencies were simply to do with their having progressive chairmen and chief officers. In those fields and those professions, there has already been debate (Plowden and Seebohm) which has prepared the ground and which can accommodate the kind of criticism that we developed. Furthermore, in some ways those agencies stand to gain from evidence of unmet need. However, we soon became aware that our resources were being swallowed up in experimental programmes which could easily be restricted to change at the field level.

We have a community education programme going in thirteen local schools and a decentralized social service experiment, both of which have put pressure for change on the face to face workers (on the classroom teacher, on the field social worker). These have resulted in some 'loosening up' of professional thinking and practice, greater interaction between clients, professionals and the local neighbourhood, and in greater relevance in what is offered by these agencies. However, we became aware that we were in danger of colluding in humanizing services which were still perpetuating more basic inequalities. More sensitive delivery of services is obviously a good thing in itself, but cannot hope to compensate for the massive inbuilt disadvantages which arise from the housing situation, the employment situation and the wider economic structure as a whole. The Coventry education committee has begun to work out some of the policy implications of what is happening in the schools programme and has now committed itself to some positive discrimination in the allocation of per capita and other allowances between schools in the city. So Hillfields children may begin to get a slightly happier education, in schools which are slightly better provided. But it is more doubtful whether any of this has been or will be able to make any significant impact on the real life-chances and opportunities of people in the area. Similarly, in the social services experiment we have been able to increase the level of resources available to the decentralized neighbourhood team. They have a slightly augmented staff, and a resource fund of £3,000 a year which they can use with local people to develop innovatory programmes to meet local needs. But it is increasingly clear to us that the social services are a bottomless pit in the inner city. Resources could be funnelled in endlessly and they would be absorbed like blotting paper, because field workers are constantly having to try to mop up the consequences of low income, poor housing, brutalizing employment, and inadequate shares of investment from the public sector.

Our experience in the field of housing and the environment has been very different, but has led our thinking in the same direction – away from managerial and technical solutions. The identification of unmet need in the field of housing has a rather different effect from that in education and social services. That problem cannot be solved by employing more staff or more housing welfare officers. It puts enormous pressure on the local council and housing department to spell out what their priorities are for the allocation of those very scarce resources. Land and housing are probably the most critical resources in Coventry at the moment.

The only fluid area for further development is the inner city. So it has become a real battle as to whether that land is going to be used for houses for working-class people who have always lived there or whether it is going to be used for public sector and private development of a city-wide kind. The area already houses the city's bus depot, the football ground, the central hospital, a staff hostel for a hotel and a number of industrial sites. So there is competition from the public sector which needs land to develop further central services and also increasing pressure from the private sector which is wanting land to build profitable office blocks and develop night-life entertainment. The local authority is thus bargaining with local people over how their area should be redeveloped while the private sector is upstaging them all by being able to pay prices for land that the local authority and local people cannot match.

The corporate planning and management system claims to provide a more rational basis for the allocation of land and housing on the basis of need. Our initial presumption, therefore, was that if we were able to feed in data about unmet need or about the negative consequences of existing policies, this would compete on equal terms with other data about need around the city. However, experience began to suggest that the planning and management system did not respond neutrally. It appeared to have within it a systematic bias in favour of certain interests – a bias which was not altogether within the control of the elected democratic system. We had to begin to account for the fact that a local authority which had managed to build an internationally famous city centre, prestige civic monuments and award winning estates had somehow failed to produce similarly efficient and well-coordinated operations in Hillfields. For a long time, we assumed that the problems were lack of data, or bureaucratic rigidity, or technical incompetence. But it became clear that the local authority is not incompetent, does not lack technical expertise; it has a highly sophisticated corporate management system which manages to serve certain interests in the city very well. The important thing was to look at whose interests were in practice being served by the operations of that system and whose interests were not – who gained and who lost from the outputs of the local authority. Coventry divides very obviously into a north and a south; a south that has large houses, wide tree-lined roads, attractive parks and open space, and a north which has congested housing, dense industry, little open space – a clear contrast between haves and have-nots. The policies and programmes of the local authority, whatever their intention, did not seem in practice to be compensating for those blatant inequalities. Indeed, in some respects, the already better-off areas and groups within the population seemed to be creaming off the main benefits. The corporate management system operated as if the whole population was homogeneous in its needs, and did not draw effective attention to questions of economic and political distribution. Plans and reports acknowledged 'priority areas' but the data was presented in highly technical, sanitized terms, projected into the future; ten-year plans, fifteen-year plans, raised to higher and higher plateaux of generality, so that any plan for Hillfields had been pre-related to the plan for the city, for the sub-region, and for the metropolitan area. The conflicts of interest were thus reconciled by being raised to a level of universality where it appeared that all people had interests in common. At the local level, it was quite clear that some areas and some sections of the population were systematically gaining while others were systematically losing.

The third insight brought home to us was the extent to which the technical management system was not really open to effective political challenge even to those who were equipped with alternative data and analysis. I have suggested that the corporate management system was serving up to the main local-authority committees a consensual view of the city based on homogenized data which obscured underlying conflicts of interest and areas of unmet need. CDP was serving up to local residents and to councillors a different view of the city based upon finer-grain data which exposed some of the inequalities and problems. But we found that the traditional democratic procedures did not necessarily provide an effective point of leverage for alternative views. We have only very small examples of this but I believe they apply more widely.

Hill's Plastics, (a subsidiary of Chrysler UK) has a small factory at the end of the two streets in the GIA (General Improvement Area). Local residents were in dispute with them about the use of the streets. They wanted the streets closed off, traffic-free, so that they could be landscaped and improved. Hill's Plastics wanted turning space for their lorries. The local-authority planning department had to decide. Residents came to feel that this issue was not being decided in the scientific, cost-benefit terms that the management system led them to believe but that it was, in practice, a hard political fight between Chrysler (UK) and a handful of residents from two streets. The model of the democratic system that we had been operating with was a naive and false one. We had assumed the democratic system to be a kind of pyramid in which all are represented but in which some people have less access to the top. Experience of struggle with local people 'demystified' this picture for us. It became clear that only a very narrow section of the decisions which were affecting the lives of the people in our area lay within the control of the democratic system, even at the apex of the pyramid. A much larger and stronger set of variables lay in sections of the economy which were not within the control of local or indeed central government. The important thing to understand was the role played by the state in mediating and servicing the interests of the private sector.

The pluralist snooker game

A man with the unlikely name of Schattschneider has said that 'the flaw in the pluralist heaven is that the heavenly chorus sings with a strong upper-class accent'. The pluralist view of the social system is a kind of snooker game in which different interest groups in society are all jostling with each other. The pluralist view is that the snooker balls are all different sizes and colours but they are all jostling in the same game. The competition is seen to be a bit unequal but the rules of the game are basically fair. The pluralist solution is to help those who are currently losing out to compete more effectively.

The early formulations of the CDP experiment implied a consensus

H

model of social change. This is based on the assumption that social problems are 'malfunctions' which can be cured by adjustments and rearrangements within the existing operating systems. The problems are defined mainly in terms of failures of coordination and communication, and the focus of change is thus on management and administration and the non-participant. The central tactic is debate.

Observation and experience in the project areas has led many CDP teams to reject this initial prescription in favour of a pluralist model of social change. This is based on the assumption that social problems arise from 'imbalances' in the democratic and bureaucratic systems. The problems are defined mainly in terms of failures of participation and representation of certain interests in the political process, and the focus of change is thus on politicians, policy-makers and the disenfranchised. The central tactic is bargaining and negotiation.

A growing awareness of 'the flaw in the pluralist heaven' has forced a number of the CDPs towards a structural class-conflict model of social change. This is based on the assumption that social problems arise from a fundamental conflict of interests between groups or classes in society. The problems are defined mainly in terms of inequalities in the distribution of power and the focus of change is thus on the centres of organized power (both private and public). The main tactic is organization and raising of levels of consciousness.

Servicing the disadvantaged outside the work-place
Analysis of social problems in terms of structural class conflict has often led to the assertion that the only possibilities for change lie in revolutionary change of control of the means of production. That kind of crude reductionism ignores the changes which have taken and continue to take place in the relationship between the traditional classes in advanced capitalist societies. In particular it ignores the changes in the relationship between private capital and the state, and (of special relevance to CDP areas) within the state apparatus itself at the local level. There has been some attention to these changes at the macro-level, but much less study of their impact in the fine-grain.

The study of small disadvantaged areas is beginning to show up some of the ways in which the fluctuations of capitalism have had consequences outside the work-place. The task is to understand better the ways in which the processes have worked to the disadvantage of particular sections of the population in concrete situations; to trace the roles played by the state, both centrally and locally; and to begin to test out some of the strategies for challenging the course of these processes. The trade-union movement has traditionally protected its members' interests in relation to inequality and injustice at the work-place. It seems to be much less well equipped to service its members in relation to what is happening outside the work-place. There are as yet few agencies geared up to service the political needs of the disadvantaged working class outside their work-place. Experience in CDP has begun to suggest some of the kinds of service that might be offered:

Information and intelligence

Help to residents in the gathering of information about their own situation (e.g. household surveys, census analyses) and about how decisions affecting their lives are made (e.g. information about the employment and investment plans of local firms; the forward plans and programmes of government departments, etc.).

Hard skills

A pool of expertise to be drawn upon by residents and their representatives on a 'hire or fire' basis. The range of useful skills include solicitor, planner, accountant, public health inspector, income and welfare rights. The aim is to demystify the knowledge which such specialists have and to share it as openly and widely as possible.

Adult education and community development

Helping groups and individuals to identify and define the issues they wish to tackle. Feeding in information and intelligence, and access to a pool of hard skills (as described above). Linking groups and individuals up with other organized movements working for similar changes. Collaborating with groups in learning about their own situation and from their experience of trying to change it.

4 Living and working in the city

Introduction

In this final section a number of papers have been included under the general heading of 'Living and working in the city'. The first five are included for the varying insights they offer into class life and culture within our cities. Banfield (4.1) draws attention to the concept of class culture and the view that styles of life operate in such a way as to give the city a distinctive form, setting in turn limits to what policymakers can achieve. Cohen (4.2) examines the way in which the culture of London's East End has been affected by redevelopment. Parker (4.3) looks at the generation of delinquency within a district of Liverpool. McInnes (4.4) sketches a description of what he takes to be working-class culture and, finally, Deakin and Ungerson (4.5) discuss the concept of the ghetto, the restriction of choices found there, and the determinants of life change for the black community in London.

Articles 6–10 shift the discussion towards work. The key paper here is that by Bowles and Gintis (4.6) which, though American, puts the finger on one of the key issues in education – the degree to which the education system's function of preparing the young for adult work roles constrains the type of personal development that education can foster. The debate is continued in the paper by Coleman (4.9) which examines the changes caused by urban industrial development and the implications of this for learning. As work has now left the home for good it has had the effect of leaving the latter less rich in learning opportunities. However, at the same time the modern workplace is denied to the young as a place for learning until they enter it as workers. Coleman suggests that educational institutions should draw on the resources of the local community and involve the young in types of activity other than purely intellectual ones, thereby helping to reduce the relationship between educational performance and family background which the current system tends to reinforce. The section ends with an article by Dore (4.10) who examines the qualification inflation that has gone on in British education and questions the rationality of the system.

4.1   The imperatives of class

Edward C. Banfield

American sociologists define social class in very different ways: by
objective criteria (income, schooling, occupation), subjective criteria
(attitudes, tastes, values), and position in a deference hierarchy (who looks
up to whom), among others. Whatever criteria are used, it turns out that
essentially the same pattern of traits is found to be characteristic of the
class. 'All who have studied the lower class,' writes Lee Rainwater, one of
those who has studied it most, have produced findings that suggest a
'distinct patterning' of attitudes, values, and modes of behaviour.[1] The
same can be said of those who have studied the working, middle and upper
classes. Each class exhibits a characteristic patterning that extends to all
aspects of life: manners, consumption, child-rearing, sex, politics, or
whatever. In the United States over the past half century these patternings
have been described – although never with the completeness that an
ethnographer would want – in hundreds of books and articles. By and large
these many accounts agree.

Various principles have been advanced by which to rationalize or
'explain' the association of the many, heterogeneous traits that have been
found to constitute each 'distinct patterning'. Probably no one of these is
best for all purposes. For the purpose here – namely, analysis of social
problems from a policy standpoint – the most promising principle seems to
be that of psychological orientation toward the future. Consequently, in
what follows much will be made of the concepts 'present-' and 'future-
orientation'. The theory or explanatory hypothesis (it cannot be called a
'fact', although there is some evidence to support it)[2] is that the many traits
that constitute a 'patterning' are all consequences, indirect if not direct, of
a time horizon that is characteristic of a class. Thus, the traits that
constitute what is called lower-class culture or life style are consequences

Source: *The Unheavenly City Revisited* (1973) Little, Brown and Company, pp. 52–63,
69–72.

of the extreme present-orientation of that class. The lower-class person lives from moment to moment, he is either unable or unwilling to take account of the future or to control his impulses. Improvidence and irresponsibility are direct consequences of this failure to take the future into account (which is not to say that these traits may not have other causes as well), and these consequences have further consequences: being improvident and irresponsible, he is likely also to be unskilled, to move frequently from one dead-end job to another, to be a poor husband and father....

It is useful to employ the same principle – ability or willingness to provide for the future – to account for the traits that are characteristic of the other class cultures as well. The working class is more future-oriented than the lower class but less than the middle class, the middle class in turn is less future-oriented than the upper. At the upper end of the class-cultural scale the traits are all 'opposite' those at the lower end.

It must be understood that the perfectly present- and future-oriented individuals are ideal types or constructs; the time horizon theory is intended as an analytical tool, not as a precise description of social reality.[3] In this it is like that familiar category of economic analysis, the 'perfectly competitive market', in which all buyers and sellers have perfect information and none is able to influence the price at which anything is sold. In the real world, of course, there never was, and never will be, such a market; that markets are *more or less* competitive is enough, however, to make the concept indispensable in economics. It is pointless to inquire how many people are 'perfectly' present- or future-oriented (lower or upper class) – undoubtedly there are none. If the concepts are useful, it is in helping one to think about behaviour that approximately corresponds to the model.

The general agreement that exists as to the content of the several class cultures does not extend to the theories about the *causes* of cultural difference and of cultural change. On the one side, there are those who stress the importance of 'social heredity'. They think of the individual as largely formed in infancy and childhood by influences that reflect the collective experience of the group: by the time he has reached adolescence, his ways of thinking and feeling have been ineradicably marked by these influences. '[C]ertain possibly critical emotional, linguistic, and cognitive patterns associated with social background are already present at the age of three,' writes Jerome S. Bruner, an educational psychologist. The young child's social background, he adds, influences the way he learns to set goals, mobilize means, and delay or fail to delay gratification.[4]

On the other side, there are those who consider these early influences relatively unimportant in shaping later behaviour as compared to situational factors like income, schooling, and social standing that are either avenues to or obstacles in the way of opportunity. Elliot Liebow, for example, in *Tally's Corner*, a book about a group of Negro streetcorner men in Washington, D.C., after acknowledging that each generation provides 'role models' for the succeeding one, goes on to assert that:

> of much greater importance for the possibilities of change, however, is the fact that many similarities between the lower-class Negro father and son (or mother and daughter) do not result from 'cultural transmission' but from the fact that the son goes out and independently experiences the same failures, in the same areas, and for much the same reasons as his father. What appears as a dynamic, self-sustaining cultural process is, in part at least, a relatively simple piece of social machinery which turns out, in rather mechanical fashion, independently produced look-alikes.[5]

Thus, when Richard, one of the streetcorner men, squanders a week's pay in two days, it is not because he is unaware of or unconcerned with his future: 'He does so precisely because he is aware of the future and the hopelessness of it all.'[6]

Obviously from a policy standpoint it makes a great deal of difference whether one emphasizes 'social heredity' or 'social machinery'. One who emphasizes the former will expect little from measures that are intended to change the individual by improving his opportunities; he will be inclined to think that one must first change the culture in which the individual is so largely formed – something that takes time – a generation or two at least – if it can be done at all. By an odd quirk of reasoning, the difficulty – perhaps impossibility – of bringing about change quickly and according to plan seems to some social scientists to justify giving the 'social machinery' theory preference as an explanatory principle even though its truth value may be less.[7]

For the present it suffices to alert the reader to the difficulty – and the relevance – of the 'social heredity' versus 'social machinery' question. Clearly the subcultures that are described below are not fixed and unchangeable. Even cultures (as opposed to subcultures) sometimes change with remarkable speed. Witness, for example, the 'cultural revolution' of China, during a stage of which once-venerated scholars were dragged through the streets by their Red Guard students. If, however, one takes at all seriously the principal insights of social science – represented by the concepts of culture, personality, and social structure – one must expect a high degree of continuity in most behaviour. Indeed, one must expect behaviour sometimes to persist in the face of conditions that offer powerful inducements to change.

The time-horizon theory does not prejudge this question. It merely asserts that the traits constituting a culture or life style are best understood as resulting from a greater or lesser ability (or desire) to provide for the future. Whether the time horizon of an individual is mainly passed on to the individual by cultural transmission, mainly an adaptation that he more or less rationally makes to the realities of his situation (poverty or racial discrimination, for example) or − by far the most likely possibility − the outcome of a complex interaction between *both* sets of forces, has to be decided (so far as it *can* be decided) in accordance with the facts of particular cases and not in the abstract.[8]

The reader is asked to keep in mind that members of a 'class' as the word is used here are people who share a 'distinct patterning of attitudes, values, and modes of behaviour', *not* people of like income, occupation, schooling, or status. A lower-class individual is likely to be unskilled and poor, but it does not follow from this that persons who are unskilled and poor are likely to be lower class. (That Italians eat spaghetti does not imply that people who eat spaghetti are Italian!) The reader is reminded also that the truth of the observations about class cultures that are summarized below does not in the least depend upon that of the time-horizon theory used to 'explain' them. If it should be shown that Richard is not present-oriented, what is crucial for present purposes − namely, that he had others like him exhibit a distinct patterning of traits − would have to be accounted for in some other way.

Strong correlations exist between IQ and socioeconomic status, and some scholars have presented evidence tending to show that they are due in large part to genetic factors.[9] Ability (or willingness) to take account of the future does not appear to have much relation to intelligence or IQ; however, it is not implausible to conjecture that some genetic factor may influence it. The position taken here, however, is that time horizon is a social, not a biological, product.

The upper class[10]
At the most future-oriented end of the scale, the upper-class individual expects a long life, looks forward to the future of his children, grandchildren, great-grandchildren (the family 'line'), and is concerned also for the future of such abstract entities as the community, nation, or mankind. He is confident that within rather wide limits he can, if he exerts himself to do so, shape the future to accord with his purposes. He therefore has strong incentives to 'invest' in the improvement of the future situation − i.e., to sacrifice some present satisfaction in the expectation of enabling someone (himself, his children, mankind, etc.) to enjoy greater satisfactions at some future time. Future-oriented culture teaches the

individual that he would be cheating himself if he allowed gratification of his impulses (for example, for sex or violence) to interfere with his provision for the future.

The upper-class individual is markedly self-respecting, self-confident, and self-sufficient. He places great value on independence, curiosity, creativity, happiness, 'developing one's potentialities to the full', and consideration for others. In rearing his children, he stresses these values along with the idea that one should govern one's relations with others (and, in the final analysis, with one's self) by *internal* standards rather than by conformity to an externally given code ('not because you're told to but because you take the other person into consideration').[11] The upper-class parent is not alarmed if his children remain unemployed and unmarried to the age of thirty, especially if they remain in school.[12] He does not mind being alone; indeed, he requires a good deal of privacy. He wants to express himself (he may carry self-expression to the point of eccentricity), and, in principle at least, he favours self-expression by others. He takes a tolerant, perhaps even an encouraging, view of unconventional behaviour in sex, the arts, and politics. He is mindful of the rights of others and wants issues to be settled on their merits and by rational discussion. He deplores bigotry (which is not to say that he has no prejudices) and abhors violence in personal relations.

It will be seen that two features of this culture – the disposition to postpone present satisfaction for the sake of improving matters in the future and the desire to 'express one's personality' – are somewhat antagonistic. Upper-class (that is, future-oriented) culture permits the individual to emphasize either theme. If he thinks that his means (money, power, knowledge, and the like) are almost certainly adequate to maintain him and his 'line' throughout the future he envisions, the future-oriented individual has no incentive to 'invest' (that is, trade present for future satisfaction) and may therefore emphasize self-expression.[13] If, on the other hand, he thinks that his means may *not* be adequate (he will think this, of course, no matter how large his means if his plans for the future are grand enough), he is likely to emphasize self-discipline so that he may acquire the larger stock of means that he thinks he needs. Insofar as he chooses the expressive alternative, the upper-class individual's style of life may resemble the present-oriented one of the lower class. But whereas the lower-class individual is capable *only* of present-oriented behaviour, the upper-class one can choose. He may, for example, do some things that require a high degree of skill, discipline, and judgment, living the rest of the time from moment to moment. Even if he lives from moment to moment all the time, he does so by choice – it is his 'thing', his mode of self-expression. By contrast, the 'true' present-orientedness of the lower class is both unrelieved and involuntary.

The upper-class individual feels a strong attachment to entities (formal organizations, the neighbourhood, the nation, the world) toward which he stands, or wants to stand, in a relation of fellowship.[14] He sees the 'community' (or 'society') as having long-range goals and the ability to shape the future. He tends to feel that it is one's responsibilty to 'serve' the community by assisting in efforts for its improvement – perhaps because, his own goals being long-range ones, he has a stake in the future of the community. At any rate, he tends to be active in 'public service' organizations and to feel a strong obligation (which he does not always act upon, of course) to contribute time, money, and effort to worthy causes.[15] (In the South the upper-class attitude in these matters is different. As W. J. Cash remarked, the aristocratic ideal of the planter became corrupted by frontier individualism, which, 'while willing enough to ameliorate the specific instance, relentlessly laid down as its basic social postulate the doctrine that every man was completely and wholly responsible for himself'.[16])

The middle class
The middle-class individual expects to be still in his prime at sixty or thereabouts; he plans ahead for his children and perhaps his grandchildren, but, less future-oriented than the ideal typical member of the upper class, he is not likely to think in terms of 'line' or to be much concerned about 'mankind' in the distant future. He, too, is confident of his ability to influence the future, but he does not expect to influence so distant a future as does the upper-class individual, nor is he as confident about the probable success of his efforts to influence it. The middle-class individual's self-feelings are a little less strong than those of the upper-class individual; he is also somewhat less desirous of privacy. Although he shows a good deal of independence and creativity and a certain taste for self-expression, these traits rarely lead to eccentricity. He is less likely than the upper-class individual to have means that he considers adequate to assure a satisfactory level of goal attainment throughout his anticipated future. Therefore, 'getting ahead' – and the self-improvement and sacrifice of impulse gratification that it requires – will be more likely to take precedence with him over 'the expression of one's personality'. In the lower middle class, self-improvement is a principal theme of life, whereas in the upper middle class, self-expression is emphasized. Almost without exception, middle-class people want their children to go to college and to acquire the kind of formal training that will help them 'get ahead'. In matters of sex, the middle-class individual is (in principle, at least) 'conventional', and in art and politics, too, he is more ready than the

upper-class individual to accept the received opinion. He has regard for the rights of others; he deplores bigotry and abhors violence. He does not, however, hold these attitudes as strongly as do members of the upper class.

The middle-class individual does not feel as strong a sense of responsibility to the community as does the upper-class one, and he defines the community somewhat less inclusively. He wants (in principle, at least) to 'belong' to a community and to be of 'service' to it, and accordingly he joins organizations, including 'service' ones. (In the lower middle class, the taste for public service and reform is relatively weak: the individual usually votes against public improvements that will not benefit him directly.) The middle-class individual, however, is less willing than the upper-class one to give time, money, and effort for public causes.

The working class

The working-class individual does not 'invest' as heavily in the future, nor in so distant a future, as does the middle-class one.[17] He expects to be an 'old man' by the time he is fifty, and his time horizon is fixed accordingly. Also, he has less confidence than the middle-class individual in his ability to shape the future and has a stronger sense of being at the mercy of fate, a 'power structure', and other uncontrollable forces. For this reason, perhaps, he attaches more importance to luck than does the middle-class individual. He is self-respecting and self-confident, but these feelings are less marked in him than in the middle-class individual and they extend to a somewhat narrower range of matters. As compared to the middle-class individual, he is little disposed toward either self-improvement or self-expression; 'getting ahead' and 'enlarging one's horizon' have relatively little attraction for him. In rearing his children, he emphasizes the virtues of neatness and cleanliness, honesty, obedience, and respect for external authority. (As David Riesman has observed, the problem in the working class is not, as in the upper middle class, to stimulate children; rather, it is to control them – 'to teach them faith, respect, and obedience, rather than independence of mind and development of talents'.[18]) If his children do not go to college, the working-class individual does not mind much. In his relations with others, he is often authoritarian and intolerant, and sometimes aggressive. He is not only a bigot but a self-righteous one. Violence and brutality are less shocking to him than to middle-class persons; indeed, he regards them – up to a point – as normal expressions of a masculine style. To the working class, the middle class appears somewhat lacking in masculinity, and the upper class – a male member of which may even weep under stress – appears decidedly feminine or 'queer'.

The working-class individual's deepest attachment is to his family (most of his visiting is with relatives, not friends). However, his relationship to his wife and children is not as stable or as close – for instance, does not involve as much companionship – as these relationships tend to be in the middle class.[19] Privacy is of less importance to him: he likes to have people around, and the noises and smells that they make seldom bother him (when he goes on vacation it is not to the country, which he finds too quiet and lonely, but to crowded resorts). The sense of sharing a purpose with others is not as important to him as it is to members of the upper classes, and when he joins an organization it is more likely to be for companionship and 'fun' than for 'service' or civic improvement. He may vote, especially if someone asks him to as a favour. His opinions on public matters are highly conventional (it does not seem to occur to him that he is entitled to form opinions of his own), and his participation in politics is motivated not by political principles but by ethnic and party loyalties, the appeal of personalities, or the hope of favours from the precinct captain.

The lower class

At the present-oriented end of the scale, the lower-class individual lives from moment to moment. If he has any awareness of a future, it is of something fixed, fated, beyond his control: things happen *to* him, he does not *make* them happen. Impulse governs his behaviour, either because he cannot discipline himself to sacrifice a present for a future satisfaction or because he has no sense of the future. He is therefore radically improvident: whatever he cannot consume immediately he considers valueless. His bodily needs (especially for sex) and his taste for 'action'[20] take precedence over everything else – and certainly over any work routine. He works only as he must to stay alive, and drifts from one unskilled job to another, taking no interest in the work. As compared to the working-class individual, he 'doesn't want much success, knows he couldn't get it even if he wanted to, and doesn't want what might help him get success.'[21] Although his income is usually much lower than that of the working-class individual, the market value of his car, television, and household appliances and playthings is likely to be considerably more. He is careless with his things, however, and, even when nearly new, they are likely to be permanently out of order for lack of minor repairs.[22] His body, too, is a thing 'to be worked out but not repaired'; he seeks medical treatment only when practically forced to do so: 'symptoms that do not incapacitate are often ignored.'[23]

The lower-class individual has a feeble, attenuated sense of self; he suffers from feelings of self-contempt and inadequacy, and is often apathetic or dejected. (In her discussion of 'very low-lower class' families, Eleanor Pavenstadt notes that 'the saddest, and to us the outstanding characteristic of this group, with adults and children alike, was the self-devaluation.'[24]) In his relations with others he is suspicious and hostile, aggressive yet dependent. He is unable to maintain a stable relationship with a mate; commonly he does not marry. ('The evidence is unambiguous and powerful,' writes Marc Fried, 'that the lowest social classes have the highest rates of severe psychiatric disorder....'[25]) He feels no attachment to community, neighbours, or friends (he has companions, not friends), resents all authority (for example, that of policemen, social workers, teachers, landlords, employers), and is apt to think that he has been 'railroaded' and to want to 'get even'. He is a nonparticipant: he belongs to no voluntary organizations, has no political interests, and does not vote unless paid to do so.

The lower-class household is usually female-based. The woman who heads it is likely to have a succession of mates who contribute intermittently to its support but take little or no part in rearing the children. In managing the children, the mother (or aunt, or grandmother) is characteristically impulsive: once children have passed babyhood they are likely to be neglected or abused, and at best they never know what to expect next. A boy raised in such a household is likely at an early age to join a corner gang of other such boys and to learn from the gang the 'tough' style of the lower-class man.[26]

The stress on 'masculinity', 'action', risk-taking, conquest, fighting, and 'smartness' makes lower-class life extraordinarily violent. However, much of the violence is probably more an expression of mental illness than of class culture. The incidence of serious mental illness is greater in the lower class than in any of the others. Moreover, the nature of lower-class culture is such that much behaviour that in another class would be considered bizarre seems routine.[27]

In its emphasis on 'action' and its utter instability, lower-class culture seems to be more attractive to men than to women. Gans writes:

> The woman tries to develop a stable routine in the midst of poverty and deprivation; the action-seeking man upsets it. In order to have any male relationships, however, the woman must participate to some extent in his episodic life style. On rare occasions, she may even pursue it herself. Even then, however, she will try to encourage her children to seek a routine way of life. Thus the woman is much closer to working-class culture, at least in her aspirations, although she is not often successful in achieving them.[28]

Each class culture implies – indeed, more or less requires – a certain sort of physical environment. It follows that a city (or district within a city) which suits one culture very well is likely to suit another very poorly or not at all.

To an upper-class individual, having a great deal of space at one's disposal is important both practically and symbolically; the demand for space, a city planner-economist observes, 'seems to be a deeply ingrained cultural value associated not only with such functional needs as play space for children, but also with basic attitudes toward nature, privacy, and the meaning of the family'.[29] Being by oneself a good deal – and therefore having room enough for privacy – is essential to the development of a well-defined self; in the middle and upper classes, but not in the working class, it is thought essential that each child have a room of his or her own. The higher a family is on the class-culture scale, the wider the expanse of lawn (or in the case of an apartment house, the thicker the walls) that it wants between it and the neighbours. Similarly, the higher the commuter is on the scale, the more important it is to him to ride to work in solitary splendour. For the lower-middle-class person a car pool will do – it is better than the bus; the upper-middle-class person, however, finds even that distasteful.

In the middle- and upper-class cultures, one's house and grounds afford opportunities for self-improvement and self-expression.[30] To the upper-class individual, it is the latter value that is usually more important: the house is the setting for and the representation of his family line ('house'). The middle-class individual is more likely to value his house for giving scope to his impulse to improve things – not only physical things (the house and grounds) but also, and especially, his own and his family's skills, habits, feelings, and attitudes. (The do-it-yourself movement is at least in part an expression of the middle-class taste for mastering skills and 'expressing one's personality'.) The middle-class individual – particularly the *lower*-middle-class one – also regards the house as a means of improving his social status; having a 'good address' helps one rise in the world.

In the upper- and middle-class cultures, the neighbourhood and community are as important as the house and are hardly to be separated from it. It is essential to live where there are good schools, for otherwise the children might not get into good colleges. Other community facilities – parks, libraries, museums, and the like – are highly valued, as are opportunities to be of 'service' by participating in civic organizations. The middle- or upper-class individual wants to feel that his local government is honest, impartial, and efficient. At the upper end of the scale, especially, he wants a sense of 'belonging' to a 'community' – that is, of standing in a fellowship relation to his neighbours (even though he may never see them) and thus of constituting with them a moral entity – not unlike the Puritan congregation of visible saints in the seventeenth century. This desire to belong to a community partly accounts for the exclusiveness of the 'better' neighbourhoods and suburbs. The exclusion of all who are not parties to the covenant (in the language of Puritanism) is a precondition of fellowship: a community, after all, consists of people who feel a sense of oneness. Where the principle of exclusion appears to be – and perhaps is – racial or ethnic, the neighbours are likely to see that in the pursuit of one of their values they have infringed upon another. Those who feel most strongly the obligation to be of 'service' and to act 'responsibly' – upper-middle and upper-class Jews, especially – often resolve the conflict by sponsoring a strenuous community effort to bring a certain number of Negroes (or whatever group is being discriminated against) into the neighbourhood.[31]

To the working class, a different set of values to accord with its life style governs the choice of physical arrangements in the city. Space is less important to the working-class family than to the middle- or upper-class one. It prefers being 'comfy' to having privacy; it is thought natural for children to sleep two or three to a room or perhaps even to a bed. Having neighbours – even noisy ones – down the hall or in a house that is adjoining or almost adjoining is taken for granted. The working-class individual has few deep friendships with his neighbours, but he likes knowing who they are and he likes seeing – and even hearing – their goings-on. (It was because the Italian working-class residents of Boston's West End took this interest in one another that Herbert J. Gans called his account of them *The Urban Villagers.*) From the working-class point of view, middle- and upper-class neighbourhoods are dull and lonely. Riding to work by oneself is no fun either; the working-class person prefers a car pool but does not mind a bus or subway.

When he must choose between more and better community facilities on the one hand and lower taxes on the other, the working-class individual usually chooses the latter. He will be satisfied if his children graduate from high school, and any school that is not a blackboard jungle will do. Parks and libraries matter to him even less than schools. He has no desire to participate in community improvement projects and no wish to feel himself part of a community, excpet perhaps an ethnic one. If his neighbours are a mixed lot, some being hardly sane and others less than respectable, that does not concern him: he is likely to take the attitude that so long as they do not interfere with him, they can do or be what they please.

To this last statement an important qualification must be attached. The working-class individual is likely to become ugly and aggressive if members of an ethnic or racial group that he dislikes begin to 'take over' his neighbourhood. He is more apt to be prejudiced than are members of the middle class and much less apt to conceal his prejudice. There is no talk in working-class neighbourhoods about 'responsibility for reducing racial tensions'.

In some areas the movement of factories to the suburban ring has led to the building of residential suburbs that are working class. Physically, these look much like middle-class ones, but in style of life the two differ sharply. The working-class suburbanite's house is not a way station on the road to something better, as is often the case with the middle class. He is also less likely than is his middle-class counterpart to forego his favourite TV programme in order to collect for the Heart Fund or 'serve the community' in some other way.[32]

The lower-class individual lives in the slum, which, to a greater or lesser extent, is an expression of his tastes and style of life. The slum, according to the sociologist Marshall B. Clinard, is a way of life with its own subculture. The subcultural norms and values of the slum are reflected in poor sanitation and health practices, deviant behaviour, and often a real lack of interest in formal education. With some exceptions, there is little general desire to engage in personal or community efforts for self-improvement. Slum persons generally are apathetic toward the employment of self-help on a community basis, they are socially isolated, and most sense their powerlessness. This does not mean that they are satisfied with their way of life or do not want a better way to live; it is simply that slum apathy tends to inhibit individuals from putting forth sufficient efforts to change the local community. They may protest and they may blame the slum entirely on the outside world, but at the same time they remain apathetic about what they could themselves do to change their world.[33]

Although he has more 'leisure' than almost anyone, the indifference ('apathy' if one prefers) of the lower-class person is such that he seldom makes even the simplest repairs to the place that he lives in. He is not troubled by dirt and dilapidation and he does not mind the inadequacy of public facilities such as schools, parks, hospitals, and libraries; indeed, where such things exist he may destroy them by carelessness or even by vandalism. Conditions that make the slum repellent to others are serviceable to him in several ways.[34] First, the slum is a place of excitement — 'where the action is'. Nothing happens there by plan and anything may happen by accident — a game, a fight, a tense confrontation with the police; feeling that something exciting is about to happen is highly congenial to people who live for the present and for whom the present is often empty. Second, it is a place of opportunity. Just as some districts of the city are specialized as a market for, say, jewellery or antiques, so the slum is specialized as one for vice and for illicit commodities generally

Dope peddlers, prostitutes, and receivers of stolen goods are all readily available there, within easy reach of each other and of their customers and victims. For 'hustlers', the slum is the natural headquarters. Third, it is a place of concealment. A criminal is less visible to the police in the slum than elsewhere, and the lower-class individual, who in some parts of the city would attract attention, is one among many there. In the slum one can beat one's children, lie drunk in the gutter, or go to jail without attracting any special notice; these are things that most of the neighbours themselves have done and that they consider quite normal.

Notes

1 Lee Rainwater, 'The problem of lower-class culture and poverty-war strategy' in Daniel P. Moynihan (ed) *On Understanding Poverty* (New York: Basic Books, 1969), p. 241.

2 For a critical review of some of the literature on 'time perspective' by a psychologist, see Vernon L. Allen's essay in the volume edited by him: *Psychological Factors in Poverty* (Chicago: Markham Publishing Company, 1970).

3 An ideal type 'is a freely created mental construct ... by means of which an attempt is made to "order" reality by isolating, accentuating, and articulating the elements of a recurrent social phenomenon ... into an internally consistent system of relationships'. Julius Gould and William L. Kolb (eds) *UNESCO Dictionary of the Social Sciences* (New York: The Free Press, 1964), p. 312.

   Most of the statements about time horizons in what follows have some empirical foundation: they employ a somewhat special terminology to report facts that have been observed by social scientists and others. The main proposition, namely, that individuals and cultures have differing orientations toward the future, is of this character; so are many subsidiary propositions, such as that present-oriented persons tend to be in constant search of sensual gratifications. Some propositions, however, are *implications* of the main proposition.

4 Jerome S. Bruner, in Sterling McMurrin (ed) *The Conditions of Educational Opportunity* (New York: Committee for Economic Development, 1971), pp. 35, 36, and 65.

5 Elliot Liebow, *Tally's Corner* (Boston: Little, Brown and Company, 1967), p. 223. For Liebow's critique of the 'cultural' approach, see his footnote p. 208.

6 Liebow, *Tally's Corner*, p. 66.

7 This presumably is what Liebow means when he writes (in the passage quoted above) that the 'social machinery' theory is '... of much greater importance *for the possibility of change*'. (Emphasis added.)

8 From a methodological standpoint, the theory advanced here has some similarity to that of Melvin L. Kohn, *Class and Conformity* (Homewood, Ill.: Dorsey Press, 1969). Kohn explains the dependent variable (life style) by an intervening one (sense of efficacy) which in turn he explains by the independent one ('the cumulative effects of educational training and occupational experience'). He dismisses the concept of time horizon as a 'stereotype' in a footnote (p. 104). 'The essence of higher class position is the expectation that one's decisions and actions can be consequential; the essence of lower class position is the belief that one is at the mercy of forces and people beyond one's control, often, beyond one's understanding' (p. 189).

9 The relation between social class and IQ is a worldwide phenomenon with the correlation between socioeconomic status of parents and IQ of children being most frequently in the region of 0.35 to 0.40. When school children are grouped by socioeconomic status, the mean IQs of the groups vary over a range of one or two standard deviations (fifteen to thirty IQ points). Arthur R. Jensen, *Genetics and Education* (New York: Harper & Row, 1972), p. 153.

10 For bibliographies of descriptive accounts of the various classes see Jack L. Roach, Llewellyn Gross, and Orville Gurslin, *Social Stratification in the United States* (Englewood Cliffs, N.J.: Prentice-Hall, Inc., 1969), ch. 4.

11 Melvin L. Kohn, 'Social Class and Parental Values' *American Journal of Sociology*, 64 (January 1959): 340, 344, 350. See also his 'Social class and parent-child relationships: an interpretation' *American Journal of Sociology*, 68 (January 1963): 475.

12 Kenneth Keniston, *The Young Radicals* (New York: Harcourt, Brace and World, 1968), p. 265. Keniston's observation was made with respect to the upper middle class.

13 This should help to explain the often-noted similarity between the life style of some 'high society' and that of the lower class. See, for example, the remarks of J. A. Hobson on 'a lower leisure class whose valuations and ways of living form a most instructive parody of the upper leisure class' in *Work and Wealth* (New York: Macmillan, 1926), pp. 155–6.

14 'To him [Bertrand Russell], a family did not only mean the people who lived under the same roof: that was what he meant by the Victorian phrase "my people". "My family" meant something it can mean only to those who have grown up with family portraits: a line stretching back to the sixteenth century, and which he hoped would stretch for many generations after he was dead. A family was a line in which the generations he knew, long as they were, were only a very small part in

which his achievement was one among a long succession.

'His concern for the posterity of the human race should be seen in the context of this sense of family posterity: of generations stretching out far beyond his knowledge.' Conrad Russell, 'Memories of my father' (London) *Sunday Times Magazine*, May 14, 1972.

15 For data on the voting behaviour of various income and ethnic groups on local public expenditure issues, see J. Q. Wilson and E. C. Banfield, 'Public-regardingness as a value premise in voting behaviour' *American Political Science Review*, 58 (December 1964): 876–87. For data on participation in organizations, see Murray Hausknecht, *The Joiners: A Sociological Description of Voluntary Association Membership* (Totowa, N.J.: Bedminster Press, 1962).

16 W. J. Cash, *The Mind of the South* (New York: Knopf, Vintage Books, 1941), p. 80.

17 *Cf.* Basil Bernstein's description of the British working class, 'Some sociological determinants of perception' *British Journal of Sociology*, vol. 9 (1958).

18 David Riesman (in collaboration with Nathan Glazer), *Faces in the Crowd*, abr. ed. (New Haven: Yale University Press, 1965), p. 254.

19 According to Lee Rainwater, in *Family Design: Marital Sexuality, Family Size, and Contraception* (Chicago: Aldine Publishing Company, 1965), p. 55, in the 'upper-lower class' (the working class as defined here):

> Though husband and wife may not go their separate ways as much as in the lower-lower class, they tend to adhere to a sharper division of labour than is true in the lower-middle class, and though they may participate together in many family activities, this seems to be more the result of default (they are thrown together in the same small home) or of a desire to keep away from unwelcome involvements outside the home than to be dictated by the values of equality and togetherness that dominate the thinking of lower-middle class men and women.

20 Although Goffman's 'romantic division of the world' cuts across class lines, there is no doubt on which side the lower class is to be found. Erving Goffman, in 'Where the action is' (*International Ritual*, Garden City, N.Y.: Anchor Books, 1967, p. 268).

21 Herman H. Hyman, 'The value systems of different classes', p. 488.

22 Cohen and Hodges, 'Characteristics of the lower-blue-collar class', p. 187.

23 Daniel Rosenblatt and Edward Suchman quoted by Anselm L. Strauss

in *Where Medicine Fails* (Chicago: Aldine Publishing Company, 1970), p. 18.

24 Eleanor Pavenstedt, 'A comparison of the child rearing environment of upper lower and very low-lower class families' *American Journal of Orthopsychiatry*, 35 (1965): 89–98.

25 Marc Fried, 'Social differences in mental health' in John Kosa, Aaron Antonovsky, and Irving Zola (eds) *Poverty and Health, A Sociological Analysis* (Cambridge, Mass.: Harvard University Press, 1969), p. 113.

26 On this and on lower-class culture, see the articles by Walter B. Miller cited earlier.

27 Jerome K. Myers and B. H. Roberts, *Family and Class Dynamics in Mental Illness* (New York: Wiley, 1959), p. 174. See also A. B. Hollingshead and F. C. Redlich, *Social Class and Mental Illness* (New York: Wiley, 1958), p. 175, and S. Minuchin *et al, Families of the Slums* (New York: Basic Books, 1968), p. 34.

28 Gans, *The Urban Villagers*, p. 246.

29 William Alonso, 'The historic and the structural theories of urban form: their implications for urban renewal' *Land Economics*, 40 (May 1964): 227.

30 James Q. Wilson, in 'A guide to Reagan Country' *Commentary* (May 1967), pp. 40–1, has described vividly the care that his generation of Los Angeles boys lavished on their cars. 'After marriage,' he continues, 'devoting energy to the improvement of a house was simply a grown-up extension of what, as a juvenile, one had done with cars.'

31 In 1972 a national poll found that among suburbanites in its sample 14 per cent said that they would be 'happy', 25 per cent that they would be 'unhappy', 57 per cent that it would 'not make much difference', and 4 per cent that they 'don't know' whether to have similar-status blacks move into their communities. The corresponding figures for addition of lower-status whites were: 10, 46, 42, and 2, and for the addition of lower-status blacks (these replies included some black suburbanites): 8, 46, 43, and 3. William Watts and Lloyd A. Free (eds) *State of the Nation* (New York: Universe Books, 1973), p. 102. In general polls have shown that the higher a person's socioeconomic status, the more likely he is to favour integration of housing, transportation, and schools, as well as other forms of integration. See Paul B. Sheatsley, 'White attitudes toward the Negro' in Talcott Parsons and Kenneth B. Clark (eds) *The Negro American* (Boston: Houghton Mifflin, 1966), p. 315.

A study of social class and voting behaviour in Little Rock found: 'The higher the social class, the stronger was support for desegregation. Conversely, the lower the social class, the greater was support for segregation.' Harlan Hahn, L. Michael Ross, and Thomas F. Pettigrew, unpublished paper, 1966.

32 *Cf.* Bennett M. Berger, *Working-Class Suburb: A Study of Auto Workers in Suburbia* (Berkeley: University of California Press, 1960), ch. 5.

33 Marshall B. Clinard, *Slums and Community Development: Experiment in Self-Help* (New York: The Free Press, 1966).

34 *Cf.* John R. Seeley, 'The slum: its nature, use and users' *Journal of the American Institute of Planners*, 25 (February 1959): 10–13.

4.2 Subcultural conflict and working-class community

Phil Cohen

Introduction

What I intend to do in this paper is to try to relate some of the theories which have been produced by academic sociologists about the working-class community to some of the concrete problems which people who actually work in those situations come up against day to day. It seems to me that the key problem for so-called community activists who are on the whole mostly middle class or fringe middle class and are located in a working-class community, especially those communities that are situated in the inner ring of large cities, is that they share an abstract identitive situation with the community but are separated culturally or subculturally from the majority of people living in the area. Community organizations that develop tend to be dominated by a combination of socially-mobile working-class people and middle-class dropouts or the 'rebel' fringe; both those groups are caught in a sort of cultural 'no man's land' between the two major class formations and they tend to view each other with an incredible degree of suspicion as a result of their respective class origins. This can lead on one hand to a kind of intellectual elitism on the part of the dropout group who view their own kind of subcultural preoccupations as being necessary for access to revolutionary change. And on the other hand it can produce a sectarian localism, a notion that unless you have been born and brought up in an area that you have no right to be there, no right to be involved, and seeing the whole thing in terms of some kind of middle-class intervention from outside. And this is something which has come up recently, when we've been trying to start Project East, which is an attempt at Community action in Bethnal Green, a district in the East End of London. One of the problems here is that community struggles do not generate the kind of structural solidarity between activists and rank-and-file which is intrinsic to struggles on the shop-floor. No one really of

Source: *Working Papers in Cultural Studies*, No. 2, 1972, Birmingham University.

the community is in the same situation as a shop steward, for example. In terms of factory struggles everyone shares a common and objective position in the production process and this isn't true, on the whole, of community struggles.

This problem leads into the main theme which I want to explore here, which is the relationship between culture and community in the perspective of a class struggle. To what extent do certain community structures generate or mediate cultural or subcultural diversity? Under what conditions does cultural diversity tend to generate class-consciousness through community structures with a consciousness which transcends local sectarian community loyalties? To what extent does the breakdown of community structures as a result of redevelopment for example, generate cultural and subcultural conflict? And what possible structures of community action are implied in answering some of these questions? It seems to me that the work of academic sociologists isn't really much help in looking at these questions or in forming them either in theory or in practice, for much of this work separates the problem into two separate fields of study: community studies, Willmott and Young and so on, and cultural studies, mainly the work of Raymond Williams and Richard Hoggart. This separation of what is a single social reality in turn leads to the theoretical production of two hypostasized entities, quasi totalities: firstly, culture, which is subtracted from community, and tends to be reduced simply to ideology or value-systems, and is analysed independently of its embodiment in actual institutions: these institutions are shaped by specific community structures and these structures in turn vary within defined limits according to the historic and socioeconomic conditions in which they operate. Secondly, community subtracted from culture tends to lose its class-specificity and can almost become a spiritual value in its own right, (a markedly strong tendency among middle-class sociologists discussing community in particular). The working-class community appears as a new kind of transcendental force in history, always the same in time or space: this overview ignores the whole complex of differences within and between specific communities, differences which are determined by macro-social structures, whether they're political, ideological or economic, and the uneven and combined development of the contradictions in these structures. It is this uneven development in particular which produces quite determinate regional variations in the physiognomy of working-class life outside production and this kind of issue is ignored in that separation process I talked about.

From the point of view of community activists then, both these theoretical tendencies fail to pose the thousand-dollar question, which is the relationship between working-class life in the spheres of production and working-class life in the spheres of consumption, or outside production: a relationship in other words, between the issue of workers' control and community control. There are two factors here, and the different sectors of the working-class are involved in each field; those who are most militant and organized at the point of production tend to be the most passive and apathetic in relation to community issues, and equally those groups which are involved in community action tend to be the least politicized in relation to the issues of the work place.

I cannot discuss this in detail here, but the sources are complex and it raises quite wide issues about the impact of advanced technology, changes in the structure of the production process and the labour force and the impact of this on the working-class ideology. This we might call the first contradiction. The second one is that institutions in which working-class culture and community organization are conjointly embodied are extraordinarily resistant to change and are often disjunctive with the changing structures in production: in other words they may correspond to earlier stages in the development of the productive forces. It is the interplay of these two linked contradictions which, to my mind, create the field of force on which any action, any political action, or political movement, has to exist. What I want to do is to explore some of these issues in the context of the East End and to take some of the insights of academic sociologists, whether in the field of community studies or cultural studies, to modify and adapt these in the light of some of the things which activists have worked out, come up with, in the course of actual community action in various situations.

The purpose of Project East [in Bethnal Green] is to enable the community as a whole, and particularly vulnerable groups within it to reorganize, to conserve what is functional in traditional working-class life, and to develop new forms of organization to meet new conditions. But before this is spelt out in more detail let's look briefly at the historical background, and social dynamics of the present crisis.

The past in the present
Since the very beginning of the industrial revolution the East End has provided a kind of unofficial 'reception centre' for a succession of immigrant communities, in flight from religious persecution or economic depression. First came the Huguenots, spinners and weavers, at the end of the seventeenth century, and still today their presence survives in surnames and placenames in the area. Then, throughout the nineteenth century there was a constant immigration of Irish, mostly labourers, and small traders from Central Europe, and in the last two decades of course Pakistanis, and to a lesser extent West Indians and Greek Cypriots. Today the East End is

indeed like 'five parts of the world, put in one place'.

Each subcommunity brought with it not just specific skills, but also of course its own traditions, and cultural values. There was no question of assimilation into a dominant indigenous culture – either that of the 'native' dockland community, or of the English ruling class. What in fact happened, until recently, was that each new subcommunity, in turn, and over time became an accepted, but differentiated part of the East End by allying itself with the longer established sections of the community against another, later subcommunity. The outsiders become established, become insiders, by dissociating themselves from an even more conspicuous set of outsiders. Perhaps it is a natural human tendency to draw the line under one's own feet; at any rate in the East End integration has proceeded by means of conflict, rather than by dissolving it.

There are three main social factors underpinning this pattern of integration – the extended kinship structures which regulate socialization in each subcommunity; secondly the ecological structure of the working-class neighbourhood; and finally the structure of the local economy. In reality these factors interact and reinforce each other – but it is important to understand them, because it is precisely the elimination of these factors, the transformation of these structures which has caused the present state of tension in the area. So let's look at them briefly, one by one.

Extended kinship networks
This is a system by which the family of marriage remains linked by an intricate web of rights and obligations to the respective families of origin, and serves as a link between them. Based in the first instance on maintaining the close relationship between mother and daughter, so that when she gets married the daughter will continue to live as close as she can to 'mum', and extending in widening circles to include uncles and aunts, grandparents, nephews and nieces, and their relations, this system virtually turns the family into a micro-community, and in fact provides for many of the functions of mutual aid and support that are elsewhere carried out by agencies in the community. Obviously such a system makes for cultural continuity and stability; it reduces generational conflict to a minimum – leaving home and getting married do not become life and death issues as they do in the nuclear family: firstly, because the extended family constitutes a much richer and more diversified human environment for the child; secondly, children tend to stay at home until they get married, or to put it another way, only leave in order to do so; thirdly, getting married does not involve any divorce between the young couple and their families, but rather recruits new members into the kinship network. And although the extended family preserves historical traditions of the subcommunity,

handing them on from generation to generation, it does not serve to insulate it from the 'outside world'. On the contrary it serves as the basis for eventual integration. For the family both becomes firmly anchored in a given locality (matrilocal residence as it's technically called) and the network is continually expanding outwards; the net result is that over time the ties of neighbourhood are extended into ties of kinship and vice versa. If everybody knows everybody else in traditional neighbourhoods it is not because they are related through interlocking kinship networks, but that schoolmates, workmates, pubmates – while they may or may not be related to relatives of one's own – will tend to be related to other mates, or mates to other relatives of one's own. But this can't be explained simply in terms of the internal dynamic of kinship – the ecology of the neighbourhood also plays a part.

Ecology of the working-class neighbourhood

The close-packed back to backs, facing each other across alley ways or narrow streets, corner shops and local pubs, the turning, all help to shape and support the close textures of traditional working-class life, its sense of solidarity, its local loyalties and traditions. And this in turn is underpinned by the extended kinship networks of the traditional working-class family, which have been so well observed in Bethnal Green.

But how does the ecology of the neighbourhood work in practice? Let's take the street as an example. In these neighbourhoods the street forms a kind of 'communal space', a mediation between the totally private space of the family, with its intimate involvements, and the totally public space, for example parks, thoroughfares, etc., where people relate to each other as strangers, and with indifference. The street, then, is a space where people can relate as neighbours, can express a degree of involvement with others, who are outside the family, but yet not as strangers, it maintains an intricate social balance between rights and obligations, distance and relation in the community. It also serves to generate an informal system of social controls. For where the street is played in, talked in, sat out in, constantly spectated as a source of neighbourly interest, it is also policed, and by the people themselves. Nothing much can happen, however trivial (a child falling, a woman struggling with heavy parcels, etc.), without it becoming a focus of interest and intervention. The presence of corner shops and pubs in the turning also serves to generate social interaction at street level, as well as providing natural settings for gossip 'cliques', which, if they do nothing else, constantly reaffirm the reality of neighbourhood ties!

The net result is that neighbours as well as relatives are available to help cope with the day to day problems that arise in the constant struggle to survive under the conditions of the working-class community. And in many areas, including the East End, institutions such as loan clubs, holiday clubs and the like developed to supplement family mutual aid, and formalize the practices of 'neighbouring'.

The local economy

Perhaps the most striking feature of the traditional East End economy is its diversity; dockland, the many distributive and service trades linked to it, the craft industries, notably tailoring and furniture making, the markets. This diversity meant that people lived and worked in the East End – there was no need for them to go outside in search of jobs. The extended family remains intrinsic to the recruitment of the labour force and even to the work process itself; son followed father into the same trade or industry while many of the craft and service trades were organized into 'family concerns'. As a result of this, the situation of the work-place, its issues and interests, remained tied to the situation outside work – the issues and interests of the community.

There was a direct connection between the position of the producer and the consumer. The fierce pride of being an East-ender was often linked to the equally fierce pride of craftsmanship and skilled labour. And it was from this section of the working class – sometimes called the labour aristocracy – that the indigenous leadership was drawn; politically conscious and highly articulate in defence of local interest, both at the community level and at the point of production. This elite group was also the most socially mobile, tending to re-emigrate from the East End to the outer ring of the middle-class suburbs; as Jewish people used to put it, the distance from Bethnal Green to Golders Green was two generations. Yet their ranks were continuously replenished as new subcommunities established themselves as part of the respectable working class. There were also those less fortunate who, for a variety of reasons, fell by the wayside, and remained permanent 'outsiders' *vis-à-vis* the 'established'. They were relegated to the ranks of the labouring poor caught in a vicious circle of poverty, ill health, unemployment and lack of education. This residual group was doubly excluded – unskilled and lacking union organization they had little or no bargaining power on the labour market; and stigmatized as 'pariahs' by the rest of the community, the scapegoat for its problems, and denied any effective voice in their solution.

At any given time, then, the social structure of the community as a whole, and of the subcommunities within it tended to be polarizing into three district strata – the socially mobile elite who monopolize leadership, the respectables, who form the 'stable backbone' of the community, and the lumpen (so called) who are often driven to petty criminal activity to survive.

The future perfect versus the historical present

The social structure we've described held until the early fifties; and then, slowly at first, but with gathering momentum it began to change, and the pattern of social integration that had traditionally characterized the East End began, dramatically, to break down. Without going into a long argument about cause and effect, it is possible to say that this breakdown coincided with the wholesale redevelopment of the area, and the process of chain reactions which this triggered. The redevelopment was in two phases, the first spanning the decade of the fifties, the second from the early sixties to the present. Let's examine the impact of each in turn.

The fifties saw the development of new towns and large estates on the outskirts of East London, Dagenham, Greenleigh, etc., and a large number of families from the worst slums of the East End were rehoused in this way. The East End, one of the highest density areas in London, underwent a gradual depopulation. But as it did so, certain areas underwent a repopulation, as they were rapidly colonized by a large influx of West Indians and Pakistanis. One of the reasons why these communities were attracted (in the weak sense of the word) to such areas is often called 'planning blight'. This concept has been used to describe what happens in the take-off phase of comprehensive redevelopment in the inner residential zones of large urban centres. The typical pattern is that as redevelopment begins, land values inevitably rise and rental values fall; the most dynamic elements in local industry, who are usually the largest employers of labour tend to move out, alongside the migrating families, and are often offered economic incentives to do so; much of the existing dilapidated property in the area is bought up cheaply by property speculators and Rachman-type landlords, who are only interested in the maximum exploitation of their assets – the largest profits in the shortest time; as a result the property is often not maintained and becomes even further dilapidated. Immigrant families, with low incomes, and excluded from council housing, naturally gravitate to these areas, and their own trades and service industries begin to penetrate the local economy. This in turn accelerates the migration of the indigenous community to the new towns and estates. The only apparent exception to planning blight, in fact proves the rule. For those few areas which are linked to invisible assets – such as possessing houses of 'character', i.e. late Georgian or early Victorian, or amenities such as parks, are actually bought up and improved, renovated for the new middle class, students, young professionals, who require easy access to the commercial and cultural centre of the city. The end result on the local community is the same; whether the neighbourhood is upgraded or downgraded, long-resident working-class families move out.

As the worst effects of the first phase both on those who moved, and on those who stayed behind, became apparent, the planning authorities decided to reverse their policy. Everything was now concentrated on building new estates on slum sites within the East End. But far from counteracting the social disorganization of the area, this merely accelerated the process. In analysing the impact of redevelopment on the community, these two phases can be treated as one. No one is denying that redevelopment brought an improvement in material conditions for those fortunate enough to be rehoused (there are still thousands on the housing list). But while this removed the tangible evidence of poverty, it did nothing to improve the real economic situation of many families, and those with low incomes may, despite rent rebate schemes, be worse off. But to this was added a new poverty – the impoverishment of working-class culture. Redevelopment meant the destruction of the neighbourhood, the breakdown of the extended kinship network, which as we've seen combined to exert a powerful force for social cohesion in the community.

The first effect of the high-density, high-rise schemes was to destroy the function of the street, the local pub, the corner shop, as articulations of communal space. Instead there was only the privatized space of the family unit, stacked one on top of each other, in total isolation, juxtaposed with the totally public space which surrounded it, and which lacked any of the informal social controls generated by the neighbourhood. The streets which serviced the new estates became thoroughfares, their users 'pedestrians', and by analogy so many bits of human traffic, and this irrespective of whether or not they were separated from motorized traffic. It's indicative of how far the planners failed to understand the human ecology of the working-class neighbourhood that they could actually talk about building 'vertical streets'! The people who had to live in them weren't fooled. As one put it – they might have running hot water, and central heating but to him they were still prisons in the sky. Inevitably the physical isolation, the lack of human scale and sheer impersonality of the new environment was felt worst by people living in the new tower blocks which have gradually come to dominate the East End landscape.

The second effect of redevelopment was to destroy what we have called 'matrilocal residence'. Not only was the new housing designed on the model of the nuclear family with little provision for large low income families (usually designated as problem families!) and none at all for groups of young single people, but the actual pattern of distribution of the new housing tended to disperse the kinship network; families of marriage were separated from their families of origin, especially during the first phase of the redevelopment. The isolated family unit could no longer call on the resources of wider kinships network, or of the neighbourhood, and the family itself became the sole focus of solidarity. This meant that any problems were bottled up within the immediate interpersonal context which produced them; and at the same time family relationships were invested with a new intensity, to compensate for the diversity of relationships previously generated through neighbours and wider kin. The trouble was that although the traditional kinship system which corresponded to it had broken down, the traditional patterns of socialization (of communication and control) continued to reproduce themselves in the interior of the family. The working class family was thus not only isolated from the outside, but undermined from within. There is no better example of what we are talking about than the plight of the so called 'housebound mother'. The street or turning was no longer available as a safe playspace, under neighbourly supervision. Mum, or Auntie was no longer just round the corner to look after the kids for the odd morning. Instead the task of keeping an eye on the kids fell exclusively to the young wife, and the only safe playspace was the 'safety of the home'. Feeling herself cooped up with the kids, and cut off from the outside world, it wouldn't be surprising if she occasionally took out her frustration on those nearest and dearest! Only market research and advertising executives imagine that the housebound mother sublimates everything in her G-plan furniture, her washing machine or nonstick frying pans.

Underlying all this however there was a more basic process of change going on in the community, a change in the whole economic infrastructure of the East End. In the late fifties, the British economy began to recover from the effects of the war, and to apply the advanced technology developed during this period to the more backward sectors of the economy. Craft industries, and small-scale production in general were the first to suffer; automated techniques replaced the traditional hand skills and their simple division of labour. Similarly, the economies of scale provided for by the concentration of capital resources meant that the small-scale family business was no longer a viable unit. Despite a long rearguard action, many of the traditional industries, tailoring, furniture making, many of the service and distributive trades linked to the docks, rapidly declined, or were bought out. Symbolic of this was the disappearance of the corner shop; where these were not demolished by redevelopment, they were replaced by the larger supermarkets often owned by large combines. Even where corner shops were offered places in the redevelopment area often they could not afford the high rents. There was a gradual polarization in the structure of the labour force: on the one side the highly specialized, skilled and well-paid jobs associated with the new technology, and the high-growth sectors that employed them; on the other the routine, dead-end, low-paid and unskilled jobs associated with the labour-intensive sectors, especially the service industries. As might be expected, it was the young people, just out of school, who got the worst of the deal. Lacking openings in their fathers' trades, and lacking the qualifications for the new industries, they were relegated to jobs as vanboys, office boys, packers, warehousemen, etc., and long spells out of work. More and more people, young and old, had to travel out of the community to their jobs, and some eventually moved out to live elsewhere, where suitable work was to be found. The local economy as a whole contracted, became less diverse. The only section of the community which was unaffected by this was dockland, which retained its position in the labour market, and, with it, its traditions of militancy. It did not, though, remain unaffected by the breakdown of the pattern of integration in the East End as a whole, *vis-à-vis* its subcommunity structure. Perhaps this goes some way to explain the paradoxical fact that within the space of twelve months, the dockers could march in support of Enoch Powell, and take direct action for community control in the Isle of Dogs!

If someone should ask why the plan to 'modernize' the pattern of East End life should have been such a disaster, perhaps the only honest answer is that, given the macro-social forces acting on it, given the political, ideological, and economic framework within which it operated, the result was inevitable. For example many local people wonder why the new environment should be the way it is. The reasons are complex; they are political insofar as the system does not allow for any effective participation by the local working-class community in the decision making process at any stage or level of planning. The clients of the planners are simply the local authority or commercial developer who employs them. They are ideological insofar as the plans are unconsciously modelled on the structure of the middle-class environment, which is based on the concept of *property*, and *private ownership*, on individual differences of status, wealth etc.; whereas the structure of the working-class environment is based on the concept of community, or collective identity, common lack of ownership, wealth, etc. Similarly needs were assessed on the norms of the middle-class nuclear family, rather than the extended working-class family etc. But underpinning both these sets of reasons lie the basic economic factors involved in comprehensive redevelopment. Quite simply – faced with the task of financing a large housing programme, the local authorities were forced to borrow large amounts of capital, and also to design schemes which would attract capital investment to the area. This means that they have to borrow at the going interest rates, which in this country are very high, and that to subsidize housing, certain of the best sites have to be earmarked for commercial developers. A further and perhaps decisive factor is the cost of land, since very little of it is publicly owned and land values rise as the area develops.

All this means that planners have to reduce the cost of production to a minimum, through the use of capital-intensive techniques – prefabricated and standardized components, allowing for semi-automated processes in construction. The attraction of high-rise developments (tower blocks outside the trade) is not only that they meet these requirements, but they allow for certain economies of scale, such as the input costs of essential services, which can be grouped around a central core. As to 'non-essential' services, i.e. ones that don't pay, such as playspace, community centres, youth clubs and recreational facilities, these often have to be sacrificed to the needs of commercial developers, who of course have quite different priorities. Perhaps the best example of this happening is the notorious St Catherine's Dock Scheme. This major contribution towards solving the East End's housing problem includes a yachting marina, a luxury hotel, luxury apartment blocks, and various cultural amenities for their occupants plus – a small section of low-income accommodation, presumably to house the families of the low paid-staff who will service the luxury amenities. And lest anyone becomes too sentimental about the existing site, Telford's warehouses, etc., it should be mentioned that the original development was by the East India Company in the early nineteenth century, involved the destruction of the homes of thousands of poor families in the area, and met with such stiff opposition from them that it eventually required an Act of Parliament to get the scheme approved!

The situation facing East-enders at present, then, is not new. When the first tenements went up in the nineteenth century they raised the same objections from local people, and for the same very good reasons, as their modern counterparts – the tower blocks. What is new is that in the nineteenth century the voice of the community was vigorous and articulate on these issues, whereas today, just when it needs it most, the community is faced with a crisis of indigenous leadership.

The reasons for this are already implicit in the analysis above. The labour aristocracy, traditional source of leadership, has virtually disappeared along with the artisan mode of production. At the same time there has been a split in consciousness between the spheres of production and consumption. More and more East-enders are forced to work outside the area; young people especially are less likely to follow family traditions in this respect. As a result the issues of the work-place are no longer experienced as directly linked to community issues. Of course, there has always been a 'brain drain' of the most articulate, due to social mobility. Not only has this been intensified as a result of the introduction of comprehensive schools, but the recruitment of fresh talent from the strata below, i.e. from the ranks of the respectable working class, has also dried up. For this strata, traditionally the social cement of the community, is also in a state of crisis.

The economic changes which we have already described, also affected their position and as it were *de-stabilized* it. The 'respectables' found themselves caught and pulled apart by two opposed pressures of social mobility – downwards, into the ranks of the new suburban working-class elite. And, more than any other section, the working class were caught in the middle of the two dominant, but contradictory, ideologies of the day: the ideology of spectacular consumption, promoted by the mass media, and the traditional ideology of production, the so-called work ethic which centred on the idea that a man's dignity, his manhood even, was measured by the quantity or quality of his effort in production. If this strata began to split apart it was because their existing position had become untenable. Their bargaining power in the labour market was threatened by the introduction of new automated techniques, which eliminated many middle-range, semi-skilled jobs. Their economic position excluded them from entering the artificial paradise of the new consumer society; at the same time changes in the production process itself have made the traditional work ethic, the pride in the job, impossible to uphold. They had the worst of all possible worlds.

Once again this predicament was registered most deeply in and on the young. But here an additional complicating factor intervenes. We have already described the peculiar strains imposed on the 'nucleated' working-class family. And their most critical impact was in the area of parent/child relationships. What had previously been a source of support and security for both, now became something of a battleground, a major focus of all the anxieties created by the disintegration of community structures around them. One result of this was to produce an increase in early marriage. For one way of escaping the claustrophobic tensions of family life was to start a family of your own! And given the total lack of accommodation for young single people in the new developments, as well as the conversion of cheap rented accommodation into middle class owner occupied housing, the only practicable way to leave home was to get married. The second outcome of generational conflict (which may appear to go against the trend of early marriage, but in fact reinforced it) was the emergence of specific youth subcultures in opposition to the parent culture. And one effect of this was to weaken the links of historical and cultural continuity, mediated through the family, which had been such a strong force for solidarity in the working-class community. It is perhaps not surprising that the parent culture of the respectable working class, already in crisis, was the most 'productive' *vis-à-vis* subcultures; the internal conflicts of the parent culture came to be worked out in terms of generational conflict. What I think seems to happen is that one of the functions of generational conflict is to decant the kinds of tensions which appear face to face in the family and replace them by a generational specific symbolic system so that the tension is taken out of the interpersonal context and placed in a collective context, and mediated through various stereotypes which have the function of defusing the anxiety that interpersonal tension generates.

4.3 Delinquency on the move

Howard J. Parker

It would be a mistake to meet The Boys at the age of sixteen without knowing anything about their childhood and earlier life experiences in Roundhouse, Liverpool. This short chapter involves a brief analysis of the delinquent activities of two younger social groups from the neighbourhood – The Tiddlers and The Ritz. Whilst unrealistically divorcing delinquency from these groups' total life style, this chapter hopefully furthers several themes.

Firstly, the innovatory and adaptive nature of delinquent action is brought out. Such processes are usually missed, because research into delinquency has of late paid little attention to longitudinal and detailed ethnographic study. Over the months the downtown adolescent hangs out all his linen. Looking at his behaviour from ground level and getting tangled up in the action allows an identification of processes withheld from the outsider, sociologist or otherwise. Secondly, the analysis to follow emphasizes the importance of the *context* of delinquency: the significance of the neighbourhood and the social organization of its adolescents is monumental, a fact which general theories of delinquency have tended to obscure.

The picture then is of different-aged peer groups being involved in delinquent action simultaneously. On occasions these groups interact, but more generally their delinquent style is distinctive and independent because of their different expectations through time. Figure I illustrates this simultaneous delinquency and its changing nature. This diagram is a crude representation of the phases of delinquent activities of the three adolescent groups studied – The Boys, The Tiddlers and The Ritz. Movement is traced over a three-year period, the second and third years based on direct participant observation, the first on formal and incidental

Source: *A View from the Boys*, 1974, David and Charles, pp.46–61.

conversations carried out fairly early in the research. The diagram has several limitations. Firstly, the three groups are not samples as such, but actual social entities or networks, and thus age distributions are not 'even'; there is no smooth numerical increase as we move from left to right and downwards. Secondly, the headings used in the diagram are illustrated only implicitly on the pages to come, since in reality transition and change do not occur evenly and exactly on a particular date. Overlap of, backtracking and withdrawal from, delinquent styles are continuous. Thirdly, these delinquent 'careers' are relevant only to the members of the networks analysed during the specific fieldwork period. 'Careers' are labelled such only because clear patterns have emerged retrospectively for these particular adolescents.[1] As we shall see, small changes in the contingency mixture might have sent individual solutions in quite different directions, either more or less proscribed.

The Tiddlers

The staff from the local primary school, which takes 90 per cent of the children from the area, see most of their intakes as leading a Jekyll-and-Hyde existence. The staff argue that there is a set of standards which demands conformity, producing consistency and thus security within the school; the kids enjoy this security and know where they stand. This, they say, contrasts with the ambiguity of standards outside, where the children are not sure how their parents, brothers and sisters and peers will act and react. The staff argue that, 'In school a kid will hand in a penny or fifty pence but he will go shoplifting as soon as school's over.'

Figure 1 Delinquency on the move

	Year One	Year Two	Year Three
The Tiddlers	Naughty	Small beginnings and petty theft	Joyriders
	8–10 yr	9–11 yr	10–12 yr
The Ritz	Petty theft	Further instrumental delinquency	Catseye Kids*
	13–14 yr	14–15 yr	15–16 yr
The Boys	Instrumental delinquency	Catseye Kings	Partial withdrawal
	15–17 yr	16–18 yr	17–19 yr

*catseye : car radios.

There is some truth in this. Compared with their highly structured day in primary school, the inner core of The Tiddlers – Frankie, Bobby, Chalkie and Tiddler himself – find the rest of their day and all their holidays without much discipline, as long as they appear at mealtimes and a stipulated bedtime there will be little adult complaint. Street life and life around the Block is full of potential excitement. One favourite activity is 'bonnies' in the 'oller', making bonfires on waste ground with anything combustible. Smoking cigarettes is also an important pastime; the easiest way to get them is to 'scrounge' them from the older lads: 'Give us a ciggy' is a phrase repeated incessantly by The Tiddlers, though they are usually rewarded only by a dog-end. Another method is to buy cigarettes – from pocket money or empty-bottle money or again by scrounging: 'Lend us two pence.'

A great deal of naughtiness involves seeing what one can get away with, knocking on doors and running away, letting car tyres down, smashing bottles and, a favourite, 'giving cheek' to adults. The adults come in all shapes and sizes, with baths-attendants, store detectives and old men being preferred. The Tiddlers will also try their luck with older boys:

Chalkie	Give us a ciggy.
Fatch	Fuck off, get your own.
Chalkie	O' fuck off yourself, you tight bastard.
Fatch	Go on, beat it, before you get kicked.
Chalkie	Come on then.

Fatch grabs hold of Chalkie who immediately submits. 'OK, Fatch, I was only messin'.'

Seeing what one can get away with soon involves stealing. That things are stolen is revealed to The Tiddlers from an early age, and at this stage the 'subcultural' effect of growing up in an atmosphere that encourages theft is quite important. Kids soon learn from each other how easy it is to shoplift. Frankie can often be seen in a local department store 'up to no good'. He is only as high as the counter and can remove goods with great ease; a little hand appears, grabs the spoils and simply disappears in the crowd. Razor blades, toothpaste, soap, cosmetics, generally make good sales around the Block. There are plenty of people who will buy something cheap without asking questions. 'Some of the women says, "If you get any more, lad, you bring them to me" ' (*Chalkie*). 'This one, she says, "Now I'm not saying go and rob none, but if you get another tin I'll take it off you" ' (*Frankie*). Tiddler, who seems to have no sense of fear at all, will simply stand outside shops offering stolen goods to passers-by.

As these kids get older they start to come into contact with Authority. Departmental-store detectives and staff are usually the first to apprehend The Tiddlers, but, given the age of the children, they can take little further action. The store staff usually end up operating a ban on those they consider 'known trouble-makers'. The kids talk of this as being 'barred out': for The Tiddlers it simply adds to the fun. Just going into a store becomes a game in itself, a further experiment in what one can get away with.

A favourite target for the little ones is the parked lorry. Confectionery vans, 'sweet lorries', are the most obvious temptations. Large numbers of goods vehicles are parked in the area with padlocks that fall off and skylights that small children can get through. Occasionally the whole neighbourhood is full of children eating mints: they have mints in their mouths, in their hands and stuffed in their pockets. The word had got round and youngsters queued up to take their share, as much as they could carry, from the van. Local warehouses are another favourite with The Tiddlers. One evening the doors of a furniture removal and storage firm's warehouse were opened, no one could remember how in the excitement. Several locals helping on a holiday playscheme at the time felt a certain responsibility for the kids involved and tried to gather them up so they wouldn't bump into the police whilst carrying stolen property. Their efforts were just seen as extra excitement – the kids simply evaded their grasp and piled into the warehouse dragging out anything and everything. Records, knives, lampshades, cartons of books, festooned the area. This activity continued till the police arrived. No one was apprehended, everyone simply vanished at the critical moment.

This particular escapade was simply expressive and experimental – though such affairs also act as apprenticeships for later more serious and dangerous operations. The occasional break-ins the youth club suffers should be seen in this light, where the kids involved know their mischief, even if discovered, would not be taken to the police. They also know the club has little to offer them in the way of valuable spoils: what the escapade does offer them is excitement and practice. Similarly The Tiddlers would appear with things of no obvious value to them which happened to be available for removal: a ladder, a bucket, a tin of paint, will always provide amusement. They can be broken up, set fire to or thrown down the tenement stairs. An umbrella doesn't have to be used to keep the rain off.

Holiday playschemes, usually run on a shoe-string, provide some stimulation and acceptable supervision for the youngsters. Even so it's usually the same old trips – not Chester Zoo again – which soon bore them. So they will chase chickens, push prams in ponds, trespass on private property, give cheek to the bus conductor, get thrown out of the swimming baths and sum up a thoroughly boring trip to the airport with the final comment, 'That was fuckin' last, the best thing about that was the robbing.'

As they get to secondary-school age, The Tiddlers take an increasing interest in adulthood. They become 'little men' before their time. Care is taken over hairstyle and dress in an attempt to look like their older heroes. The Tiddlers will smoke, swear, 'act hard', they will show you their home-made 'prison' tattoos and their razor-sharp knives. They are afraid of nobody, they claim, and to prove it will tell their seniors to 'fuckin' watch it' as long as they are out of kicking distance. The Tiddlers are allowed fairly free association with The Boys mainly for their amusement value. The Boys take considerable interest in The Tiddlers' escapades:

Joey   They're fuckin' mad, Frankie and his lot. See Frankie, he's got his hand bandaged up, he did that climbing through a barbed-wire fence on the top of Bishop's wall. I says that'll stop you robbing for a bit lad. He says fuck off, I've got this hand, haven't I?

Fosser Did you see them in that old van last week, about ten of them all piled in with Tiddler driving like a madman. They're fuckin' mad those kids ...

'Fuckin' mad' is a role type used regularly by older boys in the area to describe The Tiddlers' behaviour. In this context it means daringly dangerous without adequate concern for the consequences. More often than not the 'nutter' who's 'fuckin' mad' will suffer for his lack of strategy and consideration of the long-term consequences of his action. Hence The Tiddlers are seen as 'bound to get stuck down in a few years' and 'odds on for borstal'. At present The Tiddlers are indifferent to the outcome of their small beginnings into crime. They will tell everyone how they got caught shoplifting in a way designed to imply they are fearless even in the hands of the law:

Bobby   They take you up to the office till the copper comes. Then he gives you a warning like and then they let you go, there's nothing to it.

Chalkie They don't always let you go, 'coz this jack [policeman] took me home and told me old girl, and she fuckin' murdered me.

Whilst a lot of ten-to-twelve-year olds who live in Roundhouse fall into the 'little men' category and get involved in escapades which are strictly illegal, The Tiddlers stand out as the most reckless and acknowledged 'wild' group. Their behaviour was, by the end of Year Two, no longer simply mischief, naughtiness and 'cheek'; it was behaviour the police were, and are, concerned about. The Tiddlers are now Junior Delinquents. Early in Year Three the group got hold of a couple of large bunches of car keys. Initially they would wander around the nearby streets trying to open car doors and take what they could from inside. Stealing from cars is the stock solution for obtaining extra money used by many of the area's youth and The Tiddlers had grown up with this particular pattern, as had The Ritz and The Boys.

Yet The Tiddlers' need for money was less than that of their elders, who were interested in clothes, drinking and big spending generally. They found the simplicity and pettiness of shoplifting, once it became routine, rather boring. The desire to be adult, brave, hard, to be excited and captivated by a situation, led them elsewhere. For one thing the kids from Everomer were taking cars and riding around in them. There was even a programme on TV about how the Everomer kids were having races around their blocks in stolen cars. What Everomer could do The Tiddlers could do better. Tiddler himself was the first to learn to drive, that is to learn how to connect up the ignition and drive a car in one gear. He sat in a few cars with Bobby to begin with, by way of practice. One night I remember standing with a few of the Boys by 'The Cockle'; Tiddler and Bobby had just forced open the door of a car and were trying various keys in the ignition. The next minute the engine was revving, then it was cut out, then started again, before the two little men got out and walked coolly away, much to The Boys' amusement.

From these tentative beginnings joyriding has become a common practice amongst The Tiddlers' age group. The Roundhouse joyriding team, though not as active or sophisticated as Everomer's,[2] has built up to about a dozen early adolescents displaying varying degrees of motoring expertise. The Tiddlers have shown considerable initiative and ability in learning car-key codes, makes of cars, types of gear change and various methods of starting cars such as making a circuit with a pair of scissors. Chalkie and Tiddler are now in fact fairly safe drivers, with gear changing and improved cornering part of their repertoire. Further, it is no longer enough to take any old car; the status of the car has become relevant, with Cortinas and Marinas (which the police also drive) being highly favoured. In lots of ways these youngsters are showing a desire for the straightforward respectable status of being a car owner. They talk at length about the merits and drawbacks to various cars, the only big difference from the talk of the ordinary car owner being their addition of status concerns important to their image amongst the conversation culture.

Hence talk is often centred on how fast you've been, have you had a chase off a police car, have you had a crash, a lucky escape and so on.

The new joyriders have further influenced patterns of delinquent behaviour by leaving 'stolen' vehicles inside the tenement-block courtyards. Since the police cannot officially move these vehicles until they are reported missing, Roundhouse residents' notification to the authorities of an abandoned vehicle often appears ignored. Because the car is left abandoned for several hours and since it is regarded locally as 'lost property' which belongs to no one in particular, the little kids of the area will adopt it as a sort of mobile fortress. If left long enough the vehicle will, after its play value has been exhausted, be broken up and set on fire. This practice of one age group inadvertently handing over the car to another is common to other city neighbourhoods and increases the likelihood of the very young graduating to more daring escapades over time.[3]

Taking and driving away is not a new offence in Liverpool, although during Year Three reported offences increased rapidly until about 200 vehicles per week were being reported missing from the city area. Although the Roundhouse area, as a grid reference, shows a high incidence for this offence, this figure is due mainly to the high concentration of parked cars in the area. Nor do the adolescent joyriders account for the bulk of offences; most taking and driving away is committed by older journeymen simply wanting to get from the city centre to outlying estates. Nevertheless, joyriding became during Year Three something of a craze for The Tiddlers. Its significance in this study is that it illustrates the innovatory nature of much delinquent action. Delinquency changes in character. The Tiddlers, whilst they have been involved in shoplifting and petty larceny, in keeping with certain delinquent traditions in Roundhouse, have also broken new ground. The Boys regard such joyriding escapades with a certain amazement. They regard The Tiddlers as 'nutters' and 'madmen' because 'They're doing things now we never dared do when we were kids, they're much worse than we ever were.' (*Mal.*)

A further innovation of a more serious and potentially very dangerous nature involved a petrol bomb. This incident occurred one Sunday afternoon when a police sergeant was bending over a stolen car outside the Block. As he bent down a petrol bomb came over the wall and exploded close to his feet, not injuring him. The whole incident was watched by several of The Boys as they stood on the Corner. One of The Tiddlers who'd made the attack was able to make a simple getaway completely undetected.

There was much unconvincing talk during the next few days about a plan to stone and petrol bomb the police station, but no actual incidents took place, nor are likely to. The petrol bomb seems to have been an isolated incident. It should be seen as part of The Tiddlers' attempts to be 'gangsters' or adult as they see it. By showing hatred of the police these early adolescents were reacting to their own feelings about Authority in conjunction with the hatred that they know The Boys, those they are striving to copy, feel for the police. The Tiddlers' conception of risk and fear of Authority is relatively undeveloped; they are still spontaneous in their adventures, and would be described as 'mad' or 'got no sense' simply because they lack an adequate conception of risk as regards the consequences of getting caught, which their elders know only too well.

To a large extent, parents are unaware their children are involved in such delinquent escapades. While they know of the various goings-on they tend to feel the kids involved are not theirs. Parents will usually only take disciplinary action if proof of their child's misdemeanour stares them in the face. Thus Tiddler's mother promised his teacher after he had been caught shoplifting, 'He won't cause no more bother, I take his shoes and trousers off him when he gets in so he has to stay in and watch telly.' Chalkie has not been caught yet: 'Me mam has a good idea what I'm up to but when she asks where I've been I just say I've been in the Block or playing footy, whatever I think of.'

The Boys and The Ritz recall this same sort of parental treatment. They remember vividly their attempts to hide their 'evils' from parents and their denials when accused. Fosser recalled how 'They used to lock me in my room and take my shoes. But I'd never stay locked in boy, I'd wear any old pair of fuckin' shoes. I'd never stay locked in, I used to hate it.'

The Tiddlers, then, are growing up in much the same way as The Boys before them. Forced from an early age into the Block's social milieu with its strong expressive influences, The Tiddlers looked for things to do, things to play with, excitement and a chance to show off, like all kids. The joyriding escalation has been the solution that has come most meaningfully to them. Though they are regarded by their elders as 'madder' than they ever were, this is probably merely an impression created by the novelty of such escapades to the neighbourhood. Whilst the actual delinquent styles differentiate The Tiddlers' from The Boys' early adolescence the likelihood that they will become The Boys of tomorrow is of greater significance. The Tiddlers are known to the police with two of them already on supervision order.

The Ritz

At their age level The Ritz are again the most easily identifiable social network of friends who live in Roundhouse. Although there are individuals of the same age living in the area who are regularly involved in delinquent activities, as a group The Ritz are unique. A survey of names and addresses of fourteen-to-sixteen-year olds who attended Juvenile Court in Year Two reveals that for the Roundhouse area only seven adolescents outside the network were apprehended. Observation suggests that whilst other adolescents from the area are delinquent they usually turn to shoplifting, truancy and petty theft, most of which remains undetected. The Ritz are delinquent more often and in more serious ways, so they have tended to become known to the police; most have been convicted at least once, and by the end of Year Three up to four and five times.

Although referred to locally as a 'little gang', The Ritz are merely a peer group of friends who have grown up together and spend much of their free time together. Figure 2 represents an interpretation of the size and closer friendships of the core of the network during Year Two.

Figure 2   The Ritz

	Mal		
Sammy	Jaw	Bone	Fin
Rob	Quinsey	Toggle	Mack
	Boon	Mickey	
	Woodsey		

With the exception of Toggle and Mickey, who passed the 11 + exam and were placed in 'grammar' streams at schools outside the area, all The Ritz went to the local primary and secondary schools. With the exception of Bone and Mickey they have all grown up in the area. They all recall the same naughtiness, adventures and freedom in early childhood that The Tiddlers enjoyed. Fin recalled how 'we used to pinch things from the barrows [street traders] and round the market. Meat and fruit and that, and go to this old empty house and make a fire and sit round guzzling'. Rob and Toggle claimed they had never been involved in childhood theft. Toggle felt this was because 'My old man would have murdered me if I'd got caught then. I wasn't even supposed to go in shops at all unless I was going on a message. I never robbed at all till a couple of years ago when I started going round with this lot.'

For most of The Ritz, however, early adolescence was a time for petty shoplifting and other opportunistic theft, not always for the intrinsic value of the goods:

Jaw   Me and Quinsey done a car in for a packet of fags one night. It was only for a laugh. He said, 'I bet you wouldn't screw that car for those ciggies,' so I did.

Quinsey   We'd do cars for last week's *Echo* in those days, we weren't on to catseyes or anything then, it was just for something to do in those days.

By the end of Year Two, theft was being taken more seriously, and shirts and pairs of trousers would be taken, as would articles to sell round the Block. Jaw came on to the Corner one afternoon and rather than discuss how fortunate he was not to be 'grassed on' for selling stolen goods complained, 'We've just been all round the Block trying to flog some blouses and we only got ten bob each for them in the end.'

At this time Fin and Mal, who were physically bigger and more mature than the others, were interested in becoming more adult and getting away from 'kid's stuff'. As Figure 1 suggests, The Boys were well into 'catseyes' at this time, and Mal and Fin were attracted by this, especially because of its financial returns. These two 'worked' with some of The Boys and soon learnt techniques enabling them to 'screw' cars for themselves. Mal and Fin had an 'older' style than the other Ritz boys. Their language and image suggested their desire to be 'hard' like one of The Boys:

Fin Me and Mal are just going downtown to spend some cash, we're loaded. We did two cars this morning. The first one, I had it down me kecks and we stopped and got icecreams. We was just walking along eating these icecreams, dead cool like, when this cop car goes past with the jacks looking at us. We just carried on walking like we didn't care.

Mal and Fin tended to break away from the rest of the group and get caught up in the increased policing activities with regard to 'car attacks'. During a six-month period they made a great deal of money but were twice caught red-handed. Not sufficiently deterred by police warnings they continued till eventually they were both sent to Borstal (mid Year Three).

The core of The Ritz were not drawn into stealing 'catseyes' for several months. Year Two saw them involved in more spasmodic delinquencies. Decisions about law breaking became more personalized. Sammy and Rob for instance would not entertain the idea of 'screwing' cars, whether for loose objects or catseyes. Their reasons were mainly related to the higher chances of getting caught and the greater severity of consequent court decisions. Rob also had an idea that there was a limit to when stealing was OK and breaking car windows and ripping out radios was beyond that limit. They remained involved in little more than shoplifting, playing truant, 'borrowing' scooters and mopeds from nearby carparks and trying to get into the cinema with stolen tickets. For the rest it was opportunism as usual. Jaw had a particularly successful haul:

> I walked into this shop where there were loads of watches and
> clocks. I took a couple of watches off a stand. The woman didn't
> notice. Then she went off to get some change or something for this
> old feller. She left the till open so when this old bloke wasn't looking
> I helped myself and walked out with £19.

This was no idle boast and Jaw had a pocket full of money and the watches
to prove it. Being much smaller and younger looking than the others, he
always tried to seek their attention and would soon spend the money
somewhat over-generously to aid his acceptance.

Bone and Quinsey found themselves in trouble with the law for the
second time:

Bone   The word got round that Fleets (warehouse) had been done in, so
we went down to see what was going on. It was only mouldy old
sweets and toys, but we went in and sorted out our gear [what they
wanted to take]. I came out and went and stood round a fire on the
'oller while Quinsey took the gear back to his place. After about
five minutes two plainclothes came and said, 'We saw you handing
out sweets.' They'd got Quinsey as well. We both got done for
that, Quinsey got probation and I got scrubs.

For the most part Year Two's illegal action was made up of these
spasmodic, occasional opportunistic thefts. The Ritz were not on the prowl
for 'trouble' at every spare moment. They merely wanted things to do to
break up boring periods: perhaps a game of football or a visit to the youth
club, or if the situation arose at the right moment perhaps a car break-in.
For instance, a few of them had burgled a house outside the area when
they spotted the key left in the door and found quite a lot of cash. Woodsey
had taken a casette recorder from under the seat of a car.

This pattern only changed when The Ritz got caught up in the catseye
craze. Year Three saw 'delinquency' becoming a more important theme.
'At first we thought it was dead easy. We thought we'd never get caught.
The older boys had stacks of cash so we thought we'd get some as well.'

For about three months, the summer when most of The Ritz left school,
both they and The Boys were 'screwing' cars regularly. Mickey and
Toggle's involvement was only temporary however. As we have said they
were more academically inclined than the others, and both were awaiting
CSE results and had apprenticeships fixed for the autumn. Caught in a
carpark taking a radio, they were persuaded by the consequent police

procedures that given their prospects they would be wise to stop 'robbing'. This they have done and are both still working. For the rest however, with poor job prospects, less money and more time, screwing cars continued. The core of The Ritz of Year Three – Mal, Jaw, Quinsey, Woodsey and Boon – have become the new 'Catseye Kids', and despite several arrests are still not completely deterred, though more cautious. Their delinquent careers are following closely those of The Boys before them and will almost certainly continue to do so. A stocktaking of visits to Juvenile Court by the end of Year Three shows these five will shortly have to face decisions affecting their continued freedom. Their chances of continuing car-radio theft and enjoying the financial gains it affords will have to be weighed carefully with the possibility of a period of incarceration if they are caught again. Their convictions to date are as follows (names are not used, to ensure anonymity):

A   Discharged for loitering with intent; supervision order under a social worker for attempted theft; Attendance Centre for theft from a vehicle.

B   Police caution for shoplifting: fine for shoplifting; supervision order under a probation officer for burglary; Attendance Centre for theft from a vehicle.

C   Police caution and visit from a Juvenile Liaison Officer for shoplifting; police caution for taking and driving away a scooter; supervision order under a social worker for attempted theft; heavy fine for theft from a vehicle.

D   Police caution for burglary; conditional discharge for burglary; fine for shoplifting; supervision order under a probation officer for theft from a vehicle.

E   Supervision order under a probation officer for theft from a vehicle and resisting arrest; heavy fine for attempted theft; loitering-with-intent charge pending.

Such brief discussions about The Tiddlers and The Ritz do not do justice to their situations. The changing nature of delinquent action through time and the variations of those involved should now be clear however. Both these groups of youngsters have 'grown up' on the Corner in the sense that much of their spare time is spent knocking around the neighbourhood and becoming involved in the ideas and actions that effervesce there.

Parents, it has been emphasized, are not always in a position to offer their children an alternative to playing unsupervised. Mum, especially, tries to keep her children out of trouble, but because of a whole series of structural constraints and family contingencies is unable to offer a real alternative to young sons who pester to be allowed to play out. This is not to deny that family mismanagement and family stress occur, and affect the children, but it is the appearance of the youngsters in the neighbourhood, for whatever reason, which is of the greatest significance. The family and the home must take their place in the etiology (the search for causal explanation) of delinquency. Some parents do keep their children out of trouble, but usually by literally not allowing them out. Given that youngsters must have some freedom, and given that most family situations simply do not make such confinement feasible, however, the family in this study is relevant mainly as an agency which has only limited control over adolescent deviancy rather than as an instigator of delinquent motivation.

It is to the street-corner world in which many Roundhouse youngsters become immersed that we must look to understand the creation of delinquent action. Here views are less conservative, traditions and mythologies of great significance, and delinquency accepted as a possible means of achieving goals. The street-corner milieu, although it is an extension of parental values, also feels the need to conceal its more deviant activities from conventional residents *because* it comprehends their values as dominant.[4] This chapter has stressed that the street-corner world both transmits delinquent traditions and provides an atmosphere for innovation and creation. The street-corner adolescent thinks out and applies himself a great deal more than he is often given credit for.

Notes

1 For a critical comment on the 'career' concept see I. Taylor, P. Walton and J. Young, *The New Criminology* Routledge and Kegan Paul, 1973, p. 157.
2 See my article 'The joys of joyriding' in *New Society,* 3 January 1974.
3 This integration of age levels in a neighbourhood is also noted and discussed by James Patrick. See *A Glasgow Group Observed* Eyre Methuen, 1973, pp. 177–8.
4 Roundhouse can be seen as a condoning or tolerant neighbourhood which has accommodated the dominant meaning system to fit in with its position in society. The street-corner milieu is a further extension of this accommodation which could perhaps be regarded as a 'subculture of delinquency'. What is important is the introduction of a conceptualization which, unlike the cultural diversity perspective of the British subcultural school, allows for an overlap and cross-fertilization between versions of social morality and normative order.

4.4   Portrait of working-class culture

Colin MacInnes

Soccer
Certainly the greatest working-class achievement; for of all the games invented by the English, this is the most universal in its appeal. An educated balletomane may rightly imagine that, in watching a superb performance in a theatre, he is undergoing a profound artistic experience; yet it would doubtless not occur to him that the reactions of soccer connoisseurs to an expert game are remarkably similar, nor that their critical conversations about it can be as erudite and thoughtful as those of an admirer of the dance.

This has indeed been recognized, of late, by middle-class critics – eminent university dons among them – who now write of soccer matches (albeit a touch condescendingly) in terms appropriate to an important artistic event.

So far as affluence goes, the game, in the past decades, has undergone a magical transformation. Now players are becoming big business and, in Latin America, millionaires. As an inter-state sporting event, the World Cup is now second only to the Olympic Games.

Dog racing
Though pigeon racing is often considered, by those seeking only the picturesque, to be the working-class sport *par excellence*, dog racing would be a better choice; not only because of its ubiquity, but because, unlike soccer, it has attracted, apart from mavericks, few fans from any other class. Unlike the 'Sport of Kings' it is one in which a man of modest means may hope to train and run a winner.

Horse racing
Traditionally, the one sport – indeed, the one activity – in which the

Source: *Times Educational Supplement*, 5 October, 1973.

working and upper classes meet on almost equal terms, and do so almost to the exclusion of the middle classes. For looked at one way, racing is a matter of Royal Enclosures, millionaire stables, and the Jockey Club; looked at as realistically in another, it is the working-class preserve of jockeys, stable-boys, bookmakers and the majority of punters.It is, in fact a social hybrid, unlike show-jumping, which remains resolutely middle and upper class.

Boxing

Once, too, a sport with aristocratic overtones, in which Lord Byron took on Cockney pugilists, and Lord Queensberry formulated his Rules. Today, it has reverted to its purely working-class origins which wrestling, spurned by the cultivated, has never abandoned.

Of course, in all arts, practitioners may be found of any social origin; but we are seeking here those in which the majority of the performers, the greater part of their following, and the overall ethos of the arts, are principally working class.

Brass bands and choirs

Possibly the most conspicuous, if not the most important. There are thousands of those throughout the country, whose activities are largely neglected by the literate media, despite their social significance to millions (can one imagine, for instance, a brass-band critic of a 'quality' newspaper?). It is, indeed, through music that many who cannot, or do not wish to, achieve higher education can exercise their intelligence and imaginations. Thus, many opera and even oratorio singers are of working-class origin, their education finding a musical, rather than literate, expression.

Variety

This remains the great working-class art – the hybrid successor to the proletarian music halls, which now finds its principal outlet not in theatres, but on radio and television and, in 'live' form, in hundreds of club performances through the country. Perhaps Albert Chevalier, in the final decades of the last century, was the first middle-class artist to invade the halls – followed soon by Sir George Robey, initially a graduate in engineering. Since then, many a middle-class artist has followed their example, so that variety is now increasingly classless – that is, insofar as anything is so in England. And yet, variety remains, in its social assumptions, its subjects of myth, its objects of satire, and in its performers and admirers, predominantly working class.

Pop

It may well be that the profound disapproval of its middle-class detractors is motivated not so much by aesthetic considerations as by its enormous material success, and its conquest not only of the hearts of working-class boys and girls, but even of so many sons and daughters of their own. To this one must add, of course, a middle-class ignorance about the subject: for not until quite recently have the 'quality' press appointed informed critics to assess the great varieties of pop music. But this should perhaps not surprise us; for though the educated of today cast a kindly backward eye on the art of the old music halls, very few of their grandfathers – unless artists like Walter Sickert, or originals like Shaw or Beerbohm – ever went into a music hall at all.

Theatre and film

These have likewise seen a massive recent recruitment of working-class artists: not playing, as they might have done a generation or more ago, 'class' parts (usually comic), but almost anything, the more so as the dramatic heroes and heroines of our day are increasingly portrayed as classless or, at any rate, upper working class. This is a development – or a regression – which lovers of the drama may applaud, since it might well be thought that actors were more so before they became, from Sir Henry Irving's day onwards, knights and dames, rather than the superior rogues and vagabonds they traditionally were.

Gardening

With sport, this is the chief activity which is universally acceptable to all English classes and, at the same time, despite the English reputation for philistinism, the art most universally practised and admired. It is indeed possible to have conversations about gardening which are essentially aesthetic in their nature, with men and women of any class who would greet an attempt to discuss painting, literature or music with boredom or alarm.

The glory of English gardening may well be the aristocratic inventions of the stately homes, of the houses of rural substance, or of the patrician urban squares; always bearing in mind that most of the gardeners themselves, who interpreted their patrons' tastes, were rural workers. Yet among gardens of the urban working class, or of those who have not been exiled into towers embedded in asphalt, the passion for gardening is as strong – as are precise notions of which plants and flowers, and which arrangements of them, are most pleasing to the eye. In general, one may say that if patrician taste is for the broad sweep and the harmonious decor, the plebian one – largely, of course, for reasons of space and cost – is more for an accumulation of rather crowded colour: the appearance indeed, of many a working-class back garden, resembles, in its insistence on leaving no wasted space, the utilitarian aspect of the vegetable allotment.

Do-it-yourself
A positive mania; 'hobbies', these are usually called by middle-class people, but this suggests perhaps one, or two, sparetime activities of a recreational nature. The working-class equivalent, far more widespread, is much more immediately practical; its motivation being not so much that of 'adult play', as one useful and even financial. Thus, to sail a small boat on the South Coast is perhaps a hobby; to build your own in the garage, and then build and sell another, is a more serious sort of 'play'.

Betting-shop and bingo session
These are almost exclusively patronized by the working classes. (They are considered by middle-class critics to be somehow squalid: not so, however, expensive gambling at the races, clubs, or in overseas casinos.) The expanding holiday camps and the European packaged tour, are another working-class institution, as are the infinity of social clubs, many of them luxurious, which in no way correspond to the middle-class notion of what a club should be. Nor should we forget the public houses: which, though commercial middle-class in appropriate areas, have always been, and remain, a largely working-class place of public assembly.

For a literary version of working-class culture, the reader is invited to visit any newagent's in a popular area, and buy a copy of every periodical available (his score, even in a small shop, will be at least well over fifty).

Few indeed of these will be found to express middle-class interests and aspirations. Even a large part of the daily press is targeted at working-class readers, while the vast majority of the infinity of specialist, weeklies and monthlies portray a working-class world in a realistic or imagined form. As to books, a huge number of paperbacks (of the variety to be found in high-street stores, rather than the Charing Cross Road) are intended for the minority of the working-class masses who are casual readers.

However scrappy or superficial anyone may find this generalized portrait of working-class culture to be, he will surely admit that it is a reality to many millions, and that however alien to his own culture assumptions, large numbers of his fellow countrymen and women, though perhaps not using the word 'culture' at all, would regard it as the outward form of their social life as English citizens: and would regard any alternative cultural pattern proposed to them with scepticism, first asking whether what is offered is what they really want to be, or know about, or whether it is something alien that others are trying to impose upon them, and upon their children, against their natural interests and inclinations.

In judging all of this, I think anyone not of the working class should beware of two possible mistakes. The first is to adopt a condescending attitude to cultural artefacts and customs with which he is not familiar, and to suppose that, for this very reason, they must be valueless. The other is in an excess of romantic or guilt-ridden enthusiasm, to denigrate the authentic achievements of middle-class culture and attribute virtues to working-class culture which it has not got. For if the great weakness of middle-class culture is that it is static and exclusive, then that of working-class culture is largely that its aspirations are so limited. So the middle-class person who wishes to communicate outside his class must make the effort of imagination to step also outside his own social assumptions and try to discover by thought and, if possible, experience, what are the cultural conventions of others he is trying to understand.

4.5 Beyond the ghetto: the illusion of choice

Nicholas Deakin and Clare Ungerson

This chapter begins as an attempt at an examination of a single concept: that of the ghetto, and the extent to which it can legitimately be applied to the situation in London. Historically, the notion of the ghetto is both stigmatizing and restricting; it identifies a group which a society wishes to define as a separate entity, not forming part of the main body of that society, nor entitled to rights that are common property within it. In the past, such groups have carried a literal stigma – an ineradicable sign setting them apart: the black skin of the slave, the Star of David of the Jew. This stigma has permitted the majority to exercise control over their physical location and movement, and, in extreme cases, to destroy them.

Yet the application of the term to groups in our society now can lead not to illumination but to the generation of a great deal of heat – and heat, in turn, to haziness of outline. For it is striking how often the term is used loosely or in contradictory senses. We think that we can distinguish at least three different usages. First, and most obvious, there is the definition based on ethnic difference ('race'). There is no need to labour the point that the concept of the black ghetto has been employed freely in the British situation, often with reference to London. But in order to establish how meaningful the application of this term to the present situation is we will need to examine closely the evidence about the distribution of ethnic groups in London – a task which we will return to later. There is also another common usage, based on economic circumstances. In this usage, the term 'ghetto' is applied to deprived areas and by extension to their inhabitants. The definitions employed vary, depending on whether the focus is on deprivation in the geographical area as such – in schools, the social services available, or simply the general environment; or on the

Source: David Donnison and David Eversley (eds) *London: Urban Patterns, Problems and Policies*, 1976, Routledge and Kegan Paul, pp. 215–30 and 238–47.

individual, his income, his skills or his class – defined in socioeconomic terms. By extension, the term is also applied to certain tenure groups, conceived of as separate housing classes: it is quite common to find reference made to 'council house ghettos'.[1] Reference has even been made recently by the Chairman of one London Borough Housing Committee to 'upper-class ghettos' in part of his local authority area.

Beyond this, the term is applied more widely still, to groups distinguished by certain general characteristics, such as sex or age (references to ghettos of the old – 'Sun Cities' – or the young). Clearly at this point the usage is so loose as to become almost meaningless – unlike the other definitions we have cited in the previous paragraph, which are important enough to be worth further consideration.

But before we do consider the other usages we should also note in passing that they all appear to be based on a geographical definition – the separation of the particular group is defined spatially. It is, however, perfectly possible for a minority (however defined) to be separated from the main body of society or stigmatized in some way while at the same time being distributed evenly throughout the whole population. The 'spiritual ghetto' of a minority is a familiar concept. It can be applied to the advocates of the counter-culture as much as to the exiles and refugees who, while often spatially dispersed, still take pride in and adhere to the customs and ideologies of their lives elsewhere. Although not susceptible to precise measurement, this 'spiritual ghetto' is often of considerable importance in considering the future development of the society of which that group forms a part.

The importance of 'choice'

In general, the common usages of the term 'ghetto' imply either areas of ethnic concentration, areas of one-class concentration, areas of multiple deprivation or a combination of the three. In all these usages the concept of 'choice' plays a crucial, although differing role. This is fitting, since one of the common implications of the word 'ghetto' is that it is a place from which the inhabitants cannot escape – they have no choice but to stay within the actual or metaphorical walls of the ghetto. But the different usages imply that choices are available to the people living within the defined area. And these choices vary in kind. For example, a 'racially distinct ghetto' might exist because the people living within it wish to live together, and can do so, in areas where the services are good enough to maximize their satisfactions in other ways. The Jews of Golders Green are a good example of a group who have chosen to live together in such circumstances. On the other hand such a concentration may exist because the majority society wishes to confine such a group within certain areas. In that case, the majority society has severely restricted the choices of the minority group. In contrast, areas of multiple deprivation are areas where choice for all the inhabitants is severely restricted – not necessarily deliberately – by factors at work within the wider society. Poor schools, poor wages, bad housing and overcrowding, combine to keep the inhabitants in such conditions. Without the money to buy themselves out, or the skills to agitate for better services at home, these people are stuck almost as firmly as if their areas were literally surrounded by walls. Thirdly, in 'one-class neighbourhoods' which are not 'areas of deprivation' the concept of 'choice' has yet another emphasis. It may be, as in the commuter villages of Hertfordshire, that in middle-class, one-class neighbourhoods the occupants have deliberately chosen that it should be like that, just like the Golders Green Jews. But in working-class one-class neighbourhoods, which in London will probably be areas with a very high proportion of council housing, it is arguable that some kinds of choice are limited. For example, it is impossible even for a well-paid worker living in East London to buy a decent house in that area and thereby gain access to the considerable financial advantages attaching to owner occupation.

The significance of housing

In considering these problems of absence of choice, especially in areas of deprivation, we will need to return to fundamentals and try to answer one of the perennial and basic questions: whether the place of residence of disadvantaged groups is determined by the workings of the housing market, or whether employment is the critical factor. In the broadest terms, the pattern of the housing market has been changing rapidly over the last twenty years. Whereas twenty years ago almost three-quarters of the dwellings of England and Wales were rented, by 1967 half were owner-occupied; and of those that were not, more than half were rented from the local authority. But these changes did not take place evenly throughout the stock of dwellings. Generally, the rapid growth in owner-occupied dwellings has taken place on the periphery of our major cities and in new housing developments; the equally rapidly shrinking privately rented sector is confined increasingly to the centre of these cities. Local-authority housing is more evenly distributed between the two; but access to such housing is controlled by a series of rules operated by local authorities, which tend to restrict the access of newcomers. To be specific, there are at least six ways in which discrimination by local authorities against newcomers – and specifically coloured ones – can take place. First, in the framing of points systems for the allocation of housing from the waiting list which lay stress on local residence; second, by omitting areas of high concentration from slum clearance schemes; third, by rigid definition of the categories of persons considered eligible for rehousing; fourth, in the type of property offered to them when they are rehoused; fifth, in the assessment of their suitability for accommodation by housing visitors; and, finally, by making selective attacks on the problems of multi-occupation and thereby squeezing minorities into certain specific areas. The Political and Economic Planning report of 1967 indicated that there were grounds for supposing that discrimination is occurring under all these heads.[2]

At the same time, access to other sectors of the housing market has been severely restricted. Access to owner occupation is of particular significance, because it is often the solution which the immigrant himself would most like to adopt.[3] But the attitude initially adopted by building societies towards coloured house purchasers (especially before the Race Relations Act of 1968), and towards the type of property which is within their means to purchase, restricted their opportunities at the crucial earlier stage in the migration. Often, such purchasers have been forced to raise short-term loans at high rates of interest. The attitudes of estate agents towards black clients has been an additional restriction: often they have interpreted their role as entitling them to 'steer' coloured people to certain 'suitable' areas. That so many immigrants have been able to purchase their own property, despite a relatively low *per capita* income, is a striking illustration of the desire to escape the disadvantages inherent in housing in the private rented sector – the remaining sector open to them.

Nevertheless, it will be seen from Table I that the majority of immigrants in London are still to be found in the private rented sector, and that they are very considerably over-represented in the most vulnerable part of that sector – in furnished accommodation.

Table I   Housing tenure groups of coloured immigrants in the London conurbation

	Owner-occupiers	Renting from a local authority	Renting unfurnished	Renting furnished
All coloured immigrants	32.6	4.2	18.1	43.6
English	38.9	22.3	29.0	7.3

Source: 1966 10 per cent Sample Census.

Not only are immigrants concentrated disproportionately in one tenure group: they are also disproportionately concentrated in the inner areas of major cities. The evidence about the extent of concentration is taken from the 1966 Sample Census. There are a number of well-known objections to its use, particularly with reference to immigrants. First, this Census is, of course, out of date – we await the results of the 1971 Census which will allow us to confirm the possible trends we indicate later on. Secondly, we know that the Census seriously under-enumerated the immigrant populations. Thirdly, the smallest unit for which numbers were large enough to be significant was the electoral ward, which for our purposes may well be too large when we talk about 'areas of multiple deprivation'. Nevertheless, the 1966 Census is the latest data we have and with these caveats in mind we shall proceed to use it.

On concentration itself, the evidence is confusing. Since immigrants form such a low proportion of the London population, the proportion of one particular group living in one particular area would have to be very high indeed to fill a defined area.

As Table 2 indicates, there are some wards in London where, in 1966, nearly a quarter of the population belonged to one ethnic group. At the same time, nearly half (43 per cent) of the West Indian population of London lived in wards where they comprise less than 5 per cent of the population. What sort of areas are they where immigrants of one kind or another constitute nearly a quarter of the population? As Joe Doherty has pointed out: 'The major problem now is not "how concentrated" but "where concentrated".' In all the areas of substantial settlement, the density of occupation is high, the proportion of occupied dwellings with all facilities low, the proportion of households in privately rented furnished accommodation is high, the proportion of economically active men in skilled, semi-skilled and service employment high, while the proportion in 'other non-manual' work is low. Thus a clear picture emerges of 'typical' areas of multiple deprivation with poor housing stock, low social class, insecure tenure. This picture is most marked in Harrow Road ward where 21 per cent of households were West Indian in 1966, and very nearly half the households were lacking in one facility, nearly one-third of the households were in furnished accommodation, and nearly a quarter of the men were in service or semi-skilled occupations.

Although concentrations of unskilled workers, or poor housing circumstances are not exclusively a feature of Inner London, areas of multiple deprivation with a substantial proportion of black inhabitants are characteristically found in the inner city. These also tend to be the areas where the social services are at their least adequate. This inadequacy affects all the inhabitants of these areas – the 'twilight zones' of our major

Table 2   Major settlement of immigrants by wards, London 1966 (percentage population)

Wards with large Irish concentrations	*% Irish*	*% Asian*	*% W. Indian*	*% African*	*% Cypriot/ Maltese*
Kilburn (Brent)	24.41	2.37	6.84	2.09	0.28
Mapesbury (Brent)	22.26	4.14	1.85	3.27	0.00
Cricklewood (Brent)	18.95	3.06	3.26	2.27	1.58
Kilburn (Camden)	18.68	3.33	4.31	3.09	3.01

Wards with large Asian concentrations	*% Asian*	*% Irish*	*% W. Indian*	*% African*	*% Cypriot/ Maltese*
Northcote (Ealing)	24.41	2.89	4.56	1.44	0.17
St Mary's (Tower Hamlets)	9.30	3.67	0.86	0.12	2.08
Soho (Westminster)	8.23	1.52	0.30	0.00	1.52
Spitalfields (Tower Hamlets)	8.13	7.33	1.96	1.02	5.37

Wards with large W. Indian concentrations	*% W. Indian*	*% Irish*	*% Asian*	*% African*	*% Cypriot/ Maltese*
Kensal Rise (Brent)	21.13	6.00	0.46	1.39	0.12
Harrow Road (Westminster)	20.88	10.81	0.97	2.73	0.46
Rectory (Hackney)	14.37	3.74	1.18	1.67	0.47
Tulse Hill (Lambeth)	13.84	5.20	0.58	1.81	1.17

Source: 1966 Census
This table was taken from: DOHERTY, J., 'The distribution and concentration of immigrants in London' Race Today, 1, No. 8, December 1969.

cities where the housing stock is sinking to the end of its useful life. But there is one section of the population that suffers particularly from the handicaps imposed by residence in such areas: the children. Children in these areas are more likely to die at birth, or shortly after it, will get inferior health care at the beginning of their lives, are more likely to be run over by traffic because there are no adequate play facilities available, are more likely to catch illnesses as a result of playing among rubbish or from bad housing conditions. One investigator[4] who has recently worked in an area of this kind with a high proportion of black inhabitants stresses that the absence of adequate provision of day nurseries forces parents to place children in 'establishments' where:

> ... the children had little or no play facilities; even three year olds had no books or writing tables, nor did they get enough attention from the child-minders .... In view of the almost total absence of any formative education, it would hardly be surprising if their children did not become 'problems' during their first years at school. They will certainly require special attention, and if the teacher does not have the resources to provide special attention or fails to recognize the need for it, then their children might well start and finish in the bottom stream – today's 'problem child', tomorrow's dropout or delinquent.

The obstacles encountered by children in these areas will continue to affect them into adult life: their poverty will, in most cases, be perpetuated and transmitted to the next generation. Unable, because of inadequacies in their education, to obtain better jobs than their parents, with better pay, they cannot escape from the underprivileged area in which they were brought up, and are forced, in their turn, to bring up their families in these conditions of severe deprivation. At some point in the vicious cycle they may qualify, by operation of the points system or of the bulldozer, for local-authority housing. But entry into local-authority housing is restricted, as we have already indicated: and for inhabitants of Inner London, at least, it is often delayed beyond the span of a child's passage from birth to adulthood. Nor is decent housing a guarantee of freedom from poverty. In the light of the Housing Finance Act, the costs of decent housing may be so high as to make other areas of life very difficult indeed.

All those handicaps affect all inhabitants of the twilight zone, and coloured people are conspicuous among them. Thus we see that access to particular types and location of housing is certainly a major determinant of the quality of life, in that, with its type and location, come a whole bundle of other services and disservices, opportunities and deprivations. But the question remains: do these people have this differential access to good services, which puts them at such a disadvantage compared with the inhabitants of the leafy suburbs, because they are poor, because they are black or because of the jobs they do?

Employment and housing

There is general agreement, based initially on G. C. K. Peach's examination of migration flows,[5] that it has been the availability of jobs that has determined the distribution of coloured people among the major conurbations. Once in these areas, the coloured population are affected by a series of developments within the employment market in major conurbations. A rather over-simplified view of the current situation is this: there is a growing demand for service workers in the centre of our cities: these jobs are frequently filled by black people, particularly – in the case of London – by black women; jobs in transport, postal, hospital and catering services are comparatively low paid; the operation of discrimination in the employment market, particularly against coloured people and women, will mean that large proportions of these groups are effectively prevented from working in other industries; since they are low paid they cannot afford to purchase good housing and are forced either to pay rent or buy inadequate accommodation in the centre; moreover, they have to live near their work because fares for public transport are high, and anyway they often do shift work and go to and from work at times when public transport is not operating; they are thus made poor and forced to live in areas of multiple deprivation near the city centres.

Against this view, it is argued that – in London, at least – the opportunities for semi-skilled and skilled workers are not disappearing as rapidly as has been suggested. Nor is there any convincing evidence of a concentration of semi-skilled or unskilled workers in any specific areas. In some areas, the city has in fact generated new employment opportunities within the inner core: and other areas outside the traditional industrial belts are providing new opportunities. One specific example is Croydon, where a whole range of new jobs has become available over the last decade, and West Indians from the Lambeth area have taken full advantage of the opportunity provided.[6]

But these new opportunities, though they help to correct the impression of an inevitable decline in the inner city, can necessarily affect only a minority. The restrictions placed on coloured householders by the operation of the housing market are compounded by the additional restrictions on the type of employment available and the levels of pay.

Table 3 shows that in certain London wards where there were concentrations of immigrants, West Indian men were heavily over-represented in semi-skilled and unskilled manual work, and while a very similar proportion were in skilled work, compared to the English born men the West Indians were very under-represented in non-manual work.

Table 3 Percentage socioeconomic distribution* for different immigrant groups for selected areas, 1966: Males – selected Inner London Boroughs 1966†

Birthplace	Caribbean	Ireland	England and Wales
Number economically active‡	20 500	14 400	206 750
1 Professional workers	0.4	1.0	3.1
2 Employers and managers	0.3	3.6	8.3
3 Non-manual	4.6	13.2	22.1
4 Skilled manual and foremen	40.5	36.5	39.6
5 Semi-skilled manual	26.7	19.7	15.7
6 Unskilled manual	25.1	24.8	9.9
7 Armed Forces and inadequately described	2.3	1.2	1.2

Source: 1966 10 per cent Sample Census, Special Tabulations
  * Categories used consist as follows:

Category	Registrar General's S.E.G.
1 Professional workers	3, 4
2 Employers and managers	1, 2, 13
3 Non-manual	5, 6
4 Skilled manual	8, 9, 12, 14
5 Semi-skilled manual	7, 10, 15
6 Unskilled manual	11,
7 Armed forces and inadequately described	16, 17

† For areas covered by seven selected metropolitan boroughs (Stoke Newington, Hackney, Paddington, Battersea, Lambeth, Camberwell, Deptford). Figures for India and Pakistan born not included, because the birth-place criterion employed in the Census is misleading.

‡ Figures for the number economically active have been multiplied by ten as the size of the sample was 10 per cent of the total population.

To say that the housing market is rivalled by the employment market as a determinant of where people live is not to deny the impact of housing conditions on the quality of people's lives. Overcrowding, high rents or mortgage interest, poor maintenance, insecurity of tenure, coupled with an inability to escape from the effects of these circumstances, add up to an appalling burden for individuals and families. However, even if people are forced to live in certain areas as a result of economic factors beyond their control, there are some measures that can be taken to alleviate housing hardship, despite the operation of the broader economic and social imperatives.

Are immigrants in a special position?
A view taken by many race relations experts on this question has been neatly summarized by Elizabeth Burney. She takes the view that immigrants as a group have many of the characteristics of other deprived groups and hence suffer from all their disadvantages:[7]

> The chief losers in the battle for a fair share of housing are working-class families with young children in big cities, especially if they are newcomers supplying essential labour. Among them are the overseas immigrants, whose plight is unique only in its particular combination of circumstances. Many of those circumstances are shared with, for example: young families; large families; low-paid workers, mobile workers, shift workers; unmarried mothers; and almost any non-English-looking, non-English-speaking, non-conforming people. Any of these features is equivalent to a minus mark in the competition for housing space. Racial discrimination is perhaps the biggest single minus; but even this can generally be overcome unless combined – as it nearly always is – with at least one, if not several, of the other factors listed.

Sir Milner Holland's Committee on London Housing came to broadly the same conclusions[8] commenting that:

> The basic nature of the differences of coloured immigrants is the same in quality as that of all the newcomers to London without adequate means, arriving at a time when many local-authority housing lists are very overcrowded or even closed, and in conditions where they obtain very low priority for allocation of housing.

Others have taken rather a different view. John Rex and Robert Moore, in their study of the Sparkbrook area of Birmingham[9] argue that immigrants constitute a distinct housing class, whose access to housing is restricted as a result of competition with other classes in the city, defined by their control of access to superior kinds of housing – the suburban middle class with their access to owner occupation and the white urban working class with their access to local-authority housing. In these circumstances, the immigrant is forced back on the ethnic colony, where his needs are catered for by the immigrant landlord.

More recent evidence, from an extensive enquiry conducted in Notting Hill, enables us to examine in detail the relative circumstances of black and white in an inner urban area of a similar kind to that described by Rex and Moore. The Notting Hill Housing Survey[10] showed that a very high proportion (33 per cent) of households living in the survey area were living at more than $1\frac{1}{2}$ persons per room – black or white. Poor housing conditions, in terms of absolute numbers, affect many more whites than blacks. Proportionately, however, blacks generally suffer more. In Notting Hill, 59 per cent of the West Indians, 53 per cent of the Africans, 33 per cent of the Asians were living at this rate compared to 22 per cent of the households where the head was born in the United Kingdom. But this cannot be said to be purely a question of colour: 44 per cent of the Irish households were overcrowded – which seems to indicate the relative significance of poverty, size of household, newcomers, as opposed to the single factor of colour.

At the same time, there is no doubt that being black makes the struggle for decent, secure housing even more difficult than it is for the deprived white household. The survey showed that households with 'coloured' heads paid more rent than households with 'white' heads. It is clear that part of this is due to 'black' households being comparative newcomers and so not getting the advantage of controlled tenancies where median rents were considerably lower than in other tenures. The survey also used a device for measuring value for money in all tenures and found that furnished tenants got least value, controlled tenants the most. It is the concentration of black households in furnished accommodation which is clearly a crucial determinant of the high rents paid by coloured householders.

According to the survey, two-thirds of the West Indian households, and three-quarters of the Asians and Africans lived in furnished accommodation in Notting Hill in 1967 as compared to one-fifth of the English households. This connection between furnished accommodation and colour is not restricted to Notting Hill, it is typical of the rest of London. The 1966 Census showed that 43.6 per cent of all coloured immigrants living in London were in furnished accommodation as compared to 7.3 per cent of the English (Table 1).

The picture that emerges from these findings is not completely clear-cut. It is certainly the case that there are many more whites living in dreadful housing conditions than there are blacks. Moreover, some of the reasons why blacks find themselves in particularly bad circumstances is no doubt because they do — as Elizabeth Burney suggests — find themselves in a situation which combines many of the different features of those households that are most often found in housing need. Nevertheless, the Notting Hill evidence provides general confirmation that, as far as rent and type of tenure are concerned, colour operates as a separate handicap.

This would be less disturbing if it could be shown that the situation is improving. It is often argued that immigrant groups must expect, simply because they are newcomers, to encounter some additional difficulties in obtaining decent housing and well-paid jobs. But in fact the position of blacks in the housing market showed very little improvement between 1961 and 1966, a period in which the housing circumstances of white families living in similar kinds of areas showed a substantial improvement. When allowance is made for the change in definition of a room between Censuses, the position of Indian and Pakistani migrants, taken together, actually deteriorated.[11]

We urgently need to know whether the situation has changed since 1966: whether, for example, a large black family is likely to be in as good or bad housing as a large white family, or whether colour has become even more important as a source of differential access to better circumstances. Only the 1971 Census can answer that question: but the indications seem to be that in certain areas of multiple deprivation in London, the problems of blacks in the housing market are becoming relatively greater, particularly when account is taken of their concentration in the furnished sector.

The evidence we have available about West Indians living in London[12] shows that just over 40 per cent of West Indian households in Greater London were living in privately-rented furnished accommodation in 1966 compared with 8.6 per cent of all households. The Francis Committee has indicated that many people live in furnished accommodation not because they want to, but because they cannot get anything else.[13] It is also the tenure category from which, according to the Cullingworth Committee, some local authorities still refuse to rehouse the tenants. In Kensington and Chelsea, where 67.7 per cent of the West Indian households were in furnished accommodation in 1966, the local authority still refuses to rehouse such tenants from redevelopment areas except 'on their merits'.

This means that this sector of the housing market could be construed as the place where the significant concentration takes place. Not only does it compare badly with other sectors of the market in terms of amenities and security, but also it is very difficult indeed to move out of it, particularly if you are black and poor.

But, as we saw earlier, the Census evidence shows that a substantial proportion of West Indians are owner-occupiers. In Greater London as a whole 32.7 per cent own their houses compared to 38.5 per cent of all households, and in the eleven Inner Boroughs where 79 per cent of all West Indian households live, 28.4 per cent of West Indian households had bought their houses compared to 21.8 per cent of all households.[12] A second important point concerns the conditions in which these large groups of furnished tenants and owner-occupiers live. Haddon found that in all the boroughs – whether they had high proportions of immigrant residents or not – lower proportions of West Indian owner-occupiers were overcrowded than in any other sector. Only 12.5 per cent of West Indian owner-occupiers in concentrated boroughs were living at more than $1\frac{1}{2}$ persons per room, compared with 25.0 per cent of West Indian local-authority tenants, 30.1 per cent unfurnished tenants and 34.8 per cent furnished tenants. Thus even in areas which are afflicted by multiple deprivation, movement into owner occupation appears to be an effective way of escaping the severe overcrowding that West Indians suffer in other tenure categories. But if we turn to overcrowding patterns in the boroughs with lower proportions of West Indians, we find that movement out of the inner areas, particularly for unfurnished tenants, does not completely resolve problems of overcrowding. Even in the non-concentrated boroughs 10.4 per cent of the West Indian households were overcrowded, which is still a fairly high proportion although it compares favourably with 20.5 per cent in the 'intermediate' boroughs and 27.0 per cent in the 'concentrated' boroughs. 'Dispersal' clearly brings some comparative benefits for many, but it does not remove housing hardships for all. Thus the links between a particular form of housing hardship – overcrowding – and particular areas of concentration are not firmly established. Many West Indians continue to suffer from bad housing wherever they live.

Dispersal: the ongoing debate

In our view, the major debate that has taken place over the past few years – broadly, since Roy Jenkins produced his famous redefinition of integration in pluralist terms – about the relative merits of concentration and dispersal is based on a misconception. No amount of dispersal by physical planning or inducement will ensure that people live fully integrated lives. Everyone, regardless of ethnic origin, exercises some selection over the social contacts that they value: most people choose to live within a fairly restricted – 'concentrated', if you like – circle with broadly similar social characteristics. The important thing is that everyone should be free to choose, and to move outside such circles if they wish to do so: there should be as few constraints as possible on the exercise of choice by individuals.

To this extent, the resolution of the practical problems of limited access detailed in earlier sections are the first priority; and to talk about dispersal as a first aim of policy is to put the cart before the horse. The opportunity of freely exercising the option to disperse is not yet available; our first objective should be to provide it. This will mean making widely available information on which to base a choice, providing easier access to the particular institutions that can best provide it, and cutting down on the exercise of arbitrary powers by those who now take the crucial decisions about people's housing chances. When the options are opened up in this way, it will then be possible to talk more realistically about voluntary dispersal.

Nevertheless, although we would argue strongly for concentrating attention on short-term priorities that affect people's life-chances now, it is useful to attempt to get the long-range objectives into focus, and to consider the alternatives that may later open up. In evidence to the Cullingworth Committee, one of the present writers took the view that to argue for a policy of dispersal without any qualification was wrong, on at least three grounds. First, such a policy failed to distinguish between the different needs of different ethnic groups at different stages of the migration process. Second, it failed to allow for the fact that concentration confers certain positive benefits, especially during the earlier stages of a migration — communal support and the growth of special facilities in particular. And, third, he argued that a policy of directed dispersal is ultimately indefensible, because it introduces coercion into what should be essentially a matter of choice. The Committee, after quoting this evidence in some detail, came to broadly the same conclusions, stating that:[14]

> We are convinced that any policy of dispersal in the field of housing must be implemented with great sensitivity, with no element of compulsion or direction, and can proceed only at the pace of the needs and wishes of the people involved.

There are arguments on the other side that should not be brushed aside. First, it is clear that in certain circumstances dispersal can provide access to better material facilities. Data from 1966 Sample Census showed that the situation of those West Indians living in boroughs with low concentrations of West Indians was considerably better than that of those living in areas of high concentration (see Table 4).[15] Furthermore, it is probable that the improvement in housing circumstances would be

Table 4 **Proportion of households where head was born in
the West Indies living at different densities
(persons per room)**

Persons per room	Concentrated boroughs	Dispersed boroughs
Under 0.5	4	15
0.5–0.74	15	23
0.75–0.99	8	14
1.00	27	22
1.0–1.50	20	16
over 1.50	26	10

Boroughs of high concentration are defined as those containing more than 5000 persons born in the West Indies. Boroughs of low concentration are defined as those containing less than 2500 persons born in the West Indies.

Sources: Special tabulations by the Research and Intelligence Unit, GLC, of 1966 Census

matched by access to better educational facilities. In view of the importance of equal educational opportunity in determining the future of the second generation of black Britons, this is an important consideration. Second, it now seems likely that some of the countervailing advantages of concentration have been exaggerated. In political terms, the fact that the numerical concentrations are not as great as is generally believed effectively removes any immediate possibility that the voting strength of minorities can be used to obtain political leverage or elect candidates from minority groups to local office or to Parliament. A partial exception can be glimpsed in one or two areas of Indian settlement, though even here there are sharp intra-communal divisions.[16] Third, there is real risk of an association being made between the presence of black minorities and the existence of poor facilities in a squalid environment. Such a connection makes it easy to blame the minority concerned for creating the poor conditions with which they have to put up. If there were any serious prospect of eliminating the root causes of underprivilege forthwith, by the direct injection of substantial additional resources, this would matter less. But this seems most unlikely.

The arguments are therefore finely balanced, and no clear-cut conclusion is possible. But some misconceptions can be cleared away. In their evidence to the Select Committee, Lambeth Borough Council refer to three obstacles that have, in their experience, inhibited dispersal.[17] They argue, first, that dispersal may pose serious problems for officials and set them undesirable tasks – like setting and maintaining coloured quotas in 'dispersed' local-authority estates. Second, they argue that dispersal is still rejected as a goal by the majority of West Indians because of the risks involved in 'pioneering'. Third, they argue that the skills necessary to obtain work in a 'dispersed' area are not present.

The first objection seems to be based on a misunderstanding. A policy of scattering blacks around council estates in exactly equal-sized penny packets does not have any relationship to dispersal as we conceive it. Far more important is the breaking down of the remaining institutional barriers to the exercise of free choice. For example, it is of very great importance that categorical distinctions are not drawn between persons of different tenure categories when decisions are made about offering to rehouse residents of clearance areas. The evidence gathered by the Cullingworth Committee, and quoted above, shows that practice varies very widely. To decline to rehouse furnished tenants – among whom, as we have seen, coloured people are grossly over-represented – is to close off what will probably be the only real possibility of escape from the twilight area, thereby restricting freedom of choice in the most drastic possible way, and increasing, in all probability, the extent of involuntary concentration.

There are other constraints that hinder choice, even when people are offered rehousing. The Cullingworth Committee has drawn attention, in Chapter Three of their report, to the crucial role of housing visitors in determining where people are rehoused. At the same time, housing visitors had little or no training or common practice. In our experience, housing visitors themselves are frequently not equipped with information about the range of council housing available and the rents charged, which in turn makes it impossible for them to give the information necessary for people to make a genuine choice between types of housing and different locations. Training specifically for housing visitors and a willingness in local authorities to provide the information about rents, rent rebates and type of housing that people need to make a real choice, would be a significant step towards 'voluntary' dispersal or concentration. Local authorities could ensure that in future tenants. really do know what type of housing is available: where necessary transport should be provided so that people can have a whistle-stop tour around the estates. Such transport is already provided for their employees by firms intending to move to new and expanding towns, and a few local authorities are intending to provide such services for their residents. But, even though the distances are much smaller, we suspect there are a great many immigrants living in areas of multiple deprivation who have never seen the local-authority housing that lies in the 'leafy suburb' end of their borough. Even if, once they have seen it, they reject it in favour of greater concentration elsewhere, at least they themselves will have made that choice.

Another answer to this difficulty about dispersal that has been widely canvassed lies in increasing the opportunities for movement to new and expanding towns, which have for some time now taken 20 000 Londoners a year. On paper, many immigrants possess the skills that are at a premium in these towns – in 1966, over 40 per cent of the West Indians living in London were skilled workers. Initiatives have been taken both by local authorities and the new towns to ensure that the opportunities are more widely known among immigrants in London.

If, despite the efforts being mounted by public bodies of all kinds, coloured people continue to be, as they are now, grossly under-represented in new towns, then one conclusion would be that the persistent reluctance on the part of black and brown minorities to take the social and economic risks of dispersal from the inner city must be in part the consequence of the climate of race relations in Britain. It may be that there is an information gap (though efforts are being made to close it); there are also quite clearly some economic obstacles – though these are not peculiar to coloured people. If, even allowing for all these efforts, coloured people remain under-represented, it will be because of the anxieties to which Lambeth Borough Council refer in their evidence to the Select Committee on Race Relations and Immigration.

In these circumstances, to talk of dispersal as a policy goal is premature, and it may be that we should not only be re-examining the short-range alternatives detailed above but also fundamentally rethinking the whole broad question of race relations in Britain, and how change can be achieved.

Some conclusions

We have set out in this paper to explore an apparently straightforward issue; but our discussion of it has involved us in considering a whole series of complex issues and the deploying of a good deal of detailed evidence. But briefly, and at the risk of gross over-simplification, we would summarize what we have said so far as follows:

The distribution of housing and different types of housing tenure is of importance in determining the quality of life of black and brown people in Britain, but has to be seen within the context of constraints within the economic system: restriction of employment and educational opportunity for all groups living and working in run-down areas and industries, low wages in certain sectors and unemployment.

Moreover, immigrants are in a special position in the housing market, to the extent that discrimination on racial grounds exists and is reflected in the restrictions on the standard and location of housing available to them. But they are also the victims of the general handicaps that affect all the inhabitants of the stress areas in which they are largely to be found.

Third, we do not at present have black ghettos, in the American sense. There are, in fact, other situations in the British Isles that correspond far more closely to the American models – the Catholic enclaves in Northern Ireland, for example – and groups as grossly underprivileged as certain non-white groups in the United States, like the gypsies. But in any event the probability is that there will be an increasing concentration of coloured people in a limited number of areas. The argument as to whether this is a desirable process or not is a complex one, on which no clear-cut conclusion can be reached.

The Government has tended to concentrate on policies which might ameliorate some of the problems of grossly deprived areas, on an area basis. The Educational Priority Area programme, the Urban Programme, the Community Development Project, local-authority slum-clearance programmes, all set out to alleviate territorial injustice and deprivations. Social security payments (in particular the Family Income Supplement) and the Rent Acts are examples of efforts to counteract inequalities in the housing and employment markets. But such policies are undermined by unemployment, particularly where it is highly localized as on Clydeside, and continued insecurity for furnished tenants. Where it has had any direct policy about race relations, central government has leant towards encouraging the break-up of concentrations of immigrants, particularly in the schools, on the grounds that black and white ought to mix; and a variant of this policy has recently been canvassed at a local-authority level to encourage social class mixing by allowing private developers and housing associations access for building purposes to council-owned land. This, it is suggested, will leaven otherwise working-class areas with the necessary middle-class qualities of articulate leadership. But such attacks on concentration by public intervention, especially in the housing field, where middle-class occupation is encouraged in what could otherwise be areas of total working-class occupation, in effect maintain inequalities and deprivations by disallowing working-class claims to better housing in favour of the fulfilment of a planner's dream of 'social mix'. Thus attacks on concentration can, in some cases, actually counteract attacks on deprivation.

As far as London is concerned, the particular position of the different immigrant groups needs to be seen in the context of the broader social and economic problems of the metropolis. The apparent malaise revealed by evidence of population declining by migration, both of the skilled and unskilled; the danger that the loss of population will lead to significant damage to the economic infrastructure that sustains the capital; the contest between the prosperous and the poor for accommodation in the inner areas, where land prices are the highest in the country: all these factors may have crucial consequences.

It is true that immigrants are substantially represented among owner-occupiers. But what appears at first sight to be a form of protection against the worst consequences of insecurity produced by the workings of the housing market may in practice provide little or no protection. Many immigrant householders who have bought property in inner areas will find themselves caught up in redevelopment schemes. Even when they are not, the security that property ownership would normally confer may turn out to be illusory if adequate job opportunities are not available for the head of household. But even here many Indian families will be cushioned by the support provided by the extended family; and in many households the children of migrants will shortly be reaching wage-earning age and making substantial contributions to household income.

But although the overall prospects for black and brown people in London are not necessarily wholly depressing, it is a mistake to place too much emphasis on the aggregate performance of immigrants as a whole. The evidence so far available suggests that the effect of the economic advance that has taken place implies a tilting of the incipient colour line in this society rather than a crumbling. It is a matter for speculation whether this situation will lead to the settling in of black and brown miniroties, as a bloc, at a certain point in the social class structure of our society or whether internal ethnic divisions will result in different ethnic groups following different patterns. A picture which at first sight seems less disturbing than it is often painted may conceal the growth of a subgroup of the severely underprivileged within the general population. The Pakistani – or Bengali – single man isolated in the shrinking rented sector and contending with insecurity and rising rents; and the young West Indian couple with small children, totally unable to command the financial resources that would enable them to afford the house they want to buy, at current London prices; their problems are going to be especially difficult to resolve, in any forseeable circumstances. They are not unique: and it may well be that solutions, when they come, will be reached in the context of a concerted assault on the problems of poverty in our society. But on present indications it is difficult to see such an assault being mounted on a sufficient scale to mop up the persistent pockets of underprivilege that still disfigure London.

Notes

1 See for example HILLMAN, JUDY, (ed) *Planning for London* (1971) Penguin, p. 14.

2 DANIEL, W. W. (1968) *Racial Discrimination in England* Penguin.

3 Select Committee on Race Relations and Immigration *Housing*, Vol. 2, HMSO, July 1971, p. 68.

4 JOHN, AUGUSTINE (1970) *Race in the Inner City* Runnymede Trust.

5 PEACH, G. C. K. (1968) *West Indian Migration: A Social Geography* Oxford University Press for Institute of Race Relations.

6 MCPHERSON, KLIM and GAITSKELL, JULIA (1969) *Immigrants and Employment: Two Case Studies in East London and in Croydon* Institute of Race Relations.

7 BURNEY, ELIZABETH (1967) *Housing on Trial* Oxford University Press for Institute of Race Relations.

8 Report of the Committee on Housing in Greater London (Milner Holland Report), Cmnd 2605, HMSO, 1965.

9 REX, JOHN and MOORE, ROBERT (1968) *Race, Community and Conflict: a study of Sparkbrook* Oxford University Press for Institute of Race Relations.

10 *Interim Report: Notting Hill Housing Survey* (Notting Hill Housing Service, 1969).

11 DEAKIN, N. *et al* (1970) *Colour, Citizenship and British Society* Panther.

12 HADDON, ROY F. (1970) 'A minority in a welfare state society: location of West Indians in the London housing market', *The New Atlantis*, 2, No. 1.

13 Report on the Committee on the Rent Acts, Cmnd 4609, HMSO, March 1971, chapter 20.

14 Cullingworth Committee *Council Housing: Purposes, Procedures and Priorities* HMSO, 1969, p. 135.

15 This table, and the supporting argument, comes from DEAKIN, N. and COHEN, B. G., 'Dispersal and choice', *Environment and Planning* 2, pp. 193–201.

16 JOHN, DEWITT (1969) *Indian Workers' Associations in Britain* Oxford.

17 Select Committee on Race Relations and Immigration, *op. cit.*, Vol. 2, p. 46.

4.6   The long shadow of work

Samuel Bowles and Herbert Gintis

It is not obvious why the US educational system should be the way it is. Since the interpersonal relationships it fosters are so antithetical to the norms of freedom and equality prevalent in American society, the school system can hardly be viewed as a logical extension of our cultural heritage. If neither technological necessity nor the bungling mindlessness of educators explain the quality of the educational encounter, what does?

Reference to the educational system's legitimation function does not take us far toward enlightenment. For the formal, objective, and cognitively oriented aspects of schooling capture only a fragment of the day-to-day social relationships of the educational encounter. To approach an answer, we must consider schools in the light of the social relationships of economic life. In this chapter, we suggest that major aspects of educational organization replicate the relationships of dominance and subordinancy in the economic sphere. The correspondence between the social relation of schooling and work accounts for the ability of the educational system to produce an amenable and fragmented labour force. The experience of schooling, and not merely the content of formal learning, is central to this process.

In our view, it is pointless to ask if the net effect of US education is to promote equality or inequaility, repression or liberation. These issues pale into insignificance before the major fact: the educational system is an integral element in the reproduction of the prevailing class structure of society. The educational system certainly has a life of its own, but the experience of work and the nature of the class structure are the bases upon which educational values are formed, social justice assessed, the realm of the possible delineated in people's consciousness, and the social relations

Source: *Schooling in Capitalist America*, 1976, Routledge and Kegan Paul, pp. 125–48, © 1976, Basic Books Incorporated.

of the educational encounter historically transformed.

In short, the educational system's task of integrating young people into adult work roles constrains the types of personal development which it can foster in ways that are antithetical to the fulfilment of its personal developmental function.

Reproducing consciousness

Economic life exhibits a complex and relatively stable pattern of power and property relationships. The perpetuation of these social relationships, even over relatively short periods, is by no means automatic. As with a living organism, stability in the economic sphere is the result of explicit mechanisms constituted to maintain and extend the dominant patterns of power and privilege. We call the sum total of these mechanisms and their actions the reproduction process.

Amidst the sundry social relations experienced in daily life, a few stand out as central to our analysis of education. These are precisely the social relationships which are necessary to the security of capitalist profits and the stability of the capitalist division of labour. They include the patterns of dominance and subordinancy in the production process, the distribution of ownership of productive resources, and the degrees of social distance and solidarity among various fragments of the working population – men and women, blacks and whites, and white- and blue-collar workers, to mention some of the most salient.

What are the mechanisms of reproduction of these aspects of the social relations of production in the United States? To an extent, stability is embodied in law and backed by the coercive power of the state. Our jails are filled with individuals who have operated outside the framework of the private-ownership market system. The modern urban police force as well as the National Guard originated, in large part, in response to the fear of social upheaval evoked by militant labour action. Legal sanction, within the framework of the laws of private property, also channels the actions of groups (e.g. unions) into conformity with dominant power relationships. Similarly, force is used to stabilize the division of labour and its rewards within an enterprise: dissenting workers are subject to dismissal and directors failing to conform to 'capitalist rationality' will be replaced.

But to attribute reproduction to force alone borders on the absurd. Under normal conditions, the effectiveness of coercion depends at the very least on the inability or unwillingness of those subjected to it to join together in opposing it. Laws generally considered illegitimate tend to lose their coercive power, and undisguised force too frequently applied tends to be self-defeating. The consolidation and extension of capitalism has engendered struggles of furious intensity. Yet instances of force deployed against a united and active opposition are sporadic and have usually given way to détente in one form or another through a combination of compromise, structural change, and ideological accommodation. Thus it is clear that the consciousness of workers – beliefs, values, self-concepts, types of solidarity and fragmentation, as well as modes of personal behaviour and development – are integral to the perpetuation, validation, and smooth operation of economic institutions. The reproduction of the social relations of production depends on the reproduction of consciousness.

Under what conditions will individuals accept the pattern of social relationships that frame their lives? Believing that the long-term development of the existing system holds the prospect of fulfilling their needs, individuals and groups might actively embrace these social relationships. Failing this, and lacking a vision of an alternative that might significantly improve their situation, they might fatalistically accept their condition. Even with such a vision they might passively submit to the framework of economic life and seek individual solutions to social problems if they believe that the possibilities for realizing change are remote. The issue of the reproduction of consciousness enters each of these assessments.

The economic system will be embraced when, first, the perceived needs of individuals are congruent with the types of satisfaction the economic system can objectively provide. While perceived needs may be, in part, biologically determined, for the most part needs arise through the aggregate experiences of individuals in the society. Thus the social relations of production are reproduced in part through a harmony between the needs which the social system generates and the means at its disposal for satisfying these needs.

Second, the view that fundamental social change is not feasible, unoperational, and utopian is normally supported by a complex web of ideological perspectives deeply embedded in the cultural and scientific life of the community and reflected in the consciousness of its members. But fostering the 'consciousness of inevitability' is not the office of the cultural system alone. There must also exist mechanisms that systematically thwart the spontaneous development of social experiences that would contradict these beliefs.

Belief in the futility of organizing for fundamental social change is further facilitated by social distinctions which fragment the conditions of life for subordinate classes. The strategy of 'divide and conquer' has enabled dominant classes to maintain their power since the dawn of civilization. Once again, the splintered consciousness of a subordinate class is not the product of cultural phenomena alone, but must be reproduced through the experiences of daily life.

Consciousness develops through the individual's direct perception of and participation in social life.[1] Indeed, everyday experience itself often acts as an inertial stabilizing force. For instance, when the working population is effectively stratified, individual needs and self-concepts develop in a correspondingly fragmented manner. Youth of different racial, sexual, ethnic, or economic characteristics directly perceive the economic positions and prerogatives of 'their kind of people'. By adjusting their aspiration accordingly, they not only reproduce stratification on the level of personal consciousness, but bring their needs into (at least partial) harmony with the fragmented conditions of economic life. Similarly, individuals tend to channel the development of their personal powers — cognitive, emotional, physical, aesthetic, and spiritual — in directions where they will have an opportunity to exercise them. Thus the alienated character of work, for example, leads people to guide their creative potentials to areas outside of economic activity: consumption, travel, sexuality, and family life. So needs and need-satisfaction again tend to fall into congruence and alienated labour is reproduced on the level of personal consciousness.[2]

But this congruence is continually disrupted. For the satisfaction of needs gives rise to new needs. These new needs derive from the logic of personal development as well as from the evolving structure of material life, and in turn undercut the reproduction of consciousness. For this reason the reproduction of consciousness cannot be the simple unintended by-product of social experience. Rather, social relationships must be consciously organized to facilitate the reproduction of consciousness.

Take, for instance, the organization of the capitalist enterprise. Power relations and hiring criteria within the enterprise are organized so as to reproduce the workers' self-concepts, the legitimacy of their assignments within the hierarchy, a sense of the technological inevitability of the hierarchical division of labour itself, and the social distance among groups of workers in the organization. Indeed, while token gestures towards workers' self-management may be a successful motivational gimmick, any delegation of real power to workers becomes a threat to profits because it tends to undermine patterns of consciousness compatible with capitalist control. By generating new needs and possibilities, by demonstrating the feasibility of a more thoroughgoing economic democracy, by increasing worker solidarity, an integrated and politically conscious programme of worker involvement in decision-making may undermine the power structure of the enterprise. Management will accede to such changes only under extreme duress of worker rebellion and rapidly disintegrating morale, if at all.

But the reproduction of consciousness cannot be insured by these direct mechanisms alone. The initiation of youth into the economic system is further facilitated by a series of institutions, including the family and the educational system, that are more immediately related to the formation of personality and consciousness. Education works primarily through the institutional relations to which students are subjected. Thus schooling fosters and rewards the development of certain capacities and the expression of certain needs, while thwarting and penalizing others. Through these institutional relationships, the educational system tailors the self-concepts, aspirations, and social class identifications of individuals to the requirements of the social division of labour.

The extent to which the educational system actually accomplishes these objectives varies considerably from one period to the next. Recurrently through US history these reproduction mechanisms have failed, sometimes quite spectacularly. In most periods – and the present is certainly no exception – efforts to use the schools to reproduce and extend capitalist production relations have been countered both by the internal dynamic of the educational system and by popular oppostion.

We have identified the two main objectives of dominant classes in educational policy: the production of labour power and the reproduction of those institutions and social relationships which facilitate the translation of labour power into profits. We may now be considerably more concrete about the way that educational institutions are structured to meet these objectives. First, schooling produces many of the technical and cognitive skills required for adequate job performance. Second, the educational system helps legitimate economic inequality. The objective and meritocratic orientation of US education reduces discontent over both the hierarchical division of labour and the process through which individuals attain position in it. Third, the school produces, rewards, and labels personal characteristics relevant to the staffing of positions in the hierarchy. Fourth, the educational system, through the pattern of status distinctions it fosters, reinforces the stratified consciousness on which the fragmentation of subordinate economic classes is based.

What aspects of the educational system allow it to serve these various functions? We shall suggest in the next section that the educational system's ability to reproduce the consciousness of workers lies in a straightforward correspondence principle: for the past century at least, schooling has contributed to the reproduction of the social relations of production largely through the correspondence between school and class structure.

Upon the slightest reflection, this assertion is hardly surprising. All major institutions in a 'stable' social system will direct personal development in a direction compatible with its reproduction. Of course, this is not, in itself, a critique of capitalism or of US education. In any conceivable society, individuals are forced to develop their capacities in one direction or another. The idea of a social system which merely allows people to develop freely according to their 'inner natures' is quite unthinkable, since human nature only acquires a concrete form through the interaction of the physical world and pre-established social relationships.

Our critique of education and other aspects of human development in the United States fully recognizes the necessity of some form of socialization. The critical question is: what for? In the United States the human development experience is dominated by an undemocratic, irrational, and exploitative economic structure. Young people have no recourse from the requirements of the system but a life of poverty, dependence, and economic insecurity. Our critique, not surprisingly, centres on the structure of jobs. In the US economy work has become a fact of life to which individuals must by and large submit and over which they have no control. Like the weather, work 'happens' to people. A liberated, participatory, democratic, and creative alternative can hardly be imagined, much less experienced. Work under capitalism is an alienated activity.

To reproduce the social relations of production, the educational system must try to teach people to be properly subordinate and render them sufficiently fragmented in consciousness to preclude their getting together to shape their own material existence. The forms of consciousness and behaviour fostered by the educational system must themselves be alienated, in the sense that they conform neither to the dictates of technology in the struggle with nature, nor to the inherent developmental capacities of individuals, but rather to the needs of the capitalist class. It is the prerogatives of capital and the imperatives of profit, not human capacities and technical realities, which render US schooling what it is. This is our charge.

The correspondence principle

The educational system helps integrate youth into the economic system, we believe, through a structural correspondence between its social relations and those of production. The structure of social relations in education not only inures the student to the discipline of the work-place, but develops the types of personal demeanour, modes of self-presentation, self-image, and social-class identifications which are the crucial ingredients of job adequacy. Specifically, the social relationships of education – the relationships between administrators and teachers, teachers and students, students and students, and students and their work – replicate the hierarchical division of labour. Hierarchical relations are reflected in the vertical authority lines from administrators to teachers to students. Alienated labour is reflected in the student's lack of control over his or her education, the alienation of the student from the curriculum content, and the motivation of school work through a system of grades and other external rewards rather than the student's integration with either the process (learning) or the outcome (knowledge) of the educational 'production process'. Fragmentation in work is reflected in the institutionalized and often destructive competition among students through continual and ostensibly meritocratic ranking and evaluation. By attuning young people to a set of social relationships similar to those of the work-place, schooling attempts to gear the development of personal needs to its requirements.

But the correspondence of schooling with the social relations of production goes beyond this aggregate level. Different levels of education feed workers into different levels within the occupational structure and, correspondingly, tend toward an internal organization comparable to levels in the hierarchical division of labour. The lowest levels in the hierarchy of the enterprise emphasize rule-following, middle levels, dependability, and the capacity to operate without direct and continuous supervision while the higher levels stress the internalization of the norms of the enterprise. Similarly, in education, lower levels (junior and senior high school) tend to severely limit and channel the activities of students. Somewhat higher up the educational ladder, teacher and community colleges allow for more independent activity and less overall supervision. At the top, the elite four-year colleges emphasize social relationships conformable with the higher levels in the production hierarchy.[3] Thus schools continually maintain their hold on students. As they 'master' one type of behavioural regulation, they are either allowed to progress to the next or are channelled into the corresponding level in the hierarchy of production. Even within a single school, the social relationships of different tracks tend to conform to different behavioural norms. Thus in high school, vocational and general tracks emphasize rule-following and close supervision, while the college track tends toward a more open atmosphere emphasizing the internalization of norms.

These differences in the social relationships among and within schools, in part, reflect both the social backgrounds of the student body and their likely future economic positions. Thus blacks and other minorities are concentrated in schools whose repressive, arbitrary, generally chaotic internal order, coercive authority structures, and minimal possibilities for advancement mirror the characteristics of inferior job situations. Similarly, predominantly working-class schools tend to emphasize behavioural control and rule-following, while schools in well-to-do suburbs employ relatively open systems that favour greater student participation, less direct supervision, more student electives, and, in general, a value system stressing internalized standards of control.

The differential socialization patterns of schools attended by students of different social classes do not arise by accident. Rather, they reflect the fact that the educational objectives and expectations of administrators, teachers, and parents (as well as the responsiveness of students to various patterns of teaching and control) differ for students of different social classes. At crucial turning-points in the history of US education, changes in the social relations of schooling have been dictated in the interests of a more harmonious reproduction of the class structure. But in the day-to-day operation of the schools, the consciousness of different occupational strata, derived from their cultural milieu and work experience, is crucial to the maintenance of the correspondences we have described. That working-class parents seem to favour stricter educational methods is a reflection of their own work experiences, which have demonstrated that submission to authority is an essential ingredient in one's ability to get and hold a steady, well-paying job. That professional and self-employed parents prefer a more open atmosphere and a greater emphasis on motivational control is similarly a reflection of their position in the social division of labour. When given the opportunity, higher-status parents are far more likely than their lower-status neighbours to choose 'open classrooms' for their children.[4]

Differences in the social relationships of schooling are further reinforced by inequalities in financial resources. The paucity of financial support for the education of children from minority groups and low-income families leaves more resources to be devoted to the children of those with more commanding roles in the economy; it also forces upon the teachers and school administrators in the working-class schools a type of social relationship that fairly closely mirrors that of the factory. Financial considerations in poorly supported schools militate against small intimate classes, multiple elective courses, and specialized teachers (except for disciplinary personnel). They preclude the amounts of free time for teachers and free space required for a more open, flexible educational environment. The well-financed schools attended by the children of the rich can offer much greater opportunities for the development of the capacity for sustained independent work and all the other characteristics required for adequate job performance in the upper levels of the occupational hierarchy.

Much of this description will most likely be familiar to the reader and has been documented many times.[5] But only recently has there been an attempt at statistical verification. We will review a number of excellent studies, covering both higher and secondary education. Jeanne Binstock investigated the different patterns of social relations of higher education by analysing the college handbooks covering rules, regulations, and norms of fifty-two public junior colleges, state universities, teacher-training colleges, and private, secular, denominational, and Catholic colleges. Binstock rated each school along a host of dimensions,[6] including the looseness or strictness of academic structure, the extent of regulations governing personal and social conduct, and the degree of control of the students over their cultural affairs and extracurricular activities. Her general conclusion is quite simple:

> The major variations of college experiences are linked to basic psychological differences in work perception and aspiration among the major social class (occupational) groups who are its major consumers. Each social class is different in its beliefs as to which technical and interpersonal skills, character traits, and work values are most valuable for economic survival (stability) or to gain economic advantage (mobility). Each class (with subvariations based on religion and level of urban-ness) has its own economic consciousness, based on its own work experiences and its own ideas (correct or not) of the expectations appropriate to positions on the economic ladder above their own .... Colleges compete over the various social class markets by specializing their offerings. Each different type of undergraduate college survives by providing circumscribed sets of 'soft' and 'hard' skill training that generally corresponds both to the expectations of a particular social class group of customers and to specific needs for sets of 'soft' and 'hard' skills at particular layers of the industrial system.[7]

Binstock isolated several organizational traits consistently related to the various educational institutions she studied. First, she distinguished between behavioural control which involves rules over the student's behaviour rather than intentions and stresses external compliance rather than internalized norms, and motivational control which emphasizes unspecified, variable, and highly flexible task-orientation, and seeks to promote value systems that stress ambiguity and innovation over certainty, tradition, and conformity. Second, Binstock isolated a leader-versus-follower orientation with some schools stressing the future subordinate positions of its charges and teaching docility, and others stressing the need to develop 'leadership' self-concepts.

Binstock found that institutions that enrol working-class students and are geared to staff lower-level jobs in the production hierarchy emphasize followership and behavioural control, while the more elite schools that tend to staff the higher-level jobs emphasize leadership and motivational control. Her conclusion is:

> Although constantly in the process of reformation, the college industry remains a ranked hierarchy of goals and practices, responding to social class pressures, with graded access to the technical equipment, organizational skills, emotional perspectives and class (work) values needed for each stratified level of the industrial system.[8]

The evidence for the correspondence between the social relations of production and education, however, goes well beyond this structural level and also sheds light on the communality of motivational patterns fostered by these two spheres of social life. Juxtaposing the recent research of Gene Smith, Richard Edwards, Peter Meyer, and ourselves, the same types of behaviour can be shown to be rewarded in both education and work. In an attempt to quantify aspects of personality and motivation, Gene Smith has employed a relatively sensitive testing procedure, which he has shown in a series of well-executed studies[9] to be an excellent predictor of educational success (grade-point average). Noting that personality inventories traditionally suffer because of their abstraction from real-life environments and their use of a single evaluative instrument, Smith turned to student-peer ratings of forty-two common personality traits, based on each student's observation of the actual classroom behaviour of his or her classmates. A statistical technique called factor analysis then allowed for the identification of five general traits – agreeableness, extroversion, work orientation, emotionality and helpfulness – that proved stable across different samples. Of these five traits, only the work-orientation factor, which Smith calls 'strength of character' – including such traits as '... not a quitter, conscientious, responsible, insistently orderly, not prone to daydreaming, determined, persevering ...' – was related to school success. Smith then proceeded to show that, in several samples, this work-orientation trait was three times more successful in predicting post-high-school academic performance than any combination of thirteen cognitive variables, including SAT verbal, SAT mathematical, and high school class rank (SAT: Secondary Aptitude Test).

Our colleague Richard C. Edwards has further refined Smith's procedure. As part of his Ph.D. dissertation on the nature of the hierarchical division of labour, he prepared a set of sixteen pairs of personality measures relevant to work performance.[10] Edwards argued that since supervisor ratings of employees are a basic determinant of hirings, firings, and promotions, they are the best measure of job adequacy and, indeed, are the implements of the organization's motivational system. Edwards, therefore, compared supervisor ratings of worker performance with the set of sixteen personality measures as rated by the workers' peers. In a sample of several hundred Boston area workers, he found a cluster of three personality traits – summarized as rules orientation, dependability, and internationalization of the norms of the firm – strongly predicting supervisor ratings of workers in the same work group. This result, moreover, holds up even when the correlation of these traits with such attributes as age, sex, social class background, education, and IQ is corrected for by linear regression analysis. Edwards found that rules orientation was relatively more important at the lowest levels of the hierarchy of production, internalization of norms was predominant at the highest level, while dependability was salient at intermediate levels.[11]

Edwards' success with this test in predicting supervisor ratings of workers convinced us that applying the same forms to high-school students would provide a fairly direct link between personality development in school and the requirements of job performance.

This task we carried out with our colleague Peter Meyer.[12] He chose as his sample the 237 members of the senior class of a single New York State high school. Following Edwards, he created sixteen pairs of personality traits, and obtained individual grade-point averages, IQ scores, and college-entrance-examination SAT-verbal and SAT-mathematical scores from the official school records.[13]

As we expected, the cognitive scores provided the best single predictor of grade-point average – indeed, that grading is based significantly on cognitive performance is perhaps the most valid element in the 'meritocratic ideology'. But the sixteen personality measures possessed nearly comparable predictive value, having a multiple correlation of 0.63 compared to 0.77 for the cognitive variables. More important than the overall predictive value of the personality traits, however, was the pattern of their contribution to grades. To reveal this pattern, we first eliminated the effect of differences in cognitive performance in individual grades and then calculated the correlation between grades and the personality traits. The results are presented in Figure 1.

The pattern of resulting associations clearly supports the correspondence principle. The only significant penalized traits are precisely those which are incompatible with conformity to the hierarchical division of labour – creativity, independence, and aggressivity. On the other hand, all the personality traits which we would expect to be rewarded are, and significantly so. Finally, a glance at Figure 2 shows a truly remarkable correspondence between the personality traits rewarded or penalized by grades in Meyer's study and the pattern of traits which Edwards found indicative of high or low supervisor ratings in industry.

Figure 1 Personality traits rewarded and penalized (in a New York high school)

Partial correlation with grade = point average

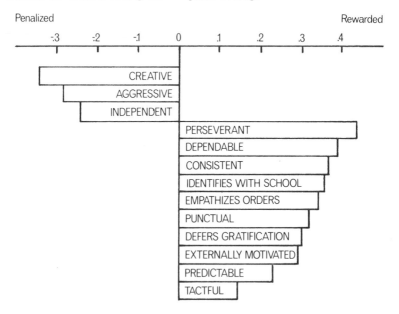

Notes: Each bar shows the partial correlation between grade-point average and the indicated personality trait, controlling for IQ, SAT-Verbal, and SAT-Mathematical. The penalized traits (left) indicate creativity and autonomy, while the rewarded traits (right) indicate subordinacy and discipline. The data are from Samuel Bowles, Herbert Gintis, and Peter Meyer, 'The Long Shadow of Work: Education, the Family, and the Reproduction of the Social Division of Labour,' *The Insurgent Sociologist*, Summer 1975. All partial correlations are statistically significant at the 1 per cent level.

As a second stage in our analysis of Meyer's data, we used factor analysis to consolidate the sixteen personality measures into three 'personality factors'. Factor analysis allows us to group together those measured traits which are normally associated with one another among all individuals in the sample. The first factor, which we call 'submission to authority', includes these traits: consistent, identifies with school, punctual, dependable, externally motivated, and persistent. In addition, it includes independent and creative weighted negatively. The second, which we call temperament, includes: not aggressive, not temperamental, not frank, predictable, tactful, and not creative. The third we call internalized control, and it includes: empathizes orders and defers gratification.[14]

Figure 2   Personality traits approved by supervisors

Correlation with supervisor rating

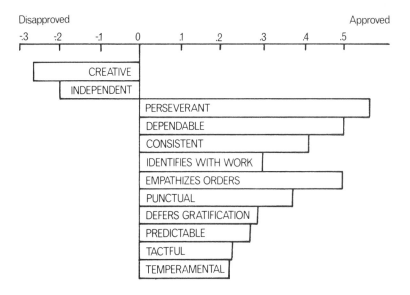

Notes: The pattern of personality traits indicative of supervisor approval correspond to those rewarded in high school. Each bar shows the correlation between supervisor rating and the indicated personality trait. The results are similar to Figure 1, except that aggressive is insignificant and temperamental significant in the sample of workers. The data are from Richard C. Edwards, 'Personal Traits and "Success" in Schooling and Work', *Educational and Psychological Measurement*, in press, 1976; 'Individual Traits and Organizational Incentives: What Makes a "Good Worker?"' *Journal of Human Resources*, Spring 1976, and are based on a sample of 240 workers in several government offices in the Boston area. All correlations are significant at the 1 per cent level.

Figure 3   Predicting job performance and grades in school from the same personality traits

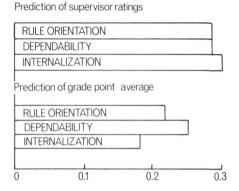

Prediction of supervisor ratings

RULE ORIENTATION
DEPENDABILITY
INTERNALIZATION

Prediction of grade point average

RULE ORIENTATION
DEPENDABILITY
INTERNALIZATION

0   0.1   0.2   0.3

Contribution to the prediction

Notes: The top three bars show the estimated normalized regression coefficients of the personality factors in an equation predicting supervisor ratings. The bottom three bars show the coefficients of the same three factors in an equation predicting high-school grade point average. All factors are significant at the 1 per cent level. The regression equations are presented in our Apprendix B.

Sources: Bowles, Gintis, and Meyer; Edwards (as Figures 1 and 2).

These three factors are not perfectly comparable to Edwards' three factors. Thus our submission to authority seems to combine Edwards' rules and dependability factors, while our internalized control is comparable to Edwards' internalization factor. In the case of the latter, both Edwards and Meyer's data depict an individual who sensitively interprets the desires of his or her superior and operates adequately without direct supervision over considerable periods of time.

Our theory would predict that at the high-school level submission to authority would be the best predictor of grades among personality traits, while internalization would be less important. (The temperament factor is essentially irrelevant to our theory and might be expected to be unimportant.) This prediction was confirmed. Assessing the independent contributions of both cognitive measures and personality factors to the prediction of grades, we found that SAT math were the most important, followed by submission to authority and SAT-verbal scores (each equally important). Internalized control proved to be significantly less important as predictors. The temperament and IQ variables made no independent contribution.

Thus, at least for this sample, the personality traits rewarded in schools seem to be rather similar to those indicative of good job performance in the capitalist economy. Since, moreover, both Edwards and Meyer used essentially the same measures of personality traits, we can test this assertion in yet another way. We can take the three general traits extracted by Edwards in his study of workers – rules orientation, dependability, and internalization of norms – and find the relationship between those traits and grades in Meyer's school study. The results shown in Figure 3, exhibit a remarkable congruence.[15]

While the correspondence principle stands up well in the light of grading practices, we must stress that the empirical data on grading must not be regarded as fully revealing the inner workings of the educational system's reproduction of the social division of labour. In the first place, it is the overall structure of social relations of the educational encounter which reproduces consciousness, not just grading practices. Nor are personality traits the only relevant personal attributes captured in this data; others are modes of self-presentation, self-image, aspirations, and class identifications. The measuring of personality traits, moreover, is complex and difficult, and these studies probably capture only a small part of the relevant dimensions. Finally, both traits rewarded in schools and relevant to job performance differ by educational level, class composition of schools, and the student's particular educational track. These subtleties are not reflected in this data.

For all these reasons, we would not expect student grades to be a good predictor of economic success. In addition, grades are clearly dominated by the cognitive performance of students, which we have seen is not highly relevant to economic success. Still, we might expect that in an adequately controlled study in which work performances of individuals on the same job and with comparable educational experience are compared, grades will be good predictors. We have managed to find only one study even approaching these requirements – a study which clearly supports our position, and is sufficiently interesting to present in some detail.[16] Marshall S. Brenner studied one hundred employees who had joined the Lockheed-California Company after obtaining a high-school diploma in the Los Angeles City school districts. From the employee's high-school transcripts, he obtained their grade-point averages, school absence rates, a teacher's 'work habits' evaluation, and a teacher's 'cooperation' evaluation. In addition to this data, he gathered three evaluations of job performance by employees' supervisors: a supervisor's 'ability rating', 'conduct rating', and 'productivity rating'. Brenner found a significant correlation between grades and all measures of supervisor evaluation.

We have reanalysed Brenner's data to uncover the source of this correlation. One possibility is that grades measure cognitive performance and cognitive performance determines job performance. However, when the high school teachers' work habits and cooperation evaluations as well as school absences were controlled for by linear regression, grades had no power to predict either worker conduct or worker productivity. Hence, we may draw two conclusions: First, grades predict job adequacy only through their noncognitive component; and second, teachers' evaluations of behaviour in the classroom are strikingly similar to supervisors' ratings of behaviour on the job. The cognitive component of grades predicts only the supervisors' ability rating – which is not surprising in view of the probability that both are related to employee IQ.

Why then the association between more schooling and higher incomes? Four sets of noncognitive worker traits are important – work-related personality characteristics, modes of self-presentation, racial, sexual, and ethnic characteristics, and credentials. We believe that all of these traits are involved in the association between educational level and economic success. We have already shown how personality traits conducive to performance at different hierarchical levels are fostered and rewarded by the school system. A similar, but simpler, argument can be made with respect to modes of self-presentation. Individuals who have attained a certain educational level tend to identify with one another socially and to differentiate themselves from their 'inferiors'. They tend to adjust their aspirations and self-concepts accordingly, while acquiring manners of speech and demeanour more or less socially acceptable and appropriate to their level.[17] As such, they are correspondingly valuable to employers interested in preserving and reproducing the status differences on which the legitimacy and stability of the hierarchical division of labour is based. Moreover, insofar as educational credentials are an independent determinant of hiring and promotion, they will directly account for a portion of this association.[18]

Finally, family background also accounts for a significant portion of the association between schooling and economic attainment. Indeed, for white males, about a third of the correlation between education and income is due to the common association of both variables with socioeconomic background, even holding constant childhood IQ. That is, people whose parents have higher-status economic positions tend to achieve more income themselves independent of their education, but they also tend to get more education. Hence the observed association is reinforced.

Indeed, there is a strong independent association between family background and economic success, illustrated in Figure 4. For the large national sample represented there, children of the poorest tenth of families have roughly a third the likelihood of winding up well-off as the children of the most well-to-do tenth, even if they have the same educational attainments and childhood IQs. What is the origin of this effect? The inheritance of wealth, family connections, and other more or less direct advantages play an important role here. But there are more subtle if no less important influences at work here as well. We shall argue in the following section that the experiences of parents on the job tend to be reflected in the social relations of family life. Thus, through family socialization, children tend to acquire orientations toward work, aspirations, and self-concepts, preparing them for similar economic positions themselves.

Figure 4 The effect of socioeconomic background on economic success is strong even for individuals with equal education and IQ

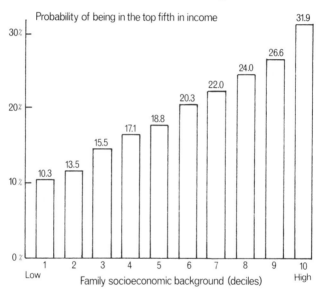

Notes: Each bar shows the estimated probability that a man is in the top fifth of the income distribution if he is from the given decile of socioeconomic background (as a weighted average of his father's education, occupational status, and his parents' income), and if he has an average childhood IQ and average number of years schooling. That is, it measures the effect of socioeconomic background on income, independent of any effects caused by education or IQ differences:

Sample: Non-Negro males from nonfarm backgrounds, aged 35–44.

Source: Samuel Bowles and Valerie Nelson, 'The "Inheritance of IQ" and the Intergenerational Reproduction of Economic Inequality'. *The Review of Economics and Statistics*, Vol. 56, No. 1, February 1974.

Family structure and job structure

Family experience has a significant impact on the well-being, behaviour, and personal consciousness of individuals, both during maturation and in their daily adult lives. The social relationships of family life − relationships between husband and wife as well as between parents and children and among children − have undergone important changes in the course of US economic development. The prospect for future changes is of crucial importance in the process of social transformation.[19]

Rather than attempt a broad analysis of family life, we shall limit our discussion to a few issues directly linked to our central concern: the reproduction of the social relations of production. Like the educational system, the family plays a major role in preparing the young for economic and social roles. Thus, the family's impact on the reproduction of the sexual division of labour, for example, is distinctly greater than that of the educational system.

This reproduction of consciousness is facilitated by a rough correspondence between the social relations of production and the social relations of family life, a corespondence that is greatly affected by the experiences of parents in the social division of labour. There is a tendency for families to reproduce in their offspring not only a consciousness tailored to the objective nature of the work world, but to prepare them for economic positions roughly comparable to their own. Although these tendencies can be countered by other social forces (schooling, media, shifts in aggregate occupational structure), they continue to account for a significant part of the observed intergenerational status-transmission processes.

However, in essential respects, the family exhibits social patterns that are quite uncharacteristic of the social relations of production. The close personal and emotional relationships of family life are remote from the impersonal bureaucracy of the wage-labour system. Indeed, the family is often esteemed as a refuge from the alienation and psychic poverty of work life. Indeed, it is precisely because family structure and the capitalist relations of production differ in essential respects that our analysis sees schooling as performing such a necessary role in the integration of young people into the wage-labour system.

Despite the tremendous structural disparity between family and economy − one which is never really overcome in capitalist society − there is a significant correspondence between the authority relationships in capitalist production and family child-rearing. In part, this is true of family life common at all social levels. The male-dominated family, with its characteristically age-graded patterns of power and privilege, replicates many aspects of the hierarchy of production in the firm. Yet here we shall be more concerned with the difference among families whose income-earners hold distinct positions in this hierarchy.

As we have seen, successful job performance at low hierarchical levels requires the worker's orientation toward rule-following and conformity to external authority, while successful performance at higher levels requires behaviour according to internalized norms. It would be surprising, indeed, if these general orientations did not manifest themselves in parental priorities for the rearing of their children. Melvin Kohn's massive, ten-year study at the National Institute of Mental Health has documented important correspondences between authority in the social relationships of work and the social relationships of the family precisely of this type.

Kohn, in a series of papers and in his book, *Class and Conformity*, has advanced and tested the following hypothesis: personality traits and values of individuals affect the economic positions they attain and, conversely, their job experiences strongly affect their personalities and values.[20] The most important values and behaviour patterns in this interaction are those relating to self-direction and conformity,[21] with individuals of higher economic status more likely to value internal motivation and those of lower status more likely to value behaviour that conforms with external authority. Thus, Kohn argues, individuals in higher-status jobs tend to value curiosity and self-reliance, to emphasize the intrinsic aspects of jobs such as freedom and choice, and to exhibit a high level of internalized motivation and a high degree of trust in interpersonal relationships. Conversely, people in lower-status jobs tend to value personal responsibility and the extrinsic aspects of jobs such as security, pay, and working conditions. Moreover, they exhibit more external motivations, a greater conformity to explicit social rules and they are less trustful of others.[22]

Kohn goes on to inquire which aspects of jobs produce these results and concludes that the statistically relevant job characteristic is the degree of occupational self-direction, including freedom from close supervision, the degree of initiative and independent judgment allowed, and the complexity and variety of the job. Thus no matter what their economic status, whether white or blue collar, individuals with the same degree of occupational self-direction, tend to have similar values and traits. Self-direction versus close supervision and routinization on the job account for most of the status-related differences in personal preferences for self-direction, degree of internalized morality, trustfulness, self-confidence, self-esteem, and idea conformity. He concludes:

In industrial society, where occupation is central to men's lives, occupational experiences that facilitate or deter the exercise of self-direction come to permeate men's views, not only of work and their role in work, but of the world and of self. The conditions of occupational life at higher social class levels facilitate interest in the intrinsic qualities of the job, foster a view of self and society that is conducive to believing in the possibilities of rational action toward purposive goals, and promote the valuation of self-direction. The conditions of occupational life at lower social class levels limit men's view of the job primarily to the extrinsic benefits it provides, foster a narrowly circumscribed conception of self and society, and promote the positive valuation of conformity to authority.[23]

There remains, however, an important discrepancy between our interpretation and Kohn's. What Kohn calls 'self-direction' we feel is usually better expressed as 'internalized norms'. That is, the vast majority of workers in higher levels of the hierarchy of production are by no means autonomous, self-actualizing, and creatively self-directed. Rather, they are probably supersocialized so as to internalize authority and act without direct and continuous supervision to implement goals and objectives relatively alienated from their own personal needs. This distinction must be kept clearly in mind to avoid the error of attributing 'superior' values and behaviour traits to higher strata in the capitalist division of labour.

Kohn then went on to investigate the impact of work-related values on child-rearing. He began, in 1956, with a sample of 339 white mothers of children in the fifth grade, whose husbands held middle-class and working class jobs.[24] He inquired into the values parents would most like to see in their children's behaviour. He found that parents of lower-status children value obedience, neatness, and honesty in their children, while higher-status parents emphasize curiosity, self-control, consideration, and happiness. The fathers of these children who were interviewed showed a similar pattern of values. Kohn says:

> Middle-class parents are more likely to emphasize children's *self-direction*, and working-class parents to emphasize their *conformity to external authority* .... The essential difference between the terms, as we use them, is that self-direction focuses on *internal* standards of direction for behaviour; conformity focuses on *externally* imposed rules.[25]

Kohn further emphasized that these values translate directly into corresponding authority relationships between parents and children, with higher-status parents punishing breakdowns of internalized norms, and lower-status parents punishing transgressions of rules:

The principal difference between the classes is in the *specific conditions* under which parents – particularly mothers – punish children's misbehaviour. Working-class parents are more likely to punish or refrain from punishing on the basis of the direct and immediate consequences of children's actions, middle-class parents on the basis of their interpretation of children's intent in acting as they do .... If self-direction is valued, transgressions must be judged in terms of the reasons why the children misbehave. If conformity is valued, transgressions must be judged in terms of whether or not the actions violate externally imposed proscriptions.[26]

In 1964, Kohn undertook to validate his findings with a national sample of 3,100 males, representative of the employed, male civilian labour force. His results clearly support his earlier interpretation: higher-job-status fathers prefer consideration, curiosity, responsibility, and self-control in their children; low-status fathers prefer good manners, neatness, honesty, and obedience. Moreover, Kohn showed that about two-thirds of these social status-related differences are directly related to the extent of occupational self-direction. As a predictor of child-rearing values, the structure of work life clearly overshadows the other correlates of status such as occupational prestige or educational level. He concludes:

Whether consciously or not parents tend to impact to their children lessons derived from the conditions of life of their own social class – and this helps to prepare their children for a similar class position .... Class differences in parental values and child rearing practices influence the development of the capacities that children will someday need .... The family, then, functions as a mechanism for perpetuating inequality.[27]

Kohn's analysis provides a careful and compelling elucidation of one facet of what we consider to be a generalized social phenomenon: the reflection of economic life in all major spheres of social activity. The hierarchical division of labour, with the fragmentation of the work force which it engenders, is merely reflected in family life. The distinct quality of social relationships at different hierarchical levels in production are reflected in corresponding social relationships in the family. Families, in turn, reproduce the forms of consciousness required for the integration of a new generation into the economic system. Such differential patterns of child rearing affect more than the worker's personality, as is exemplified in Kohn's study. They also pattern self-concepts, personal aspirations, styles of self-presentation, class loyalties, and modes of speech, dress, and interpersonal behaviour. While such traits are by no means fixed into adulthood and must be reinforced at the work place, their stability over the life cycle appears sufficient to account for a major portion of the observed degree of intergenerational status transmission.

Conclusion

The economic system is stable only if the consciousness of the strata and classes which compose it remains compatible with the social relations which characterize it as a mode of production. The perpetuation of the class structure requires that the hierarchical division of labour be reproduced in the consciousness of its participants. The educational system is one of the several reproduction mechanisms through which dominant elites seek to achieve this objective. By providing skills, legitimating inequalities in economic positions, and facilitating certain types of social intercourse among individuals, US education patterns personal development around the requirements of alienated work. The educational system reproduces the capitalist social division of labour, in part, through a correspondence between its own internal social relationships and those of the work place.

The tendency of the social relationships of economic life to be replicated in the educational system and in family life lies at the heart of the failure of the liberal educational creed. This fact must form the basis of a viable programme for social change. Patterns of inequality, repression, and forms of class domination cannot be restricted to a single sphere of life, but reappear in substantially altered, yet structurally comparable, form in all spheres. Power and privilege in economic life surface not only in the core social institutions which pattern the formation of consciousness (for example, school and family), but even in face-to-face personal encounters, leisure activities, cultural life, sexual relationships, and philosophies of the world. In particular, the liberal goal of employing the educational system as a corrective device for overcoming the 'inadequacies' of the economic system is vain indeed. We would argue that the transformation of the educational system and the pattern of class relationships, power, and privilege in the economic sphere must go hand in hand as part of an integrated programme for action.

As we have already seen, capitalist economic development leads to continual shifts in the social relationships of production and the attendant class structure. These social relationships have involved class conflicts which, throughout US history, have periodically changed in both form and content. In important respects the educational system has served to defuse and attenuate these conflicts. Thus the changing character of social conflict, rooted in shifts in the class structure and in other relations of power and privilege has resulted in periodic reorganizations of educational institutions. At the same time the educational system has evolved in ways which intensify and politicize the basic contradictions and conflicts of capitalist society.

Notes

1 Herbert Gintis, 'Welfare criteria with endogenous preferences: the economics of education', *International Economic Review*, June 1974; Alfred Schutz and Thomas Luckmann, *The Structure of the Life-World* (Evanston, Illinois: Northwestern University Press, 1973); and Peter L. Berger and Thomas Luckmann, *The Social Construction of Reality: A Treatise in the Sociology of Knowledge* (Garden City, Long Island, New York: Doubleday and Company, 1966).

2 For an extended treatment of these issues, see Herbert Gintis, 'Alienation and power', in *The Review of Radical Political Economics*, Vol. 4, No. 5, Fall 1972.

3 Jeanne Binstock, 'Survival in the American college industry', unpublished Ph.D. dissertation, Brandeis University, 1970.

4 Burton Rosenthal, 'Educational investments in human capital: the significance of stratification in the labor market', unpublished honours thesis, Harvard University, 1972; and Edgar Z. Friedenberg, *Coming of Age in America* (New York: Random House, 1965).

5 Florence Howe and Paul Lauter, 'The schools are rigged for failure', *New York Review of Books*, June 20, 1970; James Herndon, *The Way It Spozed to Be* (New York: Simon and Schuster, 1968); and Ray C. Rist, 'Student social class and teacher expectations: the self-fulfilling prophesy in ghetto education', *Harvard Educational Review*, August 1970.

6 Binstock (1970), *loc. cit.*, pp. 103–106.

7 *Ibid.*, pp. 3–4

8 *Ibid.*, p. 6.

9 Gene M. Smith, 'Usefulness of peer ratings of personality in educational research', *Educational and Psychological Measurement*, 1967; 'Personality correlates of academic performance in three dissimilar populations', Proceedings of the 77th Annual Convention, American Psychological Association, 1967; and 'Non-intelligence correlates of academic performance', mimeo, 1970.

10 Richard C. Edwards, 'Alienation and inequality: capitalist relations of production in a bureaucratic enterprise', Ph.D. dissertation, Harvard University, July 1972.

11 Richard C. Edwards, 'Personal traits and "success" in schooling and work', *Educational and Psychological Measurement*, in press, 1975;

and 'Individual traits and organizational incentives: what makes a "good"worker?' *Journal of Human Resources*, in press, 1976.

12 Peter J. Meyer, 'Schooling and the reproduction of the social division of labor'. unpublished honours thesis, Harvard University, March 1972.

13 The school chosen was of predominantly higher income, so that most students had taken college-entrance examinations.

14 We emphasize that these groupings are determined by a computer programme on the basis of the observed pattern of association among the sixteen variables.

15 This is taken from Table 3 of Edwards (1975), *op. cit.*; and Samuel Bowles, Herbert Gintis, and Peter Meyer, 'The long shadow of work: education, the family and the reproduction of the social division of labor', in *The Insurgent Sociologist*, Summer 1975.

16 Marshall H. Brenner, 'The use of high school data to predict work performance', *Journal of Applied Psychology*, Vol. 52, No. 1, January 1968. This study was suggested to us by Edwards, and is analysed in Edwards (1972), *loc. cit.*

17 See Claus Offe, *Leistungsprinzip und Industrielle Arbeit* (Frankfurt: Europaische Verlaganstalt, 1970).

18 See Ivar Berg, *Education and Jobs: The Great Training Robbery* (Boston: Beacon Press, 1971); and Paul Taubman and Terence Wales, *Higher Education and Earnings* (New York: McGraw-Hill, 1974).

19 Margaret Benston, 'The political economy of women's liberation', *Monthly Review*, September 1969; Marilyn P. Goldberg, 'The economic exploitation of women', in David M. Gordon (ed) *Problems in Political Economy* (Lexington, Massachusetts: D. C. Heath and Company, 1971); L. Gordon, *Families* (Cambridge, Massachusetts: A. Bread and Rose Publication, 1970); Zaretzky, 'Capitalism and personal life', *Socialist Revolution*, January-April 1973; and Juliet Mitchell, *Women's Estate* (New York: Vintage Books, 1973).

20 Melvin Kohn, *Class and Conformity: A Study in Values* (Homewood, Illinois: Dorsey Press, 1969).

21 Melvin Kohn and Carmi Schooler, 'Occupational experience and cognitive functioning: an assessment of reciprocal effects', *American Sociological Review*, February 1973.

22 Kohn (1969), *loc. cit.*; chapters 5 and 10.

23 *Ibid.*, p. 192.

24 The occupational index used was that of Hollingshead, which correlates 0.90 with the Duncan index.

25 Kohn (1969), *loc. cit.*, pp. 34–5.

26 *Ibid.*, pp. 104–105.

27 Kohn (1969), *loc. cit.*, p. 200.

4.7   Status of the worker

Michael Young

Golden age of equality

No longer is it just the brilliant individual who shines forth; the world
beholds for the first time the spectacle of a brilliant class, the 5 per cent of
the nation who know what 5 per cent means. Every member is a tried
specialist in his own sphere. Mounting at a faster and faster rate, our
knowledge has been cumulative from generation to generation. In the
course of a mere hundred years we have come close to realizing at one
stroke the ideal of Plato, Erasmus, and Shaw. But, if sociology teaches
anything, it teaches that no society is completely stable; always there are
strains and conflicts. Now I consider the consequences of progress for the
lower class, and particularly for those born into it.

My method of analysis is historical; the comparison I draw with a
century ago. Taylor has called that time the golden age of equality.[1] A sort
of egalitarianism flourished then because two contradictory principles for
legitimizing power were struggling for mastery – the principle of kinship
and the principle of merit – and nearly everyone, in his heart of hearts,
believed in both. Everyone thought it proper to advance his son and
honour his father; everyone thought it proper to seek out ability and
honour achievement. Individuals were riven as much as society. The
consequence was that anyone who had reached privilege behind the shield
of only one of these principles could be attacked with the sword of the
other – the man born great was criticized because, by another reckoning,
he did not deserve his fortune; and the base-born achieving greatness
could be charged half impostor. The powerful were, by this whirligig,
unfailingly unseated.

Many people were catapulted forward by their parents' riches and

Source: *The Rise of the Meritocracy*, 1958, Thames and Hudson, pp. 103–25 in Penguin
edition.

influence; not only did they benefit from the culture festooning their homes, they were sent to the best schools and colleges, dispatched on trips abroad and given expensive training for Bar, counting-house, or surgery – all the advantages, in short, which we in our day try to keep for the deserving. But since such treatment was sanctioned by only half the moral code, the beneficiaries were only half at home in their station in life. They could not say to themselves with complete conviction 'I am the best man for the job' because they knew that they had not won their place in open competition and, if they were honest, had to recognize that a dozen of their subordinates would have been as good, or perhaps better. Although they sometimes sought to deny self-doubt by too brassy an assertion of self-confidence, such denial was hard to sustain when it plainly ran against the facts. The upper-class man had to be insensitive indeed not to have noticed, at some time in his life, that a private in his regiment, a butler or 'charlady' in his home, a driver of taxi or bus, or the humble workman with lined face and sharp eyes in the railway carriage or country pub – not to have noticed that amongst such people was intelligence, wit, and wisdom at least equal to his own, not to have noticed that every village had its Jude the Obscure. If he had so observed, if he had so recognized that his social inferiors were sometimes his biological superiors, if the great variety of people in all social classes had made him think in some dim way that 'a man's a man for a' that', was he not likely to respond by treating them with a kind of respect?[2]

Even if the superiors deceived themselves, they could not their subordinates. These knew that many bosses were there not so much because of what they knew, as who they knew, and who their parents were, and went on, with wanton exaggeration, to denounce all bosses on like account. Some men of talent took pains (if contemporary novels are to be relied on) to make it known in the factory, if not in the golf club, that they had 'come up the hard way'. But who could tell for certain how far success had been accident, or lack of scruples offset lack of brains? The workmen had their doubts. They let fly with their criticism of the powers-that-be, and so kept even the able under restraint. The energy wasted on criticism and counter-criticism was colossal.

An even more important consequence of the conflict in values was that the workers could altogether dissociate their own judgments of themselves from the judgment of society. Subjective and objective status were often poles apart. The worker said to himself: 'Here I am, a workman. Why am I a workman? Am I fit for nothing else? Of course not. Had I had a proper chance I would have shown the world. A doctor? A brewer? A minister? I could have done anything. I never had the chance. And so I am a worker. But don't think that at bottom I am any worse than anyone else. I'm better.' Educational injustice enabled people to preserve their illusions, inequality of opportunity fostered the myth of human equality. Myth we know it to be; not so our ancestors.

Gulf between the classes

This evocation of the past shows how great the change has been. In those days no class was homogeneous in brains: clever members of the upper classes had as much in common with clever members of the lower classes as they did with stupid members of their own. Now that people are classified by ability, the gap between the classes has inevitably become wider. The upper classes are, on the one hand, no longer weakened by self-doubt and self-criticism. Today the eminent know that success is just reward for their own capacity, for their own efforts, and for their own undeniable achievement. They deserve to belong to a superior class. They know, too, that not only are they of higher calibre to start with, but that a first-class education has been built upon their native gifts. As a result, they can come as close as anyone to understanding the full and ever-growing complexity of our technical civilization. They are trained in science, and it is scientists who have inherited the earth. What can they have in common with people whose education stopped at sixteen or seventeen, leaving them with the merest smattering of dog-science? How can they carry on a two-sided conversation with the lower classes when they speak another, richer, and more exact language? Today, the elite know that, except for a grave error in administration, which should at once be corrected if brought to light, their social inferiors are inferiors in other ways as well – that is, in the two vital qualities, of intelligence and education, which are given pride of place in the more consistent value system of the twenty-first century. Hence one of our characteristic modern problems: some members of the meritocracy, as most moderate reformers admit, have become so impressed with their own importance as to lose sympathy with the people whom they govern, and so tactless that even people of low calibre have been quite unnecessarily offended. The schools and universities are endeavouring to instil a more proper sense of humility – what does even modern man count beside the wonders which Nature has wrought in the universe? – but for the moment the efficiency of public relations with the lower classes is not all that it might be.

As for the lower classes, their situation is different too. Today all persons, however humble, know they have had every chance. They are tested again and again. If on one occasion they are off-colour, they have a second, a third, and fourth opportunity to demonstrate their ability. But if they have been labelled 'dunce' repeatedly they cannot any longer pretend; their image of themselves is more nearly a true, unflattering, reflection. Are they not bound to recognize that they have an inferior status – not as in the past because they were denied opportunity; but because they *are* inferior?[3] For the first time in human history the inferior man has no ready buttress for his self-regard. This has presented contemporary psychology with its gravest problem. Men who have lost their self-respect are liable to lose their inner vitality (especially if they are inferior to their own parents and fall correspondingly in the social scale) and may only too easily cease to be either good citizens or good technicians. The common man is liable to sulk for his fig-leaf.

The consequences of so depressing the status of the inferior and elevating that of the superior have naturally engaged the full attention of social science. We cannot pretend that its path has always been smooth. Dr Jason's 'tadpole' argument which amounted, when stripped of verbiage, to saying that on the whole all tadpoles were happier because they knew that some of them would turn into frogs, was at best a half-truth. The young might be happier; but what of the many older tadpoles who knew they would never become frogs? The tadpoles only confused counsel. Since Lord Jason himself became a 'frog', research has proceeded more steadily.

The situation has been saved by five things. First, by the philosophy underlying teaching in secondary-modern schools. When these were started, no one quite knew what to do about the content of education for the lower classes. Children were taught the three Rs as well as how to use simple tools and to measure with gauges and even micrometers. But this was only the formal skeleton of a course without an ideology to guide it. The schools had a far more important function than to equip their pupils with a few elementary skills; they also had to instil an attitude of mind which would be conducive to effective performance of their future tasks in life. The lower classes needed a *Mythos*, and they got what they needed, the Mythos of Muscularity. Luckily they already had this in a rudimentary form, which the modern schools have been able to promote into the modern cult of physical (as distinct from mental) prowess. The English love of sport was traditional, and nowhere stronger than in the lower classes. The modern schools were not breaking with the past, they were building on it, when they encouraged their pupils to value physical strength, bodily discipline, and manual dexterity. Handicrafts, gymnastics, and games have become the core of the curriculum. This enlightened approach has achieved a double purpose. Appreciation of manual work has been cultivated, and leisure made more enjoyable. Of the two, education for leisure has been the most important. More capable pupils have been trained to participate in active games which they can continue to play when they leave school; and the others who form the great majority have been given heightened appreciation of boxing, football, and other sports displayed before them nightly on the screens in their own homes. They esteem physical achievement almost as highly as we of the upper classes esteem mental.

Secondly, the adult education movement has, in its maturity, not only maintained and enlarged the regional centres but has arranged for everyone, irrespective of previous results, to attend there for a periodic intelligence check at intervals of five years. Tests can be even more frequent at the behest of the individual. A few remarkable changes of IQ both up and down, have occurred in the middle life. Widely publicized in the popular newspapers, the reports have given new heart to many an ambitious technician. Now that psychiatric treatment is freely available in every workplace, many people with emotional blocks to the realization of their potential have been fully cured.

Thirdly, even when they have abandoned hope themselves, all parents have been solaced by the knowledge that, however low their own IQ, their child (or grandchild) will have the chance to enter the meritocracy. The solace is a real one. Psychologists have shown that parents, whose own ambitions are thwarted, invariably displace those ambitions on to their children. They are satisfied if they think that their own child may achieve what they could not achieve themselves. 'Do as I wish, not as I do,' they say. The relationship can even be expressed in quantitative terms: according to the well-known principle of compensating aspirations, the greater the frustrations parents experience in their own lives, the greater their aspirations for their children. Almost from the moment when they fail their first intelligence tests at school, children can comfort themselves that one day they will have offspring who will do better; and even when it is dismally clear from teachers' reports that the offspring too are dull, there are still the grandchildren.[4] Personal failings are not so painful if there is a vision of vicarious triumph. As long as all have opportunity to rise through the schools, people can believe in immortality: they have a second chance through the younger generation. Also, the more children, the more second chances, which helps to account for the higher birth-rate in the second half of last century, after the reforms.

The fourth saving feature has been the very stupidity which has assigned the lower classes to their present status. A common mistake of some sociologists is to impute to the lower orders the same capacity as themselves – a way of thinking akin to anthropomorphism. Sociologists would naturally be aggrieved were they to be denied their proper status. But the lower classes are the objects of study, not the students. The attitude of mind is quite different. People of low intelligence have sterling qualities: they go to work, they are conscientious, they are dutiful to their families. But they are unambitious, innocent, and incapable of grasping clearly enough the grand design of modern society to offer any effective protest. Some are sulkily discontented, without being too sure what to do about it, and find their way to the psychologist or the priest. Most are not, for they know not what is done to them.

Pioneers of dirty work
The fifth, and most important, saving feature has been the application of scientific selection to industry. The modern schools have been reproduced in industry just as surely as the grammar schools, and with consequences just as far-reaching. The starting-point is again the Hitler war. In the early years of that war the methods of distributing recruits were almost as haphazard as in industry. Only after several disasters was a more sensible practice adopted, described as follows in the words of a leading Command Psychiatrist in one of the official histories of the war:

> In allocating personnel, the basic principle should be that no man is to be employed on work which is definitely above, or, on the other hand, definitely below his ability. Any other method of allotment is wasteful of ability, or destructive of unit efficiency.[5]

What wise and far-sighted words!

By the end of the war the instruction was obeyed and very few men entering the Forces were assigned to any branch until their intelligence and aptitudes had been ascertained as accurately as the crude methods of the time allowed. Much greater efficiency was obtained in the utilization of manpower when the stupid were kept together, and the lesson was not lost on some of the better brains in civilian industry. This was long before advertisers began to include 'State IQ' (soon shortened to SIQ) in their copy; and longer still before HQ (at Eugenics House) supplied IQ certificates to authorized inquirers by teleprinter. The flower of that experiment of the 1940s was the Pioneer Corps. When this indispensable body of hewers and drawers was confined to men with IQs below the line required to get them into the Intelligence Corps, the rise in efficiency was spectacular. The morale of these dull-witted men was better. They were no longer daunted by having superior people to compete with. They were amongst their equals – they had more equal opportunities since they had more limited ones – and they were happier, had fewer mental breakdowns, *and* were harder working. The Army had learnt the lesson of the schools: that people can be taught more easily, and get on better, when they are classed with people of more or less equal intelligence, or lack of it.

Not until the 1960s did this same lesson strike home in civil life. Intelligent people used to ask themselves what they thought was a profound poser: 'Who,' they asked, 'will do the dirty work in the future commonwealth?' Those who knew the right answer apparently said: 'Machines, of course; they will be the robots of the future.' It was a good answer as far as it went, but, in view of the many jobs which can never be taken over by machinery, at best a partial one. Then as they became aware of the new and revolutionary developments in intelligence testing, aptitude testing, and vocational selection, managements realized that a permanent peace-time Pioneer Corps was a practical possibility. At first tentatively, they suggested the correct answer to the old question: 'Who will do the dirty work?' The correct answer was: 'Why, men who like doing it, of course.'

They could see the need for a kind of permanent civilian Pioneer Corps, men with large muscles and small brains (selected by other men with small muscles and large brains) who were not only good at emptying dustbins and heaving loads but liked doing it. They were never to be asked to do more than they were proved to be fit for. They were never to be forced to mix with anyone who made them feel foolish by emptying dustbins more quickly or, what was worse at that time, by consigning all dustbins to the rubbish-heap – a sure sign either of mental deficiency or genius. As I say, progressive managements were very tentative and even a little shamefaced. They were easily put off by references to Mr Huxley's gammas and Mr Orwell's proles. The managers did not see that these two gentlemen had both been attacking not equal opportunity, but the effects of conditioning and propaganda. By these means even intelligent people were to be brought to accept their fate as manual workers. We know that in the long run this is impossible, and in the short run absurdly wasteful and frustrating. The only good manual workers, we know, are those who have not the ability for anything better. Enlightened modern methods have nothing in common with these brave new worlds. But at first not all managers realized that so signally to square efficiency with justice, and order with humanity, was nothing less than a new stage in the ascent of man, brought within his reach by the early advances in the social sciences.

The Pioneer Corps was the essential counterpart of the administrative class in the civil service; its historical significance is as great as that. The success of open competition in government employment established the principle that the most responsible posts should be filled by the most able people; the Pioneers that the least responsible jobs should be filled by the least able people. In other words, a society in which power and responsibility were as much proportioned to merit as education. The civil service won acceptance far more easily – no one wanted to be blown up by hydrogen bombs or starved of foreign exchange because something less than the finest brains were ensconced in Whitehall. The Pioneers encountered far more opposition. The community of principle governing the civil service and the Pioneers was not at once recognized. The objectors, amongst them a growing number of socialists, complained of 'indignity'. A vague word, to conceal a vague concept. The brute fact is that the great majority of minds were still thinking in pre-merit terms.

In the dark England of the distant past it made the best of sense to plead for equality. In the main way that counts, in their brain-power, the industrial workers, or the peasantry, or whoever it might be, were as good as their masters. What the anti-Pioneers did not realize was that the gradual shift from inheritance to merit as the ground of social selection was making (and has finally made) nonsense of all their loose talk of the equality of man. Men, after all, are notable not for the equality, but for the inequality, of their endowment. Once all the geniuses are amongst the elite, and all the morons amongst the workers, what meaning can equality have? What ideal can be upheld except the principle of equal status for equal intelligence? What is the purpose of abolishing inequalities in nurture except to reveal and make more pronounced the inescapable inequalities of Nature?

The decisive fact was the happiness of the Pioneers, or hand-workers, as they were at first called to distinguish them from brain-workers. No one wanted to flood the chronic wards of the mental hospitals, yet that is just what industry had for many years been doing by setting substandard people to perform tasks beyond their reach. No one wanted, least of all the socialists, to cause unnecessary suffering. The principle – 'From each according to his capacity, neither more nor less' – was empirically justified. The workers were more content, and so, for the same reason, were the large middle classes with IQs broadly between 100 and 125. It was shown time and time again by the psychologists that to put a highly intelligent man on a routine job was as disastrous – reflected as it was in sickness, absenteeism, and neurosis[6] – as the obverse. Matching of intelligence and job in the various streams of society was everywhere demonstrated as the highest expression of both efficiency and humanity; as the very engine of productivity at the same time as the liberator of mankind. Without the scientific study of human relations in industry, resentment against the declining status of the lower classes, and the widening gap between them and the upper classes, would have disrupted society long ago.

The new unemployment
The axiom of modern thought is that people are unequal, and the ensuing moral injunction that they should be accorded a station in life related to their capacities. By dint of a long struggle, society has at last been prevailed

upon to conform: the mentally superior have been raised to the top and the mentally inferior lowered to the bottom. Both wear clothes that fit them, and, as I say, it is doubtful whether the lower classes would have become so docile unless they had, in fact, found the clothes comfortable. The psychologists gave the world the means of identifying people without ability. But, burdened in this way, what work were they to do? It was no use having a Pioneer Corps unless there was a job for it.

In my own special period, that is before 1963, few contemporary observers were aware that economic progress threatened to produce a new kind of selective unemployment. The trend was visible enough, if they had but looked, but this for the most part they signally failed to do.[7] Or rather they noticed one trend, that of increasing mechanization, but not its inescapable human consequences. They knew that the prime purpose of machinery was to save labour, but did not ask – what kind of labour? Mass unemployment which afflicted the clever and the stupid alike was the kind that people understood; this other kind of sub-intellectual unemployment was still hidden from all but the most discerning.

Following what was called the 'industrial revolution', when processes previously performed by hand were gradually taken over by machines, hand-work was far from being rendered redundant: machinofacture and manufacture proceeded side by side. Early machinery was a godsend to the stupid. It still had to be operated by hand, and repetitive machine-minding was well within the compass of low-grade employees, unskilled or semi-skilled. In a fairly typical mid-twentieth-century factory there was a division between the skilled men and the rest. On the one side were the trained designers and draughtsmen, the administrators and inspectors, the maintenance men and setters who provided, supervised, and repaired the machinery. On the other were the operators who fed the machine with material, pressed a few simple levers in response to a few simple signals, and extracted the material after processing; or who added a component to an assembly moving forward in a batch or on a belt. In the course of time this division became sharper and sharper, reproducing the division in society itself, with the technical staff being constantly upgraded as the machinery in their care became more complex, and the routine operators being constantly downgraded as the work for which they were responsible became more simple.

More and more was demanded of the skilled men, less and less of the unskilled, until finally there was no need for unskilled men at all. Their work was merely routine, and so it could by definition be progressively taken over and performed by mechanical means. The more simplified a job became, the more easily could it be done by a machine which would feed itself with material, press the lever, and extract the finished article. Semiautomatic became fully automatic. Displacement of low-grade labour became very rapid after the Hitler war with the development of electronics, and especially of servo-mechanisms well suited to direct industrial processes broken down into their simplest components. So marked was the progress that a new word – 'automation' – was coined for the old business of mechanization in the new form it was taking.

Displacement of labour did not at first show itself openly. The trade unions naturally did not make any distinction between clever and stupid; to them men whose jobs had been forfeit to technical change were members to be protected like any other, and they insisted that people whose jobs were taken away from them by labour-saving machinery should not be dismissed but kept on to do some quite unnecessary work, perhaps merely watching instead of 'minding' the robot at its work. The more intelligent members of the unions did not recognize that it was only the low-calibre workers incapable of doing any complicated work whose interests were menaced; sharing the general egalitarian view that one man was much like another, they identified themselves with the redundant, and supported the unions' attempts to prevent dismissals. The employers often acquiesced for the sake of good relations with their staff, or because they thought it was their responsibility, rather than the State's, to care for 'weaker brethren'. It took a very long time for employers to become fully conscious of the need to reduce labour costs to a minimum, and, until then, they did not know how heavy was the load of passengers they were carrying on their pay-roll. As late as the 1950s a large force of low-grade unskilled workers were constantly drifting in to one employment and out to another, always on the move because they were not capable of holding down a steady job anywhere. Millions changed jobs every year. The employer was perhaps aware that his labour turnover was high, but since he did not as yet test the capacity of new recruits, he had no way of knowing that the primary reason was that most had not the minimum ability required for the work. As people were not, in a period of 'full employment', registered as unemployed, except for the odd period now and then, no one appreciated the existence of this vast floating army. Very few of those endlessly moving were in fact making any adequate return for the wages they received.

Many for whom there was no place in industry came to rest in routine clerical work, or in distribution. That was a happy solution, though not a permanent one. Mechanization, starting in the factory, did not end there: offices and shops were also invaded. In the middle of the century book-keepers and typists were still common in offices; by the last quarter they had almost disappeared. Accounts were the responsibility of calculating machines and typists were no longer needed as intermediaries between the spoken and the written word. As for shops, in the middle of the century they still employed millions of people; twenty-five years later, although shop assistants had not by any means disappeared, there were certainly less of them. The large shop with its more economical use of staff had supplanted many smaller ones, the speedy spread of self-service in something like its modern form had reduced the number of assistants needed, and piped distribution of milk, tea, and beer was extending rapidly.

Domestic servants again

The Clauson Committee, which reported in 1968, took the view that by that date about a third of all adults were unemployable in the ordinary economy. The complexity of civilization had grown beyond them; owing to lack of intelligence, they could not find niches in the ordinary occupational structure and needed some form of sheltered employment. What was to be done with them? There was only one possible answer. The people who had ended their school lives either in the schools for the educationally subnormal or in the lower streams of secondary modern schools were only capable of meeting one need: for personal service. For instance, most of them could, if carefully prepared in Government Training Centres and carefully supervised thereafter, serve in public restaurants and places of entertainment, in transport and as caretakers.

That was a start. But as Lord Clauson foresaw, the lower classes would only be fully employed when large numbers of them were engaged in personal service not only outside the home, but in it. His recommendations were hotly contested in Parliament and on the hustings. But what other way was there? The critics had few constructive proposals to make. The absurdity was that many highly intelligent people were wasting much of their time performing purely menial tasks for themselves. A well-endowed person was given a long education at the expense of the State, first at a grammar school and then at a university, and when he came down he was entrusted with a highly responsible post in industry or commerce. His work should have claimed his full energies and his leisure be used for recuperation. But what happened? He spent many valuable hours not at the job for which he had been so elaborately trained, but trailing around the self-service stores buying the odd packet of potatoes or bucket of frozen fish, cleaning his flat, or cooking the fish, or making his bed. I say 'he' but of course the waste was much more widespread for the highly intelligent and hence highly educated woman. After marriage she was not permitted, such was the prevailing anarchy, to carry on the work she could so well do for society; instead, she had to pretend that she had never had a higher education at all, and try to accustom herself to behaving as though household drudgery was the proper reward for *cum laude*, in the same way as a mere secondary modern girl. That was the point – there was no need for much of the drudgery to fall to the lot of the intelligent, it was much better left to the person who would not regard it as drudgery at all because she was not capable of doing anything higher. Drudgery for the one hundred and thirty could be joy for the eighty-five. Had nothing been learnt from the Pioneers?

The critics protested that domestic service was not just service, it was servile. They had tradition on their side, but did not seem to realize how short-lived this was. For thousands of years it was the accepted thing for the upper class to have servants. They only vanished between the demise of the old aristocracy and the birth of the new; in the egalitarian age when no man was held worthy enough to deserve service from his fellows; in the interim period when no one was sure of anything except that Jack was supposed to be as good as his master. When the conditions fostering egalitarianism passed away, there was no further need for this one of its manifestations. Domestic service could be restored once it was again accepted that some men were superior to others; and done without resentment because the inferior knew their betters had a great part to play in the world and beyond, and were glad to identify with them and wait on them. Far better to perform a recognized and valuable service for an important person than to languish on the dole. Naturally, there were safeguards. No one wanted to see a return of the abuses which used to exist in the nineteenth century. All domestic servants were formally enrolled in the Home Help Corps – it topped the ten million mark by the turn of the century – and every private employer had to pay the wages laid down; provide sanitary living-space; release the servant two nights a week to attend a sports club run by the Corps; pay for a refresher course every summer; and not demand more than forty-eight hours a week except with permission from the local office. As far as female servants are concerned, the new arrangement has on the whole worked well, even if morons have sometimes done very silly things to air-conditioners. The trouble has been the men. Despite all experiments at the Corps research centres, no really adequate modern counterpart has been found for the butler and the footman of old. Male unemployment has been higher than female for forty years or more.

Summary

Under the new dispensation the division between the classes has been sharper than it used to be under the old, the status of the upper classes higher, and that of the lower classes lower. In this chapter I have discussed some of the repercussions upon the social structure. Any historian knows that class conflict was endemic throughout pre-merit times, and, in the light of past experience, might perhaps expect that any rapid diminution in the status of one class would necessarily aggravate such conflict. The questions is: why have the changes of the last century not led to such an issue? Why has society been so stable in spite of the widening gulf between the bottom and the top?

The cardinal reason is that stratification has been in accord with a principle of merit, generally accepted at all levels of society. A century ago the lower classes had an ideology of their own – in essentials the same as that which has now become paramount – and were able to use it as much to advance themselves as to attack their superiors. They denied the right of the upper classes to their position. But in the new conditions the lower classes no longer have a distinctive ideology in conflict with the ethos of society, any more than the lower orders used to in the heyday of feudalism. Since bottom agrees with top that merit should reign, they can only cavil at the means by which the choice has been made, not at the standard which all alike espouse. So much, so good. Yet we would be failing in our duty as sociologists did we not point out that such widespread recognition of merit as the arbiter may condemn to helpless despair the many who have no merit, and do so all the more surely because the person so condemned, having too little wit to make his protest against society, may turn his anger against, and so cripple, himself.

The situation has been saved by the Mythos of Muscularity, adult education, displacement of ambitions on to children, and natural stupidity. Above all by extending into adult life the main lineaments of the educational system. If, in the adult world as much as in the school, the stupid are kept together, they are not reminded at every turn of their inferiority. By the standards of the group in which they move and have their being they are, indeed, not stupid; here they are amongst their equals; they can even, in a modest way, shine in the display of their more commendable attributes. When they are amongst their equals, the great society does not press harshly upon them, nor resentments linger. They have the respect of their fellows in their own intelligence-grade. This class solidarity, provided it is not coloured with a rebellious ideology, can be, I would say certainly has been, a most valuable aid to the cohesion of society. For a time all was threatened by a species of technological unemployment, but once the Home Helps Corps was firmly established, what looks like a permanent and most constructive outlet was provided for the graduates of our modern schools.

It is not unfair to give some credit to Crosland, Taylor, Dobson, Clauson, and all the other founders of modern society for the solid way in which they built. But if we take for granted the permanence of the structure, we do so at our peril. Any sociological analysis, of the kind I have attempted in this chapter, shows full well how much depends upon an intricate system of checks and balances. Discontent cannot be totally removed even from our rational society. Here and there lurks the inferior paranoid man, harbouring resentment against some monstrous injustice which he imagines has been done to him; the romantic who hankers after the disorder of the past; the servant who feels isolated in her meritorium, even from the children whom she tends.

Notes

1 Taylor, F.G. *The Role of Egalitarianism in Twentieth-Century England*, 2004.

2 In an earlier age the sumptuary laws passed by Henry VII to force lords to eat in the same great hall as their retainers were not only for the benefit of the retainers. In modern times there is nothing to be gained from social mixing, in school, in residence, or at work, because the upper class now have little or nothing to learn from the lower.

3 This is not entirely a new realization. My colleague, Mr Fallon, has drawn my attention to an old cartoon in the *New Yorker*, an ostensibly humorous American periodical, *circa* 1954. It showed a large psychiatrist confronting a small patient, saying, 'You haven't got an inferiority complex. You *are* inferior.'

4 Three-generation interlocking of aspirations in the extended family was discussed in an interesting way by Michael Young in 'The role of the extended family in channelling aspirations', *British Journal of Sociology*, March 1967. Note the earliness of the date.

5 F.A.E. Crew, F.R.S., The Army Medical Services, HMSO, 1955.

6 An investigation made just after the Hitler war was, to judge from the Press, given insufficient attention at the time. 'The women, who were on jobs requiring skill that did not correspond with their intelligence, had a higher incidence of recent definite neurosis than those on jobs whose skill requirements did correspond: the incidence of neurosis was equally high, irrespective of whether the skill required by the job was too high or too low compared with the worker's intelligence.' Russell Fraser, *The Incidence of Neurosis amongst Factory Workers*. Industrial Health Research Board Report, No. 90, HMSO, 1947. An earlier report of the same Board said that 'severe boredom is usually found associated with more than average intelligence'. IHRB, No. 77, HMSO, 1937.

7 One notable exception was Sir George Thomson, F.R.S., in his book, *The Foreseeable Future*, 1955. See particularly the section on 'The future of the stupid'.

4.8   Factory time

Dennis Johnson

I work in a factory. For eight hours a day, five days a week, I'm the exception to the rule that life can't exist in a vacuum. Work to me is a void, and I begrudge every precious minute of my time that it takes. When writing about work I become bitter, bloody-minded and self-pitying, and I find difficulty in being objective. I can't tell you much about my job because I think it would be misleading to try to make something out of nothing; but as I write I am acutely aware of the effect that my working environment has upon my attitude towards work and leisure and life in general.

My working-day starts with that time-honoured ritual known 'as 'clocking-in'. In a job such as mine this is one of the more constructive acts of the day. For the uninitiated: a lever is pressed and, in blue ink, a time is recorded on one's card. It's so mechanical that one expects the time to be always the same. But it isn't. Just have the effrontery to be late: then you will find that your time has been stamped in RED ink. The management may condone bad timekeeping, but that blasted clock seems to shed blood in anguish.

After clocking-in one starts work. Starts work, that is, if the lavatories are full. In an hourly-paid job it pays to attend to the calls of nature in the firm's time. After the visit to the lavatory there is the tea-break to look forward to; after the tea-break the dinner-break; after the dinner-break the 'knocking-off' time. Work is done between the breaks, but it is done from habit and is given hardly a passing thought. Nothing is gained from the work itself – it has nothing to offer. The criterion is not to do a job well, but to get it over with quickly. Trouble is, one never does get it over with. Either one job is followed by another which is equally boring, or the

Source: *New Left Review* 1965; reprinted in Ronald Fraser (ed) (1968) *Work: Twenty Personal Accounts* Penguin, pp. 11–21.

same job goes on and on for ever: particles of production that stretch into an age of inconsequence. There is never a sense of fulfilment.

Time, rather than content, is the measure of factory life. Time is what the factory worker sells: not labour, not skill, but time, dreary time. Desolate factory time that passes so slowly compared with the fleeting seconds of the weekend. Monday morning starts with a sigh, and the rest of the working-week is spent longing for Friday night. Everybody seems to be wishing his life away. And away it goes – sold to the man in the bowler hat.

People who speak grandiosely of the 'meaning of work' should spend a year or two in a factory. The modern worker neither gives anything to work nor expects anything (apart from his wages) from it. Work, at factory level, has no inherent value. The worker's one interest is his pay-packet. The accent on money is understandable – after all, we are shorter of it than most. In a factory basic wage rates are usually low. Not that the management can't afford to pay more: indeed, they do pay more – but not on the basic rate. Those last few £s that bring one a little nearer the elusive 'national average wage' have to be earned under pressure. By incentive schemes, piecework, bonus, merit-pay, call it what you will, the worker is introduced to the spirit of free enterprise competition. A wage to be earned becomes a prize to be won. Payment by results they call it. And the result of the result is yet another rise in the profits.

It is possible, of course, to achieve an increase in pay through promotion. However, factory workers who attain higher status appear to do so as much by their outlook as their ability. Working-class Tories (there are more of them than many people think – and though they don't outnumber the Socialists, they are more voluble) are far more destined for glory than their Left-wing workmates. The system of promotion is hard to define; it's not so much preference as a rather subtle form of natural selection. Anyway, satisfaction with one's lot and acceptance of authority are considered by management to be more important than skill. Under our present system of industrial control this may be advantageous. But restriction of free expression, at all levels, is greatly to blame for the lacklustre reputation of British industry. Management, and to a certain extent the unions, have no time for the nonconformist. Neither, for that matter, has society.

I help to make cigarettes. I also smoke them – I'm smoking one now. Each employee of the firm for which I work receives, from the age of eighteen, a free issue of cigarettes weekly. Initiation by gift. Personally, I'd prefer the money to the fringe-benefit, but it's the cigarettes or nothing. Admitted, I could sell the cigarettes, but I don't. So I smoke; even though I agree with the medical profession about the relationship between smoking and lung-cancer. Sometimes I feel as if I'm working in an arsenal, an arsenal full of noisy machines painted green – the colour of grass – attended by green-overalled women. My workmates know little and care less about the lung-cancer side of smoking. It's a long way from the tobacco factory to the coffin. So we keep churning them out, millions a day, converting the rather attractive raw material, parchment-like tobacco leaf, into unattractive cigarettes. We make a pittance, the company makes a fortune. Other drug pedlars go to prison.

It would be wrong to assume, however, that factory workers helping to produce more worthwhile things than cigarettes find their jobs any more satisfying. They don't, and they admit it. The end-product provides no consolation to anyone who works in a factory. It is the factories, not what is made, that makes factory workers what they are. There is something about factory life that is inconsistent with man's progress through time; something retrograde. It is as if one is going down the other side of the evolutionary hill.

Factories may differ, but those working in them are all suffering from the same industrial malaise. We are all second fiddles to machines.

It gets worse, too. Complicated new machinery doesn't make the worker's job any more rewarding: the effect is the opposite. Less, rather than more, skill is required. As machines grow more complex so they become more self-reliant. They need less looking after; and they get it. As automation increases productivity it also provides management with an excuse to cut down on labour. At first the workers object to a reduction in their numbers, but nearly always they eventually acquiesce; as things stand, they haven't much choice. So where one saw a man looking vacantly at two machines one now sees him looking just as vacantly at six. This may be a greater strain on his eyes, but it certainly doesn't give him any more responsibility or food for thought.

Though men are in charge of the machines, the actual operation of them is usually done by women. Sometimes there are as many as five women to a machine. In some departments the proportion of women to men is immense: yet supervision remains the prerogative of the male. The suffragettes didn't have much effect on the factory. The women are more talkative than the men; their topics differ, too. Where the men tend to moan about pay and conditions (but won't do anything about them), the women chatter all day long about their homes, their holidays, who's in the family-way and anything else unconnected with work. Women turn their minds from the futility of factory life. Maybe they are wise. Anyway, they are much happier than the men, and more independent. They are much more likely to ask for their cards. I'd ask for mine if I was a woman with a husband at work.

The factory in which I work overlooks a cemetery. Beyond the cemetery rows of sooty houses stretch to the horizon. The prospect from the factory window reminds me of a concentration camp. And yet this is where we live: this is where we are expected to find recompense for the pound of flesh we sell to industry. One might find it necessary to work in prison, but one should not be required to live in one.

Inside the factory the prospect is just as grim. To me, anyway, though the others seem not to notice it. The workers, that is. For management, of course, are ever willing to help in the division of labour. They recognize two categories of employee: staff and worker. It is more the type of job than the importance of the work that decides one's category. To work in an office is the passport to the elite. Although we are all employed by the same firm, the staff get more money, more pension, more sick-pay, more holidays, and work shorter hours, than the workers. The supervisor and the clerk are segregated from the mechanic by pay and conditions of work. The segregation is not without the moral overtones that have become connected with the word. Staff implies status. And how some people love position. White collars are worn like halos, and the words 'I'm on the staff' spoken as a self-reference.

The staff are on the side of management. I suppose one could be radical in spite of one's job, but the staff know which side their bread's buttered on. Quite often the promotion of a worker to the staff is accompanied by a change of political allegiance. There is often a change of newspaper, too. No one, just no one, takes the *Daily Mirror* into the office. The *Express*, it seems, is OK. More a change of punishment than of taste. The staff don't mix much with the workers, either at work or outside. They think they better maintain their image by contact with their own kind. They act superior, and the worker foolishly grants them deference.

The working-class is as ready as anybody else to judge a person's worth by the job he does. Perhaps this is why even in this day and age many workers accept as predestined a class system based on heritage and privilege. The people I live and work with are those that stand to gain most from a democratic reconstruction of our society, but most of them are unaware that they deserve more from life than they get. 'Never had it so good' has come to mean 'couldn't have it any better'. The hardship that bred the character of the working-class has gone and so far nothing has taken its place as the stimulant of reform.

We are told that education is the answer to our troubles. So it is. However, working in a factory one sees that the education frequently has an effect different from that predicted. Instead of making a more intelligent worker the result is often the creation of a recruit for the middle class. Institutions for adult education, founded to bring about the spread of democracy as well as learning, now go out of their way to remain neutral and unbiased. Doctrine has become a dirty word. Consequently, the worker who gets himself an education uses it to improve himself rather than, sometimes at the expense of, the society in which he lives.

Bodies initially formed by, and consisting of, workers, such as the Labour Party and the unions, have become to a certain extent a means of escape for members of the working class with any potential. And once they've escaped they consider themselves a cut above those they have left behind. Not only do they become out of touch with their 'grass-roots' – they deny them altogether. Some think that by giving their talents to a political or sociological organization they retain their working-class affiliations. This may ease one's conscience, but workers tend to see someone who has actually ceased to work among them as someone who has made good, and from whom they can expect the worst. This may be wrong, but there is some justification for it. Time after time the worker gets a raw deal from those he has placed in a position of trust.

In the industry in which I work the worker's role is becoming more and more that of an onlooker and less that of a participant. Mechanization, though it has played a part in the achievement of a shorter working week, has led to jobs that are both dull and monotonous. The loss of dignity and restriction of talent compatible with modern factory life cause a lack of quality in the factory worker. My workmates have a sameness about them: there is an overall apathy and shortage of sinew. If the working man is to regain his sense of purpose, some compensation must be made for the enforced boredom of contemporary working conditions.

Leisure could provide this compensation, but people show little discretion in the use of their increasing freedom from work. They confuse leisure with pleasure, and pleasure with idleness. Often the best use the working man can make of his spare time is to spend his money in it. Although a person has every right to do as he pleases with time justifiably carved out of the working week, it is disheartening to see this time wasted. And it is wasted, for those that could obtain the most from leisure have been duped into regarding phoney amusement as one of the necessities of life.

However, some of the blame for this seemingly ready acceptance of trivia must rest with those who control, either directly or indirectly, the media of mass communication. We are rarely offered (perhaps 'allowed' would be a better word) anything that would be productive of serious thought. Our sense of values and formation of beliefs are controlled today as never before. About leisure, as about everything else, we get plenty of advice. Well-meaning philanthropists who rightly advocate that leisure should be used to counteract the inertia caused by modern work are often sadly out of touch with working-class feeling. Many seem to think that they can recommend a cure without first making a consultation. And what cures they suggest – teaching the middle-aged how to make pottery! We need teachers that are prophets as well. People who can initiate schemes that have logical and far-reaching conclusions. Against the empty, fruitless irrelevance of today we need inoculation, not aspirin. Factory workers waste so much time. They will waste their life, given the chance. Sometimes it's a bit pathetic. The other day I overheard two old employees who had been to the factory to receive their pensions. They greeted each other as I passed. 'How's it going, Bert?' said the first. 'Lovely, Bill,' the other, recently retired, replied. 'Anything's better than that bloody hole.' This may seem a paradoxical reference to a place where someone had spent forty years of his life. Why, if he hated the job, didn't he leave? I don't know why. I don't even know why I'm still working there myself. But I do know that people are always glad to be out of factories. Whether it be the end of the day, the end of the week, or the end of a working life, 'anything's better than that bloody hole'.

It is probably wrong to expect factories to be other than they are. After all, they are built to house machines, not men. Inside a factory it soon becomes obvious that steel brought to life by electricity takes precedence over flesh and blood. The onus is on the machines to such an extent that they appear to assume the human attributes of those who work them. Machines have become as much like people as people have like machines. They pulsate with life, while man becomes the robot. There is a premonition of man losing control, an awareness of doom. The machines seem to squat restless in their oily beds awaiting the coming of some mechanical messiah.

This is the effect it has on me; others seem immune. It is so easy to accept one's predicament and ignore the consequence. The factory provides such a surfeit of artificial sensation that one's senses become dulled. There is such an abundance of noise, odour and light, and such a provision of ready-made ideas, that factory workers lose their natural response to the finer degrees of perception. They are moved only by extremes. They laugh but they don't smile; they cry but they don't frown. They prefer exclamation to reason. The mental numbness extends to industrial relations. Workers tend to respond only to the ultimates of exploitation. Many of the middling, nagging injustices of factory life are suffered without objection. Little by little the management can accomplish a change that would have met with revolt had it been carried out *en bloc*.

The factory I work in is part of one of those combines which seem to have an ambition to become the great provider, both in and out of work, for its employees. Recreational facilities abound; but the number of people using them is small in percentage. Perhaps others, like me, resent the gradual envelopment of recreation by the umbrella of factory life. Not only recreation, either. The firm has a mania to appear responsible. Fingers of charity stretch even further into communal life. The company bends over backwards to make amends for the lethargy that the factory has produced in the worker. The effect is treated while the cause is ignored. No wonder the worker is unappreciative.

I must admit, however, that I am at the moment taking advantage of one aspect of the firm's so-called beneficence. The WEA have persuaded some of the larger firms in the district to release workers for one day a week (on full pay!) for a course in liberal studies. This, I am told, is quite an innovation. Previously, willingness to enable workers to receive technical instruction (though this is confined almost solely to adolescents) has been equalled by a reluctance to facilitate any education that would not be of direct benefit to the industry concerned. Maybe they changed their minds because they realized what the response would be. It was not very difficult to qualify for the course: mine was one of only seven applications from a firm that employs five thousand.

Anyway, I am now for the first time studying under the auspices of the WEA — the only educational establishment where the pupils are better dressed than the teachers. 'Industrial Day Release' they call it. Sounds more like parole than education. How different it is from my last encounter with learning: the secondary school I left fifteen years ago. The WEA idea is that one's relationship with the teachers should be more man to man than pupil to master. Is this an attack on the overall inferiority complex of the working class? The teachers try their hardest to be equal (or to appear to be). Outwardly they may succeed, but inwardly, in my case, they don't. I'm a sucker for anyone with a smattering of learning. Educated people are such a rarity in my life that I can't help being impressed by someone who has had the time and the inclination to think. Not that I always agree with them, but I'm impressed, nevertheless.

It is my intention to continue my studies with a period of full-time education. I hope this will lead to a more worthwhile and morally rewarding job. There are plenty of such jobs about that need doing — but no one seems very willing to help those who are prepared to do them. I have been offered six pounds a week to maintain a wife, child, and a house, while I'm away at college. Even with the best of intentions one can't support a wife and family on ideals.

Sometimes I have an urge to open the nearest door and walk and walk and walk. I feel a need to get away from this atmosphere of here and now: where all that matters is the present, good or bad, and one must make the best of it. Nobody desires change. Everyone is looking into an endless flat future and thinking they could be worse off. What a mess we are. Will there ever be any true recognition of one man from another? Will there ever be any difference that means true variety, and not just better or worse? Will the working-class ever be other than stationary, surrounded and dormant? I see few signs that the words, the ideas, the actions, to break through the siege of indifference will come from within the working-class itself.

What an insular, short-sighted lot we are. The people I know make small use of the few opportunities they are given; neither is much notice taken of advice. It seems to me that the only thing that has a rousing effect on my fellows is criticism. Often the reaction may not be that sought by the critic, but at least it's a welcome sign of life. And life is something I don't see half enough of. Perhaps I shall see more soon, because I don't intend to stay in the factory much longer. I shall not be missed – nobody is ever missed. But what of him who takes my place? Will he stick it? If he does, he will receive at the end of fifty years a gold watch – then he will be able to measure in retrospect the time he's wasted.

4.9 How do the young become adults?[1]

James Coleman

It is important to ask, along with specific questions about how schools function, more general questions about the development from childhood through youth to adulthood. Only by continuing to ask these more general questions can we avoid waking up some day to find that educational institutions are finely tuned and efficiently designed to cope with the problems of an earlier day. Among the more general questions, we need to ask how it is that the young become adults, and what are the current and changing roles of various formal institutions in that development.

There are three formal institutions that are especially important in examining the changes that are occurring in the way youth are brought to adulthood. One is the school, another is the family, and a third is the workplace. I will reserve the school till last, because changes in the other two institutions proceed from other causes, without regard for their consequences for the young, while schools are explicitly designed with consequences for the young as their primary goal. Thus the family and the workplace – together with certain aspects of society – form the environment within which the school functions.

Changes in the family
It is necessary only to give a quick overview of changes in the family's function in bringing children to adulthood, because those changes have been so great, and need only to be brought to attention. Classically, the family was the chief educational institution for the child, because he carried out most of his activities within it until he left it to form his own. That juncture in life was his transition to adult status – the transition to economic self-sufficiency and family head. The timing of this transition

Source: James S. Coleman, *How do the Young Become Adults?* Report no. 130 (May 1972), Center for Social Organization of Schools, The Johns Hopkins University, Baltimore, Maryland.

differed widely from place to place and from one economic setting to another. On an old Irish farm, it may have been age thirty-five or even older. In an industrial city, it may have been sixteen or even younger. But the transition to full adulthood has characteristically taken place when the former child married and either formed a new household or formed a sub-household within his parental family.

The family has gone through two major transitions that sharply limit its occupational training of the young. The first of these occurred when the father went out to work, into a shop or an office, and thus began to carry out his major productive activities away from home behind the closed doors of an organization. The second occurred when the mother went out to work or otherwise stopped carrying out her major productive activities in the home. Before the first transition, families contained the major productive activities of society. Thus the young learned not only the whole variety of things that one commonly associates with the family, they also learned their principal occupational skills and functions − if not in the family, then structurally close to it, in an apprentice relation.

For boys, this occupational learning within the family began to vanish as the father went out to work in a shop or an office. For girls, it continued longer, learning household work, cooking, sewing, child care from her mother, whose principal occupation that was. But by now in most families that second transition has taken place as well: the mother's principal occupation is no longer household work, for that work now occupies little of her time and attention. Either she goes out to work like her husband, or occupies herself in other activities which do not require the aid of her daughters. Even child care is minimal, as family sizes have declined. As an economist recently stated, 'the home closes down during the day'.

Thus the family as a source of occupational learning has declined as it lost its place as the central productive institution of society. But as both adults have come to carry out their central activities outside the home, they have removed other functions from the home and family as well. Friends are drawn from occupation and adult cocktail parties have replaced neighbourhood or extended family gatherings in the social life of the husband and wife. Less and less does the husband's and wife's social life take place in a setting that includes children. Some leisure activities are still carried out as a family, so I don't intend to overstate the case. But the point is that as these large occupational activities of adults moved out of the home, they took others with them, leaving it a less rich place in opportunities for learning for its younger members.

Changes in the workplace

Changes in the workplace, subsequent to its removal from the home into specialized economic institutions, have also affected the movement of the young into adulthood. The major changes have been away from small organizations to large ones; away from *ad hoc* informal hiring practices to formal procedures with formal credentials required of applicants; away from using children in secondary and service activities toward excluding them from workplaces under the guise of 'protection'; away from jobs requiring low educational credentials toward jobs requiring more education; away from loosely organized occupational settings in which workers participated with varying schedules and varying amounts of time toward a rigidly-defined 'full-time job' with a fixed schedule and fixed time commitment.

All of these trends (apart from some very minor and very recent movements in the other direction in a few of these dimensions) have led the workplace to become less available and less useful to the young until they enter it as full-time workers at the end of a longer and longer period of full-time schooling.[2]

These changes in the family and in occupational institutions have led both to become less useful as settings where the young can learn. In the family, the young remain, while the activities from which they could learn have moved out; in workplaces, the activities from which the young could learn remain, but the young themselves have been excluded. This exclusion places youth more on the fringes of society, outside its important institutions. If one is young, it is difficult to get a loan, to buy on credit, to rent an apartment, to have one's signature accepted for any of the many things that are commonplace for adults. The reason is simple: the young have no institutional base, they are a *Lumpenproletariat* outside those institutions of society that are recognized by other institutions and give legitimacy to those persons who are within them.

Before turning to changes in the school, it is important to note one central aspect of the learning that occurred in home and workplaces, and still occurs, though to a sharply reduced extent. It is learning which is variously called 'incidental learning' or 'experiential learning'. It is learning by acting and experiencing the consequences of that action. It is learning through occupying a role with responsibility for actions that affect others. It is learning that is recognized in colloquial parlance as taking place in 'the school of hard knocks'. It is not learning that proceeds in the way that learning typically takes place in the classroom, where the first step is cognitive understanding, and the last step – often omitted – is acting on that understanding.

Changes in the school
When the major educational functions were in the home, the school was an

auxiliary and supplementary institution with two functions. First, for the small fraction of the population whose occupational destination was clerical or academic, it taught a large portion of the occupational skills: languages, mathematics, philosophy, history. Second, for the large majority, it taught the basic skills of literacy and numeracy: reading, writing, and arithmetic. Then, as changes in family and workplace took place, the school began to take on two additional functions: first, to provide occupational training for the increasing fraction of occupations that seemed to require technical book learning (occupations ranging from engineering to journalism); and second, to perform some of the educational activities that were not occupational, but had been carried out to differing degrees and often with indifferent success in the family, ranging from music appreciation to civics. In addition to these explicit and positive functions, the school began to carry out an important but largely passive function as well: to house the young while the parents were off in their specialized adult activities outside the home. This is the function often derogatorily described as the 'baby-sitting' function of the school. As women come more and more into the labour force, and desire to participate even more than they do, the demand for such babysitting agencies has increased, extending downward in age to day-care centres for the very young. And as occupational opportunities for the young have lessened, the babysitting function has extended upward in age, with the universities, colleges, junior colleges, and community colleges acting as temporary holding stations on the way to adulthood.

This transformation of the schools in response to society has had a consequence that is important in considering the path to becoming adult. This is the massive enlargement of the *student* role of young persons, to fill the vacuum that the changes in the family and workplace created. The student role of young persons has become enlarged to the point where that role constitutes the major portion of their youth. But the student role is not a role of taking action and experiencing consequences. It is not a role in which one learns by hard knocks. It is a relatively passive role, always in preparation for action, but never acting. In attempting to provide the learning that had earlier taken place through experiential learning in the home and at the workplace, the school kept the same classroom mode of learning that was its hallmark: it not only moved the setting of those learning activities from outside the school to within; it changed the method from learning through experience as a responsible actor to learning through being taught as a student. There are some exceptions but the general pattern followed that of the classical school, in which a *teacher* was the medium through which learning was expected to take place. This replaced *action* as the medium through which learning had taken place in the family or the workplace. The student role, in which a person waits to be taught, became central to the young person's life.

The consequence of the expansion of the student role, and the action-poverty it implies for the young, has been an increased restiveness among the young. They are shielded from responsibility, and they become irresponsible; they are held in a dependent status, and they come to act as dependents; they are kept away from productive work, and they become unproductive. But even if we saw no signs of irresponsibility, stagnant dependency, and lack of productivity, the point would remain the same: the school, when it has tried to teach non-intellective things, does so in the only way it knows how, the way designed to teach intellective capabilities: through a teacher, transmitting cognitive skills and knowledge, in a classroom, to students.

Although the complex problems created by these changes cannot be solved easily, I believe it would be a step toward a solution if we began to conceive of matters a little differently. In particular, the problems become clearer if we wipe away the confusion between 'schooling' and 'education'. Previously, it was natural that schooling could have been confused with education – for schooling was that part of the education of the young which took place formally, and thus had to be planned for and consciously provided. But the larger part of education took place outside the school. The child spent most of his time outside the school; school was a small portion of his existence. It taught him to read and write and work with' numbers, but the most important parts of education it did not provide: learning about work, both the skills and the habits, learning how to function in society, learning how to be a father or mother, husband or wife, learning to take care of others and to take responsibility for others. Because these things were learned informally, through experience, or at least without formal organization, they could be disregarded, and 'education' could come to be identified with 'schooling'.

But much of this other education evaporates as work takes place behind closed doors and as the family is reduced as a locus of important activities. 'Schooling', meanwhile, continues to mean much the same thing that it did before, except extended in time: the learning of intellectual skills. Thus although schooling remains a small portion of education, it occupies an increasingly larger portion of a young person's time, while the remaining portion of his education is *not* well provided by ordinary, everyday, unplanned activities. Consequently, if an appropriate reform of education is to be made, it must begin with this fact: schooling is not all of education, and the other parts of education require just as much explicit planning and organization as does schooling.

Once this is recognized, then the way is paved for creation of a true educational system – not merely a system of schools, but a system of education that covers non-intellectual learning as well. If one were to go too quickly to a possible solution, or pattern for the future, he would see this as immediately leading toward a multi-track school system in which some young people concentrate on intellectual skills while others concentrate on 'practical' or 'mechanical' or 'vocational' skills. But this pattern fails to recognize clearly the impact of the above separation of schooling and education: it is not only *some* young people who need the non-intellective portions of education, it is all. Thus it is not the *persons* who must be divided into different tracks to learn different skills; it is the *time* of *each* person that must be so divided. Further, the division is not merely a division between intellectual skills and vocational or practical skills. It is a division among a variety of skills, only some of which are intellectual or vocational. If I were asked to catalogue the skills that should be learned in the educational system before age eighteen, I would certainly include all these:

1 intellectual skills, the kinds of things that schooling at its best teaches
2 skills of some occupation that may be filled by a secondary school graduate, so that every eighteen-year-old would be accredited in some occupation, whether he continued in school or not
3 decision-making skills: that is, those skills of making decisions in complex situations where consequences follow from the decisions
4 general physical and mechanical skills: skills allowing the young person to deal with physical and mechanical problems he will confront outside work, in the home or elsewhere
5 bureaucratic and organizational skills: how to cope with a bureaucratic organization, as an employee or a customer or a client, or a manager or an entrepreneur
6 skills in the care of dependent persons: skill in caring for children, old persons, and sick persons
7 emergency skills: how to act in an emergency, or an unfamiliar situation, in sufficient time to deal with the emergency
8 verbal communication skills in argumentation and debate.

This catalogue of skills is certainly not all-inclusive, nor are all the skills listed on the same level of generality. They do, however, give a sense of the scope of what I believe must be explicitly included in education.

The next question becomes, 'How is this all to be organized?' Or perhaps, 'How do we change the schools to do all this?' But the second question puts the matter wrong. My principal point, and it is the central point of the educational pattern of the future that I envision, is that we do *not* attempt to have the schools do all this. Schools are prepared to do what they have done all along: teach young people intellectual things, both by giving them information and giving them intellectual tools, such as literacy, mathematics, and foreign languages. Schools are not prepared to teach these other skills – and the history of their attempts to change themselves so that they could do this shows only one thing: that these other activities – whether they are vocational education, driver training, consumer education, civics, home economics, or something else – have always played a secondary and subordinate role in schools, always in the shadow of academic performance. The mode of organization of schools, the fact that they are staffed by teachers who themselves have been measured by academic performance, the fact that they lead in a natural progression to more and more intellectually specialized institutions, the universities and then graduate schools – all this means that they are destined to fail as educational institutions in areas other than teaching of intellectual skills.

The pattern for the future, then, as I see it, is one in which the school comes to be reduced in importance and scope and time in the life of a young person from age twelve onward, with the explicit recognition that it is providing only a portion of education. This reduction would necessarily occur, because these other skills must be learned as well – many of them by experience and practice, some of them including a little admixture of teaching.

It then becomes necessary to ask just where these other skills would be learned. An immediate response, and an incorrect one, I believe, would be to attempt to design specialized institutions to teach these things, as vocational schools were designed to teach occupational skills – incorrect because if my arguments are correct, then these activities are best learned not by being taught but by acting. Thus it is necessary to ask where the action is. The answer is clear: it is in those specialized economic institutions of society into which first men, then women, went out from the family to work. It is in the occupational institutions of society. Women have learned this through the social-psychological poverty of home and neighbourhood and have deserted the home for these workplaces.

Thus this education can appropriately take place only in the economic institutions of society – those organizations behind whose doors adults vanish while the child vanishes inside the walls of the school. Such education could not be hit-or-miss, merely placing a young person on the job or in an apprentice situation. It would be necessary to carefully lay out the skills that were necessary to learn, more carefully than I have done in the catalogue of eight skills I've listed, and to organize the young person's experiences in such a way that he learns these skills. This would involve, of course, more than one institution outside the school. And it would require brilliance both in conception and in execution if it is to work well in early days. For it involves nothing less than a breaking open of the economic institutions of society, from factories to hospitals, a removing of the insulation that separates them from the young, and giving them an explicit role in the education of the young. How this would be done will differ from society to society: in the free enterprise capitalist economy of the US, it could probably best begin by providing the young with entitlements that could be redeemed by businesses and other enterprises that try to provide the appropriate learning experiences. In other countries, it might better be done in another way. But the end result would be similar − the young would be integrated into the economic activities of society from a very early age, without stopping their schooling, but merely by stopping the dilution of schooling that has occurred in recent years. The economic organizations of society would necessarily change, and change radically, to incorporate the young − not to become schools, but to become institutions in which work is designed not only for productive efficiency, but for learning efficiency as well. The revolution necessary in society is, if I am correct, a revolution within these occupational institutions − from General Motors to government agencies − from business offices to airports.

A reorganization of education in this way would require, if it is to be effective, standards of performance and criteria to be met in the areas other than intellectual, so that the credentials of a young person would be far broader than those implied by the various diplomas and degrees that have been carried over in modified form from an early period. Some of the credentials would be based on performance tests such as those used in industries and skilled crafts today. Others would be based on performance ratings by supervisors and on letters of recommendation. For developing other criteria, inventiveness and imagination would be necessary. But the essential point is that those skills must be just as explicitly evaluated and form just as much a portion of a young person's credentials as intellectual skills do today.

There are a number of important implications to this reorganization of the path toward adulthood. If we recognize that it requires an explicit breaking open of work organizations to incorporate the young, the most direct implication is an enormous transformation of these economic institutions. Their product would be not only goods and services to be marketed, but also learning, the latter paid from public funds as schools are today. They would become much more diversified institutions, no longer preserving the fiction that nothing but production occurs within them, but recognizing that much of adults' social lives, and most of their time expenditures, takes place within them, and expanding that recognition into explicit design of this experience.

A less direct implication of this reorganization of education is that it would reduce the relationship between educational performance and family educational background or social class. In schools, the pervasive power of testing on intellectual criteria – the only real criteria the school knows – exacerbates and emphasizes the inequalities of academic background that children bring with them to school. If education is appropriately defined to include these other equally important skills, then the artificially-heightened disparity between students from 'advantaged' and 'disadvantaged' backgrounds will be reduced – but only, of course, if these other activities are carried out in their natural habitat, rather than in the school, which constitutes an uncongenial setting for them.

Finally, a still less direct implication of this reorganization of education is related to the current controversy about school integration through balancing of the races or social classes in school. That controversy, which reflects a real problem where residential segregation is pronounced, as it is in all large urban areas – cannot be solved as long as education is identified with a school building containing classrooms and teachers. It can be solved if formal education takes place largely outside the schools and in economic institutions, for it is the economic institutions that of all those in society are the least segregated by race and in which racial integration produces least friction – because it occurs in a setting with work to be done in an organized, rather than anarchic, structure of interpersonal relations.

This effect of such a reorganized system of education in integrating the society racially is not an accidental one. It arises because this reorganization is not an *ad hoc*, makeshift patching up of outworn institutions. It is a reorganization that recognizes fundamental structural changes in society – the drying up of family functions and the specialization of economic activities – and asks where in such an emerging social structure is the appropriate locus for the young, if they are to have the opportunity for moving to adulthood. The answer is that the young belong where everyone else is, and where the action is: inside the economic institutions where the productive activities of society take place.

Notes

1 This paper was presented at the American Educational Research Association 1972 Annual Meeting, 4 April 1972, Chicago, Illinois, and is published by the Center for Social Organization of Schools, which is supported in part as a research and development centre by funds from the United States Office of Education, Department of Health, Education and Welfare. The opinions expressed in this publication do not necessarily reflect the position or policy of the Office of Education, and no official endorsement by the Office of Education should be inferred.

2 There are some complications to these trends, and some statistics which

M

appear to go in the opposite direction. For example, the labour force participation rates for persons aged 16–21 enrolled in school increased between 1960 and 1970, from 35 to 40 per cent for men and 25 to 36 per cent for women. But this change reflects an increase in school-going by those who in 1960 would have been only working. The proportion of persons aged 16–21 enrolled in school was much higher in 1970 than in 1960. This increase was largely due to a lack of full-time jobs in the labour force for a greatly-expanded age cohort. Thus for many, education became the full-time activity, and labour-force participation was restricted to part-time or in-and-out work.

4.10   The diploma disease – England

Robert Dore

Training for work

It was almost entirely in the factories and mines, the workshops and mills, not in the schools, that the skills which fed Britain's industrial advance were both accumulated and transmitted. The continuity of traditional apprenticeship systems, only gradually altering in form from the eighteenth century to the present day, is proof of that. In the pioneer industrializer (unlike the situation in late-developing countries) progress was by invention or by the importation of inventions which made marginal incremental advances. Skilled workmen were able to absorb them on the job and add them to their repertoire, transmitting to the next generation a larger reservoir of skills than they themselves had inherited. Only occasionally did engineers who made the bigger leaps find it necessary to introduce deliberate training schemes – as did Boulton and Watt, who found the millwrights available to be recruited to their steam engine plant incapable of learning to work to the fine tolerances their plans required. Only towards the end of the century did technical institutes begin on any substantial scale to provide some skilled workmen with a general basic understanding of mechanical and metallurgical principles which helped them to absorb new techniques.

So it was, too, with the higher-level – what eventually became to be recognized as the professional – skills of the engineer. The engineers fully emerged to self-consciousness as a profession, distinguishing themselves from the millwrights and clockmakers who had been their forerunners, with the foundation of the Royal Institution of Civil Engineers in 1818. Their purpose in coming together and founding their society was partly to exchange knowledge and ideas, partly to define and to protect the status and good name of the engineer by control over admission. Training was by

Source: *The Diploma Disease*, 1976, Unwin Education Books, pp.18–34.

apprenticeship and self-study; proof of competence provided by work performance vouched for by one's peers.

And so, in the engineering profession, it remained until 1897. In other professions the resort to theoretical written examinations came sooner: the solicitors in 1835, the accountants in 1880. But the process of which this was a symptom — the systemization of the body of principles on which the work of the profession was based; its rationalization into a form which made it partly susceptible to teaching and learning in the classroom — proceeded steadily. Engineering became a proper university subject taught by chaired professors at Glasgow and London in the 1840s. Formal university training thus became, for members of the middle class, a short cut on the road to competence as an engineer. But still it was a short cut only insofar as one genuinely learned more quickly that which one would otherwise have had to learn in apprenticeship. The formal qualification in itself gained no recognition; it was to be several decades before the possession of a university degree helped by gaining formal exemption from the normal training requirements of the engineering institutions.

The growth of pre-career qualification

But once *that* process had begun, its acceleration in the twentieth century was rapid. It had two aspects: on the one hand the increasing willingness of professional groups to entrust to secondary schools and universities the business of training and selecting their recruits; and on the other, the gradual systematization and reorientation of the school and university system towards serving this function.

This latter involved three related changes. First was the slow, reluctant evolution of the universities' curricula, making more of the content of their courses plausibly relevant to the occupational destinations of their students. The second was the growth and systematization of secondary education parallel to, but following, the gradual systemization of elementary education. The third element was the integration of the elementary and secondary schools and universities into a single pyramidical structure, opening channels of merit competition for passage from one stratum to the next to supplement the more traditional methods of rationing educational opportunity — by fee charges and the constraints of social convention.

The story of how the universities gradually ceased to be 'comfortably monastic establishments for clerical sinecurists with a tinge of letters' (G.M. Trevelyan in Glass 1961, p. 393) is a long and complex one. The growth of medical education and introduction of engineering technology was one aspect; the latter a particularly slow, hard-fought process, even in Glasgow (Ashby 1961, pp. 466–75). The shocking discovery at the Paris exhibition of 1867 that Britain's technical supremacy was rapidly being lost helped to turn the tide, but it was not until the establishment of the new wave of civic universities at the turn of the century that the place of engineering in university education was fully established.

More generally important was the pressure to introduce 'modern studies' in the humanities and social sciences which might have some relevance to the administrative, managerial and political careers for which a large proportion of university graduates were destined. Most influential in this respect were the competitive examinations for the civil service which followed the Northcote-Trevelyan report. The standards they set had a powerful influence on the standards of university teaching. The more or less simultaneous ending of patronage in the civil service, the army and the church (leaving finance and industry (!) as the two major fields in which patronage prevailed) altered the whole significance of learning for the upper-middle class and was perhaps the most important influence tending – though in a very covert way – to 'vocationalize' university education. At the same time the expansion of secondary schools employing graduate teachers and the continuous growth of the universities themselves made the production of teachers a major vocational function of universities.

However, many professions – law, accountancy, architecture, for instance – still rely only half-heartedly on university training.

As for secondary education, the state's concern begins effectively with the establishment of a Department of Science and Art in 1858 to encourage secondary science teaching by monetary grants, and the Endowed Schools Act a decade late. By then those of the older endowed grammar schools which had not been transformed into exclusive boarding establishments for the upper class had been supplemented by large numbers of new foundations: Wesleyan and other religious schools and the so-called proprietary schools organized on the joint stock principle. These catered primarily for the middle class. The Taunton Commission of 1868, which was appointed to inquire into the health of the schools, nicely reflects the increasing extent to which education was becoming, for sections of the middle class, the major determinant of occupation and social status. The mercantile and industrial middle class, it pointed out, had property in an ongoing business to bequeath to their children; it was to other groups that the schools were of particular concern: to 'the great body of professional men, especially the clergy, medicine men and lawyers', who 'have nothing to look to but education to keep their sons on a high social level'.

It was not however until more than three decades later, with the 1902 Act, that public authorities were squarely given the responsibility of providing secondary education. Thereafter numbers in secondary schools rapidly increased: from 100,000 in 1895 to double that number at the beginning of the First World War and to well over half a million by the mid-thirties (Glass 1961, p. 392).

The third and last element of the reorientation of the educational system for occupational selection – the hierarchical integration of the three layers – was also a long time maturing. The linking of the secondary and university layers occurred first. Preparation for university entrance became increasingly recognized as an objective of secondary education. Already in 1868 the Taunton Commission had judged the quality of schools by their success in sending pupils to the universities, but only after the establishment of the civic universities did the majority of grammar schools acquire university preparatory sixth forms, and not, perhaps, until the 1960s did the importance of the sixth form in the grammar school scheme of things reach the point at which the Ordinary level General Certificate of Education, taken at the age of fifteen or sixteen, became predominantly defined in most schools as the selection hurdle for sixth-form/university entry, rather than as a terminal secondary leaving certificate.

The integration of elementary and secondary education was an even slower development. It was a long time before the argument that the national need to maximize the use of its reserve of talent combined with a nascent egalitarianism to call forth public funds. State scholarships to allow children to move from the elementary to the grammar schools which could lead on to the university started in 1907, but for a long time the flow was little more than a trickle. Still, less than 50 per cent of the pupils in grammar schools were scholarship holders in 1938. The elementary schools for the working class were allowed to add secondary-level forms, parallel to the predominantly middle-class grammar schools, and such vocational technical training as developed was concentrated in this elementary-extension sector, separate from and of lower prestige than the clerkly/university-preparatory secondary grammar-school sector (*ibid.*, p. 399).

Eventually, the 1944 Act planned, and largely brought about, the final integration of the system, but although it removed most of the economic obstacles to full working-class participation in educational pyramid-climbing, it could not as quickly remove some of the cultural obstacles – the lack of interest of many working-class parents in seeing their sons enter an educational and occupational career which they viewed either with hostility as alienating or with humility as not for the likes of them –something to aspire to which would lead only to disappointment. What proportion of the nation's parents were fully *in* the race by 1960, awaiting the results of the 11-plus grammar-school entrance tests with open or concealed anxiety, is hard to guess. It was certainly a larger proportion than in 1940; the change in aspirations and expectations had been considerable. So, consequently, was the net increase in the volume of human disappointment which each annual round of selection occasioned. And as the working class began to add its anxieties to the more intense neuroses of the middle class (for the middle-class parent, failure in the 11-plus forbode actual loss of status, not just loss of the chance to better oneself) public pressure slowly built up for the ending of selection and the establishment of comprehensive secondary education.

Today not even that issue is fully settled, while the next stage of educational evolution – the attempt to postpone even further the point of invidious selection by developing comprehensive (or at least more comprehensive) university education on the American model – is as yet only foreshadowed in vague hints in Labour Party documents. But (cataclysms apart) come it certainly will, for the more definitively important educational qualifications become in determining occupation and social status, and the more deeply rooted the ideology of equality of opportunity, and the more nationally homogeneous are Britain's parents in their aspirations to seize opportunity, the stronger will grow the pressure to have second chances and third and fourth chances – to ensure that no one has his child ruled definitively out of the race for top jobs until the last possible moment.

The inflation of qualifications

But what is the proof that academic attainment in the formal educational system *has* become more definitely important in determining career destinations? Evidence is not hard to find. Trends emerge fairly clearly if one looks at the various career guides which have been produced for ambitious young Englishmen since the end of the last century.

Take civil engineering, for example. Between 1897 and 1971 the transition from apprenticeship and mid-career qualification to *pre-career* qualification has been almost complete. Until 1897 there was no written examination of any kind. An apprenticeship, the ability to learn on the job by observation and deliberate self-study, evidence of personal work accomplishments confirmed by the grilling of a professional interview were what got one membership in the institutions and hence the right to give oneself the title of engineer. By 1897, however, the importance of basic theoretical knowledge was too obvious to be wholly denied. Soon the civil engineers had, like most of the other professions, the full three-stage range of qualifying examinations: preliminary, intermediate and final. Technical institutes oriented their courses to these, or to the higher national certificates and diplomas which were accepted as their equivalents. From the very beginning a university degree was an acceptable alternative to the institutions' own examinations; the graduate had only to acquire three years' practical experience and submit to a professional interview in order to become a full member. But in the first decades of this century the majority of entrants to the profession got there by part-time study whilst serving a practical apprenticeship – often as a 'premium-paying' pupil with special claims to be allowed to work in a variety of departments in the factory. The author of the 1926 careers guide was still advising that 'a degree of B.Sc. Engineering is a valuable supplementary qualification ... But it can never be a substitute for practical training ... Apprenticeship is still the best way of entering the engineering profession.' But he was fighting for a losing cause. The trend towards pre-career qualification throughout the century has proved inexorable. In 1935, for the first time, the number of graduate entrants into civil engineering exceeded the number of mid-career qualifiers. By 1950 the latter were becoming more and more a rarity. By 1970 they were so few in number that, together with the other members of the Council of Engineering Institutions, the civil engineers closed off the part-time qualification route altogether. Henceforth a formal degree from a university or college of technology was a necessary pre-condition for a professional career as an engineer.

Other professions have not gone quite so far in their reliance on university training. Brown's 1971 guide estimates that 60 per cent of newly qualified solicitors are graduates, but advises that 'while a degree is an asset, no one should be deterred from entering the profession because he cannot or does not wish to go to a university'. The accountants were until recently much less predisposed to encourage university study. Three years at a university gained exemption from only two of the five years required as an articled clerk – and carried the disadvantage, as the 1908 guide remarked, that the transition from the 'brightness and movement of the university to the drudgery of a first year's accountant clerk is a severe strain and may very well disgust a man'. They were recently forced to relent, however, and grant three years' exemption for a university degree.

Thus, even the professions which are most jealous to preserve their own qualification system and to stress *practical* training have been moving in the same general direction as the civil engineers. There are three parts to the trend. First, increasing reliance on certificates of general education. By 1970 the special preliminary examinations of all the major professions had been replaced by the requirement of a certain minimum cluster of passes or credits in various subjects in the General Certificate of Education, either at the Ordinary (O) or at the Ordinary and Advanced (A) levels. Secondly, that minimum level showed a steady tendency to increase, and thirdly, the requirements for on-the-job pupillage before full professional status is achieved have tended to contract.

Librarians are a good example. At the beginning of the century a librarian had to have only a 'love of books and the capacity to advise the managers as to purchases, and inquirers as to suitable works' – he had, in other words, actually to be able to do his job. By the 1930s, intending librarians were told that a school certificate was a 'useful possession'. By 1950 it was the minimal requirement. No one could be a librarian who had not continued his education to the age of fifteen or sixteen. By 1970 two A levels – an extra two years of study for the average child– were the minimum requirement, and the Library Association looks forward to the day when 'the possession of a university or CNAA degree becomes as common as possession of a GCE with A levels today' (*Library Association Research*, October 1972, p. 196). Meanwhile, the minimum apprenticeship period of three years was reduced to one (after a special two-year training in librarianship) in the 1950s and was waived altogether for university graduates in the 1970s, by which time three universities and six polytechnics were offering degree courses in librarianship (*The Times*, 18 June 1972).

Perhaps nothing better epitomizes the slow change in Britain's mechanisms and criteria for job selection than the terminology of these guides, with the emphasis slowly shifting from personal aptitude to quantitatively measurable educational achievement. The 1900 guide talks of the 'ingredients of success' (journalists need 'plenty of adaptability, energy, tact and a good constitution'). In 1910 it is still 'qualities required'. But by 1950 the comparable heading is 'educational requirements', and the 'candidates must have obtained at least ...' sort of lists rarely leave the realm of bureaucratic formality. To be sure, the system seems to be saying, two people both with Bs in history and French at A level might certainly differ in their interests and personal capacities, as personalities and as human beings. But so what? *De minimis non curat lex* – nor the bureaucratic regulations of a credential-constipated society either.

Why the qualification spiral?

Having documented this trend, the next thing to do is first to explain it, and then to analyse its consequences. First, to explain. There is, of course, a standard explanation which suits very well all those – in both the educational and other professions –who connive at the steady progress towards ever higher levels of pre-career qualifications for every profession. We live, runs this explanation, in the age of the knowledge explosion. The range of information and ideas to be mastered by any profession increases at an exponential rate. It is only natural that every profession requires individuals of greater general educational maturity than used to be the case, and a longer period of purely professional preparation before starting a career.

This is not a negligible argument. The range of general basic techniques which a civil engineer could usefully learn has increased enormously over the last century. But is that an argument why it is best to do that learning in a concentrated period of three or four years between the ages of eighteen and twenty-two rather than over ten years of part-time study combined with practical training between the ages of eighteen and twenty-eight? Who is in the best position to assess the *relevance* of what he learns: the undergraduate familiar only with laboratories and not with factories, or the factory apprentice? Why should it be that the polytechnics at least (even if not yet all the universities) have resorted to sandwich courses as a means of putting back into the pre-career qualification pattern the practical experience which apprenticeship used to provide? Does the man who does all his learning by the age of twenty-two really remember what he once learned when, after specializing for ten years in one branch, he runs at the age of thirty up against a problem in another field? And is it not odd that the argument about escalating knowledge requirements should be made to justify a system which ends formal teaching in the early twenties and then allows a man to practise for *forty years* without any obligation to learn all the exploding knowledge which has been generated since he left the university?

The case begins to look fishy. Is there no other explanation of the trend? There is, and it seems a plausible one. It runs as follows. The ability and desire to learn all that a professional engineer needs to know through apprenticeship and prolonged part-time study are rare qualities. The particular necessary combination of qualities which was needed to carry a man through that route to an engineering career – the intellectual ability, the capacity for persistance, the interest in things mechanical, the ambition for a professional career and the social assurance necessary to assume that one has a right to such a career – was perhaps found in only 2 per cent, say, or 3 or 5 per cent of the population. In 1910, when less than 1 per cent of each age group was getting into a university, the majority of that 2 or 5 per cent had no choice but to choose the apprenticeship route.

But what happens as the society gets more affluent and the university population expands to embrace, say, 5–8 per cent of each age group? Our 2–5 per cent of potential engineering apprentices are likely to be among the children who show enough talent to be encouraged by teachers and parents to aim at a university education; more of them have parents who could afford to send them to a university, more of those from poorer homes have access to scholarships. And if a man has a realistic choice between spending three or four amiable, gentlemanly, and perhaps even intellectually exciting years in a university with the assurance of coasting thereafter to full professional status and a full professional salary at the age of twenty-five, or alternatively submitting to the discipline of factory life at the age of sixteen or seventeen and sacrificing most of his leisure to part-time study for ten years, eventually to struggle through to full professional status near the age of thirty – if a man is offered that choice, which is he likely to choose? And as more and more of those with the ability and motivation to become engineers are *able* to choose the pre-career qualification route, the number whom circumstances deprive of that opportunity and who yet have the ability and drive to succeed in following the apprenticeship route gradually dwindles. So much so that that route may be closed off without danger of arousing public outcry.

And from the point of view of the officials of these professional associations, a good thing too. University graduation carries prestige, if for no other reason than because of its early association with the upper-middle classes. A profession which achieves the status of a graduate profession thereby achieves higher social prestige relative to other professions which do not – and with higher prestige goes the ability to claim higher fees for one's services.

One can give a similar account of the rise in minimum entry qualifications to, say, the library profession. Put briefly it is as follows. Fifty years ago, large numbers of people who were bright enough to be good librarians left school before the age of fifteen, and most of those who continued their education beyond the age of fifteen had access to better paid or more prestigeful jobs than librarianship. Nowadays, by contrast, most of the children who have the required level of librarian potential stay on at school until they are eighteen. (Moreover the big expansion of numbers staying at school until the age of eighteen means that they cannot all, as perhaps they could fifty years ago, expect *more* rewarding jobs than librarianship.) Hence libraries can get people with higher level certificates; and they need to recruit such people if they are to go on recruiting men and women with the same degree of librarian potential as those they were recruiting fifty years earlier. Or in other words: 'the O-level requirements were originally laid down by the professions – as the A level requirements are now being laid down – less because there was any precision about what they were measuring than in order to ensure access to what it was fashionable in the late 1950s and early 1960s, to call "the pool of ability" ' (Briggs, 1973). There are several assumptions implicit in this explanation:

1 That good librarians are, if not exactly born rather than made, at least already made by the age of fifteen, and not much remade later. That is to say that one could take a population of fifteen years olds and rank them according to their *ability to learn* how to be good librarians, from the first to the hundredth percentile.

2 That the education which the new A-level entrants to the libraries receive after, say, the age of fifteen does little of itself to enhance their potential to learn to become good librarians once they have entered a library. Likewise, that a rise in the *general* level of education does little to alter the shape of the hypothetical 'distribution of librarian potential' in society. When the school-leaving age is raised in 1990 to the age of twenty-two, there will still be, if not exactly the same bottom 40 per cent, or whatever it is, at least some not much smaller proportion of people who 'do not have it in them' to become good librarians.

3 But that the qualities which make people good librarians do *correlate* quite highly with the qualities measured by general education achievement tests – O levels and A levels – both types of performance being a function of intelligence and effort. That is to say that the 'distribution of potential for librarianship' coincides roughly with a 'distribution of general ability'.

4 If the bottom limit of the *effective recruitment range* for librarianship is relatively fixed by ability constraints, irrespective of educational changes, the *top* limit may change with the occupational structure and the relative attractiveness of different occupations. Thus the occupations generally considered more attractive than librarianship recruit a larger proportion of each age group today than in 1920. Similarly the chairman of the training committee of the Engineering Industries Association complains in 1973 that 'where we used to get A- and B-stream boys [for apprenticeships], we are now getting C and D streams, with the banks, solicitors and offices attracting the better qualified' (*The Times* Business News, 24 March 1973).

5 The responsible officials of all professional bodies seek to protect their professions from slippage of their effective recruitment range down the ability distribution. One way of doing so is to raise entry requirements. That way you are taken more seriously; if you are taken more seriously you attract higher levels of ability, and your qualificational requirements exclude lower levels of ability; thus you maintain average ability levels which in turn ensures that you are taken seriously, and the whole circular process enables you to sustain the prestige which justifies higher salaries or professional fees. After a famous local government scandal involving a public relations consultant, the President of the Institute of Public Relations wrote to *The Times* in an attempt to repair the damage. The Institute had, he claimed, a detailed code of conduct, 'a standard of ethical behaviour as high as those of the long-established professions'. His clinching argument was that 'qualification by examination is making rapid headway: although optional at present I expect it to become compulsory' (*The Times*, 30 April 1974).

In short, it is not a belief in the saving virtues of education in itself which explains why the Institute of Brewing required one A level and four O levels in 1973 compared with only five O levels in 1953, or why the Worshipful Company of Spectacle Makers should have gone from four O levels to two As and three Os over the same period (Briggs 1973). The explanation lies in the fact that educational qualifications are seen as an ability-filtering device and (precisely because they are so seen) as a prestige-conferring device. Perhaps the clearest evidence of this can be seen in the entrance regulations of those colleges of nursing which will not count as acceptable an O-level pass in such (one would have thought) an eminently relevant subject as domestic science, but require would-be nurses to show their paces in properly difficult subjects like English or maths, which better indicate whether they have the level of ability thought necessary to follow the training courses and to sustain the good name of the profession (*ibid.*, p. 83).

The process of qualification inflation described here as taking place slowly in Britain over the course of this century is, of course, the same as that taking place much more rapidly in developing countries and bidding fair, in many of them, soon to produce BA bus-conductors. There is a slight difference, however. The simpler picture is of a supply-led spiral. A surplus of graduates at one level induces them to apply for jobs one notch below what they have hitherto conventionally been entitled to. In Britain there is evidence that the spiral, though sometimes supply-led (compare the recent concern with graduate unemployment), is in part demand-led. That is to say that competitive bidding for the 'pool of ability' between professions can lead to anticipatory raising of entrance standards and a demand for, say, A-level leavers, greater than the numbers who would anyway have gone on to A level; hence many 'would-be entrants to particular professions or would-be professions, many of them highly motivated for personal or family reasons, having to struggle for a further year or two in school' (*ibid.*, p. 102) beyond the point at which (until the careers master told them what they had to do) their appetite for general education was satisfied. Either way, the essence of a qualification *spiral* is that both demand and supply factors contribute and interact to exacerbate each other. The contributions from the demand side are likely to be greater when there is a high level of competition either between professional groups for status (the situation in Britain where professional group autonomy is greater than in any other industrial country; Burrage 1972) or between private employing organizations for both status and competitive efficiency (the situation in Japan). Generally speaking, however, supply factors have been dominant both historically and in developing countries today. A brave OECD study designed to explain differences in the educational compositions of different occupational groups in fifty-three countries concluded that about 70 per cent of the variation could be attributed to 'variations in the supply of the educational system' (OECD 1971, p. 167).

Rational?

The five assumptions listed above *explain* the process of qualification inflation in Britain. Do they justify it?

It all depends on how far higher education creates as well as measures talents. When the navy advertises in the Sunday newspaper its intention to recruit graduates, it is clearly not the cognitive knowledge pumped into them at the university which counts; the navy 'is interested in any graduate who's interested in us, with a degree in either science or the humanities'. The reason is because 'we see your time spent at a university as time spent making up your own mind, thinking for yourself. And we know that you don't get a degree without a good deal of intelligence and concentration.' Which is the more important? The thinking which you have to go to a university to do? Or the intelligence and concentration which the degree test only measures, having presumably been there already? (See Little and Oxenham 1975, p. 12).

If it is chiefly the latter; if it is true that educational achievements chiefly *measure* and do little to *create* talent, that it is his first-class mind which makes an efficient Treasury mandarin or diplomat, irrespective of whether his golden youth at Oxbridge was spent getting his first-class degree in economics or in classics, then one wonders whether it is sensible for the British taxpayer to spend some £3,000 pumping a man full of Greek hexameters for three years merely in order to *assess* his likely capacity to write pithy diplomatic telegrams. Surely there must be means of making the diagnosis at an earlier stage – and other means of giving people a chance of learning to think for themselves, if it is *that* which universities add to their stature.

Many private employers do, indeed, believe that there are other means. Some of them would much prefer to get hold of highly-intelligent young men and start training them at eighteen. Many of the senior officials of the Bank of England, recruited at eighteen in the days of Montague Norman when there was, as a matter of policy, no graduate recruitment, would rather like to revert to that practice. But that option is simply not open to an individual employer. As long as most employers who are bidding for the 5 or 10 per cent most able people in each age group continue to recruit in the graduate market, no single employer could persuade a young man who was in that group *not* to go on and demonstrate that he belongs to it by getting a degree. Any young man who accepted a job at eighteen would be tying his future to that particular employer and closing off other options (apart from renouncing three years' *dolce vita* at a university). Hence (particularly since the state, not the employer, pays for it), it becomes only sensible even for employers sceptical about the real value of university education to recruit only from graduates. Attempts to alter market-established education/occupation links from the employer's side can only be made collectively. Hence the full-page *Times* advertisement of recent months urging would-be managers to go into the army rather than the university was demonstratively signed by the chairmen or directors of twenty-five leading companies (*The Times*, 11 January 1974).

So there is a gap between private and social rationality. That gap may be wide enough in Britain. It becomes far greater, disastrously greater, in the later developing countries.

The *Times* advertisement just mentioned brings us, next, to the empirical assumptions about abilities which are involved in using educational qualifications as a screening device. Is it in fact true that educational achievements do correlate with, and can be used as a proxy measure for, the sort of abilities which most employers seek and value? For accountants, computer programmers, engineers and clerks the answer is probably yes, in any country. For managers, however, the answer might vary. In Japan, where intelligence and persuasiveness and zeal have traditionally been seen as the qualities which evoke consent from subordinates, the answer might well, again, be yes. In Britain, however (as in Sri Lanka), it has been (and still, in the age of the social contract, remains) 'character' which is thought to ensure the effective subordination of the lower orders – those qualities of calm and self-assurance and judgment which were bred in men in certain *kinds* of (private) schools (not certain *levels* of schooling) or in the officer ranks of the army. Hence, in the *Times* advertisement, the chairmen of Beaverbrook Newspapers and the Ford Motor Company, the personnel directors of Whitbread and Spillers Dog Foods, proclaim their concurrence in the view that:

> Of course, we don't expect a young man from the Army to be fluent in Mediaeval French Literature or a master of Micro-Biology.
>
> But in our experience as employers, we've found that a Short-Service Commission in the Army equips a man to make the change to business management very easily.
>
> For both jobs are concerned with the handling of people and getting the best out of them, often in trying situations.
>
> (Anyone who has had to keep twenty soldiers calm when a crowd are hurling bricks at them will readily agree.)

Whether they will succeed in reversing – or changing the direction of – the qualification spiral remains to be seen. Note, however, that it is still not necessarily the formative, educative role, even of the army, which these employers value. It might still be that the army too is seen as a tester, rather than as a creator, of talent. As the chairman of a national bank is reported to have told the eighteen-year-old son of a friend who came looking for a job: 'Come back in three years' time with a good degree from a good Oxbridge college or a good chit from the colonel of a good regiment.' Note the 'good's. The reference to the 'good Oxbridge college' is also a reminder that educational records can in Britain (less so in Japan, say, or Nigeria) have other significance than as a proxy test of intelligence and effort. Ability to get into a 'good' Oxbridge college indicates the right background and manner; having been there promises possession of the right connections.

And the consequences for education?
The rationality of the system has so far been questioned from the point of view of employers and job applicants and society's collective concern with getting people into the right jobs; round pegs into round holes.

But what of the implications of the qualification inflation for the education system? It means, in effect, that over the last century in which educational certificates have come into increasing use for job selection the significance of education for those being educated has changed. In nineteenth-century England the various classes of English society went to their own schools to prepare themselves for a career to which it had pleased, if not God, at least the class system to call them. The East India Company official sent his son to Haileybury in order that he should become a good, self-respecting, effective East India Company official – should fill the place which *patronage* would give him with distinction and aplomb. The merchant's son went to school to become a better merchant. The working man's son went to elementary school to become a better – more diligent and sober and intelligent – working man.

Now, whether the knowledge one gets from schools is useful or exciting, whether the values and attitudes one picks up there are appropriate, has become of secondary importance. Schools are places where one gets certificates; O levels and A levels, passports to such and such jobs, hurdles over which one leaps to go on to more schools for more certificates as passports to even better jobs. And all are in the race. Even for the middle-class child, patronage now cuts less ice. The City and the major companies have adopted rationalized managerial recruiting procedures. Even if one goes to the army one needs that 'good chit', and if one takes the other, Oxbridge, route, one needs the 'good' degree (as well as good A levels to get there). Only the very rich who do not *need* a job, or the unambitious content with the backwater jobs which patronage can still buy (running charitable foundations for distressed gentlefolk, say) can afford to spend their time at Oxbridge merely pursuing truth and intellectual excitement without concern for certificates (assuming that it *is* truth and not the champagne breakfasts that they have come to Oxbridge for). Add to this the presence of a higher proportion of working-class students at the universities whose families could not mobilize even the most modest form of patronage. They, having faced tougher difficulties, are likely to have had even more intensive coaching at O and A level in the art of hurdle jumping, developing as a reflex action the tendency with every idea they meet to size it up for jumping height.

And if the objective significance of education for individual life chances has changed, would it be surprising that subjective perceptions of that process and attitudes to it have also changed? Is there any evidence that they have? At least one university teacher thinks there is (Bernard Crick, *New Statesman*, 6 October 1972):

> Pelican books [thirty years ago] were aimed unambiguously and enthusiastically at general adult education and the general educated reader, at people who wanted simply to inform themselves, reading on their own, or perhaps hand in hand, those who liked classes on important topics but who were not pursuing (indeed the right word) a degree or diploma. But now apparently the market is shifting with wonderfully so many more people in university or polytechnic. Most paperback publishers now aim their shotguns at the students....
>
> What I find utterly terrible about this kind of publication is the further assumption that the student is solely 'course-oriented' (only the jargon expresses the enormity), that he is not likely to be a general reader. I fear that they are right statistically. Most students do not, will not and perhaps – some kind excusing soul may prove – cannot read outside their ruddy subject. For we are not now talking about intellectuals or general readers. Most – not all, but most – are simply at university to get a degree. To adapt Dr Johnson's famous description of politics, 'reading is nothing but a rising in the world'.

So much for a political scientist's view. Similar sentiments were expressed by a chemist who described on the BBC how he rated the production of young scientists along with the production of inventions as a major objective of his research laboratory (Davis 1967, p. 577).

> It is reasonable to ask how we are adding to the process of further education already carried out – with about £10,000 to £15,000

(exclusive of lost earnings) per Ph.D. – by the universities. The answer is startling. We are undoing the effects of partial brain-washing, restoring the natural curiosity so evident in children, encouraging and purging from the system of our young lions the tranquillizers administered to them over the previous fifteen years by our educational system – tranquillizers that have made the young lions behave like young lambs.

To suggest that there is a steady process of decline in the quality of British education may seem contrary to common sense. Surely, it might be objected, with every year bringing exciting new materials and methods, the child-centred education of today, with its emphasis on problem solving, and on encouraging the child's own learning initiatives, is infinitely more imaginative and genuinely educative than schooling in Britain thirty or forty years ago. That is undoubtedly true, and at the primary level these trends, associated with declining authoritarianism and a more liberal regard for individuality, and for cooperation rather than competition, have indeed made British schools a better place. It is at the secondary and higher levels that trends in this direction are blunted, overwhelmed, by backwash from the competition to qualify. There is reason to believe that the situation at the crucial secondary level is a good deal worse in Britain than in the United States, for two reasons. First because, with a much larger proportion of the American age groups going to university and getting their more definitive labels there, secondary-level qualifications are less important. Secondly, entrance to American universities, where it is competitive and not open, is determined not by the achievement tests for the high-school diploma (the equivalent to Britain's GCE/CSE) but by the separate (and much harder to cram for) Scholastic Aptitude Tests. Whether or not these are the reasons for it, that the difference exists is certainly the impression of one schoolteacher writing to *The Times* (22 April 1975):

> Having taught history and social science in both British and American schools, it has been my experience that the exam-bound curriculum in Britain limits pupil-teacher efforts to those that are immediately measurable in some pseudo-objective sense – to readily forgettable stuffing. There is far greater opportunity in US secondary schools, at least in those I have taught in, to deal with historical and cross-cultural comparison, analysis of political, social, economic and psychological factors and interpretations of the 'whys' and consequences of events – problem-solving activities.

Some would argue that the situation in Britain has reached a point at which drastic measures are required. Lord Ashby is one of these. He would draw a careful distinction between genuinely vocational higher education in such subjects as medicine and non-vocational higher education (in the humanities and social and natural sciences), certification of which is, however, commonly used and pursued for vocational purposes (Ashby 1972):

> The motive which must be resisted is the pursuit of non-vocational higher education solely in order to get certification for a job. It is of course the employers who must be reformed first. They are doing a great disservice to higher education by using degrees and diplomas, which are quite irrelevant to the jobs they are filling, as filters for selecting candidates ... If non-vocational higher education is to serve its real purpose (which is to civilize people) it ought not to attract people who only want to be certified, not civilized. I can see only one way in which higher education systems can promote this, and it would be an unpopular way: namely *not* to certify non-vocational education.

References

ASHBY, E. (1961) 'On universities and the scientific revolution' (reprinted from his *Technology and the Academics*) in A.W. Halsey *et al Education, Economy and Society*

ASHBY, E. (1972) *The Structure of Higher Education: A world view* paper for Lancaster Conference on Higher Education, mimeo (September)

BRIGGS, A. (1973) Are your A levels really necessary? *Sunday Times Magazine* (30 September)

BURRAGE, M. (1972) Democracy and the mystery of the crafts: observations on work relationships in America and Britain *Daedalus* (Autumn)

DAVIES, D. (1967) Education for a technological society: a scarce resource called curiosity *The Listener* (4 May)

GLASS, D.V. (1961) 'Education and social change in modern England' in A.W. Halsey *et al Education, Economy and Society*

HALSEY, A.W., FLOUD, J. and ANDERSON, C.A. (eds) (1966) *Education, Economy and Society* (1961).

LITTLE, A. and OXENHAM, J. (1975) *Credentialism: speculations on careers handbooks and newspaper cuttings* paper for Lancaster Conference on Higher Education, mimeo

OECD (1971) *Occupational and Educational Structures of the Labour Force and Levels of Economic Development.*

Index

Abercrombie, Sir Patrick, 40, 86
Abrams, C., nostalgia for 'downtown',
156; 'Cold War' statements on social
mix, 159; *Forbidden Neighbours*, 153
Action Group on London Housing, 205
Adolescents, absence of social amenities
provision, 66n13, 171, 177;
imbalance of experience and myth
making, 89; absence of social matrix
for dealing with other people, 89;
enter adulthood with fixed ideas of self,
89 (*see under* Adulthood); state of
conflict between dissimilar groups, 92;
removal of metropolitan-wide controls,
92; impulse to hide from pain, 93;
defeat of mythical solidarity by need to
survive, 93–4; and experience of
meaningful conflict, 94; transition
from school to work-life, 214; social
organization and delinquency, 253;
see also Delinquency *and* Younger
generation
Adulthood, failure of the young to
achieve, 89; use of conflict and
confrontation, 90; achievement
through survival communities, 94;
generation of caring, 96; beginnings in
feelings of self-distrust and failure, 99;
delinquents and, 257; factors
influencing progress towards, 337;
reorganization of path towards, 342–5
Advertising, 23, 59
Affluent society, ability to opt out by
migration, 7, 13–14, 15, 17; and
payment for services and housing,
16–17; non-quantifiable extension of
opportunity, 40; hiding place from
achieving adulthood, 90; participation
in community problems and

experiences, 100; creation of
voluntary slavery, 100; weakens need
for sharing scarce resources, 100
African immigrants, London areas of
concentration (Table 2), 276, 281
Agricultural development, 21; based on
capitalist interests, 22, 24
Akbar the Great, builder of Fatehpur
Sikri, 8
America, 15; transition from rural to
urban civilization, 27, 73; expansion
of great cities, 29, 32–3; cultural areas
of city life, 33; areas of deterioration,
33; small town cities, 57; auto-based
way of life, 59; residential choices, 63;
numbers living in cities, 69, 70;
legislative welfare services, 80; analysis
of recent summer violence, 95–6;
socioeconomic/racial mixing, 101,
102; suburbanization of industry,
116; rights of low income groups to
government services, 118; failure of
liberal anti-poverty programmes,
132–3; territorial exploitation, 134;
transfer of capital investment away
from areas of need, 135; enthusiasm
for creative planning, 152, 156;
idealized neighbourhood unit, 152–3,
156, 159; housing and planning
legislation, 153–4; federal housing
policy, 154, 157; urban renewal
programmes, 155, 157; government
contribution to redevelopment, 174;
community patterns, 175; real estate
development companies, 176–7; good
and bad neighbourhoods, 185, 186;
whole city neighbourhoods, 189; and
street self-government, 190–1; upper
class attitudes to public services, 226;

Index

black ghettos, 288; undemocratic and exploitative economic structure, 296; changing character of social conflict, 312–3; Scholastic Aptitude Tests, 362
Architecture, 8, 9; the country house, 21
Art and design, 18, 59; influence on civic greatness, 17
Ashby, E. (Lord), 'On universities and the scientific revolution', 363
Asian immigrants, 282, 289; areas of settlement (London)(Table 2), 276, 280
Australia, town and country mix, 75
Axial Belt (the Coffin, the Hourglass), 83; geographical location, 80–1, (Figure 1a), 82, 84; % distribution of total population (Table 3a), 85; % distribution of insured (employed) population (Table 3b), 85

Baltimore, 135; rowhouses, 60
Barlow, Sir Anderson Montague, Commission on the Distribution of the Industrial Population, 83, 84, 144, 157
Barnett, Henrietta, 77
Behaviour patterns, causal analysis of socially created and culturally defined roles, 63; origin in socioeconomic/political systems, 63, 64; working class interest, 168; different rates of change and direction in US working classes, 170–80
Bell Telephone Company, 28
Benston, Margaret, 'The political economy of women's liberation', 314n19
Berger, B. M., Working-Class Suburb, 170
Berlin, Turkish immigrants, 15
Best, Dr Robin, Land Use Surveys, 72–3; and Megalopolis, 88n29
Bethnal Green, Project East study of working class community, 200, 240–2, see also London: East End
Binstock, Jeanne, 'Survival in the American college industry', 299; correspondence between social relations of education and production, 300

Birmingham, 80, 116; population, 1801, 1851, 76; central business district, 79; study of immigrants in Sparkbrook area, 280–1
Black population, southern to northern (US) migration, 32; Black Belt city areas, 32; conflict between middle class and militants, 95; and racial integration, 102, 103, 154; opposition to social mix, 157, 159, 160n1; and relocation plus improved surroundings, 170; increase in London council estates, 202; application of term 'ghetto', 271; attitude of building societies and estate agents, 274; sufferings of children, 277; job availability and distribution, 278; concentration in furnished accommodation, 281, 286; and access to better circumstances, 282; importance of equal educational opportunity, 285, 287; unrepresented in new towns, 287; correspondence between schools and an inferior job situation (US), 297
Boal, Dr, maps of Belfast, 43
Bradford, population 1951, 76
Bremen, fifteenth-century grandeur, 9
Brenner, Marshall S., 'The use of high school data to predict work performance', 305–6
Bristol, 43; population, 1801, 1951, 76
Bruges, 9; order and elegance, 17
Brunel, Isambard K., GWR, 12
Bureaucracies, tendency to become pyramids of power, 90; restructuring to create survival communities, 90, 98, 100; fallacies concerning central organization, 91; proposed removal from present directive power, 103–4; subversion of proletarian dictatorship (USSR), 133; education for dealing with, 342; filter into job selection, 353
Burney, Elizabeth, on common characteristics of working class/immigrant families, 280, 282

Cadbury, George, Bournville social mix, 158

Capital cities, as political expressions, 9

Capitalism, 20; agent of socio/physical transformation, 21; served by state and planners, 22; priority of profit motive in investment, 22; determining factors in town-and-country relations, 22; generation and distribution of wealth, 133; bars the way to income redistribution, 133; monopoly control, 134; accepted theories of its flow in relation to need, 134; localized areas of high unfulfilled need, 134–5; operation of market system in diverting funds, 135; concept of scarcity, 136; unsolved by social mix, 158; change in relationships between traditional classes, 218; social relations securing stability, 292; organization of power relations and hiring criteria, 294; effects of delegation of real power to workers, 294; domination of (US) educational system, 296; relationship between approved school personality traits and good job performance, 305; alienated conditions of work under, 308; common authoritarianism with child rearing, 308; education and, 313

Chicago, changes accompanying city growth, 28; succession process, 30–1; satellite loops, 31; central business district, 31; occupational differences, 34; immigration into, 35; public transport figures 1890–1921, 36; land values by mobility areas, 37; apartment houses, 60; dense inner-city community, 99; good neighbourhoods, 185

Chicago School, 51, 53

Children, acculturation of ethnic groups, 55; of upper-class cosmopolites, 55; of suburbia, 59, 155; and free school meals, 142–3; absence of amenities in housing estates, 171; concentration in council estates, 202; in high-rise flats, 205; class variations in attitudes towards, 226, 228, 230; influence of kinship patterns, 243; in areas of multiple deprivation, 277; association between family background and economic success, 306, (Figure 4),

307; acquisition of parental social relations, 307, 311; impact of work-related values on their rearing, 311; removal from workplaces, 339, 343–44; early role of schooling, 341; reduction of importance of social class in educational achievement, 344–5

China, People's Republic, 133, 137, 153

Chronically sick and disabled, 54, 142

Cities and towns (UK), central business districts, 75, 79; uncoordinated (private) growth, 76; high-density occupations, 76–7; transportation, 76, 77–80; negative exponential law, 77; low-density suburban housing, 79; dispersal of factory industry, 79, 116; green field sites, 79; post-war provincial redevelopment, 114–15, *see also* Suburbs

City, the, 20, 27; importance in industrial civilization, 7; escape hatch from poverty, 7; focus of social problems, 7, 13; five distinct types, 8*ff*; rising real income, 13; need for civic pride, 18; seen as overriding nature, 21; socio/physical transformations, 21; needs new forms of communication, 23; expansion as a process, 28, 29–31, (Figure 1), 30; succession aspect, 30, 47; areas of deterioration, 30, 33, 35, 36; effects of expansion on social organization, 31–5; distinction between movement and mobility, 35; attractions for the young and adventurous, 35; characteristics of central areas, 41–2; structural common factors, 43; individual perceptions, 43; disadvantages of size, 43; 'residential differentiation', 43–4; provision of shelter, 45; influences on choice of housing, 45–6; need for resources to outgrow population, 47; relationship between physical and social structure, 49n6; sociological conception, 51; siting of cultural facilities, 54; compared with the suburb, 58; demographic characteristics, 60–1; inner/outer concepts, 65; proposed

Index

Department of the Environment (DOE), 'six cities' projects, 48

Deprivation, multiple, 212; areas of, 272, 273; and multiple discrimination, 273–74; typical characteristics, 275, 277; position of children, 277

Deprived people, 14; inner-city living, 54, 56; demographic factors affecting, 55–6; exhibit anonymity, 56; low socioeconomic level, 62; causal analysis of conditions, 63; intolerable living conditions, 117; should have equal access to public services, 117, 276; slow development of political consciousness, 117–18; concept of double deprivation, 127; poor life chances, 141–2; and social mix, 158–9; contrary results of aid programmes, 213–14; suggested services, 219; lack of housing choice, 271, 273–4, 277–8; common characteristics with immigrants, 280; possible emergence of severely underprivileged group, 289; paucity of educational provisions, 298; poor anticipation of economic success, 306–7

Dobriner, W. M., (ed), *The Suburban Community*, 152

Dodson, Dr D. W., on street isolation and incompetence, 190

Domestic service, allotted task of lower classes and women, 325–6; demise in egalitarian age, 326; Home Helps Corps, 326

Dominant classes, strategy of 'divide and conquer' in maintenance of power, 293; and capitalist enterprises, 294; main objectives in education, 295; coming up the 'hard way', 316

Ecology, 115, 168, 250

Economic system, complex and stable patterns of power and property, 292, 312; foundation of stability on law and coercive state powers, 292; maintenance of détente by consciousness of workers, 293;

initiation of youth into, 294, 295, 296, 343–4; major spheres of social activity, 311; failure of liberal corrective devices, 312; occupation of much of adult social life, 345

Edinburgh, 41, 43

Education, educational system (UK), prolongation, 44; determining factor in personal development, 44, 349; and residential choice, 45–6; influence on behaviour patterns, 63; access to state and private provisions, 109, 110; and equality of opportunity, 132, 285; politically motivated, 148; battle for comprehensives, 154; and social mix, 156; unrelated to buildings, 185; and immigrant children, 277, 285; for the lower classes, 318; distinguished from schooling, 341–2; evaporation in workplaces, 341; need for explicit planning and organization, 341–2; skills to be acquired before *aet.* 18, 342; a pattern for the future, 342–5; introduction of state scholarships, 350; reorientation for occupational selection, 350–1; hierarchical integration, 350; working-class participation in pyramid-climbing, 350; qualification spiral, 360; former social gradations, 360; confers certificates not values and attitudes, 360

Education, educational system (US), legitimization function, 291; reproduction of dominance/ subdominance in economic life, 291, 295, 312; production of an amenable and fragmented labour force, 291; integrative element in reproduction of current class structure, 291, 292, basis of its values in work and class situations, 291 : initiation of youth into economic system, 295, 296; produces technical and cognitive skills for job performance, 295; and legitimate economic equality, 295; correspondence between class and school structure, 295; and discontent over hierarchical division of labour, 295; need to produce alienated forms

Index

323–4; spread to shops and offices, 324–5

Managerial class, 12

Manchester, 41, 43; population, 1801, 1851, 76; central density, 77; tentacular housing development, 78; transport, 78, 80; LA housing schemes, 79, 87n19; central business district, 79; Trafford Park, 79

Mankind, learning to deal with dissimilarities, 89–90, 94; knitting together people's social lives, 90; and conflicts and confrontations, 90, 94, 104; wish to hide from pain and disorder, 100; impulse to re-create past slaveries under new names, 100; notable for inequality of endowment, 322

Market system, and operation of scarcity, 136, 137; inherent concomitants of deprivation, appropriation and exploitation, 136, 137, 138; price system, 136, 137; competition for access to state resources, 136–7; attempts to devise alternatives based on social justice, 136–7; failure of planning to change distribution of social produce, 148, 150

Marriott, O., *The Property Boom*, 114–15

Marx, Karl, and a just distribution of income, 131, 132; and enduring alienation of workers, 169 (*A Critique of the Gotha Programme*)

Mass medium, a form of shared consciousness, 23; paradoxical set of one-way relationships, 23–4; impersonal means of communication, 51; promotion of ideology of consumption, 251; influence on working population, 334

Mass society, theory of, 52

Medical services (social justice), definition and measurement of need, 126–9; market, latent and potential demands, 127–9; application to other activities, 129

Megalopolis, area, 73, 74, 84, 88n20, 97; redefined by Taylor, 83, Meltzer, J. and Whitley, J., 'Planning for the urban slum', 113

Merchant cities, 8, 9, 10

Meritocracy, rise of, 311–12; self-approbration, 317; universal achievement, 319; apportionment of power and responsibility, 321; and social stratification, 327; attitude of meritless, 327, 328

Metropolis, Polyglot, 7–8; evidenced in New York, 12, 13–14; money-based inhabitants, 13, 16; and the deprived, 14; old and new established working classes, 14–15; tension manifested in crime, 15–16; distinction between largeness and smallness, 19

Meyer, Peter, schooling and the reproduction of social divisions of labour, 300, 302; use of factor analysis, 302, (Figure 2), 303

Middle classes, outward spread in city areas, 42, 65, 77; and downtown stores, 58–9; and property depreciation, 115; suffer less from enforced mobility, 115; hem in poorer city occupants, 116; denigration of their realm (suburbia), 155; favoured in social mix, 156, 159, 160; planning dilemma, 168; working-class upward movement, 169; end of suburban monopoly, 176; creation of bad neighbourhoods (US), 185; gentrification process, 199; background of social skills, 201; future oriented, 228; compared with upper, 228; environmental demands, 231–3; community activists, 240; provide articulate leadership, 288; work-related values and child-rearing, 310; provision of grammar schools, 349, 350

Midlands, West and East, 74, 78, 147

Milton Keynes, wrong placement, 48

Mobility, distinguished from movement, 35; resulting from stimulation, 35–6; creation of immorality and vice, 36; pulse of the community, 36, 37; and land values, 37; downward group, 54–5, 56; residential and occupational peaks, 60; and social groups, 165, 168

Motor car, the, 36, 147; a mode of

Index

relationship, 24; suburbanite uses, 58, 59; as a way of life, 59; era of privileged ownership, 80; class variations in demands, 232; and juvenile delinquency status, 258–9

Mumford, L., *The Urban Prospect*, 156, 159, 160n1

National Assistance, 142, 143
National Council of Social Service, 152
National Guard (US), 292
National Health Service, the poor and, 143
Neighbourhoods, 104, 171; upper-class detachment, 55, 62; housing and homogeneity, 60; suburban characteristics, 57, 59, 66nn9, 10; definition, 66n7; creation of diversity, 91, 155, 156; and personal relationships, 92; variations in concept and significance, 147, 152, 165; and social mix, 154, 155, 157; and community virtues, 156; US working-class attachment, 171; one-class within mixed-class communities, 172; an escape from anonymity, 174; influence of design and siting on social isolation, 178–9; results of redevelopment, 213, 247; variation in class attitudes towards, 231–3; extended kinship relations, 244; working-class ecology, 244
Neighbourhoods (New York City), idealized 'downtown' area, 156; sentimental concept, 184, 186; non-relationship between good housing and behaviour, 184–5; as organs of self-government or self-management, 185–6, 187–8, 189, 196; flaws in planners' ideal, 186–7, 192, 197; part of city life, 187–8; mutual exchange of ideas, 188–9; city streets, 189–91; function of the district, 191–2; getting help when needed, 192–3; influence on city policy, 194, 195; deteriorating island characteristics, 195–6; individual or institutional power, 196
New Communities Act 1968 (US), 154

New towns, 48, 116, 147; planning decentralization policy, 148, 156; and social mix, 156, 157, 158; density and social relations, 173; recipients of London's overflow, 205; offer nothing to worst-off, 205; employment for immigrants, 287
New York City, 12, 13; outward migration of affluent, 13–14, 15, 17; two socioeconomic working classes, 14–15; crime in, 15–16; signs of social conflict, 16; private wealth and public squalor, 17; immigration into, 35; public transport 1860–1921, 36; Lower East Side residents, 54, 194–5; accommodation in school district I.S.201, 99; Lefrak City, 101; distinction between homes and workplaces of the poor, 116; commuting patterns, 175; 'planned' neighbourhoods, 186; Park Avenue, 190; treatment of drug addicts, 194
New Zealand, Wakefield's mixed colony, 159
Niebuhr, Reinhold, 'doctrine of salvation by bricks', 185
Notting Hill Housing Survey, relative black/white circumstances, 281–2

Ornati, O., *Transportation Needs of the Poor*, 115–16
Overcrowding, social consequences, 55–6, 75n4; relief by mass transport, 77; of London immigrants, 280, 281, 283
Oxford, 43

Pahl, Ray, 'Poverty and the urban system', 41, 49n5, 109ff
Pakistanis, 15, 242, 246, 282, 289
Parents, and deviance, 265; family life/work experience correlation, 307, 308; children's inheritance of their socioeconomic background, 307; influence of work-related values on child rearing, 310, 311; social class and use of punishment, 310–11; and the meritocracy, 319; displace their

coloured people, 278
Trevelyan, G. M., and growth of
universities, 348

Unemployment, unemployed, in Great
Depression, 83; emergence of
planning, 141, 143–4; numbers living
in poverty, 142; statistics and
distribution, 144; local and central
government failure, 144;
counteraction against improvement
plans, 288; creation of a selective
group created by economic progress,
323; higher in men than in women,
326
United Kingdom, Asian and West Indian
immigrants, 15; 'residential
differentiation', 43–4; 'urban' or
'rural' personal classification, 69;
alleged urbanization, 69–70, 73; S.E.
statistics, 73; town and country
dividing line, 75; emergence of
planning, 76, 141; effects of mass
transportation, 77, 79–80; electrified
trams, 78; Great Depression, 80;
Axial Belt, 80–1; decentralization of
manufacturing industry, 116; failure
of post-war socialist plans, 132;
persistence of housing problems, 143;
regional differences of employment
and population, 144; Development
Areas, 144; belief in continuation of
national service, 152; rise in non-
white immigrants, 154; concern for
social mix, 156–7; varying approaches
to community studies, 165; economic
recovery from war, 248; professional
group, autonomy, 357; justification of
'qualification inflation spiral', 358;
use of 'character' in subduing
subordinates, 359
Universities, pictured as a survival
community, 98–9; and engineering
studies, 348–9, 351–2, 354;
evolution of occupational-based
curricula, 348–9, 351–2; professional
reliance on, 352; and exemptions from
practical training, 352; prestige
attached to graduation, 355;

entitlement to higher fees, 355, 356;
do they create as well as measure
talent, 358–60; socioeconomic
assumptions on Oxbridge graduates,
360; higher % of working-class
students, 361; alleged brainwashing
and tranquillizing effects, 362
Upper classes, outward spread of
housing, 42, 155; unmarried,
childless detachment from
neighbourhood life, 55; and social
homogeneity, 59; quasi-primary way
of life, 62; ideology of physical
planning, 145, 148; creation of bad
neighbourhoods (US), 185; highly
future-oriented characteristics, 226,
229–30; and self-expression, 227;
motivated by internal standards, 228;
attitudes towards children, 227, 232;
tolerance of unconventional behaviour,
227; subcultural group, 227;
individualism and self-discipline, 227;
duty towards community interest,
228; compared with middle group,
228; environmental demands, 232–3;
self-doubts on their superiority, 312;
results of classification by ability, 316;
consciousness of their higher calibre,
317; esteem mental achievement,
319; accustomed to servants, 326;
have nothing to learn from lower
classes, 328n2
Urban planning, 28; and expansion as a
process, 29–31; development of chain
store, 31; internal population
movements, 33; its aims and extension
of opportunities, 39–41; egalitarian
basis of choice, 40, 41; non-
quantifiable demands, 40;
involvement of people in decision-
making, 40–1; green belts, 40–1, 43,
48, 150, 205; constraints on change,
44–8; analysis of characteristics and,
63–4; endemic pyramidal power
structure, 90; assumed object, 91;
and social mix, 157
Urbanism, urbanization, nostalgic ideas
of a lost past, 25, 26; transition from
rural economy (US), 27; prevalence of
social problems, 27; variations in